OLD AND HISTORIC
CHURCHES
OF NEW JERSEY

OLD AND HISTORIC
CHURCHES
OF NEW JERSEY

Volume 1

Ellis L. Derry

Plexus Publishing, Inc.
Medford, New Jersey

Originally published in 1979 by Wm. H. Wise & Co., Inc.
This edition published by:

Plexus Publishing   Hardcover ISBN 0-937548-50-2
Medford, New Jersey   Softcover ISBN 0-937548-52-9
www.plexuspublishing.com

First printing, 2003. Manufactured in the United States of America

A CIP catalog record for this book is available from the Library of Congress.

Photographs:

   Chapters V, VI, IX, XV, XVI, XIX, XXIII, XXV, XXXI, XXXII, XXXVII by
      Ellis L. Derry
   Chapters II, III, IV, VII, VIII, XI, XII, XIV, XVII, XVIII, XXI, XXII, XXVI,
      XXX, XXXIII, XXXIV, XXXVI, XXXVIII, XXXIX, XLI, XLII, XLIII,
      XLIV, XLV, XLVI, XLVII, XLVIII by Pat Palatucci
   Chapter I courtesy of Doris and Howard Boyd
   Chapter X courtesy of Deerfield Presbyterian Church
   Chapter XIII courtesy of Crosswicks Friends Meeting
   Chapter XX courtesy of First Presbyterian Church of Connecticut Farms
   Chapter XXIV courtesy of Russell Shiveler, caretaker, Old Stone Church,
      Swedesboro
   Chapter XXVII courtesy of Barbara Steitz, church historian, South Presbyterian
      Church, Bergenfield
   Chapter XXVIII courtesy of Rev. Dr. Merle S. Irwin, Bloomfield Presbyterian
      Church on the Green, Bloomfield
   Chapter XXIX courtesy of Donna Snyder, Deacon, Old Paramus Reformed
      Church, Ridgewood
   Chapter XXXV courtesy of Cliff Patrick, Cold Springs Presbyterian Church
   Chapter XL courtesy of Reverend Roland Ratmeyer, Pastor, Old Bergen
      Church, Jersey City

Cover illustration by Gib Robbie.

To
Peggy
My Wife
Who made it all possible
With love and appreciation

Contents

Contents

Contents

Contents

Foreword

The Province of Nova Caesaria was settled by people seeking religious freedom. They came from the Old World with the hope of being able to worship God as they saw fit and not as might be decreed by some government. For those who landed on the shores of New England this dream was to some extent not fulfilled. But New Jersey, like Rhode Island, Pennsylvania, and Delaware, never established a state religion. Thus, refugees from religious persecution in the New World as well as the Old settled in New Jersey.

The Province became the haven for people of many religious persuasions. In East Jersey the Congregationalists, Baptists, Presbyterians, Dutch Reformed, Anglicans, and some Quakers found the religious climate to their liking. Even in West Jersey, which was mainly settled by Friends, Presbyterians, Baptists, Lutherans, and Moravians found a place where they could practice their religious beliefs in relative peace. On the surface it appeared that New Jersey was a state without an identity, at least a religious one. Overshadowed by the powerful cities of New York and Philadelphia, by the "country gentlemen" of Virginia, and by Puritan Massachusetts, New Jersey's contribution to the eventual principles of this nation remain largely unrecognized.

Whether by choice or geography a state religion was an impossibility. The Jersey settlers found that they could live in comparative peace with their neighbors regardless of the diverse religious practices. Tolerance became the underlying principle of the Province. Through New Jersey's example the idea of separation of church and state became a fundamental concept of the emerging nation.

This is the story of these pioneers as told by the histories of the individual churches. Men and women of such strong religious beliefs that they were willing to forsake parents, friends, and, in some cases, riches for a life of danger and hardship so that they could worship God according to their conscience. Although they were tolerant of the religious beliefs of others, they did not compromise their own principles for the sake of popularity or to gain converts. Theirs were not "social" religions.

As with any definitive work, guidelines had to be established to identify those churches to be included. Since this book deals with the old as well as with the historic churches, the age of the existing building became a primary consideration. Although no absolute date was chosen, in general the building had to be constructed no later than the broad Civil War period. It also had to be in use preferably for regular services, or at least for anniversary services. The organizational date of the church was not the determining factor. The date of the building was all-important, and this is the date shown for each church. Of prime consideration was the history itself. Those with the most interesting histories were included provided they met the other qualifications. Unfortunately, the physical limitations of the size of the book made it necessary to exclude many churches that rightfully should have been included. New Jersey is fortunate in having such a heritage.

Acknowledgments

The enthusiastic response and help of many people made this book possible. Although I should like to publicly thank each and every one, space does not permit. There were those, however, who were especially helpful, and these people I do wish to recognize. Mrs. Edith Hoelle, Librarian of the Gloucester County Historical Society, who gave so generously of her time and knowledge; my cousins, Doris and Howard Boyd, who helped in many ways, including some difficult photography; Rev. Fred Schultz, who trusted me on our very first meeting with an irreplaceable manuscript; Mr. Lamond Smith, who supplied many interesting stories; Mrs. Elizabeth Mick, who has a wealth of historical information at her fingertips; my son Douglass and his wife Martha, for their constructive comments on some of the first drafts; Dr. Lloyd George Schell, who gave so much of his time and historical knowledge; Ms. Minnie Margarita, for her special research; and especially my wife, Peggy, who literally became an "author's widow" while I spent hours at the typewriter, and who was such a help in meeting and talking to people on our field trips.

I

St. Mary's Protestant Episcopal Church

Burlington, 1703

If one were to ask the congregation of St. Mary's Church the significance of the name *Centurion,* the chances are that very few members would have any idea at all. Yet the *Centurion* was the means by which two men were brought together resulting in the founding of Old St. Mary's in Burlington. The *Centurion* was an ocean-going vessel sailing between Cowes, Isle of Wight and Boston, Massachusetts. In April 1702 George Keith booked passage and during the voyage became a close friend of John Talbot, the chaplain of the *Centurion.* Keith was being sent to the New World as a missionary by the Society for Propagating the Gospel in Foreign Parts; so it is not surprising that with the arrival of the *Centurion* in Boston in June, these two men decided to join forces. Keith immediately wrote to The Society for Propagating the Gospel in Foreign Parts requesting permission for Talbot to become his associate in missionary work in the New World. Permission was granted and Talbot received his appointment from the Society on September 18, 1702.[1]

The original commission that George Keith had received from the S.P.G. was to travel through the colonies and to suggest to the Society action necessary to establish the Church of England in this area. Therefore, as soon as John Talbot's commission was received, the two

St. Mary's Protestant Episcopal Church in Burlington, erected in 1703.

friends started their journey through Massachusetts, Connecticut, and New York, arriving in Burlington, New Jersey, on October 29, 1702.

Keith was probably attracted to this area by his previous connections with the Quakers who had founded Burlington, then known as New Beverly, in 1677. He had originally been educated for the Presbyterian ministry at Marischal College, Aberdeen, Scotland, but not finding the warmth that he was seeking in the Calvinistic theology, he became a Quaker in 1662. He was a brilliant scholar, knowledgeable in philosophy, mathematics, and Oriental languages; he was considered by Gilbert Burnet, Bishop of Salisbury, to be the most learned man in the Quaker faith. He made evangelistic tours with George Fox and William Penn through Holland and Germany.

Sojourns in prisons were not uncommon resulting from his fiery preachings and writings. After a prison term in England in 1684 he decided to emigrate to America, and was appointed Surveyor-General, arriving here in 1685. In his capacity as Surveyor-General he established a line starting from the intersection of the Old York Road and the Raritan River, going in a southerly direction to the approximate location of Holgate on Long Beach Island. This line was surveyed in 1687, dividing East and West Jersey, and became known as Keith's Line.[2]

He continued in the New World where he had left off in the Old, traveling throughout New England espousing the cause of the Friends and defending Quakerism from attacks by Increase and Cotton Mather, Congregational ministers. In 1689 he became Headmaster of the William Penn Charter School in Philadelphia, and it was here that he began to question some of the beliefs of the faith that he had so passionately advocated and defended for almost thirty years. His differences grew to the point that he was disowned in 1692 by the Yearly Meeting sitting in Burlington. This action caused the first major schism among the Quakers, as Keith had many followers and supporters. These people called themselves Christian Quakers, but were commonly referred to as Keithians. Keith traveled to London seeking the support of the London Yearly Meeting, but in 1694 this body also disowned him and Keith left the Quaker fold. By 1700 he had adopted the creeds of the Church of England and was ordained a priest by the Bishop of London.

So it is that we find George Keith in 1702 sailing on the *Centurion* as an Anglican missionary returning to the land that he had traversed so diligently in previous years for the Quaker cause. His efforts for the Church of England over a short period of time were destined to be more lasting than the thirty years he had labored for the Society of Friends. He inspired the Anglican chaplain of the *Centurion*, John Talbot, to debark at Boston and to become a missionary with him.

This was indeed providential since Talbot was to become the first Bishop of the Church of England in America.

Little time was lost by these two indefatigable men after they arrived in Burlington on October 29, 1702. On All Saints Day, November 1, 1702, they preached in the Town-House that stood at the intersection of Broad and High Streets. According to Keith's journal, Talbot preached in the morning and Keith preached in the afternoon "to a great Auditory of diverse sorts, some of the Church and some of the late Converts from Quakerism." Since the Governor of West Jersey, Colonel Hamilton, was one of the "Auditory," one wonders in which category Keith placed him. Keith's text for the afternoon sermon was John 17:3, "And this is life eternal, that they might know the only true God, and Jesus Christ, whom thou has sent."

Keith and Talbot continued to evangelize throughout the area, and by the turn of the new year were making discernable progress. By the end of February a movement for the building of a church had begun, and two hundred pounds had been contributed for this purpose. A lot was purchased on March 6th from William and John Hollingshead of Chester Township for twenty pounds and conveyed to Hugh Huddy, Nathaniel Westland, and Robert Wheeler, who had been designated trustees of the new church. This is the lot on which Old St. Mary's still stands. An earlier purchase of a piece of ground adjoining this lot was made by Nathaniel Westland, Edward Hunlike, and John Tatham on July 13, 1695 for a burial place for themselves and "free for all other Christian people, who shall hereafter be reminded to bury their dead."[3]

The cornerstone for the building was laid on March 25, 1703 by John Talbot. The church was called St. Mary's because the cornerstone was laid on the day of the Feast of the Annunciation of the Blessed Virgin. (The church was called St. Ann's in the first charter, granted on October 4, 1704 by Lord Cornbury, after the Queen of England, but a more ample charter granted by Lt. Governor

Ingoldsby on January 25, 1709 named the church St. Mary's.) Almost five months to the day after the cornerstone was laid, August 22, George Keith preached his first sermon in the new church. His text for this auspicious occasion was 2 Samuel 23: 3,4, "The God of Israel said, The Rock of Israel spake to me, He that ruleth over man must be just, Ruling in the fear of God. And he shall be as the light of the morning when the sun riseth, Even a morning without clouds; As the tender grass springing out of the earth By clear shining after rain."

The congregation's desire to use the church was so great that they did not wait until it was completed but used it for worship despite the fact that the roof was not finished, the walls were not plastered, and the structure was not floored. It was not until June 4, 1704 that the first Holy Sacrament was administered. The original church building was small, measuring forty feet in length and twenty-two feet in width. The congregation was provided with "regular Pews, below, and a fair Gallery above at the West end." Georgian in style, the construction was of brick apparently made in a nearby kiln by one of the wardens of the church, Hugh Huddy, with lime being ferried from Philadelphia. The bricks were laid by Thomas Kendall, known as "bricklayer of Rancocas Creek," and Richard Fenimore. Although there is no authoritative figure as to the total cost of the building, over 120,000 bricks were used at a cost of one pound current silver money for one thousand bricks.[5] The construction of the church left the parish a debt which was relieved by the "privy contributions of the Parish and County adjoining with abundance of other pious, & goodly dispos'd Persons, among which is the extraordinary zeal & liberality of Gov' Nicholson will always most gratefully be acknowledged by Burlington."[6] Colonel Daniel Coxe is also recorded as being a substantial giver with a gift of twenty-five pounds.

Now that a formal place of worship was established, the congregation was anxious to have a full-time spiritual leader available to them. A petition was prepared and sent to the Society requesting that John

Talbot be given orders to remain with them. Permission was granted, and in November 1705 John Talbot became the first rector of St. Mary's Protestant Episcopal Church. Not only was permission granted for Mr. Talbot to remain with the Burlington parish as its permanent rector, but funds were also supplied for a glebe for the rector's use, consisting of about six acres adjoining the church yard. It is interesting to note that of the seventeen men who signed the petition soliciting Mr. Talbot's services, six were Christian Quakers or Keithians, thus demonstrating George Keith's strong influence.

John Talbot faithfully served the church for many years, but the end of his career was to be more tempestuous than the beginning, culminating in his dismissal from the Society and an order from the Governor that he "surcease officiating." Part of his troubles developed over his intense desire to have a bishop appointed for the colonies. With this in mind he traveled to England in 1705 to appeal to the Society for a "suffragan Bishop." In his plea to the Society he said, "I have no business here but to solicit for a Suffragan, Books, and Ministers for the propagating of the Gospel." His plea was in vain, however, as no bishop was appointed, and after two years he returned to Burlington, discouraged but not giving up the fight. In 1709 he wrote to the Secretary of the Society "Hopewell has built a church and have had no minister yet...; there be many more in England but none so good as to come over and help us, that I can see or hear of. As for the account of what Indians we have converted, truly I Never saw nor knew any that were Christians indeed; but I know there are hundreds, yea thousands of our white folks, that are turned Infidels for want of looking after."[7]

For approximately twenty years Talbot continued in his efforts to have the Society appoint a bishop. His hopes were raised when a bill was presented to Parliament for establishing bishoprics in the colonies. He immediately wrote to the Secretary of the Society, "I have got possession of the best house in America for a Bishop's Seat;

the Archbishop told me he would contribute towards it and so I hope will others; pray let me know your mind in this matter, as soon as may be, for if they slip this opportunity, there is not such another to be had."[8] They did not "slip this opportunity" but sent six hundred pounds sterling to buy the house and grounds. The grounds consisted of fifteen acres of land and twelve acres of meadow. Despite these preparations no bishop was willing to settle in the New World, for none appeared.

John Talbot again traveled to England, but this time on an errand for himself. The late Dr. Thomas Tenison, Archbishop of Canterbury, left a will bequeathing one thousand pounds toward settlement of bishops in America, and until such time as bishops were appointed, the interest should be applied to the benefit of missionaries who had served in the area. One of the provisions of the will was that the missionary must be an Englishman and must be from the province of Canterbury. This was made to order for John Talbot as he was the only Englishman from the province of Canterbury serving as a missionary, and in 1721 the court ordered that the interest be paid to him.

Talbot, however, was obsessed with the notion that the colonies needed a bishop. Since none had been forthcoming, he had himself consecrated as a bishop by the nonjurors, Ralph Taylor and Robert Welton, before returning to Burlington. He kept this action secret for nearly two years. When it finally became public knowledge, a storm of controversy developed that resulted in Talbot's dismissal from the Society in 1725. His expulsion according to Talbot was "for Exercising Acts of Jurisdiction over my Brethren, the Missionaries."[9]

One of the nonjurors who had participated in the consecration of Talbot to the office of Bishop was Dr. Ralph Taylor, who had been chaplain to the Protestants at the Court of James II of France. This fact added fuel to the fires that had been kindled in earlier years by enemies accusing Talbot of being a Jacobite. On April 9, 1715 Governor Hunter wrote to the Society, "Mr. Talbot has incorporated the Jacobites in the Jerseys under the name of a Church in order to sanctify his Sedition and Insolence to the Government." Nearly two years after Talbot had been officiating as Bishop with Burlington as his headquarters, the other nonjuror, Robert Welton, arrived in America. The Governor became alarmed at the existence of an Episcopate independent of both church and state. Welton was ordered to return to England, and Talbot was ordered to "surcease officiating."[10]

John Talbot died November 29, 1727, and his death was mourned by many despite his problems with the church and state officials. The *American Weekly Mercury* reported: "Philadelphia, November 30, 1727. Yesterday, died at Burlington, the Reverend Mr. Talbot, formerly minister of that Place, who was a Pious good man, and much lamented." The Rev. Francis L. Haeks wrote, "In the history of the Diocese of New Jersey, Mr. Talbot's character and deeds will find a conspicuous place; ...the Society never had, at least in our view, a more honest, fearless and laborious missionary." During his lifetime the church had been the recipient of many fine gifts, including those from Queen Anne of pulpit and altar cloths and a silver chalice and salver for the communion table.

Rev. Nathaniel Horwood followed John Talbot as missionary to the church but was not popular with the congregation. Whether this was due to his shortcomings or the natural difficulty of following a personality as strong as John Talbot's is impossible to say. Suffice it to say that on December 3, 1729 the church wardens wrote to the Rev. Mr. Vesey of New York, "Mr. Horwood our present minister...has reduced a flourishing congregation, into almost none at all...We are informed that he had leave to stay abroad in the plantations but for three years, if so his time is well nigh spent, wherefore we shall take it extreme kind if you be pleased to signify unto him that as you are informed he and the people don't well affect one the other it would be the best way to remove with all speed, and if thereupon he tacitly goes his way, it will be well pleasing unto us."[11]

The Rev. Horwood had no choice after such an expression of dissatisfaction from his congregation but to acquiesce in leaving his charge and returning to England. However, this was not to be as he died in Burlington on July 28, 1730. No mention is made in the records as to whether or not his death was hastened by a broken heart.

The vestry then petitioned the Society to nominate and appoint the Rev. Robert Weyman. Mr. Weyman was then serving the church in Oxford, Pennsylvania, where he had been laboring with considerable success for the past eleven years. The appointment was granted, and Rev. Weyman served St. Mary's as missionary for the Society until his death on November 28, 1737.

Once again, it was necessary to petition the S.P.G., and the Rev. Colin Campbell was appointed "Minister of Burlington." Campbell had been born in Scotland, November 15, 1707, the tenth of fourteen children. He arrived in Burlington June 2, 1738, and was well received by the congregation's members, who were pleased that the Society had so soon filled the place of their late pastor. He served St. Mary's for almost twenty-nine years, relinquishing this life for a better one in 1766. During his ministry many accomplishments were recorded. The church at Mt. Holly was founded as a mission of St. Mary's, and Rev. Campbell officiated at both parishes. The Congregations of both increased, a new parsonage in Burlington was purchased, and many gifts and bequests were given to the church.

The Rev. Nathaniel Evans, missionary at Gloucester, officiated occasionally at St. Mary's until the Society could appoint a new missionary for Burlington. Twenty-nine-year-old Jonathan Odell was selected by the S.P.G. to succeed Mr. Campbell on December 25, 1766. A grandson of Jonathan Dickinson, the first President of Princeton College, Mr. Odell was born in Newark, New Jersey on September 25, 1737. He was educated for the medical profession and served as a surgeon in the British Army. This is significant as we shall see in watching his career unfold. Leaving the British Army, he returned to England and prepared for Holy Orders. On December 21, 1766, he was ordained Deacon in the Chapel Royal of St. James' Palace, Westminister, by the Bishop of London. He was advanced to Priest's Orders in January 1767.

Odell arrived in Burlington to take up his new duties on July 25, 1767, and the very next day was inducted into St. Mary's by the Governor of the Province of New Jersey, William Franklin, son of Benjamin Franklin. In October Rev. Odell reported to the S.P.G. that there were thirty-five communicants and that the church was badly in need of repair. However, it was not until 1769 that the necessary funds were raised, allowing work to be done on the building. It was common practice in those days for churches to conduct lotteries to raise such funds. Authorization for the lotteries was granted by the General Assembly by an Act of 1762. One of the vestrymen, Thomas Humloke, managed the lottery, which enabled the church to be enlarged and the repairs made. Rev. Odell informed the Society that "the Church at Burlington is completed, and is not only a comfortable building, but an ornament to the place, being 63 feet by 33. Governor Franklin was very liberal on the occasion, and his lady had made them a present of a very rich and elegant furniture for the pulpit, desk and table."[12] As was the custom of the times, the Governor was provided with a private pew with a canopy and curtains. The high pulpit and sounding board stood against the north wall, and the Holy Table and Chancel were directly in front of a large window on the eastern side. A new bell was hung in the belfry, bearing the inscription "St. Mary's Church in Burlington, 1769."

Once again the parish was in debt, brought about by its building renovations. Rev. Odell refused to accept any renumeration from the congregation until this debt was paid. He supported himself by returning to the practice of medicine while continuing his duties as rector. By 1773 the debt had been discharged and the Vestry of St. Mary's agreed to pay him thirty pounds currency, which was equal to nearly nineteen pounds sterling. The congregation at Mount Holly arranged to pay him twenty-six pounds currency, equal to about sixteen pounds sterling. He also received from the Society fifty pounds sterling so that his annual income amounted to eighty-five pounds sterling. These arrangements apparently came in the nick of time since he had married Anne DeCou on May 6, 1772.

Only a few short years of wedded bliss were in store for the rector and his bride as they were very soon to be gravely affected by the divisiveness of the Revolution. It was a violent time and feelings ran deep. Rev. Odell was an official of the Church of England, and as such had taken the oath of supremacy. He had served as a surgeon in the British Army, studied for his Holy Orders in England, and was ordained a priest in the official English church. It stretches the imagination to believe that he could have been other than a Tory with such a background.

Serious trouble started in October 1775. Two letters written by Odell and addressed to individuals in England were seized by the Committee of Inspection and Observation. These letters were turned over to the New Jersey Provincial Congress, which body declined to censure him as it was their decision the letters were not intended to influence public opinion against defense measures adopted by the colonies. Not such a benevolent attitude was taken after the signing of the Declaration of Independence. On July 20, 1776, Jonathan Odell was ordered to remain on the east side of the Delaware River within a radius of eight miles from the Burlington Court House. Such was his reputation that he was considered "a person inimical to American liberty." Despite this restriction it would have been out of character for Rev. Odell to refrain from following the dictates of his own conscience. In a letter to the Society he writes; "Since the declaration of Independence the alternative has been either to make such alterations in the Liturgy as both honor and conscience must be alarmed at, or else to shut up our Churches… It was impossible for me to hesitate a moment…to suspend our public Ministrations rather then make any alteration in the established Liturgy."

Such strong convictions did not go unnoticed by the Revolutionists who, from December 13 to 16, 1776, searched several houses in Burlington in an effort to apprehend him. Another Tory, a Quaker woman by name, Mrs. Margaret Morris, managed to successfully hide him in her home. She had recently purchased the mansion owned by the former Governor, William Franklin, when he left for Perth Amboy. Mrs. Morris reports in her journal that Odell was visiting in her home when a message was received advising him that a party of armed men was searching for him. Mrs. Morris quickly hid the good Reverend in a small room in her house that seemed to have been built for that purpose. It could only be entered through a linen closet, and in order to gain entrance all the linen had to be removed and the shelves disassembled. There was a small door at the back of the closet through which the room could be entered by stooping. The room was completely dark, with no window, but otherwise comfortable. As anticipated, the searching party arrived at Mrs. Morris's house, announcing themselves with loud knocking on the door. Mrs. Morris and the Reverend had previously agreed upon the ringing of a bell as a signal to alert him to the danger. Having a notorious refugee hiding in her own home had Mrs. Morris quite upset. In order to gain her own composure and to give the Reverend sufficient time to be properly concealed, she kept locking and unlocking the door several times. When finally she opened the door, she found half a dozen men, all armed, looking for Odell. She managed to convince them that she knew nothing of his whereabouts and got them to search an empty house nearby instead of her own.

Realizing that his situation in Burlington was untenable, Odell made his escape and took refuge with the British troops in New York, leaving behind his wife and three children, the youngest not three weeks old. Despite his difficulties, the congregation of St. Mary's thought very highly of Rev. Odell and was extremely sympathetic to his plight. In a letter written August 18, 1777, almost eight months after his flight, he expresses his appreciation for the fact that the vestry voted to continue his salary of twenty pounds currency despite his absence.

It is logical to assume that Jonathan Odell used his medical knowledge to solidify his position with the British military. This is borne out by the fact that in the spring of 1782 he made an address to a large number of distinguished officers of the British Army and Navy gathered for ceremonies in New York City.

Dr. Odell was never to return to Burlington and St. Mary's, but instead was appointed to a seat in his Majesty's Council in the Province of New Brunswick in 1784 when a large influx of American Loyalists caused New Brunswick to become a separate colony. In his position he received a salary of one thousand pounds sterling, so his loyalty to the Crown became financially rewarding.

Somehow the church managed to survive during these difficult times and to perform the necessary services to the parishioners. On November 11, 1781 James, the son of John and Martha Lawrence, was baptized. James was later to become the famous navy captain who made immortal the words "Don't give up the ship." In 1810, 1811, and again in 1821, alterations and improvements were made to the building. The extension on the eastern end was added, and the old pulpit and sounding board removed. A new pulpit was erected with a small room underneath for robing purposes. The pews were rearranged so that they ran the full length of the building.

For thirty-seven years, from 1796 to 1833, the church was handsomely served by the Rev. Charles Wharton. He died in his eighty-sixth year after earning the love and respect of his congregation. He was a brilliant scholar and a zealous and devoted Christian. In 1799 a new parsonage was built on the corner of Broad and Talbot Streets.

It was also in this same year that General George Washington died, and memorial services were conducted in St. Mary's by Dr. Wharton. In 1833 the vestry ordered the adoption of uniform pew rents which for some years had not been assessed in any systematic way. The annual rent for the eleven eastern pews on the southern side of the aisle was set at $16 each, and for the same number of pews on the northern side the rent was $15 each. For the rest of the pews the rent was established according to the distance from the pulpit. In receding order from the pulpit each pew was successively one dollar less that that immediately before it. If a person didn't mind being the farthest removed from the pulpit, he could get away with paying an annual rent of only $6.50. (If pew rents were still in vogue today, the vestry would have to reverse the procedure, since the most popular pews today seem to be those farthest from the pulpit.)

Taking Dr. Wharton's place as Rector of St. Mary's was the Right Reverend George Washington Doane, who had been consecrated as Bishop of New Jersey in 1832. St. Mary's was fortunate in securing the services of such an outstanding prelate. Similar to his predecessor, he was a brilliant scholar, a writer and poet of note, and a forceful preacher. He was fondly referred to as the "Princely Prelate" because of his dignified, courteous, and charming manner. He was definitely a man of principle, practicing what he preached. It seems that Bishop Doane on one occasion missed the last train from Jersey City to Burlington, and not wishing to spend the night in the train station sought permission to ride a freight train that was just ready to pull out. The station agent told him that this was against the company's rules and he could not give his permission. The good Bishop told the station agent that he certainly did not preach disobedience to orders, and he made no effort to undermine the agent's responsibilities by bribery or persuasion. However, he still did not wish to spend the night in the train station, so he asked the station master if freight was forwarded by weight. On receiving an affirmative answer, the Bishop stepped on the scales, paid the freight bill for his weight, and was shipped to Burlington as regular freight.

It became necessary to enlarge the church again in 1834. The entrance was changed to Broad Street and the vestibule and northern wing were added, doubling the seating capacity, and giving the church a cruciform appearance. It was at this time that the building was stuccoed, detracting from its colonial appearance. Although the building had been erected one hundred and eighty years before, it had never been consecrated. To correct this oversight consecration services were held in December 1834.

Twelve years later, on September 24, the rector presented plans to the vestry for the construction of an entirely new church structure. The old building with all its additions and improvements was no longer suited to the needs of the growing parish. Bishop Doane had secured the services of architect Richard Upjohn, who was a pioneer in the revival of Gothic architecture in the United States. He wanted a cathedral church which would reflect the fact that St. Mary's was the seat of Episcopal authority in New Jersey. On the night of the 25th, Mr. Upjohn attended the vestry meeting with Bishop Doane, and assured the board that the proposed church could be constructed for a sum not to exceed twenty thousand dollars. The rector presented a list of subscriptions which already amounted to $12,875 with an additional pledge that would make the sum $15,000. Six subscribers had pledged $1,000 each. Several pledged $750 each and there were six that pledged $500 each. Apparently the vestry was impressed as a tentative date of November 1st was set for the laying of the cornerstone.

Bishop Doane laid the cornerstone on Tuesday, November 17, 1846 just missing the original schedule by a few days. The brownstone, Gothic structure was dedicated August 19, 1854. Daily morning and evening prayers were begun along with the weekly celebration of holy communion. In 1856, St. Barnabas Free Mission was opened and the Bishop's son, Willian Croswell Doane, who was later to become Bishop of Albany, was put in charge. The cornerstone for St. Barnabas Chapel was laid by Bishop Doane on June 11, 1858, and was the last act of this sort performed by the Bishop, as he laid aside his earthly problems April 27, 1859. Shortly thereafter an Act was passed by the state making St. Mary's Church the Cathedral Church of the Diocese.[13] In addition to all his other accomplishments, George Washington Doane also wrote hymns. The best known of these is "Safely Now the Light of Day" written in 1824. Other well-known hymns written by him are "Thou Art The Way; to Thee Alone" and "Fling out the Banner! Let It Float." The son not only followed his father into the priesthood but also inherited his song-writing ability. That famous hymn, "Ancient of Days," was written by William C. Doane in 1886.

Although the debt originally incurred in the building of the new church had been steadily reduced, it was not until the early months of 1864 that it was finally liquidated. Partly responsible for generating the final enthusiasm to pay off the debt were sisters of the parish, Mary and Margaret McIlvane. They promised to present a chime to the church as soon as the debt was paid. The chime consisted of eight bells, which were cast by Messrs. Mears & Stanbank of London. The bells arrived in Burlington in 1866 and were hoisted into place immediately. They pealed forth their joyful music for the first time that Easter morning. Many gifts have been made since, including the Lych Gate erected in memory of Stephen Germain Hewitt, the exquisite stained glass windows given just before the turn of the century, a Litany desk in memory of DeTracey Hudson Rich, and a Credence Table in memory of Miss Sarah B. Woolman. George Hewitt built the beautiful colonial gateway in memory of his wife Elizabeth and Daughter Anne. An historic step was taken under Rev. Lewis, who became rector in 1914, when the pew rents were discontinued.

The mortar and stone of the 164-foot steeple deteriorated over the years, and in 1972 it was necessary to do a major overhaul. Richard

Murphy of Philadelphia was hired as architect-in-charge with Dominic and Luigi Ventresca, the stone masons. The old mortar was replaced with new cement, and about 100 stones were so eroded that they had to be removed. The new stones used in the renovation were Wilbertha sandstone from a quarry in West Trenton. The same type of stone was used in the original construction. Stones varying in weight from 25 to 300 pounds were cut to fit at the church site and were raised mechanically to the steeple, where the stone masons fitted them into place. To accomplish this task it was necessary to erect a scaffolding with steel stairs and platforms at various levels. The cost of the steeple renovation was about $75,000, almost four times the original cost of the entire church.

Even though the congregation had built a beautiful cathedral church, it did not forget Old St. Mary's, which had served the community so well for one hundred and fifty years. At a meeting of the vestry on April 6, 1875, a committee was appointed to secure a plan and to devise the means by which the old church could be converted into rooms for a Sunday School and other parish purposes. Architect William D. Hewitt was commissioned and submitted plans and specifications to the vestry at their meeting of July 12th. Subscriptions were obtained and the contract let in September for $5,091 with James Wilson the master builder and William A. Goodher the mason. The work started promptly on the 12th of the month and was completed so that the Benediction of Old St. Mary's could be held in February on the day of the Feast of the Purification. A large congregation assembled for this solemn occasion, and at 10 o'clock the old bell bearing the date 1769 was rung once more, announcing the opening of services. At the close of the colorful ceremony the congregation slowly left the old church, with the chimes of St. Mary's playing "Home Sweet Home," "Carol, Carol, Christians," and "Let the Merry Church Bells Ring."

The old church holds many memories for those interested in its history. Christmas was always a festive occasion. The church was dressed with laurel, spruce, and pine. The sexton bored holes in the tops of the pews about two feet apart and then inserted a branch of laurel followed by spruce and then box. Wreaths of running pine were draped over the pulpit and reading desk and twined around the chancel rails. The two beautiful chandeliers of cut glass were filled with wax candles, with additional wax candles being placed appropriately throughout the church. All those who entered were caught up in the joyous gaiety of the Christmas message.

Old St. Mary's was the first church in America to introduce the old English custom of the "Waits." At midnight on Christmas a number of young men would visit the Episcopal residence, the homes of the clergy and prominent parishioners, saluting them under their windows with Christmas carols and ushering in the remembrance of Christ's birth with song.

But Old St. Mary's had a larger destiny to fulfill. One hundred twenty-two years after the congregation moved into their beautiful, new cathedral church, tragedy struck as a devastating fire left nothing standing except the walls. On April 15, 1976 the roof burst into flames, and before the holocaust was over the building was ruined. Only the walls were left standing. The exquisite walnut interior went up in flames, the magnificent stained glass windows were smashed, but the eight large bells which arrived from England in 1866 miraculously escaped damage. Old St. Mary's was called upon to house the congregation once again until the new church could be rebuilt. In the words of Father Greene, "We're moving everything over to the old church. We left there in 1854 to come into the new church, but now we're going back."

Expressions of sympathy were received from people near and far. The disaster evoked the concern not only of people connected with the church, but of others who had no affiliation except their love for the beautiful, the sacred, and the historic. Contributions were received from the parishioners and local businessmen as well as from people all over the United States. Plans were made for the church's restoration with an anticipated cost of over one million dollars. Fifty-four percent of the value of the burned-out building was obtained from the insurance company, a special project committee was formed to work on fund raising activities, and the possibility of securing governmental grants was explored. Reconstruction work was started, and the target date for completion is Easter 1979.

1. *History of Burlington New Jersey*, by William E. Schermerhorn.

2. *Burlington: A Provincial Capital*, by George DeCou.

3. Ibid.

4. *History of the Church in Burlington New Jersey*, by Rev. George Morgan Hills.

5. *Early Brickmaking in New Jersey*, by Harry B. and Grace M. Weiss.

6. Governor Nicholson was the Governor of Virginia.

7. *History of the Church in Burlington New Jersey*, by Rev. George Morgan Hills.

8. Ibid.

9. Ibid.

10. Ibid.

11. Ibid.

12. Ibid.

13. *History of Burlington New Jersey*, by William E. Schermerhorn.

II

Friends Meeting

Woodbury, 1715

It was late in the evening and Ann Whitall sat alone in the living room of her home, knitting by candlelight, her husband absent, the help not around, and her children tucked safely in bed in the upstairs bedroom. A slight sound distracted her reflections. Glancing toward the open staircase, she saw a pair of shoeless feet disappearing around the landing. Dropping her knitting on the table, she sprang up the stairs and found a man on his hands and knees trying to crawl under a bed in the northwest bedroom. Grabbing him by the feet, she pulled him out from under the bed and demanded to know what he was after. Upon his churlish reply "nothing," she told him that this was no place to be hunting it, slapped him in the face, and marched him downstairs, all the while lecturing him on his sinful nature.[1]

Ann inherited her fearlessness from her Quaker ancestors, who had suffered physical torture rather than give up their religious beliefs. One of these early Quakers was Henry Wood, who had been cruelly beaten, persecuted, imprisoned, and had lost the sight of one eye. Although he was about eighty years old at the time, he decided to leave Bury, Lancashire, England, which was his home, and migrate to the New World where he could enjoy the freedom to worship in his own way. Before leaving England with his son John, his wife

Woodbury Friends Meeting, erected in 1715.

Alice, and their children, he purchased three hundred acres of land from Edward Byllynge located on the south side of the Woodbury Creek, then known by the Indian name, Piscoyackasingz. Shortly after their arrival in Philadelphia in 1681,[2] son John borrowed a canoe from an Indian and paddled his way to the mouth of the Woodbury Creek, continuing up the stream until he reached a place of such natural beauty that he decided to locate his home in that area. According to legend, within a week John had completed a crude log cabin and returned to Philadelphia to escort his family to their new abode. Others of like religious beliefs followed them, for Henry had brought with him from the Monthly Meeting of Friends at Clithrice, Lancashire, England the following certification: "To Friends in

America of the Monthly Meeting where it may fall to the lot of Henry Wood and his son John to inhabit. This may satisfy you that the above named Henry Wood and John Wood, with their families, going to these parts is with the consent of Friends. And we further certify you that they have been faithful to their testimonies and are in good report among Friends in several parts of this nation. So with our dear love to you remembered, desiring your loving assistance to those our dear Friends, we rest your Friends in truth."

The first order of business for the newly arrived Quakers was to establish a Meeting. It was their strong religious beliefs that had brought them to the New World in the first place, so their first concern, after their families were provided with shelter from the elements, was to hold worship services. It was not necessary to have a formal house of worship, so the log cabin of John Wood served as the meeting place for these pioneer Quakers. The Quakers lived side by side with the Indians in a spirit of mutual respect, the wisdom of which was to be proved on more than one occasion. One such occasion was the time the settlement ran short of food, so the men decided to travel to Burlington for supplies. After they had gone a storm arose, preventing their immediate return, and provisions that were available for the women and children when the men left were soon depleted. An Indian squaw, learning of their plight, supplied them with venison and other staples to last them until the men returned.

Patriarch Henry Wood died October 19, 1686, and son John Wood became a leading citizen, serving in the legislature and other public offices. About this time there are vague references to a meeting house having been established called the Shelter. No records exist firmly establishing this as fact, and some historians think that this was simply the name given to John Wood's home. The earliest recorded birth of a child to English parents was that of Constantine Wood, daughter of John and Alice Sale Wood on July 24, 1683. The earliest recorded marriage took place in the "Shelter." Joshua Lord, son of Jesse Lord of England, married Sarah Wood, daughter of John and Alice Sale Wood, in 1689.

Joshua Lord settled in the area as did Henry Tredway, Thomas Gardiner, William Warner, Thomas Matthews, John Ladd, and George Ward. On May 25, 1696, John Wood deeded a lot seventy by one hundred feet to Thomas Gardiner, William Warner, and Joshua Lord as trustees to be used for a meeting house and burying ground. There are no positive records that a meeting house was built, but the graveyard was established. However, the settlers in the area were farmers, and they gradually moved inland where the soil was more productive. By the year 1715 the Friends had decided to build a permanent meeting house in the village. An original deed dated September 15, 1715, states that: "John Swanson of Philadelphia conveyed to John Ladd, Henry Wood and John Cooper, yeoman, all of the County of Gloucester, Western Province of New Jersey, trustees, one acre of ground...lying on the west side of Woodbury Creek some distance up the hill from the swamps of Woodbury Creek...in trust to erect a meeting House upon." The cost of this land was three pounds, two shillings current silver money. Construction of the meeting house was started in the fall of 1715 with John Cooper, an influential man in the community, as the builder. The joists were fifty-one feet in length, fifteen inches thick, and ten inches wide, all hand-hewn. To this day they are sturdy and well-preserved, with the tool marks still visible. It was a red brick building interlaced with blue bricks to break the monotony of color. The interior was simple, in keeping with the Friends philosophy of no frills, with plain paneling in the back of the facing benches, wide wooden planks for the floors, and sturdy, hand-made wooden benches, some of which are still in use. Galleries were erected on the west and south sides of the building. Tin sconces lined the walls, each holding one tallow candle. Originally it was known as the Red Bank Meeting, then the Woodbury Creek Meeting, and finally Woodbury Meeting.

The Meeting continued to grow and additional land purchases were made in 1757, 1764, and 1801. All together just under 2.5 acres were purchased. In typical Quaker fashion the men sat on one side of the aisle and the women on the other. Their business meetings were held separately, and when matters of joint concern arose, representatives would be appointed from each Meeting to meet together, discuss the matter, and report back to their respective business assemblies.

The Quakers, as with all sections of an organized society, were great in appointing committees. On February 7, 1766, Joshua Lord, Joseph Gibson, Jr., and David Cooper were placed in charge of the graveyard. It was their duty to determine the eligibility of the people who wished to be buried there. In order to preserve the space for the members of the Friends Society who were paying for its upkeep, the following rules were adopted:

1. Every person in membership is to be admitted.
2. Every widower and widow whose last wife or husband lies there, unless lives have been openly profane and dissolute, is to be admitted.
3. Every person who professed with the Friends, and was of an orderly life and steady in attendance with the Religious Meetings is to be admitted.

The Revolutionary War disrupted the peaceful life of these Quakers, as it did their brethren in other communities. The meeting house was used as a commissary depot and hospital during the battle of Red Bank. Job Whitall, in his diary, mentions his experience: "Eleventh Month 7, 1777, went to Woodbury Meeting, and found it was in use as a hospital for sick soldiers, but Friends had a solid satisfactory meeting out of doors." There were a number, though, who were quite disturbed over the use of the meeting house by the soldiers, and they wrote a formal letter of protest to General Varnham advising him that they had built the house at their expense and for the sole purpose of meeting together to worship Almighty God, and calling on the General to return the building to its intended purpose. The letter was effective, for on the 30th of the month the house was restored to the Quakers for their use.

In the same year the Battle of Red Bank took place, and the name of Ann Whitall again appears in the pages of history, witnessing her stoutness of heart and stubbornness of spirit. She had been married in 1739 at the age of 23 to James Whitall, only son of Job and Jane Sidon Whitall. They started married life without wanting much in the way of the world's blessings. They lived on a ninety-acre farm located on the east bank of the Delaware River, seven miles below Philadelphia. Their marriage was blessed with six sons and three daughters. She was a devout person, and, despite the demands on her time in running the household and in caring for a "passel of children" with their fevers and sicknesses, managed to attend worship services regularly. So devoted was she that once she rode all the way to Haddonfield for Quarterly Meeting on horseback through a driving rainstorm. Not so with her husband and children. In her diary she bemoans her husband's endeavors to escape attending services: "Hannah and I went to meeting alone, and her father would not go with us. But it is my lot to go alone, or none must go. Oh, it is my mind that any may contrive their business so as to go to meeting constantly, if they will. But, oh! This going when he has a mind, or once a month. Once a month! When 6th day meeting comes then more earnest at work than ere a day in the whole, whole week!" Sometimes her husband would tease her, questioning whether she were any better than he since she had not escaped being thrown and kicked by her horse even while she was on her way to Meeting!

But to return to the Battle of Red Bank and Ann Whitall. The British troops were in Philadelphia, but General Washington wished to make it impossible for them to remain there by depriving them the free use of the Delaware River. Fort Mercer was built in the Whitall's apple orchard. The lumber from their barn was used to build the stockade which was constructed within three hundred feet of their house. When the British tried to force passage through the Delaware River, the Americans opened fire. Ann, who was 61 years of age at the time, was urged to flee the house, but she replied: "God's arm is strong and will protect me. I may do good by staying."

So she remained alone in the house while the battle raged and the cannon balls were falling all around. Calmly she stayed in her upstairs sitting room working at her spinning wheel as she would on any other day. That is, she remained there until a twelve-pound cannon ball from a British vessel on the river passed through the heavy brick wall on the north gable of the house, crashed through a partition at the head of the stairs, and lodged in another partition near where Ann was spinning. Conceding divine protection a little more certain elsewhere, she retreated to the cellar where she continued her spinning until called upon to nurse the wounded and dying.[3]

Do good by remaining she certainly did. She went among the wounded caring for their needs and easing their pain as best she could, regardless of whether they were British or American. She could not resist, however, chiding the British about coming to America to cause pain and suffering. One of the wounded who was taken to the Whitall home was the British Commander, Count Donop, who was mortally wounded early in the battle. He was buried between the fort and the Whitall house where his grave was marked by a modest stone until 1874. By then the erosion of the river bank forced the owner of the Whitall estate to reinter the remains elsewhere.[4]

Ann lived another twenty years after her participation in the Battle of Red Bank, dying September 22, 1797, aged 82. Her husband, James, despite his errant church ways, outlived Ann by eleven years, dying September 29, 1808, aged 92. With his sly, teasing, good humor he probably enjoyed having the last word!

By 1783, concern arose over the adequacy of the meeting house, and on the 11th a committee reported to the Monthly Meeting that an enlargement of the facilities was considered necessary. James Whitall, Jr., John Jesops, and Aaron Hewes were placed in charge of securing the necessary materials. Aaron Hewes was also given the job of receiving the money that was subscribed. It was decided to add an additional twenty-six feet to the length of the building, thereby doubling its size, and to add two new galleries to match those of the original building. Within two years the addition was completed, and a committee consisting of David Cooper, Samuel Ladd, and Phineus Lord was pleased to report on October 7, 1785 that more money had been subscribed than was necessary. The total cost was 1,167 pounds, 5 shillings and $4\frac{1}{2}$ pence leaving 7 shillings and $5\frac{1}{2}$ pence remaining in the treasury. The addition had been so skillfully added to the old building that the harmony of design gave the entire building the appearance of having been built all at the same time. The simplicity of Quaker desires had been incorporated into the addition as in the original, and no adornments were included which might mar the plainness of the Quaker meeting house. However, Joshua Evans, who visited the Woodbury Meeting in 1798, apparently thought otherwise. He records in his diary: "Next day I had some close labor at Woodbury Monthly partly on account of superfluous workmanship in the building of the addition to the Meeting House. I had also to speak of the growth of pride and superfluity in other buildings, and riding in fine carriages which have painting of different colors and carvings that occasion them to be more costly and not more useful." Apparently Joshua Evans objected to what he considered the "ornateness" of the paneling in back of the facing benches as well as the lifestyles adopted by a few of the brethren. Possibly the wagon sheds that were built in 1796 to accommodate the horses and wagons of those attending First day services caused Joshua Evans to be concerned. These were constructed at private cost, and each Friend who desired such a shed had to pay $14.25 for its use.

Woodbury Friends Meeting

The great schism that afflicted the Society of Friends in 1827–28 was felt at Woodbury. Elias Hicks, a deeply religious Quaker, had founded a Quaker community in Virginia based on the thinking of Voltaire and Paine's *Age of Reason*. Hicks' teachings began to influence many Friends, rousing intense feelings of antipathy among the Orthodox members and causing a schism that was to divide so many Friends congregations. As a result, most Friends community meeting houses were taken over by one group, with the other sometimes building their own place of worship. Not so in Woodbury. Here they shared the same place of worship by simply partitioning the building, with each branch using one side. The partition was moveable so that the entire meeting house could be used for special occasions by either branch. For First day services the Hicksites worshipped on the east side and the Orthodox on the west side. This arrangement was followed for more than a century, until 1927 when the two branches began meeting together once a month.[5] The first joint worship service was held on June 28, 1927. This worked so well that three years later they agreed to unite for services each First day. By 1954 the Hicksite and Orthodox Monthly Meetings united to form the Woodbury Monthly Meeting of the Religious Society of Friends.

The meeting house was originally lighted by means of homemade candles set in tin sconces attached to the walls, which were later replaced by kerosene lamps. At first the only heat was that supplied by each individual worshipper, such as in a heated brick or foot stove. Eventually stoves were installed, and when the meeting house was partitioned because of the separation, there were two stoves in the center aisle on each side of the partition. The stoves nearest the facing benches burned coal while the other two burned wood. There were no other conveniences which are thought so necessary today. In those days when Quarterly Meeting was held and it was necessary to feed a large number of people, the third floor was set up as a kitchen. It contained a large table and a coal range. Tables were put up in the galleries where the people were fed the noon meal. All of the water had to be carried in from neighboring houses since there was no running water in the meeting house. The men carried the water up two flights of stairs and built the fire and the women prepared the food. As a result of these tasks there was good fellowship and no one realized that they were being inconvenienced. But progress must be served, and in 1951 the Monthly Meeting approved plans for the renovation of the west end of the old meeting house. Four rooms were partitioned off, one for an oil heating system, two for wash rooms, and one for the kitchen. The old stoves were removed, a new floor was laid over the old random-width boards, plumbing was installed (making running water available), the galleries were made into classrooms for the First day school, and, finally, the last concession to modern-day conveniences, the old wooden benches were given away or sold. Those who decry the modernization of cherished heritages rejoice over the fact that the east side remains the same as the day it was built in 1785, except for the back gallery which is now used as a classroom for First day school. Time has aged the woodwork beautifully as no paint has ever been applied to it.

This venerable old meeting house has been in continuous use by Friends since it was first erected. Unfortunately, membership has dwindled to about 80 people with only about 20 active, but services are still held every First day.

---

1. *Ann Whitall – The Heroine of Red Bank,* by Isabella C. McGeorge.

2. *History of Gloucester, Salem and Cumberland Counties,* by Cushing & Sheppard.

3. Ibid.

4. Ibid.

5. *The History of Quakerism,* by Elbert Russell.

III

Friends Meeting

Seaville, 1727

eligious freedom! That privilege, much sought after by the early colonists, and so hard to find elsewhere, was one of the main reasons for the settlement of this area. These people had left the Old World because they were not allowed to worship as they pleased, and to establish this cherished freedom in the New World. However, they found that the New World was no better than the Old in this respect, and they were forced to flee from New England to Rhode Island to Long Island and, finally, to the Jerseys. Here at last they found the freedom they sought.

According to the early records, people were living in the Cape May County area by 1685. They earned their livings as shipbuilders, fishermen, and farmers. Strange as it may seem to us today, some of them were whalers, also. In fact, whaling was the first occupation for the settlers in the Cape May area. The Dutch were the original whalers, but it was the English who made it a successful commercial enterprise. These hardy Englishmen ventured into the Delaware Bay in small boats to harpoon whales weighing as much as 250 tons!

Thus, it is not surprising that there were many nationalities among the first families to establish the Friends Meeting now located at Seaville. John Townsend's ancestors had come from England as early

Seaville Friends Meeting, erected in 1727.

as 1640, settling in Boston. However, they had a habit of speaking out against the practices of the times, such as witchcraft, suppression of speech, and imprisonment for harboring dissenters. This was one of the families that found it necessary to flee to Rhode Island and then Long Island to escape persecution. John Townsend learned of the Friends settlements in the Jerseys and brought his family to the Great Egg Harbor region sometime during the 1680s. Unfortunately, the exact date is not known. He settled his family at Ocean View after obtaining a grant of 640 acres from the West Jersey Society.

Christopher Leaming came from England to Long Island in 1670. He was a successful whaleman and became familiar with the Cape May area during the winters while on whaling trips. In 1691 he moved his family to the Cape May region. He and John Townsend had been close friends when they both lived in Long Island. It was Christopher who helped John build his house. When not whaling, Leaming was a cooper and coffin maker.

The Corson brothers, John and Peter, came from Long Island in 1680 on a whaling vessel, and settled in upper Cape May in what now is Palermo.

In New Amsterdam the church fathers were all powerful, and they were troublesome to the Quakers. Remmer Garretson, along with his wife Rebekah, arrived in 1693 to settle near Beesley's Point. They had been driven out of Long Island by the authoritarian actions of the church officials of New Amsterdam. Rebekah was a devout and staunch Quaker.

All of these families were among the founders of the Friends Society that eventually became the Seaville Monthly Meeting.

Probably as early as 1693 meetings for worship were being held in John Townsend's home at Ocean View. Some of the worshippers lived north of the Great Egg Harbor River, and this meant crossing that large body of water each First day. However, the Quakers, as practical people, always manage to find practical solutions to their problems. They purchased a boat under joint ownership with each family sharing the cost. This boat came to be know as the "Business Boat" because many a business meeting was held during the crossings concerning the affairs of the Friends Meeting. The boat traveled from Somers Point to Beesley's Point, and then it was a long horseback ride to Ocean View for the faithful.

Because of these obvious hardships, Rebekah Garretson offered her home at Beesley's Point as a place to hold First day services. This offer was gladly accepted, particularly by those Friends living north of the Great Egg Harbor River, but the records, unfortunately, do not shed any light on the exact date when the meeting place was changed. It was probably about the year 1702, as this is the year generally accepted as the date the Meeting was officially established. It became part of the Great Egg Harbor Monthly Meeting along with Meetings at Tuckahoe and Galloway.

For about twenty-five years they had no meeting house in which to hold their worship services. Most of this time they met in Rebekah Garretson's home, but they also held meetings in the home of Richard Somers. Finally, it was decided that a meeting house should be built. The following is taken from the minutes of the Great Egg Harbor Monthly Meeting: "3rd month 29th 1717 Rebekah Garretson it is concluded to build a Meeting House by Jacob Garretson and Jacob Garretson agrees to give one acre of land for the servis of s'd meeting, which house is to be built this fall." Jacob Garretson was the son of Rebekah Garretson, and it was on the plot of ground given by him that a meeting house of cedar siding was erected in the fall of 1727.[1] Because the walls had originally consisted of one thickness of white cedar boards, it was known as "The Old Cedar Meeting House." It remains today much as it was in 1727. The old oak beams with the adz marks still visible are the original beams. The straight wooden benches, colored by age and polished by long use, accommodated the early worshippers. Wooden buttons and door latches on the inner portals, along with the heads of hand-made, wrought iron nails showing noticeably in the benches, add greatly to the centuries-old look of this ancient meeting house. Even some of the original wide-planked flooring is still in use. Around 1890 the old cedar boards, worn satin smooth by the ravages of time and weather, were covered with new siding.

Around the year 1731 the meeting house was moved from Beesley's Point to Seaville, where it is still in active use. The records leave much to the imagination since they do not indicate the reason for the move. Just as the place of worship was originally changed from Ocean View to Beesley's Point to accommodate the majority of the worshippers, so the meeting house was now moved to Seaville where there was a large colony of Friends. In connection with this move there is an interesting legend. Regretfully, it cannot be proved by the records, but has been passed on from one generation to another. Since modern-type roads were nonexistent in those days, the logistics of such a move presented considerable problems. According to legend, the building was cut in half and moved in two parts. One body of belief has the meeting house being moved by water, and an examination of a map indicates that such a move was very likely. In fact, this may have been the simplest means of transportation. Another theory is that the two parts were moved over the dirt road that roughly paralleled the present Route 9.

As was the custom with the Quakers in those days, and, in fact, with most other sects as well, the private lives of the members were as much a concern of the entire membership as their religious activities. At the Monthly Meeting held fourth day of the fifth month, 1740, the minutes contain the following statement: "At Preparative Meeting Robert Smith and Edmund Somers are appointed to assist the women Friends in dealing with Deborah Seeds on ye account of selling drink and return on our next meeting as they find. The meeting adjourned to ye usual time and place." Robert Smith and Edmund Somers faithfully discharged their assignment as recorded by the minute of the next meeting: "At our Monthly Meeting held at Cape May for Cape May and Egg Harbor this 4th day of ye 6th month 1740 at Preparative Meeting Robert Smith and Edmund Somers reported that they did assist the women Friends according to appointment." Unfortunately, our curiosity as to the solution arrived at is not satisfied as no further details are recorded.

The tragic separation of the Friends Societies did not take place at Seaville. There was no separation since all the members were of the Hicksite persuasion. Therefore, there was no division of property, no dividing the meeting house into Orthodox and Hicksite sections, and no separation of friends and families. At the time of the Separation, generally speaking, Friends in the rural areas were Hicksites, and those in the urban and city areas were Orthodox. Since Seaville was definitely a rural area, it is not surprising that all the members of this Meeting were Hicksites. One of the stories in vogue in those days was that Orthodox Friends owned two horses and a carriage, while Hicksite Friends only owned one horse.[2]

Toward the end of the 19th century the meeting house was no longer used on a regular basis. The Meeting became to all intents and purposes a closed Meeting. By 1937, however, annual Meetings were held the last First day in August, mainly for the convenience of those Friends who were vacationing at the shore. Interest began to revive, and Meetings were held every First day during the summer months. By 1957 there was sufficient interest to warrant First day services throughout the year, and the Meeting was reorganized as a Monthly Meeting under the care of the Salem Quarterly Meeting. According to one devoted, life-long member, Seaville Meeting is now filled with "convinced Quakers" rather than "birthright Quakers," and, as a result, the Meeting is now very active.

Registered as an historic site, this quaint, old meeting house remains a visible symbol of our forefathers' quest for that freedom which they considered most precious—religious freedom.

---

1. Some histories erroneously give the year as 1716.

2. See Chapter on Friends Meeting, Woodbury.

IV

First Presbyterian Church

Tennent, 1751

It was a black period in Scotland's history infamously known as "Killing Times." The Black Watch of King Charles II swept over the country seeking the Covenanters, who were mainly Scotch Presbyterians who hated prelacy. Charles II had tried to force prelatic religious worship on his subjects, and the Covenanters refused to abide by his orders. They held that no man could usurp the prerogatives of Christ as head of the church, and they were willing to die for their beliefs. They did just that! For twenty-eight years, from 1660 to 1688, they were hunted down, thrown into prison, sold as slaves, banished from the country, and deprived of their property, and all because of their unbending religious beliefs. It is estimated that 18,000 Covenanters were either killed or banished during those horrible twenty-eight years.

One of them, George Scott, led 200 brave men and women on a voyage to escape the torture and prisons of Scotland to the New World, where they hoped to find peace and the freedom to worship God as they saw fit. They sailed from Leith on September 6, 1685 on the vessel *Henry and Francis*. It was a disastrous voyage that lasted one hundred days before they landed at Perth Amboy in December. Disease and fever plagued these hardy voyagers, and by the time the

The First Presbyterian Church in Tennent, built in 1751.

journey ended, sixty of their number had perished, including George Scott and his wife. Discouraged, ill, and poverty-stricken, the little band of 140 men and women faced the perils of an unknown land inhabited by savages, which they had ironically sought for peace and freedom, fleeing from a so-called civilized, Christian country.

Some of them settled around the Amboys while others moved on to the fertile land of what is now Monmouth County. Here they held their services in private homes without any interference. They read the Scriptures, sang psalms, taught the children, and were led in prayer by one of the leaders. Soon they decided to build a house of worship, and for the location selected a piece of ground with a slight elevation. In line with the freedom they were enjoying, the hill was called "Free Hill," which evolved into "Free Hold" and the modern name "Freehold." The structure was necessarily crude, built of logs in approximately 1692. This became known as "Old Scots Church." There is no record of its actual size, but years ago there was a depression in the land about 20 feet square which tradition has credited to be the location of Old Scots Church and which would indicate its approximate size.

That such a building existed by the year 1705 is evidenced by a book at the County Clerk's office in Freehold containing the minutes of Monmouth County from 1688 to 1723. This record proves that the building existed by the year 1705, but it could have been erected prior to that date. The site of this building was at a place called Topenamus. Walter Ker obtained a deed for fifty acres in Topenamus in 1689–90, and in the same year he secured a deed for an additional thirty acres. According to legend, the first meeting of the Philadelphia Presbytery was held in Old Scots Church on December 28, 1706. At that meeting John Boyd was ordained; he was the first known pastor of Old Scots. Thus, Old Scots had the distinction of hosting the first know meeting of a Presbytery and the first recorded Presbyterian ordination in America. Besides ordination, a candidate for the ministry had to be "qualified." If he was not in the communion of the Anglican Church, the candidate was obliged to take an oath that he would not teach the doctrine of Transubstantiation, and that he agreed with the doctrine of the Trinity as taught by the 39 Articles of the Anglican Church. Once he took this oath he was considered "qualified." Rev. Boyd was qualified on May 29, 1706.

Rev. Joseph Morgan ascended the pulpit of Old Scots Church after the death of Rev. Boyd and was its minister from 1709 to 1729. At the same time he was the preacher for the Brick Church of Marlboro, which later became the First Reformed Church of Freehold. He was qualified to preach in both the English and Dutch languages. He was something of a free spirit. At that time Monmouth County was wild, undeveloped country, and horseback riding was the accepted mode of travel. Rev. Morgan astonished his parishioners by riding around the countryside in a two-wheeled carriage drawn by his horse. It was the first of its kind in the county. Apparently he liked the "good" life, because in 1736 the Presbytery disciplined him for the use of strong liquor. Later he became a missionary along the Jersey coast.

When Rev. Morgan vacated the pulpit in 1729, Walter Ker took it upon himself to travel to Neshaminy, Pennsylvania to persuade John Tennent to become the pastor of Old Scots. John Tennent's father had started the famous Log College in Neshaminy where John Tennent was educated. It is not surprising that Walter Ker shouldered this responsibility since he was one of the original Covenanters, having come from Scotland when he was 29 years old under sentence of perpetual banishment. From the beginning he had been one of the leaders of the group that formed Old Scots.

An interesting story is told of his trip to Neshaminy. It was harvest time, and the grain was ripe in the fields. Ker had left his fields to seek a new minister for the church. In Ker's absence his neighbors harvested his grain and stacked it in the fields. His neighbors, however, suffered a tragic loss of their crops through bad storage, and Ker's grain was all that survived. In appreciation for his neighbor's help Ker supplied the seed from his grain the following spring so that his neighbors could plant again.

Ker's trip to Neshaminy was successful, and John Tennent became the third pastor of Old Scots. He was called on April 15, 1730 and ordained on November 19th in Old Scots Church. Tragedy was once again to strike this pioneer church. Like Rev. Boyd, John Tennent was only to preach two years, dying on Sunday, April 23, 1732. Before his death, however, he was to enjoy the privilege of preaching in their new building.

By 1730 Old Scots Church was inadequate, and the congregation decided to build a new sanctuary. The elders met at the house of

Charles Gordon on Monday, July 29, 1730. After a full discussion as to the merits of repairing and enlarging the old church or of building a completely new sanctuary, the vote was cast for a new meeting house "between Walter Ker's Barns and Rocky Hill Bridge." This became the first sanctuary on White Hill, which got its name from two old and beautiful white oak trees growing on the summit. John Davies was the chief carpenter. William Redford Craig built the pulpit as his contribution. The iron furnishing and the iron weathervane were forged on the anvil of Benjamin VanCleve.

The elders may have had their say at the meeting, but it was Janet Rhea who decided the actual location of the new meeting house. The original plans were to build on the lower side of the hill. However, Janet had other ideas. She was a strong-minded woman who had been one of the original Scotch Covenanters who sailed on the *Henry and Francis*. Gathering the small cornerstone in her apron, she marched to the top of the hill and announced, "Who ever heard of going doon to the hoose of the Lord, and not going oop to the hoose of the Lord?" The meeting house was built where Janet placed the cornerstone. Not even the elders wished to argue with her. The first service in the new meeting house was held April 18, 1731.

Rev. William Tennent, Jr., brother of John Tennent, became the fourth pastor. He, too, was educated at the famous Log College of his father. Because of some unusual experiences, he became know as a mystic. He had apparently died of a fever. The mourners had gathered for the funeral when a young doctor noticed a slight tremor under the arm. Upon the insistence of the doctor, the funeral was postponed. For three days and nights the doctor never left the body, but no further signs of life developed. The mourners again arrived for the funeral, but the doctor pleaded for more time. Finally, when no more time was to be allowed and the service was about to begin, Rev. Tennent opened his eyes. The astonished mourners tried to feed him nourishment, but his jaws were stiff and could not be opened. In desperation the doctor pried his jaws open enough to allow a straw to be inserted. Slowly, Rev. Tennent recovered.

Since he had literally returned from the dead, he was asked what heaven was like. He said he saw a great multitude in the height of bliss, his own troubles were ended and he had a feeling of complete and total peace. When he was about to join the multitude, he was advised that his time had not come and that he must return to earth. He cried out against being returned to the world, but to no avail. When he opened his eyes and saw that he was indeed back in the world, he fainted. During the first stages of his recovery, he had no recollection of things past, not even knowing his name. He remained in a state of ecstasy for some time, but gradually his memory returned. He continued his active ministry until his death at 72 on March 8, 1777. He was buried beneath the floor of the White Hill church.

Rev. Tennent preached in both Old Scots, which became known as the Upper Meeting House. Services were finally discontinued in Old Scots with Rev. William Tennent the last preacher to officiate there. During his pastorate the White Hill church was rebuilt and enlarged to meet the congregation's expanding needs. The interior arrangement remained unchanged. There were no stoves to provide heat on cold Sabbath mornings. The women brought foot warmers, which were tin-lined boxes in which live coals were placed. Box pews kept out the drafts and kept in what little heat was provided by the foot warmers. The only aid in the singing of psalms was a pitch pipe. In June 1797 Jonathan Forman, William McChesney, Thomas Coock, and David Sutphin were appointed as clerks in reading and singing the psalms. During the pastorate of Rev. VanDoren the acceptance of music in the church services had advanced to the point that a choir was formed. Around 1856 a melodeon was installed, followed by a pedal organ and then by a modern pipe organ. In the early part of the 19th century the Watts Hymnal was used, later replaced by the official hymnals of the Presbyterian Board of Publication.

Tennent First Presbyterian Church

Old Tennent, as the sanctuary on White Hill became known, did not escape the ravages of the Revolutionary War. The church and the parsonage were in the thick of the Battle of Monmouth, which took place on June 29, 1778. Cannon balls pierced the walls of the church; a round shot tore through the roof of the pastor's study in the parsonage. Fortunately, he wasn't there at the time. After the battle the church was used as a hospital by the American soldiers. Blood from wounded and dying soldiers stained the pews. The pastors of Old Tennent were strong supporters of the Revolution. Rev. William Tennent was an ardent patriot, and Rev. Woodhull was a chaplain in Washington's Army and supposedly took part in the Battle of Monmouth.

Known by many names—Upper Meeting House and the Freehold Church because of its location, Old Red Church because of its once flaming color, Tennent Church because of the famous Tennent ministers, and, finally and fondly, Old Tennent Church—here indeed is historic ground. Scotch Covenanters, who were driven out of the homeland by torture and persecution, made their new home a shrine of Presbyterianism. Under their auspices was held the first meeting of a Presbytery and the first ordination of a Presbyterian minister. They contributed enormously to the Great Awakening and to the eventual freedom of their adopted country from the Old World. Their ministers were active and ardent supporters of the Revolution. It is no wonder that Old Tennent Church is considered not only a shrine of Presbyterianism but of freedom itself.

V

St. Michael's Protestant Episcopal Church

Trenton, 1753

The sturdy sailboat *Shield*, which was the next vessel after the *Kent* to bring immigrants from the Old World up the Delaware River to Burlington, dropped anchor on October 19, 1678. Most of the passengers were Quakers who had come to the New World to escape the persecution they had suffered in their homeland. One of these, Mahlon Stacy, was to play a large part in the establishment of Trenton. After landing in Burlington he traveled north and laid claim in 1679 to land in the area now known as Trenton. He settled just south of Assunpink Creek adjacent to the falls of the Delaware River. Here it was that he established the first permanent settlement by building a grist mill in 1680. The settlement soon became known as The Falls due to the eight foot drop of the river at this point. In 1703 Mahlon Stacy died, and his son, Mahlon Stacy, Jr., sold the family homestead, along with 800 acres, in 1704, to a Philadelphia merchant named William Trent.

In the early years of the 18th century William Trent became a prominent citizen of the Province of New Jersey. He was appointed to the legislature in 1721 and became Speaker of the House and finally Chief Justice of New Jersey. After purchasing the land from

St. Michael's Protestant Episcopal Church, built in 1753.

Mahlon Stacy, Jr., he named the area Trent's Town from which has evolved the modern name of Trenton.

In 1719 the Township of Trenton was formed from a part of Hopewell Township. It is in Hopewell that St. Michael's has its origins. On April 29, 1703 John Hutchinson conveyed two acres in trust to Andrew Heath, Richard Eayre, Abial Davis, and Zebulon Heston. The purpose of the trust as stated in one of the deeds was to reserve the ground for the construction of a public meeting house as well as for a burial place. Funds which were voluntarily contributed made it possible to build a church which became known as the Hopewell Church, around the year 1704. Although the deed was addressed "To all Christian people" it wasn't long before the Church of England laid claim to the building, and people of this persuasion occupied it until St. Michael's was built in Trenton. Since there were no other churches nearby, it became the first Christian church in the Trenton area. Rev. John Talbot often officiated, and in 1720 Rev. William Harrison was appointed missionary for the Hopewell Church along with the care of the Maidenhead Church. This was too arduous a task for him, and in 1723 he left for a church on Staten Island. The Hopewell Church was abandoned about the year 1755 after St. Michael's was built. In 1838 the congregation sold the land, the meeting house having long since disappeared.

The land on which St. Michael's now stands was deeded to the parish by John Coxe. This was bought by him at a public auction on October 27, 1742 for 48 pounds, 10 shillings. He had purchased it from James Trent, eldest son of Willian Trent, on January 29, 1729. So this parcel of land was owned in turn by Mahlon Stacy, the Quaker who arrived on the *Shield*; William Trent, for whom the town was named; James Trent, the eldest son of William; James Neilson; John Coxe; and finally St. Michael's, which at that time was known as the Church of Trenton.

Not until 1761 does the name St. Michael appear in the minutes of the church. The date its name was officially changed is not known, but it can be surmised that it happened about September 29th. This was the date the church was dedicated, the day of the Feast of St. Michael and All Angels.

Construction of the building was started in the autumn of 1747 and probably finished in 1753. In 1749 they had run out of funds and it was necessary to run a lottery, which raised 393 pounds, 15 shillings. This allowed them to finish construction of the new church. By April 30, 1755 it is mentioned in the minutes that they not only have a church building but that they have a minister. Rev. Michael Houdin was living in New York when the communicants at Trenton wrote to him beseeching him to be their minister. In their letter they mentioned that the closest Anglican minister was far away in Burlington, and the people in Trenton were sadly in need of the services of the Anglican church. Rev. Houdin wrote to the Society for the Propagation of the Gospel in Foreign Parts, which was the agency in England that appointed and supported Church of England missionaries, and they approved of his move to Trenton as their missionary in that area.

Rev. Houdin was born in France in 1705 and had been a priest in the Roman Catholic Church and Superior of a Fransican convent in Montreal, Canada. He had been ordained by the Archbishop of Treves on Easter Day, 1730, and Easter Day 1747 he made a public announcement of what he considered the errors of the Church of Rome. He received Holy Communion according to the precepts of the Church of England, and afterwards took the oath of allegiance and subscribed to the 39 Articles of the Church of England.

The progress of the French and Indian Wars was to have a profound effect upon the career of Rev. Houdin and his relationship with St. Michael's. In 1759 William Pitt, Prime Minister of England, assigned General James Wolfe the task of capturing Quebec. Rev.

Houdin's knowledge of the Canadian terrain was of tremendous importance to the British commander, and he immediately appointed him as his personal guide. When General Wolfe ordered the troops to move out, Rev. Houdin found himself accompanying the General on his way to Quebec. Concerned about the Society's reaction to his absence from his missionary post, Houdin wrote to them explaining that he really had no choice as he was ordered by the army commander to be his personal guide. When General Wolfe was killed in the Battle of Quebec, Rev. Houdin asked for permission to return to Trenton. However, his request was refused. At the end of the war he was sent as a missionary to New Rochelle, New York, to minister to the many French refugees. He remained there until his death in 1766.

Rev. Auger Treadwell became rector of St. Michael's on April 4, 1763. He was a graduate of Yale College and had become a teacher in a small, private school in Flushing, New York, where he was active as a lay reader in the Anglican church. He was so effective as a lay reader that the congregation sent him to England in December 1762 to be ordained. It was after his ordination that he was sent to St. Michael's as the Society's missionary.

Even though he was stationed in Trenton, Rev. Treadwell had a soft spot in his heart for the people at Flushing. According to a letter written to the Society by the rector at Flushing, Rev. Treadwell traveled to Flushing, forced his way into the church, and held services. In his own defense Treadwell explained to the Society that he had been invited by the church wardens, and that they had assured him that it was proper for him to conduct services in the church.

As to his affairs at Trenton, Rev. Treadwell reported that about 20 families attended church services regularly and that they contributed willingly to his support. This contribution, willing as it was, amounted to only 20 pounds sterling per year. In addition to his duties at Trenton he also held services at Maidenhead and

Allentown. Treadwell had but a short pastorate, dying at the age of 31 on August 19, 1765.

After his death the church was without a minister for a number of years. Finally, the Society appointed Rev. William Thompson, an itinerant missionary in Pennsylvania serving the communities of York, Carlisle, and Cumberland. He arrived in Trenton in June 1769, when he received a friendly reception, but found the people rather indifferent to religious services after being without them for so long. In a short time, however, he was able to report to the Society that he was much encouraged as the church was filled with worshippers each Sunday morning.

In his travels he visited the small village of Princeton, known at that time as Prince Town. He found there a large Presbyterian college attended by about 100 boys. In the village were a number of people anxious for the services of the Church of England as were some of the boys who were attending the Presbyterian college. Rev. Thompson offered to minister to them on weekdays, an offer which they gladly accepted. A subscription was started for the purpose of building a small church, and Thompson believed that they would succeed since 130 pounds were subscribed immediately. However, the difficulties caused by the upcoming war made the task extremely formidable, and it was not until 60 years later that an Episcopal church was formed in 1833.

It was not only at Princeton that the war with England disrupted the normal course of events. In Trenton the vestry found it necessary to close St. Michael's completely until the end of the war. On Sunday July 7, 1776, the day before the Declaration of Independence was publicly proclaimed from the steps of the court house, the vestry suspended services.

This temporary suspension of services remained in effect from July 7, 1776 until October 1783—seven years. The alteration referred to in the Resolution of the Vestry was the prayer for the King of England contained in the church's liturgy. The patriots demanded that it be removed, a condition to which the church officials could not agree.

St. Michael's suffered considerable physical damage during the war. A detachment of Hessian troops under Colonel Rahl's command was quartered in the church prior to the Battle of Trenton. After peace was declared, St. Michael's filed a claim for damages to the church property amounting to 173 pounds, 4 shillings. There is no record that this claim was ever paid. However, the vestry did not wait for action on the claim, but took steps to put the church in condition so that services could be resumed.

On August 30, 1815 the Annual Convention was held at St. Michael's. At that convention the Rt. Rev. John Croes, D.D., was elected the first Bishop of New Jersey. This event caused a decided change in the spirit of the Episcopal Church in New Jersey since New Jersey was the ninth state to receive a bishop of its own. St. Michael's had the honor of hosting this historic event.

Over the years, repairs, alterations, renovations, and extensions were made to the original building. Side galleries were added in 1844, increasing the seating capacity to 250 people. A major enlargement took place in 1871. These alterations were under the direction of George T. Pearson, a Philadelphia architect. Before the work was finished the church was practically rebuilt, except for the front facing Warren Street. The cost of these alterations amounted to $7,000. Again in 1886 extensive changes were made consisting of a rearrangement of the aisles, the reupholstering and repainting of the interior, the addition of a new vestry room, and the painting of the exterior of the church. During this time the congregation held Sunday services in the Ferry street Chapel. In 1903 the chapel was sold to the Salvation Army for $5,600. In 1924 the women of the church undertook a very important task. Time and weather had played havoc with the names and inscriptions on the old tombstones. At a cost of $1,500, the women had the stones cleaned and the inscriptions recut so that they were legible again. In 1931 the bishop dedicated the church yard.

St. Michael's has always ministered to the needs of the people in its parish. These needs have changed as the area evolved from its rural beginnings to the office and factory complex it is today. The concern the church has shown for its people over the years is just as true now, even though the ethnic background is changing.

VI

Friends Meeting

Mount Laurel, 1760

Among the dissidents in England in the late 17th century who were dissatisfied with their treatment was William Evans, whose son was destined to become the first white settler in a large area in South Jersey called Evesham. William Evans was a member of the Society of Friends and was looking for a place where he could worship God according to the dictates of his own conscience. Charles II, King of England, had granted the entire area of New Jersey to his brother, the Duke of York. In 1559 the Duke of York sold East Jersey to Sir George Carteret and West Jersey to Lord John Berkeley, each paying two thousand pounds for their share. Berkeley in turn sold the southern half of his portion to John Fenwick and the northern half to Edward Byllinge. Byllinge immediately offered tracts of land of 1,000 acres, more or less, and found a ready market of buyers in the unhappy Quakers. So the scene was set for the arrival in South Jersey of the Quakers who were to be the main colonizing force in this area in the late 17th century and early to middle 18th century.

The first boat to leave England for the South Jersey shores was the *Kent*, which arrived in 1677. William Evans joined the next boatload of immigrants who sailed on a small sailboat, the *Shield*, arriving

The second-largest sassafras tree in New Jersey
is located on the Mount Laurel Friends Meeting grounds.

October 10, 1678. Although the *Kent* had arrived first, the *Shield* was the first boat to sail all the way up the Delaware River to Burlington. The *Kent* had anchored thirty miles downstream, and the passengers had to reach Burlington by rowboat and the strength of their own arms. Captain Towes, skipper of the *Shield*, however, decided to risk the dangers of going aground in the narrowing Delaware. His courage was vindicated as the *Shield* successfully navigated the river and dropped anchor off the town of Burlington. To prevent the boat from swinging with the tide a line was tied to a Buttonwood tree on shore. Unlike the Buttonwood tree in Moorestown to which Henry Warrington hitched his horse, this Buttonwood tree is no longer in existence, but a plaque marks the historic spot. Since it was winter, the passengers remained on board their small sailboat that evening for protection from the elements. It was a wise move. As so often happens in this part of the country, a drastic change in the weather took place that night with cold Canadian winds sweeping across the river. By morning the river was frozen, and the passengers were able to walk ashore on the ice.[1]

At this point in time historical records become a bit hazy, and it cannot be definitely stated exactly how long William Evans remained in Burlington. Suffice it to say that Evans stayed in Burlington for a comparatively short period of time, and then settled on a 323-acre tract of land on the northern side of Rancocas Creek, then known as Northampton River.[2] Historical records are also strangely silent concerning his family. Yet we know he had a son, for in 1687 he located 300 acres in Evesham Township on which his son, William, settled shortly after his marriage to Elizabeth Hanke in 1693.[3] There is a romantic story concerning the manner by which William and Elizabeth reached Evesham. Obviously there was no such thing as public transportation, and the only means open to them was euphemistically called "shanksmare." Contrary to what it might sound like, "shanksmare" meant they traveled on their own two feet. They followed the old Indian Trails through the woods with the watchful eyes of the Lenni Lenape Indians peering at them from behind the trees and bushes, and with no assurance that one of them would not let loose with an arrow. The fact that they traveled unarmed was taken by the Indians as a sign of friendship.

They walked along these trails until they came to the base of the mountain peak on what is now Mount Laurel Road. Cold weather was coming and to protect themselves from the approaching winter they dug a cave and made camp. This act signified the founding of Evesham Township. According to one story the Evanses walked along the trails until they collapsed from fatigue and exposure. The Indians found them and took them to a cave where they nursed them back to health by supplying them with corn meal and venison. In the spring, the Evanses, with the guidance of the Indians, built a small cabin of mud bricks. During the summer the cabin burned down, and they once again took shelter in the cave for the winter. In the spring they built a new home, this time a log cabin near the site of the present Friends Meeting House.

By 1695 enough Friends were living in the area to warrant their petitioning the Burlington Monthly Meeting for permission to set up a Meeting at Evesham. The Burlington Monthly Meeting was slow to act since permission was not granted until 1698. The first recorded meeting of the Evesham Friends was in 1694 when they met in William Evan's home. Monthly Meeting undoubtedly continued in his home until the Burlington Monthly Meeting acted on their petition and granted permission for them to establish a regular meeting.

Once permission was granted a meeting house was immediately erected. Probably very small in size and undoubtedly built of logs cut from trees in the surrounding area, it is supposed to have been built very near the site of the present meeting house. Since this was erected slightly before the one in Moorestown, it was the first place of public worship in this section of the county.

According to an old deed dated 1717, William Evans transferred one acre and thirty-two perches[4] to the Society of Friends for the purpose of meeting and for a place to bury their dead. William Evans died December 25, 1728. The family Bible, which had been brought over from Wales, was left to his son, Thomas Evans, who wrote this inscription in the flyleaf: "Thomas Evans, his Bible, which I give to my sons and grandsons and not to be sold but to go from one family to another as they may have a mind to read in it. Then to return it to the oldest son or grandson and to be kept in good order." The Bible was printed in 1572 during the reign of Queen Elizabeth and was known as the "Bishop's Bible."[5]

Mount Laurel Friends Meeting

The eastern end of the present meeting house was built in 1760 with the aid of the Indians, with whom the Friends had lived in peace and harmony since their arrival in the area. The meeting house was built of Jersey sandstone quarried in the mount across the street. This is the same mount where William and Elizabeth Evans dug their cave upon arrival in the area. The mount has had a succession of names, originally called Mount Pray, which may have been the Indian name for it. Later it was called Mount Evans after the original settlers, then Evesham Mount and finally Mount Laurel. Miss Hannah Gillingham, a teacher at the Friends School, was responsible for giving the Mount its present name. She called it Mount Laurel in appreciation of the laurel that grew in great profusion over the land. The village government officially adopted Mount Laurel for its name in 1849 when the post office was established.

Besides sandstone, ironstone was also quarried in the mount and used in the construction of the meeting house. Ironstone is stratified rock and similar in appearance to sandstone. It was usually found about twelve inches below the surface. An ingenious method was developed to determine its location. Firm rock would be located by means of a sharp pointed rod. The strata of rock would then be uncovered and stones of the required size cut out with pointed iron pins shaped somewhat like harrow teeth.

By the time the Mount Laurel Meeting House was built the population of Evesham consisted mainly of Quakers, who have always been known as liberty-loving pacifists. They built their meeting house to be able to worship God as their own consciences dictated without harassment from outside forces. However, they were to enjoy the quiet solemnity of their meeting house for little more than a decade before the harsh and divisive strains of the American Revolution were to engulf them. Both the colonial militia and the British Army, under the command of General Clinton, marched through Mount Laurel on the way from Philadelphia to Monmouth. They reached Mount

Laurel June 19, 1778, and used the meeting house as a bivouac area. A wing of the meeting house that has since been torn down was used by the British troops as a commissary. However, there is no record of any great damage being done to the meeting house by either the colonial militia or the British troops.

With the advent of independence Evesham Township settled down to a simple agrarian existence. Again the activities of peace filled the daily Quaker lives. The meeting house was filled to overflowing so that it was necessary to add the western end in 1798. Built of the same sandstone and in the same architectural design, the two buildings look to be one. The end wall was taken out and the sidewalls extended to nearly double their original length. At the time of the unfortunate separation in the Society of Friends in 1827–28 the Orthodox Friends occupied the old part of the meeting house and the Hicksites the newer section.[6]

Times have changed and the number of Quakers in the area has gradually diminished. Although the meeting house is maintained in excellent condition, it is now used for First day services only during the summer months. Since the interior has not been changed to any great extent, the Friends have found it impractical and certainly uneconomical to heat the two-story building with the small stove that was once considered adequate. Rather than attempt to keep the Mount Laurel Meeting House open during the cold winter months, the Friends attend other, more modernized, Quaker Meeting houses in the vicinity.

Before leaving the Friends in Mount Laurel, it might be interesting to trace the origin of the name for the area. A number of people who originally settled in this locality had come from Evesham Borough or Township in England. It was a fertile area on the north bank of the Avon River and noted for its market gardening. Nearby is Stratford-on-Avon where Shakespeare lived. Since they loved their old homeland and the area to which the first settlers migrated reminded them so much of it, they simply adopted the name and called their new land, Evesham.

---

1. *A History of Evesham Township,* by Maurice W. Herner.

2. *Moorestown and Her Neighbors,* by George DeCou.

3. Ibid.

4. One perch equals 30.25 square yards.

5. *Traditions of Old Evesham Township,* by William R. Lippincott.

6. See Chapter II on Friends Meeting, Woodbury.

VII

Neshanic
Reformed Church

Neshanic, 1762

"The lowlands above the Raritan are the handsomest, pleasantest country a man can behold." So spoke Cornelius Van Tienhoven, Secretary of New Netherlands, in 1650. So thought many Dutch families as a good number of the early settlers migrated from Long Island and New Amsterdam. These pioneers built churches in the Raritan Valley as soon as they had erected their homes and ploughed the fields. They became the earliest permanent residents of Somerset County except for the native Indians.

The date the first settlers arrived in the area of Neshanic is not known, but there are records as early as 1683 that a John Bennet owned a large tract of land on the south bank of the South Branch of the Raritan River. In 1718 a church called Noortbrensch was built at the confluence of the two branches of the Raritan River. We can assume that these first white settlers spread over the area which is now Neshanic. The Noortbrensch Church, according to tradition, was destroyed by fire in 1737, and the congregation built its new church near the site of the present Readington Church. It was to these two churches that the early residents of Neshanic traveled for their spiritual needs until 1752.

Neshanic Reformed Church, erected in 1762.

By this time many more settlers had arrived in the Neshanic area, and they felt capable of supporting their own services. Traveling to Readington was a long and arduous journey over very primitive roads with the added danger of fording the South Branch of the Raritan River, especially during times of heavy rains. A group of Neshanic's most prominent citizens petitioned the Noortbrensch consistory for the privilege of starting their own church. Rev. John Frelinghuysen, who was the minister for the Noortbrensch Church and the churches of Raritan, Six-Mile Run, and Sourland, was the son of Theodorus Jacobus Frelinghuysen, pioneer minister of Somerset County. The elder Frelinghuysen was a minister in Holland when asked to become pastor at "Rarethans." At the time Frelinghuysen thought this was part of Flanders. He agreed to become their minister without realizing that "Rarethans" was in the undeveloped New World across the ocean. How fortunate for America that he lived up to his word, even when he found out where the place was located, since his descendants have been prominent statesmen, lawyers, ministers, and soldiers.

The petition was approved on August 25, 1752 upon the condition that Dominie Frelinghuysen serve as minister for this new congregation. The first elders were Bernardus Verbryck and Abraham DuBois. The first deacons were Johannes DeMott and Cornelius Low. During the next few years the people met for Sunday services in private homes or barns until they could accumulate sufficient funds to start their own church building. Although the building was actually started in 1759, the deed for the ground was not given until March 1, 1760. It was signed by John and Lawrence DeMott in the presence of Cornelius Lott and Abraham Voorhees. The land was part of the farm owned by Johannes DeMott and George Brokaw. After the Revolutionary War a new deed was drawn in 1798 so that there could be no doubt as to the legality of the ownership of the land under the new government.

Construction of the church building was started in 1759. Stones, shingles, and boards were hauled to the site as late as 1761. Trenches for the foundations were dug in April 1761, and the walls were erected in 1761–62. An excellent record of the masons who worked on the job was kept. Ten masons were involved and their pay in 1761 was 5.5 shillings per day. By 1762 inflation had set in, and their pay rose to 6 shillings per day. The total working days were 533, not counting the time put in by the apprentice. Unskilled labor was paid at the rate of 3 shillings per day. During the building of the church 73 gallons of rum were consumed by the workers. This indicates that rum was supplied as a daily ration, as it was with Washington's troops during the revolution.

The work on the church moved very slowly. Dirck Low spent five days framing the windows. It wasn't until October of the same year that Dirck VanAlen cut the glass for the windows, and two weeks passed before he and Issac Runyon did the masonry work on the window frame behind the pulpit. More supplies were hauled to the church site than were needed for its actual construction. In September 1762 Johannes DeMott sold 38 bushels of lime and 13 panes of glass. At the same time Dirck Low sold glass, lime mortar, and a window frame.

By the winter of 1762 the walls were up, the windows in, and the roof on. Although the interior was not completely finished, it was possible to hold services within the building. No further work was done on the church until June 1772, except for replacing a few broken window panes. The cause for this long delay is unknown. Whether it was lack of funds or the uncertainty by the gathering storm of the approaching Revolution must be left to our imagination. However, by December 15, 1772 the galleries were built. Proof of this is the receipt given by Jos. B. Cook, Jr. on December 14th in the amount of 49 pounds current money for the carpentry work to be done on the eastern side of the "Kark" and on the pulpit. On December 15th a receipt was given by Cornelius Lott for the carpentry work done on the western side for 38 pounds, two shillings, and seven pence current money. At last the work was completed and the two managers Dirck Low and Johannes DeMott turned in their final report on December 28, 1772. The total cost for building the church was 985 pounds, 17 shillings, and 9 pence. Of this amount, almost 800 pounds had been spent by the close of 1762.

Although Rev. John Frelinghuysen had supported the Neshanic group in separating from the Noortbrensch Church and had been one of the first contributors to fund for building the Neshanic Church, he did not live to see it completed. He died on September

15, 1754, at the tender age of 27, in Long Island on the way to a meeting at Coetus.

From 1754 until 1758 the Neshanic congregation was without the services of a minister. As was the custom in the Dutch Reformed Churches, the voorleser conducted worship services when a minister was not available. Rev. Jacobus Rutsen Hardenbergh came in 1758 and ministered to the Neshanic congregation during the construction of its church building. For two winters during the Revolutionary War, Dominie Hardenbergh and General Washington were neighbors, the Dominie living in the parsonage and Washington next door in the Wallace house.

An interesting story is told of the marriage of Jacob Hardenbergh. He was a ministerial student studying under Rev. John Frelinghuysen, who was conducting classes at the parsonage. The students could not have attended classes at the parsonage without getting to know the Dominie's wife, Dinah Van Bergh Frelinghuysen. After Rev. Frelinghuysen's death, his widow planned to return to Amsterdam, which had been her home prior to her marriage. One day prior to her departure young Hardenbergh came to see her, and much to her amazement, proposed marriage. She is reported to have exclaimed, "Why child, what are you thinking about?" He was 17 and she was 30. The story goes that the next day when she was ready to leave for the vessel that was to carry her down the Raritan River to the port of Perth Amboy, a violent storm arose which caused her to abandon her plans for the time being. Since sailings to Holland were few and far between in those days, young Hardenbergh had time to press his suit. For whatever reasons—the hardship of the trip back to Holland, the ardor of young Hardenbergh, or the storm that prevented her from sailing as planned— widow Frelinghuysen decided to stay and marry young Hardenbergh.

In fact, Dinah Frelinghuysen's life had been greatly influenced by storms. She was the daughter of a Dutch merchant whom John Frelinghuysen had met when he was in Holland studying for the ministry. When it was time for him to leave Holland and return to the colonies, young Frelinghuysen asked for her hand in marriage. Her father was opposed to the idea of his daughter marrying someone who would take her so far from home. John sailed for America without Dinah, but he was no sooner out to sea when a violent storm arose and forced the ship back to port. Taking this as an act of Divine Providence, John went to see Dinah and convinced her that it was God's will that they should marry. Apparently these arguments were more than Dinah's father could overcome. Dinah and John were married and sailed for Raritan.

It is no wonder then that the widow Frelinghuysen considered the storm that prevented her from sailing back to Holland another sign of Divine intervention in her life. Since the two circumstances were so similar, she could hardly be blamed for giving young Hardenbergh's proposal second thoughts.

After being ordained in 1758, Rev. Hardenbergh served the churches of Neshanic, Millstone, Bedminster, and Readington. On March 2, 1761, at a meeting held at the house of Johannes DeMott, the consistories of Neshanic and Millstone, feeling that the two churches could support their own minister, issued a call to Rev. Johannes Martienis Van Harlingen. This action met with the approval of Dominie Hardenbergh, as he was present at the meeting of the consistories. His forthcoming trip to Holland to bring back his widowed mother-in-law probably precipitated this action by the two consistories. Rev. Van Harlingen remained with the Neshanic Church for thirty-three years until his death in 1795. He preached exclusively in the Dutch language and was a highly effective, evangelical preacher. He was a patron of learning and a member of the first board of trustees of Queens College.

During Van Harlingen's pastorate, there was considerable agitation for worship services in the English language. On November 24, 1769, a petition was presented to the consistory requesting such services.

Serious consideration was given to the petition by the consistory, but it was discovered that the petition could not be approved because of the conditions imposed by the deed. The consistory did not feel that it had the right to change the fundamental basis upon which the church was founded. However, this did not stop the agitation, and by January 1774 the consistories of Millstone and Neshanic met to consider a joint call to Rev. Christian Foering. Two-thirds of his time was to be spent at Millstone and one-third at Neshanic. His preaching at Neshanic was to be in the English language. A subscription list was circulated to all members of the Neshanic church in an effort to raise the money to pay Foering's salary, but sufficient funds were not obtained. However, some arrangement was reached as the church records indicate that on January 1, 1775 he was president of the Neshanic consistory and in April of the same year was its scribe.

Foering was an ardent patriot, a fact which eventually caused his death. His father died while serving a period of compulsory service in the German army, and his mother decided that her son would not be subjected to the same conditions. When he was 7 years old, she strapped him to her back, skated across the Rhine River, and brought him to America. As a minister, Foering was an inspiring preacher. One of his sermons espousing the revolutionary cause was so powerful that a company of soldiers was immediately recruited from the congregation. This so infuriated the British that they sent a detachment of soldiers to capture him. Forewarned, he escaped into the woods. He had to remain in hiding for some time during the terrible winter of 1778–79. When he was finally able to return home, he had a severe cold which turned into pneumonia, causing his death shortly thereafter.

On the 6th of April 1775, just thirteen days prior to the battles of Lexington and Concord, a charter was granted the "Reformed Protestant Dutch Church of New Shannick in Hillsborough in the County of Somerset and province of New Jersey. "The charter was given by King George III and presented in Perth Amboy by William Franklin, Governor of New Jersey. The people listed in the charter are Johannes Martienis Van Harlingen, Philip Van Arsdalin, Cornelius Sebring, Martinius Hooglandt, Joshua Coshun, John Ver Bryck, and John VanDyck. The presentation of the charter twenty-three years after the Revolutionary War raises many questions. Were most of the members of the church at that time Tories? In view of the political events taking place, were they simply being precautionary, making sure that the church property was recognized by the British Crown? After all, no one could possibly have foreseen at that time the final defeat of the powerful British Army. The answers to these questions must be left to speculation, as there is no explanation to be found in the records of the church.

In 1780 another fiery preacher, Solomon Froeligh, was called jointly by the Neshanic and Millstone churches. He was to serve along with Rev. Van Harlingen. His duties were to preach two Sundays at Millstone and one Sunday at Neshanic. The Millstone congregation was to supply him with 160 bushels of good wheat, and Neshanic 108 bushels. He served for only six years, but was destined to gain fame at his next charge for his part in what became known as the Hackensack Insurrection.

Once again Dominie Van Harlingen was left to carry on by himself. He did his best to preach some sermons in English, which was a foreign language to him. This trying time for him as well as the congregation lasted eight years, until Rev. William Richmond Smith was called. He was to preach two Sundays at Neshanic and one Sunday at Millstone. Smith took up his residence at Flagtown so that he was the first minister to live within the area of the Neshanic congregation. Neshanic paid him a yearly salary of $200 and Millstone contributed another $125. Some years later, after eight children had been born to Rev. Smith and his wife Rachel Stidham, Neshanic increased his salary to $325 per year.

The longest pastorates were served by the Reverends Gabriel Ludlow and John Hart. Altogether these pastorates lasted for 101 years of active ministry from 1821 to 1922. If the fourteen years that Rev. Hart served as pastor emeritus are included, then these two ministers accounted for 115 years of service to the church. Gabriel Ludlow came to Neshanic at the age of 24. Young in years he may have been, but it wasn't long before he had to display the wisdom of Solomon. In those days the minister was consulted about all matters whether they were temporal or spiritual. Shortly after he took over the ministry of the Neshanic church he had to render decisions in such mundane matters as a stolen pig, a half bushel of stolen watermelons, and a claim for a dowry apparently due a new bridegroom!

He soon developed a reputation as a very outspoken man. At a funeral service which he was conducting, after giving his condolences to the bereaved members of the family of the departed, he leaned over the pulpit, and gazing at the face of the corpse, said, "but as for the deceased, I believe the less said about him the better."

Rev. John Hart was called in 1875. He graduated from Rutgers in 1869, from the New Brunswick Theological Seminary in 1872, and was licensed to preach immediately after his graduation by the Classis of Philadelphia. He served the Reformed Church of Locust Valley on Long Island until he accepted the call from Neshanic in the spring of 1875. He died in 1936 at the age of 93 after a long and illustrious career.

The Neshanic Reformed Church is the oldest and the only original Reformed Church building in New Jersey still used by the congregation. Riding down historic Amwell Road on which the church stands, one can still agree with Cornelius Van Tienhoven when he said in 1650, "The lowlands above the Raritan are the handsomest, pleasantest country a man can behold."

VIII

Old Pittsgrove
Presbyterian Church

Daretown, 1767

"In the name of the Almighty, Eternal Jehovah, God the Father, Son, and Holy Ghost. We, who are Christian Protestants of the Presbyterian denomination inhabiting Pilesgrove, and the neighboring places in Salem County, in West New Jersey, in America: Acknowledging and truly lamenting our sinful and woeful state in Adam's fall,…

"We do, therefore, by the grace of God enabling, sincerely forsake all our sinful ways…

"And we do, hereby, solemnly renew our baptismal engagements by that covenant to be the Lord's people, both we and our seed…"

So stated the Church Covenant drawn up by Rev. David Evans and signed by forty-nine people on April 30, 1741. David Evans had received a call from the people of Pilesgrove and Quihawken (Penn's Neck) on May 27, 1740 to be their minister, and after considerable thought had accepted. He apparently was not pleased with conditions as he found them, and after laboring among them for about a year decided that a formal declaration of their faith was necessary. The original settlers had been immigrants from East New Jersey, Connecticut, and Long Island and were of many religious persuasions. At first they had met in members' homes and then had built a rough

Old Pittsgrove Presbyterian Church, erected in 1767.

log meeting house in the vicinity of Woodstown. Desiring a pastor, they had appealed from time to time to the Presbytery of Philadelphia, which was the nearest ecclesiastical body. The Presbytery's records indicate that supplies had been sent to them as early as 1720, and eighteen pounds had been allotted for preaching in Pilesgrove and Gloucester. When Rev. David Evans arrived on the scene he decided that the church should be organized in the Presbyterian faith. Thus, he drew up the Church Covenant adhering closely to the Calvinist tenets, and the signing of this document is considered to be the beginning of the Pilesgrove Presbyterian Church.

An argument had been brewing for some time with the Presbyterian Church of Deerfield over the location of the Pilesgrove

Meeting House. The population had been moving inland, and the Woodstown area was no longer convenient. However, the prospects of another church being built in the area from which Deerfield drew its members was not the least bit enticing to them. Presbytery had encouraged a union between the two groups, but neither was interested. Finally, after considerable debate, the Presbytery authorized the congregation of Pilesgrove to build their own church, but the objections of Deerfield were also recognized. Presbytery stipulated that Pilesgrove could build a meeting house no closer to Deerfield than nine miles. Actually Pilesgrove had already selected a site which was approximately six miles from Deerfield and Presbytery upheld their appeal to build there.

At a cost of forty shillings current money of New Jersey two acres of ground were purchased from Louis DuBois for a graveyard and meeting house. The deed of sale was executed January 1, 1742, and the same time a "Declaration of Trust and Performance Bond" placed upon Eleazer Smith, carpenter, and Jacob DuBois, blacksmith, the responsibility to hold in trust the two acres of ground.

"To and for the only Use, Benefit and Behoof of the Presbyterian Congregation at the foresaid Pilesgrove, for a Burying yard and Build thereon a House for the Publick worship of God, and a School House for lawful use and Christian Book Learning, and a convenient Stable, or such Buildings as the said Congregation shall judge necessary and convenient for the said Use, and for no Other Uses Whatsoever, Save only for the Use of the Said Presbyterian Congregation."

This document was signed by Eleazer Smith and Jacob DuBois in the presence of Cornelius Nieukirk, Barent DuBois, John Rose, and David Evans. A log meeting house was built near the center of the graveyard, but, unfortunately, no records exist to establish the date or the cost. This log structure became known as the "New Missionary Meeting House."

At this time the Presbyterian denomination was torn asunder by a theological dispute which divided the church into two camps known as "Old Lights" and "New Lights." The "Old Lights" followed closely the teachings of John Calvin, and the "New Lights" were more liberal in their views. Rev. Evans remained with the "Old Lights," and as long as he lived, Pilesgrove remained on the side of the "Old Lights." He was their minister until November 1750 and died on February 4, 1751 in his 69th year.

On December 12, 1752 Nehemiah Greenman, a licentiate of the New York Presbytery educated by David Brainerd, the missionary to the Indians, arrived in Pilesgrove and began to preach as a candidate for settlement. On Wednesday, December 5, 1753 he was ordained and installed. Participating in the services were the ministers Richard Treat, Andrew Hunter, and Charles Beatty. He was to be minister for twenty-six years, a period marked by much dissension and unpleasantness. It was also a period when great strides were made by the church. In August 1764 the church glebe was purchased, and in 1767 a new brick meeting house was built to replace the cedar log meeting house that was badly in need of repair and inadequate for the needs of the congregation. The new meeting house was a model of colonial architecture and a considerable accomplishment for the poor farmers that made up the membership. It was a two-story, red brick building with two doors leading into the auditorium that housed fifty-two box pews. In the front, opposite the center pews, was a high pulpit with a sounding board. A balcony ran around three sides of the auditorium. The floors under the pews were constructed of wide planking and the aisles were of red brick.

Most of the difficulties between Rev. Greenman and the congregation arose over the failure of the people to pay the minister's salary and to provide the agreed-upon allotment of grain. Until 1726 the method was not very satisfactory, and it was finally decided that Elders Jacob DuBois, David DuBois, and Joseph Van Meter, along with Rev. Greenman, should call on the congregation in an endeavor to have them submit their estates to be rated in such a manner that adequate funds would be assured to meet their obligation to the minister. This system worked for a number of years, but Rev. Greenman found himself in difficulties again in 1776 when, in desperation, he requested that a commission visit the church to implore the people to live up to their obligations. At that time the church was in arrears by fifty pounds and had not supplied the agreed amount of wheat.

It was during this period of his ministry, 1770, that the area where the church was located separated from Pilesgrove Township and became known as Pittsgrove, being named in honor of William Pitt, the English statesman that was friendly to the colonies. From that time on the church was known as the Pittsgrove Presbyterian Church.

Trouble still plagued Rev. Greenman and the congregation. A serious crisis developed as a result of the Revolutionary War. In 1778 a British Regiment, 1,200 to 1,500 strong, marched into Salem, having camped the previous night near Sharptown, about one hour's ride from Rev. Greenman's home. He well knew the peril that faced Presbyterian ministers at the hands of the British, so the same night that they marched into Salem he fled to Egg Harbor. He left his Pittsgrove congregation stranded, and on April 6, 1779 the congregation presented charges to Presbytery outlining all their grievances:

> Mr. Greenman, January 1, 1778, read from the pulpit a paper charging them with premeditated design of defrauding him of his just dues, etc.
>
> He has not administered the Lord's Supper since April 1, 1777.
>
> Has not called a session in this congregation since 1774, when requested to call a session has declared there was none.

He moved March 17, 1778, to Egg Harbour, and stayed there six months without consulting the congregation, and never returned to preach a sermon, and did offer to contract with some people of Egg Harbour to preach for them for one or more years.

For a number of years neglected to catechize the youth and neglected pastoral duties.

Has written reproachful and injurious letters.[1]

For his part Rev. Greenman complained that the congregation had been guilty of injustice and inhumanity in not collecting the back payments due the 17th of March, 1778. Also, that when he fled from the enemy, they did not send him his salary nor quota of wheat, nor did they pay these amounts when he returned on September 2, 1778. Presbytery acquitted the people of the charge of injustice and inhumanity, and a special effort was made by the congregation to settle the amounts due Rev. Greenman.

There seemed to be no end to the disagreements between Rev. Greenman and the congregation. When the parsonage needed repairs, both refused to take any action. On April 8, 1779 Rev. Greenman filed a complaint with the Session against Jacob DuBois, one of the deacons, Presbytery healed the differences, but by now the congregation had reached the limit of its endurance and asked for the dissolution of the pastoral relationship, stating that Greenman's usefulness had ended. Rev. Greenman concurred and the relationship was dissolved. The finality of this act eased the tension, and the congregation committee asked that Rev. Greenman be appointed to supply them as much as possible until a new minister was found. Presbytery appointed him to supply one-half of his time and as much more as may be convenient to him and the people promised to give him generous compensation. Thus the troubles were peacefully settled, and

Rev. Greenman supplied the congregation until his death, just three months later on July 25, 1779.

During the next thirty-three years the church experienced many difficulties. Depreciation of the currency due to the demands of the Revolutionary War and the exhaustion of the land before the benefits of marl were discovered impoverished the farmers. Internal dissensions resulted in short pastorates and long vacancies. During this time the pulpit was occupied about nineteen years and vacant about fourteen.

The period started propitiously when the Rev. William Schenck was installed on Wednesday, May 3, 1780. He was a learned man, interested in education, and during his pastorate started a school which became known as Pittsgrove Log College. Despite the poverty of the times, the school flourished and families from a considerable distance away sent their young men to be educated there. In 1781 the graveyard was enlarged, extending as close to the stream as would be suitable for burying, and enclosed by a fence consisting of all new posts and many new boards.

In 1783 the Session promised Rev. Schenck 100 pounds yearly or its equivalent, but he suffered the same frustrations that plagued Rev. Greenman—lack of payment. A letter by him tells the pitiful story: "We have no wheat or corn, and flour for only two weeks."[2] Despite these hardships there was great love and respect mutually shared by the congregation and the minister. According to legend he left the pastorate because of the lack of financial support. If this was true, he was gracious enough in his letter to the congregation to state that his only cause for complaint was the poor health of himself and his family, expressing at the same time his pleasure in the fact that they had lived together in peace and harmony and that many wounds were healed during his ministry. He left the pulpit in June 1786.

Rev. Issac Foster arrived in 1791 and served until 1794. He was followed by the Rev. Samuel Laycock, and once again problems between the minister and the congregation erupted. In April 1795, after he had served as stated supply since the previous October, the congregation issued the call and Rev. Laycock accepted. Installation took place in August. Just over two years later, on October 17, 1797, a petition from several members of the congregation requested the dissolution of the pastoral arrangement. Presbytery disapproved but decided to meet at Pittsgrove to investigate the reason for the request. On Tuesday, December 5th, Messrs. Davenport, Osborn, Clarkson, and Laycock, along with five Elders from the church, assembled and for three days considered the charges against Rev. Laycock. The use of intoxicating liquor and the purchase of strong drink were the main charges. Previously Rev. Laycock had declared from the pulpit that he and his wife had agreed not to keep alcholic beverages in their home except at harvest and hay time. In his defense to the charges he stated that the gallon of rum he had purchased was bought at late hay time. Mrs. Louderbach, one of the petitioners, testified that on the previous August the Rev. Laycock and his wife were at her house along with four other guests when she set out a decanter of spirits about two-thirds full (whether a quart or a pint decanter she could not recall). When the Laycocks left only a gill remained in the decanter although she did not observe Rev. Laycock behaving in a manner unbecoming a minister. Presbytery found the charges unwarranted although a serious admonition was given him and the people advised to study the things that make for peace.[3] In April 1798 letters were received by Presbytery from a number of individuals reporting divisions and animosities between the minister and the congregation. Finally, a petition signed by forty-six communicants asked that the pastoral relationship be dissolved. Presbytery acquiesced since it was obvious that Rev. Laycock had lost his influence with the congregation even though nothing appeared to mar his character.

Peace still was not to come to Daretown. The congregation was to experience tumultuous times with two more ministers before finding the satisfying relationship that they sought. Rev. Buckley Carll was installed October 16, 1799. He was an impulsive individual deeply involved in the politics of the day. With the debates between the Federalists and the Democrats reaching fever heat, most of the members of the congregation sided with the Democrats. Since Rev. Carll was an avid Federalist, he gave up his charge in 1803 because of the strong feelings which ran through the congregation. On October 15, 1805 a call was presented to Rev. John Clark through the Presbytery of Hudson, New York. Unknown to Pittsgrove, Rev. Clark had apparently told his congregation in Pleasant Valley, New York that he would return if he regained his health. His health restored, Rev. Clark requested in April 1808 that the pastoral relation with Pittsgrove be dissolved. Presbytery agreed although not endorsing Clark's reasons. The Pittsgrove congregation was very much upset and wrote to the Session of the Pleasant Valley Church. That Session replied: "If you have involved yourselves in building, you will be provided the better for another minister, and in this we are not to blame. Mr. Clark is a man of veracity and honor, and we hold him to his promise."[4]

For the next four years the pulpit was vacant, but then the congregation, which had had so many periods of strife, was finally to enjoy a long, continuous ministry under a man who brought harmony and peace. The Rev. George Washington Janvier was ordained and installed on May 13, 1812. He had supplied the church from June 1811, and the call was issued in October. He was pastor for nearly 47 years when, in October 1857, because of the infirmities of old age, he resigned his charge amid the tears and sobs of an affectionate people. When he assumed his pastoral duties the membership was 98. When he resigned it was 547. He was the first Moderator of the Presbytery of West Jersey, and in 1864 Lafayette College conferred on him the honorary degree of Doctor of Divinity. His last public act was to assist his successor, Rev. E. P. Shields, in laying the cornerstone of the new church on July 14, 1864. On June 9, 1865 he died in his sleep at the age of 82.

On June 2, 1858 Rev. Shields was ordained and installed as pastor. It was during his ministry that the church building now used by the congregation was built. In the spring of 1863 a building committee was appointed, consisting of Charles Wood, John R. Alderman, James Coombs, Enoch Mayhew, Benjamin Burt, George Coombs, and John W. Janvier. On July 4th the committee signed a contract with Joseph Allen, a builder and contractor of Salem, New Jersey. The cornerstone was laid on July 14, 1864, and the building was to be completed in one year. But the Civil War was in progress, some members of the congregation had enlisted, the cost of building materials had skyrocketed, and the workers were demanding higher pay. Four years elapsed from the signing of the contract before the new church was completed. Including projecting tower and recessed pulpit, the dimensions were fifty-one by ninety-one feet. The total cost, including furniture and a bell for the tower, was $25,336. It was dedicated on a stormy day, August 11, 1867 with the Rev. Charles W. Shields, D.D. of Princeton, New Jersey preaching the dedicatory sermon. That night a terrific crash was heard, and it was discovered later that the ceiling of the old brick church had caved in. After a pastorate of thirteen years the Rev. Shields resigned, to the regret of the congregation, to accept a call from the church at Cape May City.

After the new church was built the old brick church gradually deteriorated because of disuse. In the 1890s it was repaired somewhat so that it could be used for concerts and festivals. In 1920 a floor was laid over the balcony to make a basketball court and meeting room for the Boy Scouts. In the late 1930s restoration work was done on the stones in the cemetery, wherein lie twenty-six Revolutionary War veterans, a new driveway was installed and maintenance work was done on the building inside and out. In 1971 the brick aisles were sandblasted and the outside brick walls painted. In the balcony, which extends around three sides of the auditorium, are several benches used as pews in the 1741 cedar log meeting house. In the keystone over one of the doors the following inscription can be seen:

N.G.
V.D.M.
1767
P.G.C.

The initials N.G. are those of Nehemiah Greenman, pastor when the church was built, V.D.M. stands for Verbi Dei Minister—minister of the word of God, 1767 is the year the church was built, and P.G.C. are the initials of Piles Grove Church.

The old brick church is included in the New Jersey Register of Historic Sites, and anniversary services are conducted in it once a year. A blast from the old conch shell heralds the start of the worship service, a custom that started before the 17th century.

Not to be forgotten is the Old Pittsgrove Log College that stood in the cemetery during the pastorate of the Rev. William Schenck. After considerable research this old landmark was reconstructed on the same location and with the same materials. A concession was made, however, to modern construction methods when the hand-hewn timbers were notched and assembled at Birdsboro, Pennsylvania, then knocked down and reassembled on the site. The restored Log College was dedicated Sunday, April 30, 1972.

---

1.   *History of Pittsgrove Church,* by Rev. Allen Brown.

2.   Ibid.

3.   A pamphlet entitled, *Pittsgrove Log College.*

4.   Ibid.

IX

Christ Church

Shrewsbury, 1769

In one of the loveliest spots in the Garden State stands Christ Church, amidst the sycamore trees that once marked the old Mohawk or Minisink Trail of the Lenni Lenape Indians. The original settlers named it Shrewsbury in memory of the town in England of the same name where many of them had come from. The original pioneers were a varied lot as far as their religious beliefs were concerned. A number were Anglicans, some were Quakers, others Presbyterians, and still others fortune seekers with no particular beliefs.

The first service of the Church of England of which there is any record took place on October 24, 1702. This service was conducted by the famous missionary, George Keith, who had been sent to the New World by the Society for the Propagation of the Gospel in Foreign Lands (S.P.G.). His diary records the fact that on this date he preached to a group of people gathered together in a house in Shrewsbury. As early as 1703 thought was given by these people to building a church, but there is no evidence that they went ahead with their plans. Efforts were made to secure the services of a full-time missionary, but to no avail. At that time the S.P.G. could not afford to support a missionary for just this area. However, the Rev.

Christ Church in Shrewsbury, erected in 1769.

Alexander Innes, a chaplain for the British Army, took upon himself the care of these people. He was not financed by the S.P.G., but the Society probably contributed something to his support. Apparently he was a man of some means as upon his death he left twenty pounds to the churches of Shrewsbury, Middletown, and Freehold. His personal library of 179 volumes of religious and classical works he left for the use of the ministers of the Church of England.

Although Rev. Keith thought very highly of Alexander Innes and repeatedly wrote to the S.P.G. about the fine work that he was doing, he was not regarded in such high favor by everyone. Before coming to Shrewsbury he had fled New York (about August 1689), apparently to escape the persecutions of Jacob Leisler. Leisler had written to King William and Queen Anne that Rev. Innes held opinions contrary to the Protestant faith. He was accused of being a papist. Whatever fault Jacob Leisler found in Innes was not shared by the people of Monmouth County. He was looked upon as a man of great piety who sacrificed his own personal comfort in traveling about the wilderness to look after the needs of the people.

Service by the Reverends Keith, Innes, and Talbot, another missionary, were conducted in the private homes of the congregation. In 1706 Nicholas Brown donated the ground on which the present church now stands. The deed is dated May 20, 1706, and was executed in the presence of Thomas Bills, John West, Samuel Dennis, and Joanna Grunt. It was not acknowledged, however, until July 9, 1714, when Nicholas Brown, along with one of the witnesses, Samuel Dennis, appeared before Thomas Gordon of Her Majesty's Court to formalize the transaction. About 1715, the first stone and brick building was erected facing Sycamore Avenue, northwest of the present building. Unfortunately, the records of the parish from 1702 to 1732 have been lost, so very little is known about the activities of the church during those years.

Rev. John Forbes served the three churches of Shrewsbury, Middletown, and Freehold from 1733 to 1736. On October 29, 1734, he reported to the S.P.G. that he had found many worshippers homesick for the services of the Church of England. He also reported that there was "one very fair and handsome Building for a church," and that there were three other places where he had to officiate which required considerable traveling "not without Fatigue and Expense."

For the next eight years, from 1737 to 1745, Rev. John Miln was in charge of the churches in Monmouth County. He had been appointed by the Society in 1727 as missionary to the Mohawk Indians in New York. He was well received by the Indians, and his work with them was very successful. The commanding officer of Fort Hunter thought highly of Rev. Miln, attributing the civilized manner of the Indians to the Christianizing work of the missionary. His efforts were far less successful, however, with the good folk in Monmouth County. In 1745 he was actually dismissed from the services of the Society as a result of charges of neglect and ill conduct brought against him by his congregation.

The Rev. Thomas Thompson was appointed by the S.P.G. to succeed Rev. Miln. Thompson arrived in New York on May 28, 1745. After preaching in New York and Elizabethtown, he journeyed to Trenton, where he took the required oaths before Governor Lewis Morris. Upon his arrival in Monmouth County, he received anything but a warm welcome. Rev. Miln was still in charge and reluctant to leave. A group in the congregation supported Rev. Miln, contending that he had been abused and misrepresented. This group favored his retention. A majority of the vestry favored Rev. Thompson, and so the church was badly split. Sixty members of the congregation signed a paper expressing their determination to bar Rev. Thompson from holding services. The controversy peaked when Rev. Miln informed Rev. Thompson that violent means would be taken to eject him if he should attempt to hold religious services in the church.

Feeling that prudence was better than valor at this time, Rev. Thompson traveled to Freehold, where he was met with no opposition. He notified the Society of the situation, stating that Miln's friends in Shrewsbury were mainly those who were dissenters and people who were disenchanted with the church. In his report to the Society he was fair in pointing out that Rev. Miln had mended his ways. He had given up the use of strong drink, and was faithful in visiting the sick and needy. However, he also mentioned that Miln neglected church services and ridiculed those who sought his advice on matters of conscience. On November 24, 1746, the secretary of the Society wrote to Rev. Thompson advising him to take legal action against Miln if he continued in his efforts to retain wrongful possession of church property at Shrewsbury and Middletown. How this explosive situation was finally resolved is unknown, as no further reference is made to it in the available records. Apparently the recalcitrant groups at Shrewsbury and Middletown withdrew their opposition to Rev. Thompson and he was allowed to take charge.

Needless to say, he did not find the going very smooth in the beginning. Gradually, however, he was able to woo the antagonistic members to his side. Eventually he was able to report that the services were well attended each Sunday.

His interest in the Negro race, which eventually led him to Africa as a missionary, was kindled at this time. He noted their interest and desire to be educated. He spoke to their masters, urging them to instruct their slaves in the catechism. On certain Sundays he instructed them in church and visited them in their homes. After sufficient training, he baptized them and admitted to communion those who accepted the Christian faith.

He became especially interested in a black man at Crosswicks who had been convicted of an atrocious crime and sentenced to death. He visited the Negro for two weeks and found him completely uncooperative in the beginning. Rev. Thompson persevered, and before the time of the Negro's execution arrived, the convicted criminal repented his crime, was baptized by Rev. Thompson, and given communion.

In 1751, Rev. Thompson's request to the Society to be its first missionary to Africa was approved. In closing the account of his missionary efforts in Monmouth County he expressed a quiet satisfaction over the change in conditions from those which he found when he first arrived. A substantial number of baptisms had been performed, and a number of Anabaptists, Quakers, and Presbyterians came to hear him preach on Sundays. He hoped that a few of these had been converted from the error of their ways. Besides preaching at Shrewsbury, Middletown, and Freehold, he had traveled to Manasquan and Cranbury, as the people there were without the help of any clergy. The congregations were no longer split into factions; they were united and flourishing, and the problems that he had faced upon his arrival were now resolved. He could leave with a free mind, feeling confident that his work in this area had been successfully accomplished.

The transfer of pastoral responsibilities was completed without incident. For the next 25 years, Christ Church was to have the services of a much beloved pastor. Rev. Samuel Cooke had graduated from Carus College in Cambridge, England and had come to America in 1750 after his appointment by the Society. But these were eventful years. The turbulence which finally erupted into the Revolutionary War was increasing in intensity. Most of the ministers of the Church of England were staunch loyalists, and Rev. Cooke was no exception. His loyalist feelings would eventually make it necessary for him to flee his parish.

Along with a change in leadership comes a change in philosophy. This is as true of churches as it is of any other segment of society. Rev. Thompson had enthusiastically supported the Society in its efforts to educate the youth by supplying a schoolmaster. Rev. Cooke held opposing views. Under Rev. Thompson, Mr. Christopher Robert

Reynolds was the Society's schoolmaster in Shrewsbury. Thompson thought so much of him that he persuaded Reynolds to spend a year teaching in the Pines. When the schoolmaster's job became open in 1760, Rev. Cooke objected strenuously to a replacement. On November 5, 1760 he wrote the Society advising the members that they would receive a petition from the Shrewsbury congregation requesting that the Society's support for a schoolmaster be continued. Rev. Cooke objected, stating that he believed the money spent for a schoolmaster could be better utilized and that in Monmouth County it was a needless expense. His ire arose from the fact that the people were unwilling to contribute towards the support of the minister, but were not only willing but anxious to contribute toward the support of a schoolmaster so their children could be taught reading, writing, and arithmetic.

By April 1769, plans had already been made for the construction of a new church. The old church was by now unable to accommodate all those who wished to worship. Rev. Cooke's observation in 1760 concerning the congregation's unwillingness to contribute toward their religious obligations certainly did not hold true in 1769. Five hundred pounds current money of the Province of New Jersey had been contributed for the erection of the new building.

The plans were prepared by Rev. William Smith, a priest and architect of Philadelphia. These plans called for a building sixty-two feet long, thirty-eight feet wide "with posts as high as timber on the spot will admit of." There must have been a good stand of timber as the height turned out to be 24 feet. It was built to accommodate about 400 people. It was a frame building, very plain on the outside and with a modest little steeple. On top of the steeple was an old iron crown. The interior was that of an old English country church. The Chancel at the southern end was raised about four feet from the floor with the pulpit just in front of it. The windows were of stained glass, and the one behind the chancel was considered one of the most beautiful in

America at that time. It was the gift of George DeHart Gillespie of New York, who had many ancestors buried in the church yard.

The discord between the mother country and the colonies delayed the completion of the building. Imports were restricted, and the inability of the builder to obtain nails and glass delayed the construction for about three months. The nails were finally made at Shrewsbury, although at a cost of almost twice that of the English nails. Apparently they waited for the glass to arrive from England, as no mention is made of making the glass at Shrewsbury. Rev. Cooke complained that this delay prevented him from holding services in the new building during the winter months of 1770. He acknowledged, however, the generosity of the Presbyterians in offering their meeting house until such time as the new building was completely ready. When finished, the new church had cost 800 pounds. On April 12, 1774, Rev. Cooke announced that the entire cost had been paid through the generous support of the congregation and other interested parties.

Over the years, twenty-four priests have served the parish, and many renovations and improvements have been made to the building. The matching crystal chandeliers which still hang in the church were given by Dr. Smith Cutter shortly after 1840. He had brought them from his house on Barclay Street, New York City, in 1839, when he moved to Shrewsbury. Originally they were lighted by candles. The church had never been consecrated, since it had been built before the Revolution. This omission was corrected by a service performed by Bishop Doane on January 16, 1845. It was on the occasion of the reopening of the building following extensive repairs and the addition of an organ. Until 1853, Shrewsbury and Middletown had been one parish. An act of the Legislature in 1853 divided the townships, and Shrewsbury became a separate parish. In 1869, the centennial anniversary of the laying of the cornerstone was held. It was attended by President Ulysses S. Grant.

Christ Church cherishes many unusual features. The steeple bell was cast in France in 1788 and sent to a Roman Catholic Church in Santo Domingo. At the time of the revolution in the Dominican Republic it was sent to New York and purchased by a Mr. Van Zandt of Little Neck, Long Island. He presented the bell to his church, but there was a hill between his house and the church which prevented him from hearing the tolling of the bell. He, therefore, sold the bell to Rev. Eli Wheeler in 1825. Rev. Wheeler had the bell sent to Christ Church, where it hung in the great oak tree in the church yard until the belfry base was added to the front of the church in 1874. Because of its history the bell is fondly known as "Old Eli." It has a bas-relief on the fleur-de-lis, the French coat of arms, and the date 1788 inscribed on it.

The canopied pew in the northeast corner was for the sole use of the Royal Governor. In 1844 an organ was obtained and placed in the Royal Governor's pew. The organ was removed in 1874, and the pew is now maintained in the manner as when the Royal Governor occupied it. The canopied pew in the southeast corner was maintained for the rector's family. All the other pews belonged to the members of the congregation, who paid an annual rent for their use. This practice was continued until 1845, when the pews became free.

A unique feature of Christ Church is the Royal Crown. An iron English crown, it sits high above a weather vane and a gilt ball representing the earth. It is believed to be the only church in the United States retaining the Royal Crown atop the steeple. Patriotic citizens, during the Revolution, fired upon it, trying to knock it down. Even though it was less than fifty feet from the ground, they were unable to dislodge it. However, the ball below it was riddled with bullet holes. Failing in these efforts, they decided to burn the church. A pile of straw was set afire in the hallway, but William Parker, a Quaker from the meeting house across the street, happened by and smothered the fire with his coat.

One of the proudest possessions of Christ Church is its Vinegar Bible. This was presented to the church in 1732, during the pastorate of Rev. Cooke, by Robert Elliston, who was Controller of His Majesty's Custom House in New York City. The Bible was printed at Oxford, England in 1717 by John Baskett. It was so full of errors that it was referred to as "A Casketfull of Printer's Errors." It earned its popular name from the error in the title of the parable of the vineyard, which is printed as "the parable of the vinegar." This Bible was used in Christ Church for more than a century and a half, until it was placed in the display case in 1916.

X

Deerfield Presbyterian Church

Deerfield Street, 1771

This is a story of a people firm in spirit, independent in mind, and resolute in purpose; and that purpose was to worship God as they saw fit, and they would not be deterred from their goal regardless of the hardships created by their single-mindedness of purpose. These early settlers did not need nor depend upon the inspiration or guidance of an eloquent cleric to lead the way in their spiritual lives. There was no indecision, no vacillation in what they believed, even though there were many periods when they were without a pastor and had to rely upon their own resources. These people were Calvinists and strongly schooled in their beliefs. The session governed the congregation and the people obeyed.

In the latter part of the 17th century, pioneers came from New England and Long Island, settling along both banks of the Cohansey River and founding the towns of Fairfield and Greenwich. One of these hardy pioneers, Benjamin Davis, made his home along the banks of the Delaware River at a place called Ben Davis Beach, now known as Sea Breeze. A point of land jutting into the Delaware River is still identified on maps of New Jersey as "Ben Davis Point." In the year 1725, Benjamin Davis purchased 1,000 acres of land from Colonel Cox, the land speculator of Burlington, paying ten shillings

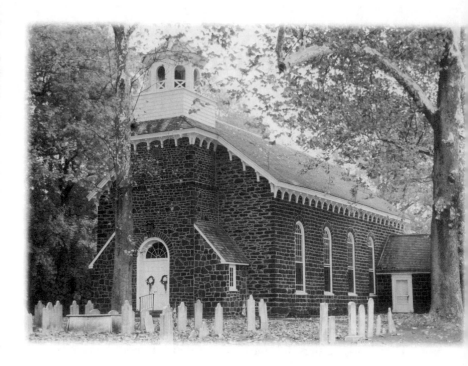

Deerfield Presbyterian Church in Deerfield Street, built in 1771.

an acre. This land had originally belonged to that part of Fenwick's holdings that extended from the Cohansey Creek to the Maurice River, and was located in the northwest section.

Since Ben Davis was the first major landowner, he had the privilege of naming the area. There are some interesting fables as to the origin of the name Deerfield. The first has a beautiful sylvan touch to it, but probably very little basis in fact. This theory contends that Mr. Davis, while inspecting his newly purchased holdings, found a large herd of deer grazing in the lush green of the savannah, automatically suggesting the name. The second, less romantic, supposition is that Mr. Davis had not seen the land before purchasing it, and when he gazed upon some of the treeless acres and contemplated the price he had paid, exclaimed that it was a "dear field" indeed. The third and most likely surmise is that the name was brought to West Jersey from New England, as were those of Fairfield and Greenwich.

Mr. Davis moved his family to Deerfield, and by 1732 a sufficient number of people were living in the area to justify the erection of a log schoolhouse, which stood just across the street from the present site of the church. Since most of the inhabitants were Presbyterians from the Fairfield and Greenwich communities, and since it was inconvenient to travel regularly to these towns for worship services, they formed a Presbyterian Society and met in the log schoolhouse for worship. By 1737 the schoolhouse had become inadequate for this purpose, and it was evident that a structure for religious activities was necessary. No records exist concerning the acquisition of the land needed for this purpose. However, a deed dated 1771 implies that the land was donated by Abraham Garrison: "land which Mr. Abraham Garrison did in his lifetime give for a burying ground to said Society, on which the Old Meeting House now stands." Whether the land was given or whether it was purchased is of little import. The important fact is that eighty-five acres were acquired, and a log building was erected to serve the spiritual needs of the people in the year 1737.

An interesting sidelight is that since these people were of Puritan extraction they did not call their congregation a church but rather a Society, and they did not call their building a church but a "meeting house for public worship." In keeping with their Puritan schooling they were afraid of any kind of sentimental attachment which might become idolatry. For this same reason the interior of the log meeting house was bereft of any adornments or comfort.

It was not until 1746 that the Deerfield Society installed a pastor. One could have been obtained sooner, but these people were Calvinists with strong convictions. Contrary to the origins of many colonial churches, the Society was not formed because of the inspirations or exhortations of any one preacher, but by their own desires and persuasions; they were not dependent upon a pastor to keep the congregation alive. In 1738, one year after the erection of the log meeting house, the Philadelphia Presbytery was anxious to settle David Buckingham as pastor of the Deerfield and Pilesgrove congregations, but Deerfield was opposed to the arrangement. Even though they had built a church and had no pastor for it, they would not sacrifice their principles for the convenience of having a minister. From time to time supply pastors were afforded them, but in the absence of a minister, the people attended regularly and conducted services according to the established order of the Society. Benjamin Davis wrote in his diary in 1790: "Nor were the public exercises of religion omitted when no supplies were given. Some always appeared who had firmness and zeal to conduct exercises of prayer and praise, and profitable authors were read to which there was a decent attention and which we hope to have been blessed, for the good of souls." Among the supplies who preached at Deerfield during this period were well-known graduates of the Log College in Neshaminy, Bucks County, Pennsylvania. These included Samuel Blair, Gilbert Tennent, Samuel Finley, John Rowland, and Charles Beatty. All of these men adhered to the "New Lights" movement, and their influence was undoubtedly responsible for the Deerfield Society linking itself with this more emotional, revivalistic group.

Finally, the Deerfield society secured the services of a pastor, although they had to share him with the Greenwich Presbyterian Church. The Rev. Andrew Hunter was born in Ireland in 1715, taken on trial by the New Brunswick Presbytery in 1744, and licensed to preach in 1746. He was ordained and installed as the pastor of the Deerfield and Greenwich congregations on September 4, 1746. The joint arrangement required Rev. Hunter to spend two-thirds of his time in Greenwich and one-third in Deerfield, preaching every third Sunday to the Deerfield congregation. As remuneration for his efforts, Rev. Hunter received a yearly salary of seventy-five pounds, twenty-five of which was supplied by Deerfield. In 1752, the Deerfield Society purchased from James Abit a tract of land containing fifty acres to be used as a parsonage farm. Apparently the Deerfield members of the session had not given the Greenwich congregation advance notice of their intention, and a storm of protest erupted when it was finally made known. The Deerfield Society was accused of "seeking to drive Mr. Hunter away."[1] Despite the furor, the pastoral arrangement continued for another eight years. Rev. Hunter served the Deerfield Society for fourteen years, after which the joint arrangement was finally terminated because of the dissension that had developed between the two congregations.

The Deerfield parish found itself again without a pastor until 1764, when the Rev. Simon Williams agreed to serve as stated supply. He was offered a salary of seventy pounds per year and a promise to cultivate the farm for him until he could secure the necessary help. On May 22, 1765 a call was presented to him through the Presbytery to become their pastor, and he indicated his willingness to accept. Apparently there was some dissension, as his ordination was postponed several times by Presbytery and once by Rev. Williams, since the call was no longer unanimous. However, the call was renewed on April 9, 1766, but at the same time a petition was presented, signed by several members of the congregation against the call. Due to this situation, the Presbytery decided against the ordination and Rev. Williams was given a letter of dismissal to a church in New England. Once again Deerfield's pulpit was declared vacant.

An insight into the personality of Rev. Williams that might explain why a unanimous call could not be obtained from the congregation is given in the diary of a later minister. Rev. R. Hamill Davis wrote: "Mr. Williams once rode his horse to a certain house in the parish, and approaching the lady of the house, informed her he had selected an appropriate text for use at her funeral. In reply to her question he answered, "you will find it in Acts 9: 31, 'Then had the churches rest.'" According to Mr. Davis, Rev. Williams' statement was probably a well-earned rebuke, as the woman was a mischievous gossip who had stirred the pastor's ire. Possibly from personal experience, Rev. Davis goes on to state that "the sin of which that woman was guilty has unsettled more pastors than all other sins combined."

On Tuesday, June 9, 1767, the Rev. Enoch Green was ordained and installed as pastor. He had been licensed to preach in 1761 and had been active in the Egg Harbor area. He was the first minister to occupy the brick parsonage that had been built on the parsonage farm in 1764 during the difficulties with the Greenwich church. It was in this parsonage that Enoch Green conducted his famous classical school, preparing young men for college. Two of his pupils who later became famous were Phillip Vickers Fithian and Joseph Bloomfield. Bloomfield later became the first lawyer in Bridgeton, an officer in the Continental Army, Governor of New Jersey, and had a town named for him.[2]

The "log meeting house for public worship" had now been in use for forty years, and the congregation realized that a new meeting house was necessary. Shortly after Enoch Green's installation the people started gathering stones for the new meeting house they intended to build. On Saturday, May 25, 1771, a triangular piece of land containing approximately one-third of an acre was purchased from Daniel Ogden and Azariah Moore for the sum of ten shillings. The stones collected were Jersey sandstone, which is a combination of sand and pebbles bound together by iron ore. Nowhere in the Deerfield area does this stone occur in sufficient quantity to qualify as a quarry. In order to obtain a sufficient number of stones to construct their new building, it was necessary for each family to scour their own and adjoining properties to find the stones. These were then taken to their homes where they were squared and prepared for use by the women of the household. When a sufficient number were ready, they were brought to the church site and put into place by the men so that, stone by stone, the walls were eventually raised. Upon examining the structure it can be discovered that the large, regularly formed stones were used on the south side and the side facing the road. The irregular stones were used for the walls on the sides toward the north and the stream, not ordinarily seen by the casual passerby.[3]

Originally the building was rectangular in shape with dimensions of thirty-eight by forty-eight feet. Inside, the ceiling was arched, and the high, octagonal pulpit on the west side of the sanctuary was reached by a narrow staircase. Above it was a sounding board suspended by a rod. Immediately below the pulpit was an area fenced with a low, paneled partition which was known as "The Circle." Except for the sermon the service was conducted from this area. Benches were provided for the choir master, who led the congregation in singing paraphrased psalms. The deacons also sat in this area during holy communion. The aisles were paved with bricks. Box pews were supplied for the comfort of the worshippers with the floors under the pews being made of "pine, grooved and ploughed smooth." A gallery was constructed on three sides with stairs rising from either side of the south entrance. The main entrance was on the east side and was graced with double doors. At a later date a flat ceiling was installed, probably to conserve heat. The interior was whitewashed, in keeping with the custom of that period. No ornaments of any kind were permitted, as the people were to gather together for the purpose of worshipping God and not to be distracted by works of art or other objects. In keeping with their stern views there was no tower and no bell. The deed for the land contained a clause that hopefully would insure the continuation of doctrine as it was accepted in that day: "To be held by said Society and its successors as long as they adhere to those thirty-three Articles agreed upon by that Godly and Reverend Body of Divines in the Year of our Lord One Thousand, six hundred and forty seven at Westminster in Great Britain, as it may be seen at large in the Books Intitled the Confession of Faith with the Longer and Shorter Catechisms."[4] The deed was witnessed by the Rev. Enoch Green and Fithian Stratton, who was later to leave the church and become a Methodist preacher.

Enoch Green served the Deerfield congregation for nine years, in what was apparently a very cordial relationship. He, along with the Rev. Andrew Hunter, who was still pastor at Greenwich, was an ardent supporter of the Revolutionary cause. He volunteered as a chaplain in the Continental Army, immediately contracted "camp fever," and died on December 2, 1776. He was buried in a place of honor beneath the floor of the meeting house, indicating the high esteem in which he was held by the congregation.

Casting about for a successor of stature equal to the Rev. Enoch Green, the congregation approached the Philadelphia Presbytery in April 1777 "for as much of Mr. Brainerd's pastoral labours as may consistently be offered them." This refers to John Brainerd, brother of the famous missionary to the Indians, David Brainerd. The people knew that the Tories had burned Rev. John Brainerd's house in Mt. Holly because of his loyal support of the Revolution, which made it impossible for him to continue his work with the Indians in that area. Rev. Brainerd gladly accepted the offer, and moved into the parsonage left vacant by Rev. Enoch Green's family. He was never installed as pastor of the Deerfield church, however, probably because he expected to return to his work with the Indians. He remained as stated supply until his death on March 18, 1781. He was also buried beneath the church toward the southern end, so greatly was he regarded by the congregation during their short acquaintance with him.

It was during the ministry of the Rev. John Brainerd that the Methodists came into the picture. Fithian Stratton, who was a witness to the deed transferring title to the Deerfield Society for the ground on which the stone church was built, had now become a Methodist minister. He sought permission from the session to hold Methodist services in the church. Since he had incurred the displeasure of the session by becoming a Methodist minister, the session refused his request, stating that it was not conducive to the health of the congregation to permit Methodist teachers "with whose principles we are unacquainted" to preach within the bounds of the Presbyterian church.[5]

The church was now to go through a period of tribulation that was to last until 1795, fourteen years. For three years after Rev. John Brainerd's death, the church was without a pastor. In 1783, Rev. Simeon Hyde accepted the call, but seven weeks after his installation he died and was buried in the church yard. Another period of three years went by before another minister could be secured. Mr. William Pickles was installed June 20, 1786, but the congregation would have fared better had he never been called. He served for little more than a year before the church was required to take the unpleasant step of complaining to the Presbytery of his drunkenness and scandalous conduct. Although the Presbytery had endeavored to satisfy themselves of Mr. Pickle's qualifications before his installation, they and the congregation had been misled by his excellent gift of speech. A committee of Presbytery conducted his trial from November 20–24, 1787, which resulted in his suspension and later removal from the ministry.

Another eight years were to go by before this little parish was to find a pastor. During that period, however, they were not idle. An additional piece of property was acquired in 1792 from Uriah Davis and his wife, Sarah. This property was immediately north of the church and crossed the road to form part of what is now the "Chapel Yard." It consisted of slightly more than 1.5 acres, and the Society paid eight pounds and thirteen shillings "in gold and silver money."[6]

The congregation was to be fortunate in its next selection of a pastor. The Rev. John Davenport was ordained and installed August 12, 1795, and was to faithfully serve the church for the next ten years. He was born in Freehold, New Jersey in 1752, graduated from Princeton College in 1769, and served parishes in Long Island and Bedford, New York, before coming to Deerfield. Under his leadership the first roll of church members was made on June 6, 1801. The membership at that time was eighty-five, and during his ten years sixty-four persons were added to the church roster. The session in 1796 adopted a Covenant which set forth the requirements for church membership. It was a strict document requiring of the members a "conscientious performance of Christian duties... to exercise a Christian watchfulness and inspection over us... and to submit to the same from us – to subject yourself to the government and discipline of Christ in this his church..." It was undoubtedly due to the strictness of this document that the congregation of Deerfield could be said to consist of two parts. In the first group were those who had agreed to abide by the strict terms of the Covenant and were members of the Society. In the second group were those who had rented pews for their families and attended services regularly, participated in the life of the church and served on the committees, but were not willing to take the final step of becoming members of the Society. Even though they were not members, their contribution to the church was real and vital. Can there be any doubt as to which of these two groups most modern day Presbyterians would belong?

The congregation continued to be active, regardless of whether or not it had the services of a pastor. In 1810 another three-quarters of an acre was purchased for one dollar from the same Uriah Davis who had sold the church a parcel of land in 1792. By 1819, the old parsonage was beyond repair, and the congregation decided to build a new one, to be financed by selling the timber on the parsonage farm. The Rev. Francis S. Ballentine was the first pastor to occupy the new parsonage, which was built across the road from the old brick manse constructed in 1753.

By 1858 the old church had become outmoded in design and a new building program was begun. The architect was D. A. F. Randolph, who drew up plans radically changing the appearance of the old church. Twenty-five feet were added to the north end, with a recess to accommodate the high pulpit. Five tall, arched windows with thirty-six panes of clear glass replaced the previous windows and the east entrance. The brick floor was removed and a wooden floor installed. The gallery across the north and east sides was taken down and a vestibule built beneath the gallery on the south end with a four-fold door giving access to the sanctuary. The curved ceiling was restored, but the room was heated by means of stoves placed in each corner. Except for the lowering of the pulpit platform at an unknown date and the removal of the pew doors in 1884, the church remained this way until the next renovation period in 1907.

At the time of these changes thought was given to the building of a chapel, but nothing came of it until 1878, during the pastorate of the Rev. Edward P. Heberton. A building committee consisting of Elmer Biddle, Robert Moore, Moses Peacock, and Edward O. Leake was formed. The Bridgeton firm of Conover & Ackley was hired, and the chapel was built for the sum of $1,270. Sufficient pledges were obtained so that the building was debt-free upon completion. Immediate steps were taken to furnish the new chapel, which was accomplished at a cost of $324.40.

Expenses for Furnishing Materials for Chapel

Material for Seats (benches)	$108.00
Labor putting seats together	10.00
Lamps	70.00
2 Stoves, including extra pipe	29.11
Pulpit	8.00
Chairs	24.00
Carpet	18.00
Blinds (inside shutters)	46.34
Freight	5.32
Sundry Articles	3.70
Oil Cloth	<u>1.93</u>
	$324.40[7]

The congregation continued with its acquisitions as opportunities arose. In 1884 they purchased approximately an acre of land from Elijah Parvin in the southern part of the village for $400. On this land they built a new parsonage, costing $3,287.65, including a barn, woodshed, henhouse, and fencing. In 1904 property belonging to the estate of George Leake became available. The administrator of the estate was a member of the church, Edward O. Leake. He arranged the sale to the church of 8.17 acres for the sum of $770. This land was dedicated as a new cemetery, and in 1927 the stone posts were erected. In keeping with the New England frugality inherited from their Puritan ancestors, the congregation realized the cost of this property many times over by renting the portion not needed for a burial ground.

The original views of the founders concerning the appearance of their house of worship had long since disappeared, and the dream of the congregation was to have a tower and bell added to the church. This drastic step was taken in 1907 and dedicated on June 19th of that year. For forty years the people were satisfied with things as they were, but by 1947 the urge to add one more piece of equipment to increase their enjoyment of worship services became overpowering. They wanted a small pipe organ. Hannah M. Coles was appointed chairlady of the committee to raise fund for the project. Every member, active or otherwise, was approached to make a pledge toward the organ fund. One of the inactive members was Charles F. Seabrook of the well-known Seabrook Farms. Undaunted, Hannah Coles and Melvin Mixner called on Mr. Seabrook. This visit ignited an interest and activity that was to continue for the rest of Mr. Seabrook's life. Initially he pledged to match whatever sum the congregation raised.

When the church building was examined, the church members were horrified to learn that major repairs would be necessary, including the replacement of termite-infested floor joists. The estimate of the cost for these repairs came to $10,000. By this time Mr. Seabrook had resumed full participation in all phases of church life, and he brought in his architect to suggest what might be done to appropriately renovate the building. A drastic renovation was the result. The old leaded windows were replaced with colonial type sash, glazed with a reproduction of the original hand-blown glass, stone was used to pave the interior of the church in place of the wooden floor, and radiant heat took the place of the old stoves. Eventually the church was stripped to the original stone walls and roof. In providing an access passage to the new organ chamber, the body of Rev. Enoch Green was transferred from beneath the floor of the church to a new grave in the church yard. By this time, the contagious enthusiasm of Mr. Seabrook had spread to all members of the congregation. A revitalized choir rehearsed each week under the direction of Lowell Ayers, Director of Music of the First Church in Bridgeton, and new robes were purchased for the choir and pastor.

While the renovation of the church continued, the organ committee searched the area for a suitable instrument, finally settling on one made by the Aeolian-Skinner Organ Company. However, this was during the period immediately following World War II, and manufacturers still had not been given permission to resume production of consumer goods. Tin to be used for organ pipes was not available. Once again Mr. Seabrook was equal to the occasion. He bought an unused organ from a theatre on Chestnut Street, Philadelphia, and had it disassembled and the pipes shipped to the organ factory so that the tin could be reclaimed. At last, the great day arrived when the renovation was completed and the pipe organ installed. On Sunday, October 26, 1947, rededication services were held. Calvin H. Moore, representing the congregation, turned over the keys of the restored building to the Honorable Stacy Robbins, representing the Presbytery of West Jersey. The drive for funds to buy a small organ had precipitated a building program that totaled in excess of $70,000.

Shortly after the church had been rededicated, Pearl Buck, the famous authoress, while touring the Seabrook Freezing Plant, expressed a desire to visit the church that Mr. Seabrook had built for his workers. When it was explained that the church building had been in existence since 1771, and that every member of the congregation had contributed to its renovation, Mrs. Buck lost interest and declined to visit the church.

Most churches are formed after a community has been established. The Deerfield Presbyterian Church has the distinction of being in existence before the community. In fact, it was the existence of the Presbyterian church and the log school house in the area that was the justification for the gradual formation of the village. Not until 1803 was this area sufficiently populated to warrant a postal designation. That year it was named Deerfield Street, which is still its official name. The name Deerfield Street was chosen to distinguish it from a Deerfield in northern New Jersey. Today's descendants of the stern Calvinist founders still maintain the faith of their fathers and the rugged individualism that kept their church alive despite periods of hardship and dissension. In the words of Elder F. Alan Palmer, "We have returned to our Calvinist beliefs."

---

1. *The Presbyterian Parish of Deerfield Street, 1737–1971,* by F. Alan Palmer.

2. See Chapter I on St. Mary's Episcopal Church in Burlington for further reference to Joseph Bloomfield.

3. See Chapters XVI and XXIV, respectively, on Old Stone Church, Fairton, and Old Stone Church, Swedesboro, for other churches built of Jersey sandstone.

4. *The Presbyterian Parish of Deerfield Street, 1737–1971,* by F. Alan Palmer.

5. *Deerfield Presbyterian Church, 1737–1847,* by Clyde M. Allison.

6. *The Presbyterian Parish of Deerfield Street, 1737–1971,* by F. Alan Palmer.

7. Ibid.

XI

Friends Meeting

Greenwich, 1771

ohn Fenwick, the "convinced Quaker" who had brought a shipload of refugees, mainly Quakers, from England, in 1675, to Salem, had great plans for the village of Greenwich. It was to have streets 100 feet wide, and was to be called "Cohansey," after the river along whose banks it is located. The river played a large part in the development of the town. It was deep enough to allow access to ocean-going vessels, a fact which was responsible for Greenwich becoming a port of entry for the colonies in 1701. Pirates are said to have roamed the area, and, according to tradition, Blackbeard and Captain Kidd buried their treasures along its banks. It was by means of this river that many of the early settlers arrived, as travel by boat was often easier and more convenient than traveling overland in those early days. Samuel Bacon sailed up the river in 1682 looking for a homestead location, and Bacon's Neck derives its name from this ancient mariner. He had sailed all the way from Barnstable, Massachusetts looking for a suitable place with favorable weather, rich soil, and the political freedom to live his own life as he chose.

By the time the town was laid out, John Fenwick was sleeping in what is now an unknown grave, but some of his plans were carried out. The main street, called Great Street, was constructed 100 feet

Greenwich Friends Meeting House, built by the Hicksites in 1857.

wide, as he had directed. But in naming the town he did not do as well. Instead of Cohansey, the settlers called the town Greenwich, in all probability after Greenwich, Connecticut, from whence many of the original settlers had come in search of religious freedom. There seems to be a difference of opinion today as to the proper pronunciation of the town's name. A descendant of one of the original settlers explained it this way: "Newcomers, those who have only 'lived' here for 100 years or so, pronounce it 'Greenwich.' Those of us who have lived here for about 300 years pronounce it 'Gren-ich.'"

Mark Reeve, who had arrived with Fenwick, bought a sixteen-acre plot of ground on August 9, 1686, near the wharf on the Cohansey River.[1] On December 4, 1686, Reeve sold the acreage to Joseph

Browne. On Christmas day, 1693, Browne sold a section fifty feet wide and fifty-five feet deep to Charles Bagley for a small consideration for the purpose of building a meeting house. "Whereas, Mark Reeve, of Caesarea River, yeoman, by deed of Dec. 4, 1686, sold to said Joseph Browne 16 acres in Greenwich, now he sells to Charles Bagley a lot 50 feet on the street and 55 feet deep, for the only use, service & purpose of a Meeting House & graveyard for these people he calls Quakers." The consideration on which the sale was consummated was that Charles Bagley, his heirs and assigns shall pay "yearly and every year the sum of 6 pence" to Joseph Browne. Caesarea was the name that Fenwick had given the Cohansey River. His desires were not to be followed in naming the river anymore than they were in naming the town, however, as the settlers referred to the river by its Indian name—Cohanzick.

From the time of Samuel Bacon's arrival until Charles Bagley bought a lot from Joseph Browne in 1693, the Quakers had been holding worship services in private homes. With more Friends arriving it had been felt for some time that a meeting house should be built. According to the minutes of the Salem Monthly Meeting dated the 29th of November 1686: "It was ordered by the Meeting that seeing friends of Cohansey did not appear at this meeting according to this meeting ordered them, as concerning the establishing a meeting house amongst them it is thought convenient by friends that the meeting bee kept at Joseph Browne's house if hee and his wife bee willing every first day." The Quakers were wont to move deliberately and without haste as the minutes of the Salem Montly Meeting on the 26th day of May in the year 1690, almost four years later, reports: "Anthony Woodhoouse of Cohansey came to this meeting and there proposed to this meeting that the friends in that place was about to build a Meeting House and they desired some assistance from friends of this meeting." Not to be hurried, the Salem Monthly Meeting took no action for almost another four years. At the Monthly Meeting held the 29th of January 1694 the Salem Monthly Meeting "ordered 4 pounds to be given to the friends of Cohansie to help to build them a meeting house."

Time apparently was not of the essence as, even with the help of the Salem Monthly Meeting, it was not until 1698 that the first meeting house was built, even though the Preparative Meeting was established in 1694. Unfortunately, little is known about this place of worship, except that it was a log cabin erected on the same site where the present Orthodox meeting house now stands. It was not by accident that the Friends had selected this spot close to the river. A group of Quakers lived on the Fairton side of the river, and they had no meeting place. The Friends rowed their boats up the river from a place called Lanning's Wharf, which is about a mile below the meeting site. This was not considered an inconvenience, as they had deep religious convictions—after all, they had suffered many persecutions because of their beliefs—and to go to Meeting by rowboat, despite the wind, rain, or snow, was nothing out of the ordinary. Families who comprised the early Greenwich Meeting included such names as Stewart, Test, Reeve, Davis, Tyler, Bacon, Dennis, Horner, Brick, Wood, Sheppard, Miller, and Haines.

This log building served the needs of the Quakers from 1698 to 1771, when a beautiful brick meeting house was built on the same site overlooking the Cohansey River. The front of the meeting house faces Greate Street, while the back faces the river about 200 yards away. This building remains today as it was in 1771, with practically no changes. The interior is typical of the Friends meeting houses built during the colonial period. Comfort was not encouraged, as this was thought to be worldly and would detract from the spiritual mood engendered by the "Quaker Meeting" of quiet reflection. Hard wooden benches with straight backs and no cushions were the seats for the worshippers, facing benches on an elevated platform in front were for the elders, wide oak planks provided the flooring, and panels divided the men's side from the women's section, with separate entrances for the men and women. On the grounds outside many beautiful sycamore trees were planted. Sycamore trees are found at all Quaker meeting houses, and this is another example of the practical side of the early Quakers. These trees grow tall and broad and provide a great deal of beauty as well as shade from the hot sun. They also act as a lightning rod during electrical storms, thereby protecting the meeting house and serving a practical purpose.

Services in those days lasted many hours. Families had come on foot, by boat and on horseback, and they were not going to leave until they had received sufficient spiritual nourishment to last them through the coming week.

From 1771 to 1827, Quakers worshipped in this meeting house without any serious problems. But by 1825, the teachings of Elias Hicks, a deeply religious Quaker who had founded a Quaker community in Virginia according to the thinking of Voltaire and Paine's *Age of Reason*, began to have its effect. The Greenwich Friends were divided by the Separation in 1827–28 that affected the entire Society of Friends. Feelings had become so intense that they could no longer worship together. The Orthodox Friends, being the more numerous, kept the meeting house, and the Hicksites moved out. The Hicksites worshipped in individual homes until 1831, when they bought an unused, frame, Methodist meeting house. They had already purchased a plot of ground from Benjamin Tyler and his wife, Hope, fronting on the main street 1.5 miles northwest of the Orthodox meeting house. The frame building was then moved to this new site. The Hicksites conducted their worship services on the first floor of the building, and a school was run on the second floor by Sarah B. Owen. In 1857, a brick meeting house was built a few rods south of the frame building on three-quarters of an acre of ground also purchased from Benjamin Tyler. This meeting house was a replica of the one built in 1771 and used by the Orthodox Quakers, except smaller in size. There was a concession to more modern ways, though, as they had a stove which dispelled the chill on cold winter days. This stove was called a "flirt," and it was considered rather hilarious that there was a flirt in the Quaker meeting house. In the early 1950s some more worldly people wanted to install central heating. According to a life-long member, this suggestion almost split the Meeting once again. More moderate heads prevailed, however, and a space heater was purchased, which took care of the cold, and also satisfied those who wanted to maintain the historic atmosphere of the old Quaker meeting house.

A descendant of one of the original settlers became a member of the Friends Meeting in a rather unusual way. According to his story, his father, a Quaker, had married a Presbyterian, and in deference to her views the family attended worship services for many years at the Presbyterian Church. One Sunday morning, however, at the conclusion of the service, the Presbyterian minister admonished the congregation about lingering around the church after services, claiming that this was the time the devil was most active. The minister had no sooner stopped talking when the Quaker father stood up in church and exclaimed, "If the devil is so active around here, this is no place for me." With that he started out of the church, and the boy began to follow. The mother grabbed the boy by the seat of the pants and pulled him back to the pew. However, from that time on, the whole family attended the Friends Meeting, giving the devil no further opportunity to corrupt its members.

By 1938 the intense feelings which had caused the Separation in 1827–28 had started to subside. The two groups began having committee meetings to find a means of healing their differences and becoming one group again. In the tradition of the Quakers, action was not taken with undue haste. As a result, it was not until fifteen years had gone by before they could reach an agreement. By this time the Hicksites were the stronger branch, and it was agreed to meet in the Hicksite meeting house. The Orthodox membership had declined drastically, and the Hicksite Friends took over the responsibility of maintaining the 1771 building.

Only occasional meetings are held in it now, but because of its historical significance it is maintained in perfect condition by the Hicksite Friends with help from the Cumberland County Historical Society. The present day Friends have a more tolerant attitude toward their disagreements than the Friends of the early 1800s. Today they have in effect agreed to disagree as far as doctrine is concerned, and each person can believe in accordance with his own persuasion.

---

1. *History of Gloucester, Salem and Cumberland Counties,* by Cushing and Sheppard.

XII

Friends Meeting

Salem, 1772

nder the friendly arms of an oak tree many centuries old, John Fenwick met with the chiefs, or sachems, of the local Indian tribes to purchase the land for what later became known as Fenwick's Colony. Even though he had already purchased the land from Sir John Berkeley for 1,000 pounds, who in turn had received it from the Duke of York, Fenwick met with the Indian chiefs to pay them for the land since they were the inhabitants. Fenwick was a member of the Society of Friends, and it was in keeping with their religious beliefs to deal honestly with the Indians. Undoubtedly, Fenwick also realized that his small band of colonists needed the protection of friendly Indians if they were to survive in this wild country.

John Fenwick was born in Northumberland County, England, in 1618, and served in Cromwell's army as a major of cavalry. In 1665 he joined the Society of Friends and endured many of the persecutions to which the followers of that sect were subjected. It was in this period that West Jersey was offered for sale by Lord Berkeley, and in 1673, Fenwick purchased it for himself and another Quaker, Edward Byllinge. The territory now comprising Salem and Cumberland Counties became his, and he immediately made preparations to settle in the New World. Inducements were offered to other Quakers,

Salem Friends Meeting House, constructed in 1772.

and the idea of escaping the persecutions in England was attractive to a number of them.

In July 1675, John Fenwick, at 57 years of age, set sail on the *Griffith* with his children, his servants, and associates. After a trying 2.5 months at sea, the *Griffith* sailed up the Assamhackin, known now as the Salem Creek, and on the 5th of October, 1675, anchored at the site of what is now the City of Salem. After fleeing from persecution in the Old World, overjoyed at the end of a long, perilous voyage, and thankful for their good fortune in landing at such a pleasant spot, they named their new home "Salem," meaning peace. This was the first English settlement in New Jersey. Most of those who had sailed with Fenwick on the *Griffith* were Quakers, the most prominent of whom were Robert, Samuel, and Edward Wade; Samuel Nicholson; Nathan Stuart; Edward Champney; Samuel Hedge; Richard Guy; John Thompson; John Smith; and John Adams.

Fenwick was determined that they would start their new life on friendly terms with the natives so that Salem would indeed be the peaceful place they sought. It was with these thoughts in mind that Fenwick called the chiefs of the Indian tribes together under the spreading arms of the oak tree, and repurchased from them the lands he had already bought from Lord Berkeley. Territory roughly equivalent to Salem and Cumberland Counties was acquired.[1] By demonstrating his consideration for the rights of the Indians, Fenwick obtained their friendship and secured the opportunity for the small band of settlers to live in peace with their neighbors. All of this took place seven years before the more publicized dealings of William Penn with Indians of Pennsylvania.

Having traveled this far and enduring the hardships of an ocean voyage for the privilege of worshipping God as they saw fit, these early settlers immediately arranged to hold their meetings in the home of one of their members until such time as they could construct a meeting house. Samuel Nicholson had built a log house near the old oak tree under which the treaties with the Indians had been signed, and it was in this house that the Friends met regularly twice each week. On occasion they would meet in the homes of Robert Bane, Richard Guy, and Robert Wade. The Monthly Meeting began in 1676, when "At a meeting held the first day of sixth month, 1676, it was unanimously consented thereto that the first second day of the week, in every month, the Friends within the town of New Salem in Fenwick's Colony, and all Friends belonging thereunto, do monthly meet together, to consider of outward business, and as such as have been convinced, and those that walked disorderly; that they may, with all gravity and uprightness to God, and in tenderness of spirit and love to their souls, be admonished, exhorted, and also reproved, and their evil deeds and practices testified against, in the wisdom of God, and authority of Truth, as may answer the wisdom of God within them."[2] This was signed by, among others: Samuel Nicholson, Robert Lanes, Robert Wade, Edward Wade, Richard Guy, Issac Smart, John Fenwick, and Richard Johnson.

The Friends were desirous of building a suitable meeting house, but for unknown reasons had a difficult time agreeing on an acceptable location. On June 2, 1678, Richard Guy, Edward Bradway, Issac Smart, and Edward Wade were appointed a committee to select a site for the meeting house and burying ground. Their efforts were fruitless. On January 5, 1679 another committee was formed, consisting this time of Edward Wade, James Nevill, John Maddox, and George Deacon, to negotiate with Samuel Nicholson and William Penton for their houses and plantations in Salem, and also "to see Ann Salter, widow of Henry Salter, about her lot of ground." The records do not reveal the problems encountered, but they were of such a nature that it was necessary a month later to appoint a different committee, this time to investigate the suitability of Edward Bradway's house and grounds. No progress was made by any of these committees, and, in December 1680, almost two years later, still another committee was formed to investigate the purchase of a lot from Edward Champney.

Three years after the formation of the first committee no decision had been reached, for reasons which we can only surmise. Whether the various sites investigated were not considered suitable or convenient, or whether an acceptable price could not be agreed upon, is left to speculation.

Finally, on June 6, 1681, Samuel Nicholson and his wife Ann deeded sixteen acres of land on Wharf Street (now West Broadway) to the Salem Monthly Meeting, in consideration of twelve pounds for a meeting house and burial ground forever. The deed for the sixteen acres also included his log dwelling, in which the Friends had been meeting. John Thompson of Elsinboro, and Richard Zane of Salem were immediately authorized to repair the house and fit it for occupancy by the Society. About a year later the same persons were engaged to enlarge the house by adding sixteen feet to its length and increasing its height, so that it would be large enough to accommodate all who came to worship. For some reason this was never done, and in 1683, Benjamin Acton was appointed to build the addition, including stairs and chimney. In 1687 it was floored with a "good clay floor." During this period the Yearly Meetings were held in alternate years in Salem and Burlington, a custom that continued until 1707. The need for a good road through the wilderness between the two towns resulted in the construction of the famous King's Highway, which was laid out by surveyors as early as 1681.

Meetings were held in Nicholson's old log house until 1700, when a new meeting house of brick, the first of its kind, was built, a few yards east of the old oak tree. By 1769, this meeting house had become too small to accommodate those who wished to worship. Ephraim Tomlinson reports in his journal for the spring meeting that "fully 300 persons were obliged to remain out-of-doors for want of room." That same year a new structure, sixty-five by forty-two feet, was being considered, but it was not until 1772 that the new meeting house was built. With the help of 250 pounds contributed by Greenwich, Alloways Creek, and Pilesgrove Meetings, land was purchased, in 1770 from Thomas Hancock and Roger Johnson, on Fenwick Street, (now East Broadway), opposite Margaret's Lane (now Walnut Street). William Ellis, an architect from Philadelphia, drew the plans, and in 1772, the new brick meeting house was built. At the same time the old one was torn down and meetings were held in the court house until the new one was ready. Benjamin Acton was the builder, and the cost is given in one account as 415 pounds and slightly over 425 pounds in another. The cost for the iron work, nails, and glazing amounted to more than the combined cost of bricks, stone, lime, and workmanship.

The walls were 18 inches thick, and glass from the first glass factory in the United States, Wistarburg, was used for the windows. Huge hand-hewn beams fastened with wooden pegs were hoisted into place with a cable-and-pulley apparatus. Roman numerals were cut into the rafters so they could be properly matched when hoisted into position. The "pews" were long wooden benches made of two twenty-foot planks. The two rear doors were called "saddle doors." Their sills were built three feet from the ground so members could dismount from their horses without getting their feet wet.[3] The meeting room was divided by a partition as it was customary for men and women to meet in separate rooms. For Quarterly Meetings the partition was removed. Other doors in the building were called "witches cross" doors, as they were made with six panels forming a cross. The fence at the sidewalk and along one side of the front yard was made from New Jersey bog iron, as are the covers of the two wells in the front yard. Firemen in the early days drew water from these wells to fight local fires.

The meeting house was completed just as the sparks of the Revolution began to sputter. The meeting house was not damaged by either the Continental troops or the British army, contrary to the experience of many other Quaker meeting houses; nevertheless, the British maintained their headquarters in front of the Quaker building. On March 16, 1778, Colonel Mawhood entered Salem just as a funeral procession was on the way to the Friends burying ground. He promptly commandeered all the horses in the procession except the one belonging to the widow, a Quaker lady named Fogg.

A possible explanation for the fact that the Salem Meeting House was not destroyed by the British was the sympathy for the British cause expressed by the Salem Quakers. Quakers from Salem as well as Philadelphia conducted a "hot" war of their own with those they dubbed "the rebel canaille." Richard Wistar, of Wistar glass fame, was extremely loyal to the British, and he married his second wife, widow Mary Gilbert, in the Salem Friends Meeting House on August 4, 1776, just one month after the Liberty Bell at Bridgeton pealed for the Declaration of Independence.[4]

Not all Quakers of Salem County, however, were such ardent Tories. Anthony Sharp espoused the Revolutionary cause. When the British were near his house, he lay concealed in his barn. Later he went to Fort Ticonderoga where he attained the rank of Colonel in the American army.[5]

Because of the infamous massacre of patriot troops at Hancock's Bridge, the local citizens cried out for retaliation against the British. Since the war was not over there was little they could do about it except vent their anger on those who had aided the enemy. On September 26, 1778, the Salem County Grand Jury retuned indictments against those persons who had borne arms or otherwise helped the British cause. Following the indictments, the Court of Oyer and Terminer met in Salem on November 30th and continued until December 19th. On many occasions the Court met in the Friends Meeting House. Despite this swift action by the Court, the hatred, particularly toward those who had guided the British to the scene, did not die easily. As late as 1825, a member of the Sayre family, who had had a relative murdered at Hancock's Bridge, had not forgotten nor forgiven. He was captain of a small vessel sailing between Salem and Philadelphia. One night he became drunk and fell into the Delaware River at the Market Street wharf. A young man standing on the wharf jumped into the river and saved Sayre's life. Upon being rescued Sayre discovered that he owed his life to the son of Jonathan Ballinger, who had been one of the guides for the British. When he became aware of this fact, Sayre said he "would be damned if he would owe his life to such a double damned scoundrel as the son of a

Ballinger." Whereupon he threw himself back into the river, but was rescued a second time.[6]

The turmoil caused by the preaching of Elias Hicks, the Long Island farmer, was felt in Salem as it was in practically all Quaker settlements.[7] In 1827–28 the Meeting was split into two factions—Hicksite and Orthodox. The Hicksites maintained the old meeting house, and the Orthodox, after worshipping in a school house on Walnut Street until 1837, built their own meeting house on West Broadway, opposite the old burying ground.

But the story of the Salem Meeting House and its burying ground would not be complete without relating the piteous tale of one family whose father was buried therein. A German-Catholic family had settled in Salem in the fall of 1844, and because they were too proud to let their needs be known, existed through the winter in abject poverty.

With the arrival of spring the husband became ill and died. As there was no Catholic cemetery in the area, the Friends, with their usual concern for those in distress, offered the widow a plot in their burying ground. Their kindness was gladly accepted, but then a new problem arose. The widow, being a staunch Catholic, could not allow her husband to be buried without the rights of the Catholic Church. Since there was no priest in the vicinity, she requested that a certain prominent citizen, who was not a Catholic, perform the ceremony. He replied that he could not conscientiously perform such a ritual. The widow, misunderstanding his reasons, assured him that the Pope would forgive him. Since he did not feel qualified to act, he finally persuaded her to conduct the service herself, since she was a good Catholic. After some moments of reflection she decided that this was the best solution.

As the mourners gathered at the grave, the brave widow stepped forward, took a spade-full of earth and consecrated it. Without hesitation she went through the solemn burial service of the Catholic

Church in such a reverent manner that tears were brought to the eyes of many a hardened spectator. She concluded the service with an appropriate prayer for her departed husband. Turning from the grave she headed home with no idea as to how she would provide for her children. The peculiar circumstances of the burial, however, received widespread attention, and the courage of the widow tugged at the heart strings of many a person. As a result the story had a happy ending, as immediate relief was provided for her and her children.[8]

Still in regular use more than two hundred years since it was built, this venerable old meeting house stands as a testimonial to the courage and faith of those early Quakers who fled the persecutions of the Old World to find the religious freedom that they sought in the New World.

---

1. *The History of Gloucester, Salem and Cumberland Counties*, by Cushing & Sheppard.

2. *Minutes*, Salem Monthly Meeting.

3. See Chapter XIII on Crosswicks Friends Meeting.

4. *The Glass Gafers of New Jersey*, by Adeline Pepper.

5. *The History of Gloucester, Salem and Cumberland Counties*, by Cushing & Sheppard.

6. *History of Salem County, New Jersey*, by Joseph S. Sickler.

7. See Chapter II on Friends Meeting, Woodbury.

8. Ibid.

XIII

Friends Meeting

Crosswicks, 1773

It was Sunday morning and all through Burlington and Mercer Counties youngsters were awakening to the savory aroma of Taylor's Ham cooking in the kitchen. This had become a typical Sunday breakfast in colonial times for the Crosswicks area, just as baked beans and brown bread were the typical Saturday night supper in Boston. Although it could be prepared in any number of ways, the favorite was to broil two slices of Taylor's Ham and serve them with a poached egg on top. This was a Sunday breakfast that would satisfy anyone, including the hardy farmers of that early age. Since 1906, Taylor's Ham has been known as Taylor's Pork Roll, probably named for John Taylor, who lived near Crosswicks and first ground the ham for market in 1856. The progenitor of this Taylor was a man of the same name who had been a fighting Quaker as a Captain in the Continental Army. His name was Samuel Taylor, and he was one of the early settlers along Crosswicks Creek.

Crosswicks Creek separates the Township of Chesterfield and the picturesque village of the same name from Mercer County. It takes its name from the Indian "Crossweeksunk," meaning "a separation." The town of Crosswicks was settled by English Quakers in 1677 upon their arrival from England on the *Kent*, which had brought a number

Crosswicks Friends Meeting House, built in 1773.

of Quakers to Burlington. The first recorded meeting for worship was held in the house of Thomas Lampert that same year. Meetings for worship continued to be held in the homes of Friends, including Francis Davenport, William Biddle, Edward Rockhill, and Ann Murfries. By 1684, the Friends Meeting was formally organized, as recorded by the minutes of the Chesterfield Monthly Meeting: "At our monthly meeting of Francis Davenport's house near Crosswicks Creeke the place now called Chesterfield in West Jersey ye 2nd of ye 8th month 1684 it is agreed that weeke day meeting be kept every fourth day." The Monthly Meeting was established in 1684, and the first notice of a burial is that of Mary, daughter of Anthony and Hannah Woodward, who was interred on January 13, 1686.[1]

Crosswicks Friends Meeting

The first meeting house, built in 1693, was of frame construction, unusual for that period since most of the structures were built of logs. Francis Davenport's house, where the Monthly Meeting was established, was a log house. This first meeting place for the Friends was built on land purchased from Samuel and John Bunting, and stood at or near the graveyard close by Crosswicks bridge. John Green was the builder. A minute of the Monthly Meeting gives the details: "At a monthly meeting at the Meeting house in Chesterfield ye 4th day of ye 11th mo. 1693, the committee reported that it had settled with John Green about the meeting house building and according to agreement paid his 41 pounds 2 shillings, also paid for lime 6s 8d." As the Quakers were great lovers of horses, arrangements were made on January 3, 1697 to build a stable to house the horses during meetings. The dimensions of the stable were eighteen by twenty-four feet with the sides clapboarded and the roof shingled with oak shingles. This stable was used by the Quakers for their horses for 137 years, until it was finally torn down in 1834.

The frame meeting house built in 1693 was used by the Friends for only a short period of time before it became inadequate. By 1706, twenty-three years after their arrival, their houses built, their farms established, they now had more time to devote to improving their worship facilities. The original meeting house was torn down, and a larger one erected, one more suited to serving the needs of the growing community. This time the meeting house was built of brick. Arrangements were made with William Mott for the supply of 40,000 bricks at a cost of forty pounds. The minutes of the Monthly Meeting tell the story: "At a Monthly Meeting of Friends held at their meeting house in Chesterfield ye 2d day of the 3d month 1706, William Wood and Francis Davenport acquaints this meeting that they have agreed with William Mott for 40000 Thousand of Good Bricks to be made for 40 Pounds with which the meeting is satisfied and desires yt they will take Care to make Articules of their agreement." Two hundred bushels of lime were furnished by John Farnsworth, but the cost is not mentioned. Samuel Bunting, Francis Davenport, William Wood, John Tatum, and Robert Wilson were appointed to select a carpenter. They decided on one of their own members, Tatum, but the cost of his labors is not recorded, nor is the actual date the meeting house was completed and ready for use, but it was probably the fall of 1707. This meeting house served the needs of the Friends for almost fifty years, but by 1753, it was no longer large enough for the growing number of Friends, and a substantial addition was made to it at that time.

This proved to be only a stopgap measure, however, because on February 4, 1773, another committee was formed to consider the advisability of an additional enlargement. The Friends formed large committees, and this was no exception. The members were Anthony Sykes, John Bullock, Amos Middleton, Thomas Thorn, James Lawrie, Joseph Horner, Benjamin Clark, Joseph Duer, Jonathan Wright, Edward Rockhill, Stacy Potts, Caleb Shreve, Amos Wright, and Samuel Saterthwaite, Jr. Between February and July, the committee came to the conclusion that it would not be practical to add another addition to the old meeting house, and that a new one should be built. Favorable reports had been received about the meeting house at Buckingham, Pennsylvania, and Stacy Potts, Benjamin Clark, James Odell, and Abraham Skirm were commissioned to visit it and submit their recommendations. After examining the meeting house at Buckingham they reported that a similar one could be built for 750 pounds. After considerable discussion, the Monthly Meeting took the following action: "At a monthly meeting of Friends held at Chesterfield ye 7th of ye 10th month 1773 this meeting taking into consideration the building of a new meeting house agreeth to and authorized the committee which was appointed to take subscriptions for that service to get or agree for materials in order to carry on said building and also to collect the money which is subscribed for that purpose and to report to next Monthly Meeting." Abel Middleton and Isaiah Robbins were appointed managers, and Caleb Newbold was named to assist them in procuring materials. Amos Middleton was also appointed treasurer to receive the collections and to pay the managers.

The managers did their job well, as a large, commodious, two-story brick meeting house was built, one of the largest in South Jersey. Today it has an air of quiet dignity which speaks of an age when affairs of men were less harried and people took time to pause from their weekday chores to seek the "inner light." When completed it was almost an exact duplicate of the one in Buckingham. The outside dimensions are sixty-eight feet, ten inches, by forty-three feet, eight inches. The brickwork is Flemish Bond, except for the north side, which has black-header bricks. The original flooring, which was laid with wide, heavy planks with closely spaced joists, is still there. A gallery about sixteen feet wide runs around three sides of the building. On the north side the gallery is only about three feet wide, below which are the facing benches for the ministers, elders, and overseers. The meeting room is divided by movable shutters, which can be closed for the Monthly Meetings. During worship services the men and women sat on opposite sides of the room separated by an aisle. The side used by the men is easily identifiable by the initials carved on the backs of the benches in the gallery. There are no "artistic" carvings on the women's side. Providing heat for the building is a huge, box-like stove bearing the name "Atsion." This stove was built of Jersey bog iron and cast by the furnace at Atsion, New Jersey, which was a flourishing town at that time. The stove was purchased in 1772 for 8 pounds, 4 shillings, and 4 pence, and, according to a framed letter hung near the stove, Stacy Potts was charged with the responsibility of collecting the cost from the members. This stove is one of three such stoves still known to exist in New Jersey, the other two being in the Old Broad Street Presbyterian Church in Bridgeton.

The woodwork is native cedar, practically free of knots. The nails are hand-wrought, and the benches are made of oak.

The sill for the rear door is elevated several steps above the floor level, which is an unusual piece of construction, the purpose of which has been explained in two ways. One explanation is that it was used to assist horseback riders to dismount from their saddles and enter the building. The difficulty with this thought is that it leaves someone outside to take the horse to the stable. The other explanation is that the higher entrance was to facilitate the handling of coffins in and out of the meeting house, and was, therefore, a "coffin door."[2]

The quiet dignity of this venerable old meeting house was shattered during the Revolutionary War. On June 17, 1778, the British left Philadelphia on their way to New York, marching in three detachments—one going through Mount Holly, one through Columbus, and one via Bordentown. The Bordentown column reached Crosswicks on June 23rd and attempted to navigate Crosswicks Creek over a drawbridge nearby. The Colonial troops in that vicinity, under the command of General Dickinson, had been withdrawn, with the exception of three regiments under the commands of Colonels Frelinghuysen, Van Dike, and Webster. In order to impede the crossing of the creek by the British, the Americans had torn up the planking and raised the draw so that the bridge was unusable. When the British reached the drawbridge, they immediately began repairing it and a skirmish took place. An American named Clevenger was killed as he cut away the last sleeper. The American forces stationed on the Woodwardsville side of the creek fired several cannon balls that struck the meeting house walls. One of these, a three pounder, lodged itself in the north wall under an upper window. For a number of years this relic of the Revolution was safeguarded by a family who had removed it from the wall when the meeting house was being repaired a few years after the skirmish. Later it was restored to its original place in the wall and cemented there to secure it from falling out. It is still there, and is one of the tourist attractions of the meeting house.

The date of the erection of the meeting house, 1773, appears in the western gable, and it was the western end of the building that was occupied by the American forces shortly after the Battle of Trenton. Still visible in the woodwork are the marks of axe and rope, as well as a number of rings on the floor made by musket barrels. Even during the time the building was being used as a barracks, Sunday services were still held. The soldiers rearranged the benches each Sunday morning to accommodate the worshippers.

At the time of the Separation of the Friends in 1827–28, the meeting house remained in the possession of the Hicksite branch.[3] The Orthodox Friends met at Joseph Hendrickson's house on Buttonwood Street until they built a frame meeting house on the Bordentown Road in 1831. A school was conducted on the men's side until 1853, when the meeting house was moved north and converted into a school house. In 1854, a brick meeting house was erected on the former site and used until the Meeting was laid down.

When the Society split into two branches there was a disagreement over the ownership of the school funds. The treasurer of the fund was an Orthodox Friend, and he refused to turn the money over to the Hicksites. The fund amounted to two thousand dollars, so the Hicksites took the case to court. The trial was held in Trenton before the Chancery Court, the verdict being in favor of the Orthodox branch.

At Crosswicks, as in other communities, the Friends lived together peacefully with the Indians. However, differences between the white man and the red man gradually developed, and the State Legislature appointed a committee to investigate the grievances of the Indians. The most serious of these grievances was the Indian claim that they were constantly being cheated by the white man. In February 1758, a conference was held in the Crosswicks Meeting House at which

Teedyescong, Chief of the Lenni Lenape Tribe, was present. He was the last of the great Indian Chiefs who ruled the Delawares living in Eastern Pennsylvania and New Jersey. He had been converted to Christianity by early Moravian missionaries in 1750. Besides taking on the white man's religion, he had also taken on one of the white man's curses. He became a victim of the white man's "firewater," and in 1763 burned to death in his wigwam while in a drunken stupor.

In August 1975, tragedy struck in the form of a devastating storm. A landmark of the Crosswicks Meeting came crashing to earth with a thunderous sound like a cannon shot heard throughout the town. The famous white oak tree that had been standing on the Meeting grounds since 1682 was the storm's victim. It had a girth of over 17 feet, and had been entered in the Hall of Fame for big trees in Washington, DC on March 1, 1921. Justifiably proud of this magnificent tree, the Crosswicks Friends had enjoyed vying with the Salem Friends over the merits of their respective white oak trees. This unfortunate storm settled the contest, leaving the Salem white oak unchallenged as the oldest and largest in South Jersey.

Until 1934, this Meeting was known as Chesterfield Preparative Meeting at Crosswicks. Now its official name is Crosswicks Meeting of the Religious Society of Friends.

---

1. *Historical Sketches of Friends Meetings*, by T. Chalkley Matlack.

2. See Chapters XII and XI, respectively, on Salem and Greenwich Friends Meetings.

3. See Chapter II on Friends Meeting, Woodbury.

XIV

Friends Meeting

Mount Holly, 1775

etticoat Bridge, Battle of Iron Works Hill, and John Woolman —the names of two Revolutionary War battles and the name of the greatest American Quaker totally opposed to war certainly don't have much in common, yet all three contributed significantly to the history of Mount Holly, where the Friends Meeting House is the outstanding historical landmark. Built in 1775, it was used as a slaughterhouse and commissary by Hessian troops when they occupied the town, and as a meeting place for the State Legislature when prudence decreed that it should leave Trenton because of the activities of the British Army. Having no greater desire than to live in peace and harmony with their fellow man, the Mount Holly Friends were destined by fortune to be placed in the thick of the Revolutionary War. But young blood runs hot, be it Quaker or other, and thirty-two Friends were disowned by the Society for their war activities.

The first Friends Meeting House was built in 1716 at the foot of the northern slope of Mount Holly, formerly called Cripp's Mount. Authorized by Burlington Monthly Meeting on "ye 2nd day of ye 11th mo, 1715," the meeting house was a brick building located on the west side of Woodpecker Lane, opposite the Woodlane Cemetery, at

Mount Holly Friends Meeting House, erected in 1775.

the junction of the roads leading to Jacksonville (then known as Slabtown) and Burlington. Prior to this the Friends held worship services in private homes, including those of Restore Lippincott, who lived in the east end of town, and Daniel Wills Jr., whose home was near Eayrestown. Restore Lippincott was a member of the committee authorized by the Burlington Monthly Meeting to obtain the title to land on which to build a meeting house, but for some unknown reason Daniel Wills, Jr. was not. The other members of that committee were Richard Eayres, Samuel Lippincott, John Burr, Thomas Haines, and James Lippincott.

By 1742, there were enough Friends in the village of Mount Holly that they debated the wisdom of traveling to the outskirts of town for

First day services, particularly during the cold, blustery winters that gripped Mount Holly in those days. The Burlington Monthly Meeting was petitioned for permission to hold worship meetings in the homes of Friends, and permission was granted, but only for the winter months. The brick meeting house on Woodpecker Lane continued to be used until 1763. During this time it was not only used by the Friends for worship services, but also by the town fathers for meetings of the Township Government, permission for which had been granted by the Friends until a town hall was built in 1747.

Growth of the town along the Rancocas Creek made the building of a meeting house nearer the center of population a necessity. Again the Burlington Monthly meeting was consulted, and in their meeting on April 4, 1763, permission was granted for the Friends of Mount Holly "to build a meeting house in such place and manner as they can agree upon." This second meeting house, known as "Little Meeting House," was built on Mill Street behind John Woolman's tailor shop and was reached by Meeting House Alley. It was the place not only used as a section of worship but as a schoolhouse. This was the meeting house that John Woolman attended, and, as suggested by the Quaker historian Amelia Mott Gummere, he probably taught school there. Even though the Little Meeting House was built in the center of Mount Holly, the Woodpecker Lane Meeting House was still maintained. Apparently this was a more commodious place of worship, as the Burlington Monthly Meeting of May 7, 1770, stipulated that the meetings were to be held "at the Meeting House out of Town" when prominent Quaker ministers were visiting.

A touching story is told of a Negro slave who very much wanted to be a Friend. He was courting a Negro servant named Dido, and both of them wanted to be married according to the custom of Friends. The Society of Friends, however, did not admit Negroes at that time. John Woolman, who spent most of his adult life preaching against slavery, came to the aid of the young couple. He arranged for them to meet in a Friend's home where the Friends marriage ceremony took place on May 3, 1768. In 1814 William Boen, who had by then been freed by his master, was admitted to membership in the Society of Friends.[1]

By 1775 the need for a larger, centrally located meeting house combining the services offered by the Woodpecker Lane Meeting House and Little Meeting House on Mill Street was recognized. The Burlington Monthly Meeting authorized the building of the present Friends Meeting House on land purchased from John Brainerd at the corner of Main and Garden Streets. The foundation was built of iron-stone[2] from a quarry on the South Branch of the Rancocas River. Joel Fenton's brick-works in Burlington furnished the bricks,[3] the lumber was rough-sawn by a gate mill, the planing was done by hand, the mouldings were worked out of solid lumber, and the frames and windows were all constructed on the site. Local men provided all the labor. Michael Rush, who was to do the county courthouse under architect Samuel Lewis twenty years later, did the woodwork for the meeting house.

Once the new meeting house on Main and Garden Streets was finished and ready for occupancy, the trustees petitioned the Burlington Monthly Meeting for permission to dispose of the Little Meeting House. Permission was granted in April of 1776, with the idea that the building and forty-foot square lot were to be sold and the proceeds used by the Friends for defraying the costs of the new meeting house. At the same time the Mount Holly Monthly Meeting was "set off" from Burlington Monthly Meeting. The following Preparative Meeting became part of the Mount Holly Monthly Meeting: Mount Holly, Rancocas, Springfield (Copany), Upper Springfield, Arney's Mount (Shreve's Mount), and later on Vincentown.

Erected to serve the peaceful needs of the Mount Holly Friends, the meeting house was completed at a time when these needs coincided with other less peaceful needs of the colonies, and the meeting house was put to some uses never intended by the Friends. The Declaration of Independence had just been signed and the Revolutionary War was under way. By December 1776, the British and Hessian troops were all through the area, and on December 23rd, Mount Holly witnessed the Battle of Iron Works Hill. The iron works was engaged in casting cannon balls, soup kettles, and other necessary articles for the American Army.[4] On December 20th, the Hessian Captain Johann Ewald led a force of ninety men out of Bordentown by way of Black Horse (Columbus) and Slabtown (Jacksonville). A party of "rebels" about 200 strong met the Hessians, at a place later called Petticoat Bridge, on December 22nd. This was a bridge across the Assiscunk Creek, and was so named, according to local legend, because the neighborhood women destroyed the bridge upon the approach of the King's troops. A short engagement developed, but the Hessians, being badly outnumbered, had to retreat. Early the next morning, 2,000 reinforcements, led by the Hessian Commander, VonDonop, met the Americans under Colonel Griffin, and drove them back to Mount Holly. That afternoon Colonel Griffin regrouped his forces on Iron Works Hill. An artillery battle ensued, but the Colonials could not withstand the superior forces of VonDonop and retreated toward Moorestown. VonDonop and his Hessian troops destroyed the iron works and ransacked the village, taking whatever cattle and provisions they could find. They used the meeting house for a slaughterhouse and butcher shop, and some of the old benches in the meeting house show the marks of the cleavers used in cutting the meat. Around one pillar in the western end of the meeting house are the rope marks where they hauled up the bullocks. Quaker Aaron Smith, who had been meditating in the meeting house, was chased out and had his Bible literally kicked down the street.[5]

The Hessians remained in Mount Holly until December 26th. That morning a dispatch rider reported the Battle of Trenton to VonDonop, who immediately pulled his troops out of Mount Holly to go to the aid of the British in Trenton. He was too late, of course, but if "all things work together for good for those who love the Lord," then the Quakers of Mount Holly can be reassured that the desecration of their meeting house played an important part in General Washington's victory at Trenton by distracting troops who otherwise would have been used to repulse Washington's surprise attack.

For the next year and a half Mount Holly was apparently free of British soldiers. In June 1778, however, General Clinton evacuated Philadelphia and started marching his troops toward New York City. The British Army reached Mount Holly on Saturday, June 20th, and camped there for the weekend, just eight days before the famous battle of Monmouth Court House. This time the Friends Meeting House was billeted for the British soldiers, and the English officers used the Woodpecker Lane Meeting House as a stable for their horses.

The historic roles played by the Friends Meeting House, however, had not yet run their course. Two sessions of the State Legislature were held there in November 1779. The State Legislature had fled Trenton when the British troops threatened to invade New Jersey from Staten Island. They held all of their meetings in Mount Holly from November 8 to December 26, 1779, and legislative sessions were held there on November 15th and again on November 17th. Apparently these meetings were held without the sanction of the Friends, since no mention of them is made in the Friends records. The meeting house was probably commandeered by the State Government. Despite the fact that war was still going on, Governor William Livingston proclaimed Thursday, December 9th as Thanksgiving Day. This proclamation was made from Mount Holly on November 9, 1779, but there is no record that the Friends Meeting House was used for this Thanksgiving purpose. How fitting it would have been had the Governor issued his Thanksgiving Proclamation from the Mount Holly Meeting House.

Mount Holly Friends Meeting

This Separation of the Friends in 1827–28 caused by the preaching of Elias Hicks affected the Mount Holly Meeting as it did practically all other Friends Meetings.[6] The Hicksites kept possession of the meeting house, and the Orthodox faction built a small, frame meeting house on Buttonwood Street north of Brainerd. The Orthodox meeting was "laid down" many years ago, and the meeting house was used for a time by the public school and then by the town as a community center.

By 1850, with the Friends prospering and growing in number, the meeting house had to be enlarged. A gallery was added which increased the seating capacity by fifty percent. To do this, it was necessary to raise the roof six feet. Zackariah Reeves was in charge, and he used screw jacks to do the job. The ceiling beams are twelve-inch square timbers, mortised and anchored at the center, locked into the rafters and additionally braced with collar beams for extra strength. In 1879, the old fence along Garden Street and some of the horse sheds were taken down. A school was started in 1893 using the west end of the meeting house for its classrooms. The school was maintained only a few years. In 1896 the present iron fence was erected and the brick sidewalk laid. The west side of the meeting house was remodeled in 1919, removing the youths' galleries, and flooring over the entire area provided a place for First day school classes. Galleries in the east end were leveled and floored over at a later date, preserving the ceiling structure and providing space for kitchen facilities. Modern methods of transportation made the horse sheds an anachronism, and these were removed in 1930.

---

1. *The Historic Rancocas,* by George DeCou.

2. See Chapter VI on Mount Laurel Friends Meeting House for comments on ironstone.

3. *Early Bricklaying in New Jersey,* by Harry B. and Grace M. Weiss.

4. *Crossroads of Freedom,* by Earl Schenck Miers.

5. Ibid.

6. See Chapter II on Friends Meeting, Woodbury.

XV

Friends Meeting

Arney's Mount, 1775

A t the intersection of the road from Mount Holly to Juliustown and the Pemberton-Jobstown Road 2.5 miles northwest of Pemberton stands a quaint old Friends meeting house. Gracing the highest land in Burlington County, it was built in 1775 to serve the needs of the Friends living in the surrounding country-side. Whether this was the first meeting house built by Friends in the area seems open to debate, and the records are conflicting. According to the minutes of the Burlington Monthly Meeting dated August 3, 1743: "Sundry Friends belonging to the upper part of Mount Holly meeting made application in writing to Burlington Monthly Meeting for liberty to hold a meeting for worship on the first day of each week during the winter season at the 'meeting house'[1] now standing near Caleb Shreve's mount, which the meeting had under consideration." This would indicate that a meeting house was already in existence. This view is supported by Dr. Henry H. Bisbee in the *Historical Names* series, published in the *Burlington County Times*, December 4, 1969: "The first meeting house at this spot was built of logs and was erected circa 1743." George DeCou in his very informative book, *The Historic Rancocas*, quotes Ephraim Tomlinson's journal: "On the 20th day of 6th mo., 1771, I was at the marriage of my son-in-law, John

Arney's Mount Friends Meeting House, built in 1775.

Gardiner, at the log meeting house hard by Julytown." Yet DeCou also quotes in the same book a lease dated July 30, 1743, which seems to indicate that the meetings were held in a schoolhouse: "Jonathan Hough, son of Daniel Hough, leased for a term of fifty years to Caleb Shreve, John West, Michael Atkinson, Joseph Lamb, Julius Ewing, Jacob Shinn, Abraham Merritt, James Langstaff, yeoman, and Benjamin Carter and Issac Cowgill, planters, one acre of land for the use of a schoolhouse near the improvements of Nathan Wilson, at the crossing of the great road leading from Bridgeport (Mount Holly) to the new dwelling house of the said Jonathan Hough, with the road that leads from John West's gate to Hanover road, they paying therefore a yearly rent of one penny if demanded; this acre lay at the N.E.

end of Caleb Shreve's Mount." DeCou connects this schoolhouse as the place of worship by the Friends Meeting by an extract from the minutes of the Burlington Monthly Meeting dated December 5, 1774: "To the monthly meeting of Friends of Burlington: We the subscribers with others having obtained liberty of holding a meeting for religious worship near Shreve's Mount have hitherto met in a schoolhouse which we find very inconvenient for that purpose..." The History published by the Mount Holly Friends Meeting, which is now responsible for the care of Arney's Mount, mentions only the schoolhouse as the first place of worship, and ignores completely other references to a log meeting house.

This author prefers to accept both positions. From 1743 there is the record of the Burlington Monthly Meeting referring to a "meeting house now standing near Caleb's Mount," which is very specific. The reference to the schoolhouse being used as a place of worship comes thirty-one years later, dated 1774. It is also very difficult to overlook the specific reference to a "log meeting house," written by Ephraim Tomlinson in a private journal dated 1771. It seems logical to assume that a log meeting house did exist between 1743 and 1771, and that it was destroyed, probably by fire, between 1771 and 1774, when the first mention is made of meeting in a schoolhouse.

Arney's Mount was originally called Shreve's Mount, for Caleb Shreve who owned the surrounding land. The name was later changed to Arney's Mount after an early settler named Arney Lippincott.

Seven Friends—Jacob Shinn, Francis Shinn, William Lovett Smith, Restore Shinn, Samuel Shinn, John Coate, and James Smith—asked the Burlington Monthly Meeting for permission to obtain the ground and to build a meeting house. Permission was granted and better than one acre of land was obtained from Jonathan Hough, Jr. for the sum of one shilling. The meeting house was built by Samuel Smith in 1775 of native sandstone quarried locally on the mount, and is one of only two meeting houses built of native sand-stone in the county.[1] The meeting house was small by today's stan-dards, consisting of one room with inside dimensions thirty feet square. Luxuries such as pews were nonexistent in those days, and the worshippers sat on benches with a wooden board for a back rest. The benches were held together by handmade, riveted iron bolts, and were arranged around the center of the room, those in the rear being ele-vated. In the center was an oval, washtub-style wood stove used for heating. There was a gallery to handle overflow crowds which could be reached by let-down stairs. The gallery was supported by pillars turned from solid wood.

Fire struck on February 17, 1800, and destroyed the roof and much of the woodwork. Fortunately, there had been a heavy snow-storm and the floor was saved by throwing snow on it. Once again, in 1809, fire, that nemesis of early settlers, almost destroyed the meeting house, burning out the interior and leaving only the stone walls standing.

The steep hill to the rear of the meeting house was used for a bury-ing ground, and this was enclosed with a wall of native sandstone in 1860. It is said that those who lost favor with the Meeting were buried outside the wall! According to the early custom of Friends, graves were not marked. Records were kept of rows. Later, markers were used, and some bear dates earlier than the formal establishment of the Meeting. Many of the stones are from the old mountain pit, and are crudely inscribed, probably by relatives of the deceased.

Problems with the young people took place in those days just as they do today. Henry Charlton Beck, in his enchanting book, *More Forgotten Towns of Southern New Jersey*, tells of the troubles encountered by Sarah Shinn, a descendant of one of the original trustees. It seems that Sarah invoked the displeasure of the Meeting in 1830 when she married a Mr. Davis, "contrary to the established order of the Society." Apparently she had failed to obtain the Meeting's approval for the wedding, and after consideration, the Meeting forwarded the case to the Monthly Meeting in Burlington for disposition.

Marrying outside the Meeting was frowned upon, and this, apparently, was the situation of Barclay White, clerk of the Meeting. It seems that he had married his first cousin and that the wedding was performed by a magistrate. White was ordered to hand over all his books and was removed from his position of clerk.

Arney's Mount Meeting stands as it did in 1775, at the crossroads near the foot of the mount, the surrounding farm land still undisturbed by encroaching civilization. In its heydey in 1776, Arney's Mount Meeting boasted a membership of fifty-three adults and fifty-one children, but with the passing of the years the area changed and the worshippers dwindled. The Preparative Meeting established in 1776 was laid down in 1871, although the meeting house was still used occasionally for worship and First day school. After 1941, meetings for worship were held twice monthly, but now there is only an annual ceremonial service held each Easter morning for which Friends from miles around come to renew their faith through association with the past. The old benches and the interior woodwork are still in their natural state, but grown more beautiful with the patina of time. Maintained in excellent condition by the Mount Holly Meeting, Arney's Mount Meeting House is a monument to the faith that sustained the early settlers.

---

1.   See Chapter VI on Mount Laurel Friends Meeting.

XVI

Old Stone Church

Fairton, 1780

Lured by the rich soil and milder climate of southern New Jersey, Puritans from New England migrated to this area in the 17th century, the exact date of their arrival being unknown. What is known is that by 1680 these hardy pioneers had erected a church at a place they called "New England Town Crossroads." The "church" was really a log cabin, small in size and very primitive, with practically no comfort for the worshippers except shelter from the elements. It was built on the south bank of the Cohansey River where the old graveyard still stands, about one mile west of the present Old Stone Church. The old documents and records were destroyed by fire so very little can be told about the building or the congregation. Its charter designation was as "The Presbyterian Church Congregation at Fairfield," but it was familiarly known by any one of many names; Old Fairfield, Old Christ's Church, Cohansey Church, and the Old New England Town Church. The first minister to preach in the log church was the Rev. Thomas Bridges. Little is known about him except that he was born in Hackney, England in 1657, and received the rights to locate 1,000 acres of land wherever he wished from the West Society of England. He chose the area of Cohansey for his land,

The Old Stone Church in Fairton, erected in 1780.

but how long he remained and whether anyone succeeded him before 1708 is uncertain.

Joseph Smith, a Harvard graduate licensed to preach, met the Presbytery in 1708, and was ordained and installed in the log church in May 1709. Apparently he did not fare very well, as he soon returned to New England complaining of negligence in his support by the congregation. Samuel Excell then came to Cohansey, but in 1711 the Presbytery notified the congregation that according to information in their possession he was not suitable to continue the work of the ministry. No reason is given as to why he was ordained and installed in the first place, so we can only assume that the debasing information must have come to the attention of the Presbytery at a later date. Howell Powell next arrived at the banks of the Cohansey, and he served the congregation until his death in 1717.

By this time the old log church had served its purpose, and what is described as a "comfortable" frame building, shingled on its sides and roof, was erected in its place. It stood on the southeast corner of the old graveyard, and was provided with benches for the "comfort" of the worshippers. An Irishman, Henry Hook, was installed as pastor in 1718, but he was openly rebuked and suspended by the Presbytery for some nefarious deed about which we are not informed. Some of the first men who came to the colonies as ministers and missionaries were not of the best character, and were actually adventurers rather than men of God. The Fairfield church was to experience another such situation in the successor to Henry Hook. Noyes Parris, a graduate of Harvard, preached to the congregation from 1724 to 1729. Facing charges of misconduct, he ungraciously resigned and returned to England.

The church was to do better with its next try. Daniel Elmer came from Connecticut, and was ordained and installed as pastor in 1729. Although he was truly a man of God and preached there until his death in 1755, the life of the church was anything but serene. In 1741 the Presbyterian Church was torn asunder by a theological dispute which divided the church into two parts called "Old Lights" and "New Lights." Rev. Elmer adhered to the "Old Lights," but the congregation was split with about one-half supporting the cause of the "New Lights." Even the minister's son, who was married and living in Cedarville at the time, was attracted to the "New Lights," and would pass by his father's church on a Sunday morning on his way to Greenwich to hear Rev. Andrew Hunter, a practitioner of the "New Lights." The home that Daniel Elmer had erected next to the church burned just before his death in 1755, thus destroying all the old records of the church.

Following the death of Rev. Elmer, the church was without a parson until 1756, when the Rev. William Ramsey was ordained and installed December 1, 1756. The congregation purchased a parsonage in Sayres Neck with 150 acres for the new minister and his wife. Rev. Ramsey was an eloquent speaker, and the church flourished during the fourteen years that he was pastor. Unfortunately, he died in 1771 at the early age of thirty-nine. Under his ministry the church was once more united, this time on the side of the "New Lights."

Rev. William Hollinshead was installed as pastor in 1778, but prior to this it had become evident that a new building was necessary. Theophilus Elmer was appointed treasurer to raise the necessary funds. He called on all the members of the congregation and received donations of cattle, poultry, sheep, geese, and even feathers, which were sold at public auction. Ground was purchased in 1775, and the deed recorded in Burlington May 18th. Upwards of 189 loads of stone and 800 feet of lumber were collected and stored on the newly purchased lot.[1] By now, though, the war-drums of the Revolution were heard throughout the land, and the thoughts and efforts of the people were directed toward the fight for freedom. The people put up with the old frame building, even though it had become so dilapidated that in good weather the benches were taken outside and placed under a large white oak tree where Rev. Hollinshead conducted services. At that time the membership consisted of seven ruling elders and ninety-four members. The congregation felt the wrath of the British when all the stones and lumber assembled for the construction of their new church were seized by the British to build a wharf along the Cohansey River.

By 1780, the people were ready to start the building of their badly needed church. The following subscription paper was circulated:

"We, the subscribers, whose names are hereunto annexed, do each and everyone of us, bind ourselves, our heirs, executors and administrators to pay or cause to be paid, unto the person or persons appointed or to be appointed as managers for building said house, the several sums annexed to our names, to be paid either in labor or materials necessary to be used in the building at the same price that articles of the like quality might have been purchased for in the year 1774, to be applied in building an house on the aforesaid lot of ground where the materials are provided for building the same.

"The one-half to be paid any time, when the congregation shall think proper to proceed to build, and the other half to be paid when the walls shall be finished, which, if not paid in labour or materials aforesaid, then we do hereby engage to pay the same in money, allowing the year 1774 as the standard, at such a sum as shall make up the depreciation at the time the money shall be called for and paid.

"In testimony of all which we have hereunto set our hands, with the several sums thereunto annexed.

"N.B. What money had been paid by any subscriber, to be deducted out of his subscription when payment is made."[2]

With the uncertainties of the value of money caused by the Revolutionary War the author of this document was wise to set the year 1774 as a standard. It is not only in the present day that erosion of paper money values is a problem. The total subscribed was 488 pounds, 17 shillings and 10 pence, with Jonathan Elmer the heaviest contributor, having pledged 40 pounds. The second was Theodotia Anderson, with a pledge of 37 pounds, 10 shillings.[3]

Since money was not as readily available as physical labor, many of the men worked out their subscriptions traveling six to eight miles to the church site. The first stone was laid Friday, May 1, 1780, and the walls and roof were completed by June 14th of the same year. Although the church was not completed until 1781, the first sermon was preached in it on Thursday, September 7, 1780, such was the yearning the people had for a suitable house of worship. Constructed of field stone, it was a two-story building of the colonial meeting house design. According to one legend, the five-sided pink stone high up in the gable was given to the church builders by the Indians as a good luck token. Inside, the aisles were paved with brick. Originally the only accommodations for the congregation were the primitive benches, but later boxed-in pews were added. The flooring under the pews was wooden planking. In the center of the church at the front was a high, canopied pulpit reached by a narrow staircase. From this vantage point the preacher could keep a watchful eye on the worshippers in the gallery as well as on those on the first floor. The gallery that went around three sides of the building was supported by gracefully turned wooden beams. For the first eight years no provision of any kind was made to take the chill and dampness out of the air. This was left to the ingenuity of the individual worshippers, many of whom brought heated bricks or foot stoves on which to rest their feet. Two Franklin stoves were later installed in the middle of the two aisles with their pipes joining in the center and extending through the ceiling. The seating capacity was three hundred, and this venerable old building saw many a service when it was literally "filled to the rafters." As was the custom in those days, the pews were rented to the highest bidders. Those seats downstairs brought an annual rental of 65 pounds, 10 shillings, and those in the galleries, about 36 pounds. The church realized an annual income of better than 100 pounds from pew rentals.[4]

The church was incorporated on August 4, 1783, by a special act of the legislature, which required the trustees to take the oath of adjuration of the British rule, the oath of allegiance to the United States and an oath to faithfully perform their duties. The same year Rev. Hollinshead left, having guided the congregation successfully through its building program.

In 1785 the trustees adopted a rule that any member absent from their meeting should be fined a sum not exceeding five shillings unless a satisfactory reason was given. Another rule adopted made the trustees responsible for any debt that was more than a year overdue unless the debtor had become insolvent. Needless to say, this had the effect of increasing the tempo of collections, but in some cases legal action was taken to collect overdue pew rents.

In 1788 there arrived in Fairfield a young man just turned thirty who was to have a profound and lasting effect on the congregation, and, in fact, on the entire community. His name was Ethan Osborn, and he had ridden on horseback all the way from Litchfield, Connecticut to preach on trial at the Old Stone Church. He had attended Dartmouth College, served in the Continental Army under General Washington, and was licensed to preach in 1786. As was the custom in those days, the trial preaching period for a new minister was six months. The congregation did not believe in rushing into an arrangement that they might regret later on! The following record is found in the trustee's book for March 11, 1789: "It was agreed to pay 15 shillings hard money per week for the keep of Mr. Osborn and horse." Successfully passing his trial period, he received the unanimous call of the congregation, and was ordained and installed Thursday, December 3, 1789, by the Presbytery of Philadelphia. He was to be their beloved pastor for an unprecedented fifty-five years!

When Rev. Osborn took over the Fairfield charge, the communicants were numbered at 125. Under his inspired leadership the number increased to 336 by 1831, and not a pew on the main floor nor a bench in the galleries remained unrented. The session, the governing body of the church, was increased from seven to nine members shortly after Osborn's arrival. Discipline was administered by this august body, and in most cases the congregation submitted to its decisions. Cases which would now go to a civil court were adjudicated by the session. Religious matters were, of course, their primary concern, and violations in this area were swiftly dealt with. Offenses such as failure to keep the Sabbath, absence from public worship, neglecting to have their children baptized were matters of grave concern to the session. If the offender was found guilty, discipline was meted out, usually including some form of public penance. In Rev. Osborn's notes he mentions that "the intoxicating cup is the chief cause" requiring discipline.

In 1800, and again in 1816, the trustees purchased additional ground to enlarge the graveyard. In 1810, the trustees obtained a deed from James D. Westcott, as agent of John Bellers of London, confirming the right and title of the congregation to the possession of three acres of land, commonly called "the old burial ground," purchased originally on June 10, 1747. The deed was recorded on June 5, 1811, in the Clerk's office of Cumberland County.

The beloved pastor labored with, ministered unto, and watched over this large flock until 1844, when he offered his resignation in the 86th year of his life. It was felt by all a "mournful necessity." His pastorate had been like his own life, tranquil in nature and full of the blessings of the Holy Spirit. Even the question of the Old and New Schools was handled in an amicable fashion. His feelings were with the New School, and about one-half of the session and congregation were with him. Lengthy deliberations were held before they decided to withdraw from the Presbytery of West Jersey. The formal step was taken on May 11, 1840, and they became connected with the Third Presbytery of Philadelphia on May 13th and built a church in Cedarville.

At the time of Ethan Osborn's resignation there was but one living worshipper who was a member of the church when he arrived. He had buried all but one of those who had composed his flock at the time of his installation. He had seen the children of two generations, baptized with his own hands, take the places of their fathers in the church. To the members of his church he was an institution. The following minute was adopted by the Presbytery April, 1844, when they dissolved this pastoral relationship:

"For fifty-four years Father Osborn has ministered to this branch of Zion, during which time a degree of harmony and friendship has subsisted between pastor and people, and a success has attended his ministry, highly creditable to them, and happily illustrating the beauty and importance of a permanent pastoral relation. Now, late in the evening of his life, the eighty-sixth year of his age, after having been permitted to enjoy, in connection with his labors, several revivals of religion, and having buried all but one of those who composed his flock at the time of his installation, and after having seen the children of two generations, baptized with his own hands, succeeding to the places in the church vacated by their fathers, he comes with undiminished regard for his people, and in the unabated enjoyment of their confidence and affection, to commit his united and happy charge to the care of this body. The Presbytery commend this church for providing that their worthy and venerable pastor may continue to lean upon their arm while he lives, and recline on their bosom when he dies, and hope that other churches may follow their example."[5]

At the time of his resignation there were three elders and one hundred and thirteen members, the decline having been caused by the exodus of the Old School adherents. Even though he had relinquished the responsibility of the church, he continued to worship with the congregation and to take part at frequent intervals in the Sunday services.

On November 18, 1845, the Rev. Beriah B. Hotchkin was installed as pastor, and talk of building a more modern church began. After several discussions and preliminary meetings it was decided on March 16, 1848, to proceed with the building plans. A lot was contributed by John Trenchard, and the size of the building was determined to be thirty-eight by fifty-two feet. A building committee consisting of John Trenchard and Theophilus E. Harris was formed, and they reported on March 20, 1850, that the new church was completed at a cost of about $2,250, of which $278.58 was still due the contractors.[6] At a congregational meeting held in the Old Stone Church the following action was taken:

"Resolved, That from and after the fifth Sabbath of March, 1850, the regular public worship, held by this congregation, be transferred from the house now used for the purpose, to the new church in Fairton.

"Also Resolved, That the public worship of Almighty God, conducted by the pastors and elders of this congregation on Sunday and other days appointed for the purpose, in the new church in Fairton, should be regarded as worship performed by this congregation according to all their compacts and agreements to unite in such worship as a particular congregation."

Who else but the revered patriarch of this old church could be chosen to preach the last sermon? Henry Charlton Beck describes the scene in his book, *Forgotten Towns of Southern New Jersey*, as "The preacher was still active at ninety-seven when he preached his farewell sermon in the Fairfield Church. The congregation was distributed tightly in the lined pews, many had chairs in the aisles and many others were compelled to stand huddled by the doors. Father Osborn mounted to the pulpit, unassisted. When he concluded he came down with a look of triumph, as if he had closed some valiant chapter of his life. He had closed the book of a church's service as well, but he did not know it then."

Although Mr. Beck credits Rev. Osborn with being ninety-seven years old at the time, actually he was a "mere" ninety-one. He lived almost another eight years after his final sermon, receiving his last "call" on May 1, 1858. He had lived a life dedicated to God for ninety-nine years, eight months, and ten days. He is buried in the graveyard of the church he loved and served so faithfully, where "his children in the flesh and in the spirit lie around him."

The Old Stone Church is listed by the Library of Congress as a National Historic Site. It has been faithfully maintained by the Fairfield Presbyterian Church. It is used now only on special occasions and for evening services during the summer.

Fairton Old Stone Church

1. *History of the Old Stone Church*, by Rev. Samuel R. Anderson.

2. *Bicentennial Celebration of the Old Stone Church*, by A. M. Heston.

3. Ibid.

4. *History of the Early Settlement and Progress of Cumberland County New Jersey*, by Lucius Q. C. Elmer.

5. *History of the Old Stone Church*, by Rev. Samuel R. Anderson.

6. *Bicentennial Celebration of the Old Stone Church*, by A. M. Heston.

XVII

Trinity Episcopal Church

Swedesboro, 1784

lthough the Swedes were among the first settlers in New Jersey, very little remains to commemorate the colonies they established. One of the finest memorials to their heritage is the Trinity Episcopal Church in Swedesboro, built in 1784 and still in use today. But much history took place before the building of this church.

The first body of Swedish immigrants reached the Delaware Valley area in 1636. They settled near what is now known as Wilmington, Delaware at a place they called Christina. It was the intent of the King of Sweden to Christianize the area, so, along with the first settlers, he sent a Lutheran minister, Roerus Torkillus, to establish the state religion of Sweden. He was followed by another pastor named John Campanus Holmenis.[1] During the seven years from 1636 to 1643, the Swedish Governor, Johan Printz, whom the Indians called "Big Tub" because of his size, established forts to protect the colony at Christina. Since these forts were on the Jersey side of the Delaware River, the settlers were encouraged to stake out farms in the area from Penn's Neck (Churchtown) to Raccoon (Swedesboro).[2]

It was necessary for the Swedish settlers in West Jersey to cross the Delaware each Sabbath for religious services, but for a short period of seven months, a Lutheran minister, Israel Holgh Fluviander, resided

Swedesboro Trinity Episcopal Church, erected in 1784.

at Fort Elfsborg, a few miles south of Salem. He, therefore, became the first resident minister in New Jersey.[3]

The weekly trip across the Delaware River taxed even the intense religious devotion of these early settlers. By the end of the 17th century, this discontent had become serious, and created the situation into which stepped a colorful character named Lars Tollstadius. Lars arrived in the Delaware Valley in 1701 without the consent of the Consistory of Upsala.[4] Even though he lacked the slightest documentary proof of his theological qualifications, he was warmly received by Rev. Andrew Rudman of Gloria Dei Church at Wicacoa (Philadelphia), who was in poor health and only too happy to accept the assistance offered. Tollstadius's career seemed doomed to an early demise, however, with the arrival of Johan Sandel, who had been appointed the first Provost of the Swedish churches in America by the Upsala Consistory. Sandel knew Tollstadius, having met him in England, and knew that he was acting without the authority of the Consistory. He immediately relieved him of his duties and ordered him to leave the country. Lars was not the type to meekly submit to such authoritative action, and instead of leaving the country, crossed the Delaware River and stayed with some friends in Raccoon. It did not take much persuasion on his part to convince the Swedish residents of West Jersey that it was to their advantage to have a resident minister rather than to cross the Delaware each Sunday, or worse yet, to forego religious services waiting for one of the rare visits of the minister from across the river.

It was not long before enough members had been weaned from the Wicacoa and Christina churches to start the Raccoon parish. Twenty acres of land were purchased from John Hugg, Jr., a Quaker and sometime High Sheriff and Chief Justice of Gloucester County. Hugg had bought the land from John White, son of William White, who had brought the Quakers to Salem and Burlington. William White had secured all the land where Swedesboro now stands and had bequeathed it to his son John.[5] The original survey for this plot of ground was made by Richard Bull, and on September 1, 1703, an additional 80 acres were purchased. The cost for the 100 acres was 12 pounds. Sometime between September 1, 1703 and June 17, 1705 the first church was built. The exact date of its erection as well as its dimensions have been lost to history. It is known that it was built of cedar logs, and that it was consecrated on the third Sunday after Trinity, June 17, 1705, with Lars Tollstadius as the first minister.

Unfortunately for Lars, his career was not to have a happy ending. He was constantly the center of strife and discord with the Swedish ecclesiastical authorities. In 1706 he became embroiled in a scandal concerning the unmarried daughter of Ollie Oarson. He was bound over to the Burlington Court for trial. Before this august body could meet his empty boat was found near where the Raccoon Creek meets the Delaware, and his body washed ashore on the Pennsylvania side nine days later. It was never determined whether his death had been an accident or suicide. His sudden and tragic end brought to a close the stormy career of this controversial figure.

Since the parishioners of Raccoon had presumed to start a congregation and to build a church without proper authorization from the Swedish ecclesiastical officials, they received no help in finding a new pastor. Finally, Rev. Jonas Auren, who had been sent from Sweden in 1696, agreed to take charge of the parish. He was an excellent but eccentric man who, for the previous ten years, had been engaged in secular activities. He had developed strong views concerning the sanctity of the seventh day of the week and observed it as the Sabbath, although he preached to the congregation on Sunday. Not wishing to continue the strife with the sacerdotal powers and realizing that it would take many months to obtain proper approval from Sweden, the people suggested that Auren obtain permission from the Governor of New York as the next best thing. The Governor granted his official sanction and approbation, and so, instituted by civil authority, Jonas Auren began his pastoral duties, which lasted until his death in 1713.

Finding itself now in the good graces of Sweden, the Raccoon parish had the help of the Bishop of Skara in securing a new minister. Rev. Abraham Lidenius was appointed and became the pastor of the united congregations of Raccoon and Penn's Neck. In 1715, the church was repaired, replastered, and white-washed, so that it was anything but a primitive log building. In 1719, a vestibule was built in front of the door and a schoolhouse was erected. Since Rev. Lidenius had two congregations to minister to, the question of a parsonage soon arose. Although the Raccoon congregation had its own church and land, Lidenius would not advise them to build a parsonage there. His salary was small and he needed land on which to grow crops for his own support. He considered the ground too poor and sandy to be suitable for farming, and he would not settle there. He suggested instead that they obtain a residence between the two congregations that would make his ministry more convenient and the land more suitable for farming. The Swedes were not to be pressured into a hasty decision, however, and they deliberated over this question, discussing it at every parish meeting for almost eight years.[6] Finally it was decided that Goram Kyn's farm was suitable, being situated about six miles from Raccoon and nine miles from Penn's Neck. The farm consisted of 117 acres and was purchased on March 21, 1720, at a cost of 145 pounds.[7] A two-story building was erected and the land cleared for grain. A major reason for the delay in purchasing Goram Kyn's place was the fact that cash was scarce. Rev. Lidenius was confronted by the same problem faced by all colonial missionaries—and even modern day ministers—the difficulty of securing adequate funds not only for his own upkeep, but for the repair of the church building and graveyard. Donations of food, materials, and labor by the congregation generally had to suffice. Lidenius complained often and at length about the situation, and finally an agreement was signed by 52 members of the congregation pledging various amounts toward his support, and that these pledges were to be collected twice a year. After serving the congregations faithfully for ten years he was recalled to Sweden.

The Consistory of Upsala appointed the Rev. Peter Tranberg to succeed Lidenius. On his way from Sweden to Raccoon, Tranberg stopped in England, and while there the Society for the Propagation of the Gospel in Foreign Parts, which was an arm of the Anglican church, agreed to pay his traveling expenses and to give him $1,000 toward his support. Peter Tranberg remained over fourteen years in the parish, residing on his own farm while the glebe land was rented. During his pastorate a gallery was built, which could be entered only by a stairway outside the church. In 1731, the communion service of old beaten silver, which is still in use today, was purchased. An innovation begun by Tranberg not enthusiastically endorsed by the congregation was the renting of pews. The parishioners detested this change so much that, when Tranberg left, they would not approach Sweden for a replacement.

No new pastor was obtained until 1747. In the interim, the people became indifferent to religious services. The pastorless condition of the Raccoon church was a boon to the Moravians, who were now in the area actively propagating their views.[8] Mr. Paul Bryzelius was a Moravian, but since he was also a Swede, a group in the Raccoon church desired to secure his services as pastor. A Sunday in 1744 was appointed for him to preach in the Raccoon church. On the designated day a large gathering assembled, one part to get him into the church, a second part to keep him out, and the third part to watch the fun. Since those opposed to his entering the church had the key, it seemed that the advantage was theirs. Those in favor, however, were not so easily thwarted. A few members of this group crept around to the back of the church, and, breaking a window, gained access. They immediately opened the front door and a fight ensued, but those opposed held the day, and as a result no services were held. This fracas created quite a scandal, and the church fathers took immediate action. The church wardens were deposed, and all Moravian ministers were forbidden to conduct services in the church. Because of this dissension a small segment of the congregation left the Raccoon parish and was instrumental in building a Moravian meeting house in 1747 at Oldman's Creek.

The Consistory sent the Rev. John Sandin to be pastor of the parishes at Raccoon and Penn's Neck. He arrived March 29, 1748, and after six pastorless years the congregation eagerly received the new minister. Their joy was short lived however, as the new pastor died on September 22, 1748, six months after his arrival. Another period of being without a pastor was to be their lot, this time for four years. The people were fortunate, though, for living in their midst was the famed Swedish professor and naturalist, Peter Kalm. It was he who named our mountain laurel which still honors him with its Latin name, Kalmia. While living in the area he bemoaned the absence of a favorite Swedish food—rutabagas, or Swedish turnips. (About thirty years later the last Swedish turnips were sent to America.) According to Kalm the Swedes and Indians lived together on friendly terms. His journal records the story of a friendly wager between the Swedes and a young Indian brave. The Swedes claimed that the Indian could not overtake a frog in a foot race if the frog were given a two-leap handicap. The Indian accepted the challenge and the contest was on. The Swedes took a large bullfrog and heated its posterior with a torch. With this persuasion the frog took off with a mighty leap, and the poor Indian brave never had a chance. During the time when the church was without a settled pastor, Peter Kalm was the lay reader and kept alive the religious spirit in the congregation.

In November, 1749, Mr. Erick Mathias Unander was sent from Sweden to minister to the combined parishes of Raccoon and Penn's Neck. In those days such a trip was a major undertaking, and he was not installed until June 1751, on the tenth Sunday after Trinity. He continued his ministry until 1756.

For the first time a native born son was to serve the congregation. The Rev. John Abraham Lidenius, son of the third pastor Abraham Lidenius, born at Raccoon, educated in Sweden, succeeded Erick Unander as minister of the united parishes of Penn's Neck and Raccoon. He served the parishes from 1752 to 1762, after which he taught school in Raccoon. He was followed by the Rev. John Wicksell, who spent twelve years at Raccoon and then returned to Sweden. Before returning, however, he made a lasting contribution to the life of the parish as well as to the education in the area. He was the first to see the possibilities of the banks of the Raccoon Creek as a place for a town, and he gave Swedesboro its name. He built the rectory in 1765 and started the building of the school house. Since the school was built on ground owned by the church, he wrote the lease allowing the school to use the land. He used the words "free schooling" in the lease, which is perhaps the earliest record of free schooling in this part of New Jersey.

The end of the Swedish influence in the life of the colonies was now fast approaching. The final period was the rectorship of Nils or Nicholas Collin. He arrived in Raccoon on May 19, 1770, and preached for the first time in the log church on Whitsunday. The text was "God is Love. 1 John, 4:8. Subject: The blessedness of God's love as compared to the love of the world." In his journal he stated: "As I will probably spend most of my time in this congregation, and as I will, in all likelihood, through the province of God Almighty become their regular pastor, I made a more careful inaugural address here than at the other places..."[9]

Collin was born August 2, 1746, in Fundbe, Sweden where his father was pastor. He entered the University of Upsala at the tender age of 13. The studious life of the scholar appealed to him, and, although theology was his major subject, he studied biology, mathematics, and philosophy. By 1768, he had finished his theological studies and with his brilliant record could easily have been appointed assistant to some pastor in the State Church of Sweden. But he had other plans. His was an adventurous spirit, and he craved an appointment to the Swedish mission on the Delaware. He was ordained on December 20, 1768, and on May 19, 1769, his official appointment was made by the Council of State. Anticipating favorable action by the Council, he had already obtained his traveling money for his trip to Philadelphia from the government. Collin's friends strongly advised against this "foolish" adventure, considering America as a wild and dangerous country where the Indians were stalking about with their scalping knives ready to pounce on any unwary intruder. Collin however, was young, full of life and energy, and looked forward with great anticipation to his life in the New World.

By July 1769 he had booked passage on a vessel headed for London, where he arrived on September 5th. His description of the trip vividly portrays the fortitude a traveler needed in those days: "For six weeks I lay and rocked between Stockholm and London, during which time I ate pea-pudding and salt meat three times a day in company with ugly tars. There was often quite a melancholy music in my stomach, which was not accustomed to such a feast, especially as the poor fellow never could retain the meagre gifts…"[10]

Collin's enforced stay in London awaiting passage to Philadelphia was apparently enlivened by the company of young English girls as attested to by his letter to Jan Biornstierna, librarian at Upsala: "In London I had to go and sniff evil coal smoke for three months through lack of opportunity to get across. There I usually felt badly and would hardly have lived through it, if it had not quite often been refreshed by the kisses of beautiful girls. There as well as in America is the pleasant custom always to kiss a lady on the first visit."[11] Besides such pleasant diversions, he devoted serious effort to the study of the English language, which was to stand him in good stead during his years in the colonies.

Finally, in March 1770, he obtained a berth on a vessel headed for Philadelphia, and after a trying voyage of seven weeks, arrived on May 12th. Tarrying here only long enough to present letters of recommendation from William Penn to the Governor of the Colony, he proceeded to Raccoon. Arriving in Raccoon on the 19th of May with no place to stay, he became the guest of Johan Wicksell, pastor of the parish. After preaching his inaugural sermon on June 3, 1770, he preached in English on July 8th. This was unusual for a pastor who had just arrived from Sweden and made an excellent impression on the congregation. By this time the parishioners were a liberal mixture of Swedes and English, and the Swedish tongue was fast losing its original monopoly. Always the student, Collin's life in America was devoted to five main interests: his religious work, his scientific studies, his inventions, his collections of botanical specimens, and his studies of history, politics, and philosophy.

Collin was made rector of Raccoon and Penn's Neck parishes in October 1773. He took over what appeared to be a dying church. The building was in poor condition, and the parishioners rarely came to services. About two hundred people in the area still understood Swedish, but they were indifferent and often hostile not only to the Swedish church but to all religion. Through untiring efforts he gradually built a strong congregation. He devoted all his time to the church work, visiting and comforting the sick at all hours of the day and night, preaching two and three sermons on Sunday, presiding over innumerable prayer meetings, and traveling on horseback as far as Maurice River, a distance of thirty miles. Even with his arduous efforts in his church work, he did not neglect his interests in the academic area. He read extensively and borrowed books from the Philadelphia Library Company. With the aid of Mr. Matthew Huston, a schoolmaster in Swedesboro, he started a circulating library, which was probably the first public library in West Jersey. He collected botanical specimens, made observations on the weather, gathered information about animals, insects, trees, bushes, and plants, all of which he sent to Sweden.

This idyllic life came to an end with the Revolutionary War. These years were extremely difficult for Collin. He was accused of being pro English, came close to being shot as a spy, experienced extreme poverty since his rector's pay from Sweden could not get through, and the pursuit of his studies became difficult and hazardous. Both British and American forces marched through the area, using the church and parsonage for the convenience of the troops. On February 4, 1777, he was taken prisoner by an officer of the militia whom he describes as "a man of a rather bad character, and his religion, if he really had any, was Moravian."[12] Collin lays the blame for his arrest to "an old Swede, who had always been a worldly minded person, and his son-in-law, a Presbyterian,"[13] who were Magistrates under the new government and had given the order to the officer. The combination of a worldly Swede, a Presbyterian Magistrate, and a Moravian officer was a force too strong for Collin to cope with. He was given fifteen minutes to get ready for a one-hundred-mile journey. He was guarded by an armed force with loaded guns and fixed bayonets. "I often expected death, especially as many were drunk and fired several salvos for their own amusement…"[14] Fortunately for Rev. Collin, they had only traveled about six miles when another magistrate arrived; this time a friendly German Lutheran, Doctor Otto, who secured Collin's release by posting bail. On the following day Collin was presented with a difficult decision. He was given the choice of going to a prisoner-of-war camp or taking the oath of allegiance to the new government. Either choice was intolerable, since the first would mean the abandonment of his rectorship, and the second was impossible since he was a Swedish citizen. After lengthy negotiations he was able to persuade the authorities to modify the oath, allowing him to remain neutral and not to be compelled to do anything which would jeopardize his Swedish citizenship.

This was by no means his last war time escapade. Apparently undaunted by his short period of captivity, he went with a few friends to inspect a fort about twelve miles from Raccoon which the Hessians had attacked and had been repulsed. "Some rascals accused me before the Commander and made him believe that I was a spy, especially as I was clever enough to make drawings of the fort."[15] Collin's scientific mind and his penchant for recording his experiences in great detail were to get him into serious trouble this time. His naiveté in making drawings of a military fort is hard to understand, and it was almost unbelievable to the fort's defenders. He was arrested and threatened to be hanged immediately. What made the threat particularly convincing was the spectacle of two men being led right then to the gallows. Fortunately, Collin was a convincing speaker, and this situation brought out his most persuasive talents. He reminded the commander of the requirements of international law and offered to prove his innocence by securing certificates from the most prominent citizens. His arguments were compelling, and he was released upon his solemn oath that he would surrender upon demand.

Both of these events took place in 1777. In February 1778, General "Mad" Anthony Wayne became his house "guest" for one night. An American detachment of 300 men passed through Raccoon, and Collin describes them as "miserably clothed, some without boots, others without socks."[16] General Wayne did not arrive until midnight and took up quarters in the parsonage. According to Collin: "He was a well-bred gentlemen and showed me great respect."[17] He left the following morning, but the British had learned of his presence. At 11 A.M. a regiment of English infantry came in a running march in an effort to capture him. Once again Collin had a narrow escape, seemingly brought about by his apparent inability to take the Revolution seriously. Upon the arrival of the British troops, Collin left the parsonage to present his credentials to the English commander with the request that he be not molested. When Collin emerged from his house to approach the commander, he failed to hear the guard order him to stop. The Reverend led a charmed life, since once again he escaped death's beckon by the failure of the guard's rifle to fire.

With the end of the conflict Collin could now devote his time to the new church. The building had suffered much during the war, and was actually beyond repair. It should have been replaced many years before, but during the war years such a project was useless even to consider. Early in 1783, Collin discussed the possibility with the leaders of the congregation. As there was general agreement with the necessity of replacing the old log building, it was decided to go ahead with the project. Rev. Collin's persuasive powers were once again called upon to convince the members to commit themselves to the sacrifices that would be required. At a Sunday morning service in the summer of 1783, he laid before the congregation all the compelling reasons he could think of: "how unchristian and shameful and dilapidated the interior of the church was; how unreasonable it would be to refuse such an expenditure, when they had contributed so little to the support of the clergyman, but for a long time enjoyed the noble generosity of the Swedish Crown; that a respectable church would be a strong and precious link of union between the members of the congregation and a noble pledge of brotherly reconciliation after a long, miserable and bloody period of dissension, a splendid means of gaining increase and addition from outsiders; that it should further the cultivation of the country and give the congregation general esteem and political influence; and finally that it would be a worthy monument over their dead friends and relative parents, wives, husbands, and children, who had found their last resting place in the sacred earth around the church."[18]

Collin had not been a student of human nature for nothing. He issued a personal invitation to over twenty of the most active members to meet at the parsonage. As a result of this meeting over 300 pounds was subscribed. With this auspicious example almost 300 more pounds were pledged by the general membership. By diligent effort and personal calls on the individual members of the congregation Rev. Collin was able to obtain total pledges of 1,200 pounds. On these visits he was often accompanied by the same Doctor Otto who had secured his release from the British by paying his bail. Knowing that the enthusiasm with which a pledge might be given would not necessarily be matched with the same enthusiasm in fulfilling the pledge, the wily minister worded the subscription so that payment could be lawfully collected. The agreement also guaranteed the right to a seat in the church for himself and his heirs as well as a burial place in the graveyard, took away the rights in the new church of anyone who refused to help, and made it mandatory that the pastor would be appointed by the Swedish Crown. As can be imagined, a considerable effort was necessary to convince enough members to sign such a pledge and for a sufficient amount of money. Collin displayed remarkable foresight as he realized that such an expenditure would keep those that were lukewarm active in the church, and that if the Swedish mission in the New World were discontinued, the church would remain a worthy monument to Sweden.

By autumn of 1783, the plans were drawn following Collin's ideas, and efforts were started to obtain the necessary materials. A contract was made with Felix Fisher for enough bricks to build the church at a delivered price of one pound, seventeen shillings, and six pence per thousand.[19] Many problems were to beset them, though, before the new church was completed. It wasn't until May 1784 that some of the bricks were ready and the work actually started. It was the middle of November before the roof was erected as the bricks for the gable walls were spoiled by frost and rain and had to be dried in a small oven at the site. By December 23rd the roof was completed and the work was discontinued because of winter weather and not resumed until May 1785. The money subscribed did not come in as it was needed, and the workmen had to take their pay in trade at the stores owned by the church officers. By March 1786, the benches, balconies, and windows were all completed, but the paneling of the arched ceiling and the whitewashing and painting of the walls still remained to be done. The entire cost of the new church was 1,298 pounds, which did not include the tower and spire.

With the church completed to the extent of being usable, Rev. Collin severed his connection with the parish. The Swedish parishes were in a chaotic state when he took charge of them in 1773, and when he left in 1786 after sixteen years of hard work, they were prosperous, and the membership had greatly increased, as had the interest in church work. The church building at Raccoon was the best in that part of the state and a splendid monument to the determination of its pastor and the dedication of the people.

It was difficult to find a successor to the Rev. Collin. As a result, the church again found itself in a pastorless state for a few years. During this time the Rev. John Wade, a Lutheran minister, conducted services without being a settled rector. As all connections with Sweden were now dissolved, this can be regarded as the beginning of the English-speaking history of the church.

On October 24, 1789, the Rev. John Croes, then a candidate for holy orders in the Protestant Episcopal Church, was engaged to officiate on trial as the lay reader for six months. On January 24, 1790 he was called to the pastoral charge on condition that he obtain a regular ordination in the Protestant Episcopal Church. The only record of the act of the parish in attaching itself to the Diocese of New Jersey is found in the minute of April 8, 1792. The minute is in the hand-writing of Mr. Croes and affirms the fact that the parish had united with the Episcopal Church since the ending of the Swedish mission. When he took over the pastoral duties of the Raccoon church his salary was 145 pounds and later was increased to 200 pounds per year.

Rev. Croes remained as rector for eleven years from 1790 to 1801, and was later to become the first Bishop of the Diocese of New Jersey.

At a meeting of the vestry on April 3, 1838, it was decided to build a tower and steeple. The construction was completed in 1839 at a cost of $2,941.88, of which only $621.67 was obtained by pledges. The parish had sufficient invested funds at that time to defray the balance of the cost. Important changes were also made to the interior of the church. A vestibule was built, the old pulpit was moved back, and instead of a middle aisle the pews were rearranged so that there were two side aisles. The pews were the box type, with individual gates about three feet high. Such closed-in pews were necessary in those days to protect the worshippers from drafts as the building was unheated. The worshippers brought foot stoves or heated bricks on which to rest their feet to fight the cold. The lectern was unusual in that it was a huge golden eagle with outstretched wings on which the bible was held.

This magnificent building, the dream of Nicholas Collin, is still in use today. On May 23, 1964, the site of the first Swedish church in New Jersey was dedicated as New Sweden Park. Among the treasures of the church are the beaten silver communion service purchased in 1731 and still in use; two bibles, one a Swedish bible presented by Gustaf Adolf, King of Sweden, and a 1599 bible published by Queen Elizabeth's own printer which is one and a half inches thick weighing several pounds; a Charter presented to the church by John Penn; an elaborate scroll map of the church property made in 1828; and an unusual organ which had a large iron wheel connected to a plumber's valve, designed so that water power would operate the bellows. This is the same organ the church proudly uses today, although the iron wheel and plumber's valve have been replaced by electricity.

Although the church has not been connected to the Swedish Crown since Nicholas Collin turned over the rectorship to John Wade, neither the Swedish Crown nor the congregation has forgotten their former ties. A bible and a large Swedish flag were presented to the church in 1926 by King Carl IV through the Swedish Consulate in New York. But the banner day for the entire Swedesboro community was April 8, 1976, when King Carl XVI Gustaf of Sweden visited the church and dedicated a granite marker commemorating this historic event.

---

1. *A Historical Sketch,* by Rev. F. D. Hoskins.

2. *Religion in New Jersey,* by Wallace N. Jamison.

3. Ibid.

4. *Notes of Old Gloucester County, Vol. 3,* by Frank H. Stewart.

5. *Notes of Old Gloucester* County, *Vol. 1,* by Frank H. Stewart.

6. *A History of New Sweden,* by Israel Acrelius.

7. *A Historical Sketch,* by Rev. F. D. Hoskins.

8. See Chapter XIX on the Moravian Church at Oldman's Creek.

9. *The Journal and Biography of Nicholas Collin,* by Amandus Johnson.

10. Ibid.

11. Ibid.

12. Ibid.

13. Ibid.

14. Ibid.

15. Ibid.

16. Ibid.

17. Ibid.

18. Ibid.

19. *Early Bricklaying in New Jersey,* by Harry B. and Grace M. Weiss.

XVIII

Friends Meeting

Burlington, 1784

"Strong liquor was first sold to us by the Dutch and they were blind, they had no eyes, they did not see that it was for our hurt. The next people who came among us were the Swedes who continued with the sale of strong liquor to us; and they also were blind, they had no eyes, they did not see it to be hurtful to us to drink it, although we know it to be hurtful to us; but if people will sell it to us we are so in love with it we cannot forbear it. When we drink it, it makes us mad, we do not know what to do; we then abuse one another, we throw each other into the fire. Seven score of our people have been killed by reason of drinking it since the first time it was sold to us. Now there is a people come to live among us who have eyes, they see it to be for our hurt. They are willing to deny themselves the profit of it for our good. These people have eyes, we are glad such a people are come amongst us, we must put it down by mutual consent; the cask must be sealed up; it must be made fast; it must not leak by day or by night, in the light nor in the dark, and we give you these four belts of wampum which we would have you lay up safe and keep by you to be witnesses of this agreement that we make with you."

So spoke Ockanickon, according to tradition, at a conference held by the Friends in Burlington in 1678. This was the second conference

Burlington Friends Meeting House, built in 1784.

held with the Indians since the Friends arrived on the shores of the Delaware in 1677. The problem of liquor was considered so important and of such grave consequences to the Indians that all eight Sachems or Kings living in the area attended the conference. The Quakers had been especially anxious to live in peace and harmony with the Indians, and had taken special pains to buy the land that they used and to treat the Indians justly in all transactions. Therefore, it was especially important that the liquor problem be solved before it became a disruptive force. The Burlington Monthly Meeting has as the second item on its agenda the question of "selling rum unto the Indians." As a result of this concern and with the cooperation of the eight Indian Sachems, steps were taken to prevent the sale of liquor to the Indians.

The Quakers sailed from England on the *Kent*, arriving in the wilderness which was the New World in 1677. They immediately held their first worship service in a tent fashioned from one of the sails of the *Kent*, praising God for watching over them on their perilous journey. For the curious Indians watching these strange people it must have been a remarkable sight. Another shipload came in 1678, and, by 1681, at least 1,400 colonists, mostly Quakers, had come into the colony.[1] New Beverly, later to be known as Burlington, was established in 1677. The first arrivals set about building shelters for themselves and immediately began holding worship services in their homes. Existing records give us the names of some of these early pioneers: Thomas Gardner, Thomas Budd, Christopher Taylor, James Wills, John Woolston, and Robert Young.

By 1681, a year before William Penn set foot in the New World, Burlington had become a thriving community designated by the Colonial Assembly as the West Jersey Capital and the official port of entry. It was not surprising then, to find the Quakers in need of a meeting house. A plot of ground had already been donated by Bridget Guy, widow of Richard Guy, one of the first Quaker settlers in Salem who had migrated to Burlington. At a Monthly Meeting held in the home of Thomas Gardiner on December 5, 1682, it was ordered that a suitable house be built, forty feet square, and that the contract be given to Francis Collings. He was to be paid 160 pounds. Construction was started in 1683, but problems developed and the meeting house was not ready for occupancy until 1687, and was not completed until 1692. In an effort to explain the long delay the following romantic tale has been told: It seems that Francis was too busy courting his second wife to properly attend to business. Mary Gosling, the widow of Dr. John Gosling, was the object of his attention rather than the Friends meeting house, and as a result the meeting house suffered. Apparently Mary took a lot of persuading, as they were not married until 1686, and Collings could then attend to the business of the day. A less romantic explanation is found in the fact that Francis Collings was the bricklayer and builder for the area, and he had also agreed to build the courthouse in Burlington. Both jobs were probably more than he could handle at the same time. George DeCou, in his book *Burlington: A Provincial Capital*, describes the extra persuasion that was needed to prod Francis Collings into fulfilling his contract: "George Hutchinson & James Budd are willing to take ye Trouble upon them to Endeavour to Cause Francis Collings to perform his Covenants in building ye Meeting house & Court House to ye Finishing of what he undertook in ye Case." Apparently their prodding was not too successful considering that this resolution by the Burlington Monthly Meeting was made on May 7, 1685, and yet it was two years before the meeting house was ready for occupancy and seven years before it was completed! For whatever reason, Mary Gosling or the courthouse, Francis Collings was not a man to be rushed.

The meeting house was a frame structure, hexagonal in shape, with a steep, pitched roof and a cupola of the same design.[2] Although lovely in appearance, it was completely impractical for the area. The first winter convinced the members that it was impossible to heat the high roofed meeting house, and it was consequently abandoned during the winter for more comfortable worship services in the homes of Friends. Just four years after the meeting house was completed, the Burlington Monthly Meeting decided that holding worship services in the meeting house during the summer and in the homes of Friends during the winter was not ideal. On March 4, 1696, it proposed that a winter meeting house should be built as an addition to the hexagonal meeting house. The walls were to be a brick-and-a-half thick, raised from the ground one and a half feet "with Good Sound Stone," double pine floors, thirty feet in length and the width to be equal to one of the hexagonal sides of the original building. A huge open fireplace heated the entire building during the cold weather, although it was still the custom for people to carry with them foot stoves that were so necessary in those days to make a protracted stay in a cold room bearable. Such a large open fireplace with a huge fire in it provides warmth and comfort, but it is also hazardous. The building was badly damaged by fire in 1740, but it is not known whether the fireplace was the culprit or whether the damage was caused by a general fire in the area. The brick walls suffered little damage, however, and so the meeting house was restored to use.

In 1716, a brick meeting house was erected on East Broad Street to serve the needs of the Yearly Meeting. The Yearly Meetings were first held in Burlington, long before Philadelphia became the seat of Quakerism. This building stood on the site of the Baptist church and was forty feet long and thirty feet wide, with walls ten feet high. Ten pounds of West Jersey money was paid to Thomas Wetherill for a sixty-foot square plot of land on which the meeting house was built.[3] The Yearly Meeting was held in this building until 1760, when it was moved to Philadelphia. The building was used as a schoolhouse from 1722 to 1792, when the Friends school on York Street was built.

By 1773, the hexagonal meeting house was no longer adequate for the growing needs of the Friends in the area. For nearly one hundred years this picturesque meeting house had provided the Quakers with a suitable place to worship God in the freedom which their ancestors had sought when they fled England. During this time it was also used for secular purposes, as the court tried cases there and students attended school in the building.

The Quarterly Meeting, held in Chesterfield (now Crosswicks) on May 26, 1783, authorized the Burlington Friends to build a new meeting house to sufficiently accommodate their needs. A committee of twenty-five was named to draw plans and specifications and to report back. This took them until January 1784, at which time they were sanctioned to proceed with the building "when a sufficient sum is raised." Quakers have always been practical businesspeople, and this commonsense approach was not lacking, even in the building of their house of worship. The new meeting house closely followed the specifications of the Crosswicks Meeting House. The outside dimensions were sixty-five by forty feet, the walls were twenty feet high and twenty-four inches thick to the ceiling. The beams were hand-hewn, forty-two feet in length and twelve by ten inches in size. No nails were used in the construction, and the frame was mortised and fastened with wooden pegs. Separating the men's section from the women's side were movable shutters which could be raised and lowered by pulleys. Prior to the beginning of this century the men and women held separate business meetings. Since the business meetings were always preceded by a worship service, there was no shuffling of seats when the business meeting started as the men and women were already seated on separate sides of the shutters. It was a simple matter to just lower the shutters.

The High Street meeting house was built in front and just to the south of the old hexagonal meeting house, which remained standing until 1792. The new building was capable of seating 550 worshippers. Inside were the facing benches on which the elders and ministers sat, and the rough benches for the congregation. A gallery extended around three sides of the building, and some of the benches in the gallery were more primitive than those on the main floor, having no back supports at all. The initials of some of the young worshippers are carved in the backs and seats of a few of the benches, reminding us that the young in those days were not much different from the young of today. How ingenious they must have been to accomplish such a feat, since worship service was a solemn occasion and their demeanor was carefully supervised by their parents and watched by the stern eyes of the ministers and elders.

The meeting house remains today very much as it did when originally constructed. The porches which now adorn the front and the southern end were not part of the original building. Most of the doors, iron latches, and window fasteners are originals. Even some of the glass panes, those which are iridescent, could very likely be part of the original construction. The brick wall on High Street was erected in 1807 and took the place of a solid board fence. The dining room and kitchen were added circa 1904. The dining room walls are decorated with the sconces used in the old meeting house. There is also the pine table, built in 1698 for the use of the clerk, which has become the traditional place for present-day brides and grooms to sign their wedding certificates.

The Burlington Monthly Meeting covered a large area, including the Particular Meetings held at Shackamaxon and Chester, Pennsylvania, the Falls of the Delaware, Hoarkills, and Newcastle. Even Friends on Long Island expressed a desire in 1681 to be considered members of the Burlington Monthly Meeting. In 1699 there were 832 landowners in West Jersey, of whom 266 were Quakers. In fact, the Friends were more numerous in Burlington County than in all the other counties.

Fortunately for local historians, and for those of the general public who may be interested, the records of the Burlington Monthly Meeting have been well preserved. Many interesting anecdotes can be found therein. One cannot help but wonder how John Tomlinson and his wife would feel today after being censured by the Meeting because they had not been attending. It seems that the Friends were offended by women speaking in public. Surely they would be aghast at the freedoms women enjoy today. In 1704, the Meeting passed an Act in support of the Friends who could not bear arms. It sent a list of over one hundred names to officers of the militia, certifying that those men were members of the Society of Friends and were opposed to bearing arms in accordance with the principles of the Friends. However, such action did not stop the course of history, and during the Revolutionary War the meeting house was seized and used as a military barracks. Isaac Collins, the Burlington printer who is buried behind the meeting house, printed a quarto bible, which was the first one printed in America. Biblical scholars considered it the most authoritative one at that time.

Unable to alter the course of events leading to the Revolution, they were also unable to stop the course of history that led to the Separation of the Society of Friends in 1827–28.[4] The group known as "Orthodox" continued meeting in the High Street Meeting House. The other group, known as "Hicksites," met in a building that stood at the northwest corner of York and Union Streets. At their Monthly Meeting held in November 1844, it was decided to secure a lot for the purpose of building their own meeting house. According to a deed dated March 1, 1845, Thomas Longstreth and his wife conveyed to Charles Ridgway a lot on South High Street. The price was $800. The records indicate that Charles Ridgway was an excellent businessman, as he sold all but about one acre three days later for $1,100. The records also indicate that he was an excellent Friend, as he turned over to the trustees the profit of $300 as well as the parcel of land. An additional $1,534.86 was raised by subscription, making a total of $1,834.86 available for the construction of the Hicksite Meeting House. The lot fronted eighty-five feet on High Street with a depth of 414 feet.[5] The meeting house was built well back from the street, and the first meeting for worship was held on August 1, 1845. The building was leased in 1910 to the Polish Lithuanian Congregation of Burlington for $10 monthly with an option to buy at a price of $22,900. The Polish Lithuanian Congregation held services in it until 1936, when the building was demolished.

Many notable people are buried in the graveyard behind the High Street Meeting House. Issac Collins who printed the quarto bible, James Kinzey, Chief Justice of New Jersey, and Dr. Joseph W. Taylor, the founder of Bryn Mawr College, are but a few whose graves can be easily recognized.

Apparently the agreement the Friends made with the Indians in 1678 and to which King Ockanickon is supposed to have given his approval with a gift of four wampum belts was well kept. Upon his death in 1681, Ockanickon was buried in the Friends' cemetery. Not only was there a large gathering of Indians for this solemn and tragic occasion, but many of the Quakers showed their great respect for this fine leader and friend by attending the funeral services. Unfortunately the exact location of his grave has been lost to history. It is presumed to be near the marker erected in 1931 commemorating the 250th Anniversary of the Founding of the Philadelphia Yearly Meeting. Although it is doubtful that the agreement to stop the sale of liquor to the Indians was actually kept, there can be no doubt that an earnest effort was made, as King Ockanickon became a fine friend to the Quakers, helping them to live in peace with their copper-colored neighbors.

_____

1. *Burlington: A Provincial Capital,* by George DeCou.

2. *History of Burlington, New Jersey,* by William E. Schermerhorn.

3. *Burlington: A Provincial Capital,* by George DeCou.

4. See Chapter II on Friends Meeting, Woodbury.

5. *Burlington: A Provincial Capital,* by George DeCou.

XIX

Moravian Church

Oldman's Creek, 1786

It was a cold, wintry Sunday morning, January 23, 1744, and a large crowd had gathered outside Old Swedes Church in Swedesboro. A feeling of excitement filled the air. The crowd was anxiously awaiting the start of Sunday morning services. This was unusual, for the church had been without a regular pastor for almost four years, and many had become indifferent not only to church attendance but to the whole subject of religion during this time. For the previous year a young Swede, Moravian Peter Bryzelius,[1] had been holding services in the church and had been accepted by a majority of the congregation. A Moravian preaching in the Swedish church did not meet with the approval, however, of the Swedish Lutheran authorities, and the Rev. Gabriel Naesman, recently sent from Sweden to take charge of the church at Wicaco (Philadelphia), was on his way to Swedesboro to rid the church of this usurper.[2] The feeling of anticipation mounted as the time for services neared, and the crowd was not to be disappointed. The Rev. Naesman arrived and publicly denounced Bryzelius and those members of the congregation who had allowed him to preach in the Lutheran church. A fight followed between those in favor of allowing Bryzelius to preach and those opposed. The group opposed to Bryzelius had taken possession

Moravian Church at Oldman's Creek.

of the church, and they were able to prevent his followers from entering. Bryzelius continued preaching in the nearby Friends meeting house to large audiences, and from this nucleus the Moravian Church at Oldman's Creek was finally formed.

The immediate beginnings of the church at Oldman's Creek can be traced to an estate in Saxony, Germany owned by Count Nicholas Louis von Zinzendorf. In 1722, he offered the persecuted Moravians asylum on his lands, where they built a village called Hernhut (The Lord's Watch). The Moravians are sometimes referred to as Hernhuts. Zinzendorf was ordained a minister in 1734 and consecrated as a Bishop of the Church in 1737. He became acquainted with Augustus Gottlieb Spangenberg, who was a professor at the

Oldman's Creek Moravian Church

University of Jena. Spangenberg became so impressed with Zinzendorf and the Moravians that he resigned his professorship, moved to Hernhut, and was consecrated as a Bishop in 1744. He was soon to direct the activities at Oldman's Creek.

By this time the Moravians had already established a colony in Savannah, Georgia, in 1735, but abandoned it in 1740 when they made their way to Pennsylvania. Here they founded the cities of Bethlehem, Nazareth, and Lititz. From these settlements the Moravian missionaries traveled to areas that were without the services of any minister of the Gospel. Included in their missionary work were the towns of Raccoon (Swedesboro), Penn's Neck, and Maurice River.

Count Zinzendorf followed the brethren to America, arriving in New York on December 2, 1741, and in Philadelphia December 10th. The next year, several boatloads of Moravians followed the Count to Philadelphia. During the long, tedious voyage, they formed a church government known as "Sea Congregations"[3] to continue their church services and to maintain discipline. The first group to arrive consisted of 56 members and landed in Philadelphia in June 1742. One of the immigrants was Paul Daniel Bryzelius. He was commissioned by the Count for special duties in the Jerseys. Learning that the area of Raccoon, Penn's Neck, and Maurice River was without a settled pastor, Bryzelius immediately visited Reverend Peter Tranberg, the Lutheran minister at Christina (Wilmington) and volunteered to minister in the area. Tranberg was, of course, delighted, since there was a dearth of available talent; and without bothering to secure official approval from the Consistory at Upsala, he delegated the spiritual care of the area to Bryzelius. He was assigned three Swedish Lutheran churches and one German Lutheran church which were located at Raccoon, Penn's Neck, Maurice, and Cohansey. He preached his first sermon in the home of Goran Kyn at Maurice River. Raccoon was the major station and, since he had received a call from thirty-three members of this congregation, he settled there with his family.[4] Things went well for about a year, until Rev. Gabriel Naesman arrived from Sweden and took steps to remove Peter Bryzelius from the Swedish church.

The disturbance that was caused by his action resulted in a number of men being thrown in jail. Since this was a religious and not a civil matter, the affair was referred to a jury of 25 men. While they were deliberating, Bryzelius continued to preach in the nearby Friends meeting house. Rather than render a verdict, the jury advised Bryzelius for the sake of peace to refrain from preaching any longer at Raccoon.[5]

Many Swedes, however, remained loyal to the Moravian beliefs and petitioned Bishop Spangenberg for a minister. Missionaries were sent to the area, among them Abraham Reinke, Henry Sensmann, Owen Rice, Matthew Reutz, and Lawrence Nyberg. When they preached at Oldman's Creek, they were entertained by George and Jane Avis. According to tradition, this couple donated the land on which the first Moravian church was built. The ground lay between two branches of Oldman's Creek, formerly called Oldmutz River,[6] and along King's Highway, now Sharptown Road. Besides the ground, George and Jane Avis also donated a large amount of lumber for the construction of the church. At a later date, after the congregation had grown, Bishop Seidel of Bethlehem bought one and a half acres along King's Highway from the Avis' for five pounds. There is a deed dated January 22, 1767, covering this transaction and giving the boundaries as "a hickory, small white oaks, a chestnut and two posts" of unspecified wood, indicating the variety of timber on the land as well as the lack of permanent markers.

In 1747, construction of a log church was begun under the leadership of the first pastor, Lars Nyberg, but it was not until August 31, 1749 that it was dedicated by Bishop Augustus G. Spangenberg.[7] The building was 24 feet square, but there is no record of its interior design and furnishings. It was undoubtedly similar to the Moravian churches described by Bishop Hamilton in his paper, *Moravian Activity in New Sweden and its Vicinity*: "having the interior completely ceiled with boards that were smoothed with hand labor, as were those of its flooring. Small rudely made window sashes doubtless held the few panes of glass that lighted the plainly furnished room. Behind an unpretentious table stood a quaint chair of ancient pattern. Possibly a feeble spinet furnished the instrumental accompaniment of the voices of those who sang the solemn chorals of the fatherland. The seats of the worshippers, the sexes sitting apart, were plain wooden benches, as like as not without even the superfluity of backs for support..." The flooring, which was just the dirt of the ground, was kept scrupulously clean and spread with fresh white sand before each Sunday service.

At the time of its dedication it was called "the Moravian Church of Pilesgrove at Old Man's Creek." There were twenty-nine members including the following: George Avis; Nicholas Dalberg and wife; Charles Dorsan; Andrew Holstein; Lawrence Holstein, Sr. and his son Lawrence, Jr.; Larse Hopman; Michael Kett; Mons Kyn; Peter Lauterbach; Adam Lehberger; Samuel Lynch; Christopher Linmyer; Bateman Lloyd; Obediah Lloyd; Alexander Mueller; John Roalin Samson, a slave; Garret Van Immen and wife; Andrew Van Immen and wife; Jechoniah Wood and Jeremiah Wood.[8] Curiously, Jane Avis is not mentioned as being a member, even though she and her husband are credited for donating the land and entertaining the missionaries. The church was completed just nine years after the Moravians came to Pennsylvania and founded the city of Bethlehem.

This log building was to serve the people's spiritual needs for forty years. During that period many important events were to take place in the life of the church as well as the country. In the early years the affairs of the church were apparently under the control of a mission board at Bethlehem. Many ministers served the congregation, and, on March 15, 1755, under the leadership of Reverend Ernest Gambold, steps were taken to form a Moravian Society. On April 17, 1755, the first Society meeting was held, and on April 24th, George Avis, Obadiah Lloyd, and William Guest were chosen stewards.[9] It was eight years later, however, on November 28, 1763, before the church at Oldman's Creek was dedicated as a Moravian Congregation.[10] The Revolutionary War was fought throughout the area, and the church bore silent witness to the passing of colonial as well as British troops. According to the diary of Pastor Frederich Schmidt, twenty American militiamen took possession of the parsonage on the night of December 5, 1777. On February 25, 1778 over 2,000 British troops passed through Oldman's Creek on their way to Salem, taking with them whatever they could carry. A simple entry in Pastor Schmidt's diary for May 10, 1778 speaks eloquently of the longing for peace and the need for spiritual sustenance felt by those involved in war: "Many militiamen at church." Despite the hardships and privations of this period, the congregation had steadily grown so that by the end of the war in 1783 it numbered 134 members.

In 1783, Francis Boehler succeeded Frederich Schmidt, who had guided the church through the difficult years of the Revolutionary War. By this time the old log building had become inadequate for the needs of the communicants and was sadly in need of repair. The need for a new building was discussed on Thursday, January 13, 1785 at a congregational meeting. Agreement was reached that a new building was necessary, and a building committee was appointed to oversee the project. It was decided to build the new church on the eastern side of the cemetery, and 200 pounds had already been collected toward the expenses. In October 1785, the first stones were hauled to the construction site, and on June 1, 1786, the foundation was laid. The building operations went well, and in two months the walls were raised and the roof in place. Construction slowed down after that due to the worsening economic conditions, and, in 1787, depression hit. Many people could not pay their subscriptions, and those who did, paid in paper money, which was honored for about half its face value. Encouragement in the form of contributions from the mother church in Bethlehem, Pennsylvania buoyed the spirits of the little group, and the vision of a new church was never lost. On Sunday, June 28, 1789 the last service was held in the log building, and the following Sunday, July 5, 1789, the same year that George Washington was inaugurated as President, Francis Boehler conducted the first service in the new church. Dedicatory services were conducted the same day by Bishop J. Ettwein.

The new church was built of brick in the simple, unadorned colonial meeting house style of architecture, of which it is an authentic example. Two wide doors centered on the front wall a few feet apart are reminders of the days when men and women were separated during worship. From the outside it has the appearance of a two-story building, but the upper as well as the lower windows all open into one large room. Though the windows are not particularly large, the lower ones have 24 panes each and are protected by paneled shutters. A date was inscribed at one time high up in the gable, but that part of the wall fell out many years ago and was rebuilt, so the date is no longer there. Inside, the congregation was "pampered" with the "comforts" of wooden benches. A stove with a pipe leading to the ceiling took the chill out of the air. At the front was a communion table, behind which the pastor sat while delivering the sermon. The church was built to accommodate 150 worshippers. Pastor Boehler's diary lists some of the things which the church owned: "a basket and two bottles for the use of the Lord's Supper, a glass cup, a small white bowl for baptism, 39 cups for love feasts with 2 small baskets, and a treasury box."

Rev. Boehler's wife, Anna Catherine, died shortly after their arrival at Oldman's Creek, and the congregation petitioned the church authorities to permit him to remain and to send a married couple as his assistants "for having become single, he could no longer discharge the requisite duty toward both sexes."[11] For awhile the church prospered, and Rev. Boehler was able to report to the Moravian Conference in 1786 that the services were well attended, including among its congregation Presbyterians, Methodists, and Quakers.

After ten years of service to this little church Rev. Boehler was succeeded by Rev. Frederick Moering, who was pastor from 1793 to 1798. The fortunes of the church, however, had reached their peak under Rev. Boehler, and it was necessary for Rev. Moering to report that services were not well attended. From 1798 to 1800 the church was without a pastor, although Rev. John Meder of Philadelphia occasionally occupied the pulpit and administered the sacraments. In 1801, Rev. Samuel Towle was appointed as pastor and remained for almost two years. Rev. Casper Freytag served the congregation from 1802 to 1803, and was the last regular pastor.

Although it is not clear from the records, it appears that the church and the parsonage were abandoned by 1804. In 1807, the Methodists used the meeting house, much to the disapproval of Andrew Vaneman, who "thought it my duty to go there and forbid their keeping any more meetings there till I write to Bethlehem to know what is to be done with the Meeting House as I know it was built for a place of serious worship."[12] Apparently Brother Vaneman was not impressed with the Methodists. Bethlehem concurred with Brother Vaneman, and the church stood idle for many years. Noting the deplorable condition of the church, the Rev. Johan Woart, Rector of Trinity Episcopal Church in Swedesboro, discussed the situation with the Moravian authorities in Bethlehem. As a result, in 1836, a petition was signed by fifteen members of the Oldman's Creek Moravian Church requesting that the property be turned over to the Trinity Episcopal Church in Swedesboro if the wardens and vestrymen were in agreement. The church property was deeded to the Episcopal Diocese of New Jersey the same year. On Thursday, April 26, 1838 Episcopal Bishop Doane consecrated the old Moravian

Church to the worship of Almighty God. The church was renamed "Zion Chapel Maoravia" and services were once again held in the church, following repairs. After Rev. Woart left Swedesboro, services at the Oldman's Creek Church were held infrequently, and once again the church was abandoned. On July 1, 1877 Henry Shivler started a Sunday school there, which he conducted for about 30 years.

In 1907, the Gloucester Historical Society became interested in the building because of its historical significance. On a beautiful Saturday afternoon, August 31, 1907, 800 people attended dedication ceremonies, at which time a tablet was secured to the walls of the old church. The honor of unveiling the tablet was given to Henry Shivler, who had been conducting Sunday school classes in the old building since 1877. The formal presentation of the tablet was made by Honorable John Boyd Avis of Woodbury, a descendant of George Avis, who had donated the land for the original log church in 1747.[13] In 1948 the Gloucester County Historical Society obtained custody of the building and necessary repairs were made for its complete restoration. The balcony, robing room and other additions and alterations made by the Episcopalians were removed so that the church now appears as it did during the Moravian services. It is fitting that this church was restored since it had the longest life of any of the Moravian churches in New Jersey. Every summer special services are held, at which time the public has an opportunity to relive an interesting part of early New Jersey history.

---

1. Spelled "Brycelius" in some historical accounts.

2. See Chapter XVII on the Trinity Episcopal Church in Swedesboro.

3. *Moravian Church at Oldman's Creek*, by George B. Macalitioner.

4. *Moravian Church at Oldman's Creek*, by M. F. Oerter.

5. *Notes on Old Gloucester County*, by Frank H. Stewart.

6. *Historical Sketch*, by F. D. Hoskins.

7. *The Moravian Church at Oldman's Creek*, by Paul Minotty.

8. *Notes on Old Gloucester County*, by Frank H. Stewart.

9. *The Moravian Church at Oldman's Creek*, by Paul Minotty.

10. Ibid.

11. Ibid.

12. Ibid.

13. *Swedesboro News—August 29, 1957.*

XX

First Presbyterian Congregation of Connecticut Farms

Union, 1788

"Give 'em Watts, boys," rang out the cry from the fighting parson. The occasion was a battle between the British and American forces on June 23, 1780. The British had marched from Elizabethtown on their way to Morristown, where General Washington and the American Army were encamped. Word had reached Washington and a small detachment of American troops met the British at the small village of Springfield. During the ensuing battle, the American forces had exhausted their supply of wadding used to ram down the powder and shot. Realizing the seriousness of the situation, Rev. James Caldwell dashed into the church and brought arms full of Watts hymnals, tossing them to the troops and shouting out his now famous cry, "Give 'em Watts, boys."

As early as the summer of 1667, a number of families had moved from Connecticut to New Jersey. The land they chose for their new home was a fertile area with an abundance of streams. Since most of them were farmers, good land and plenty of water were essential considerations. They named their new location Connecticut Farms, probably because the land reminded them of their former home. The names of these original settlers were Ball, Bearing, Bond, Bonnel,

The First Presbyterian Congregation at Connecticut Farms in Union, erected in 1788.

Crane, Earls, Hays, Headley, Jaegers, Littel, Meeker, Potter, Searing, Terrill, Thompson, Winans, and Woodruff.

On Sunday morning they traveled to Elizabethtown to worship at the First Presbyterian Church, a distance of four or five miles. Most of them were Puritans, and when they lived in Connecticut they had undoubtedly worshipped according to the Congregational beliefs. The Congregationalists were strong in New England while the Presbyterians were active in New Jersey.

Traveling to Elizabethtown every Sunday during the heat of the summer and the cold of the winter required people of strong faith and perseverance. These settlers were indeed men and women of strong convictions, for they continued their weekly trek for over 60 years. In 1730 they decided it was time to have their own house of worship. A frame building was erected on a hill along the main road. The church was chartered in the same year and belonged to the Presbytery of Philadelphia. By 1734 they secured their first pastor, Simon Horton. He served the congregation until 1746, when he accepted a call from the church in Newton, Long Island. He was an ardent Whig who proclaimed the cause of the colonies against the mother country and helped establish the reputation of the Connecticut Farms Church.

Things went along smoothly for the next thirty years. Four ministers served varying periods of time without any unusual event taking place. The sixth minister, Rev. Benjamin Hait (Hoyt), was installed during the winter of 1765–1766 and guided the church through most of the turbulent Revolutionary War days. He died on June 27, 1779 while still serving the church.

To fill the vacant pulpit the Presbytery sent the Rev. James Caldwell, minister of the First Presbyterian Church of Elizabeth, to be the interim pastor. Forces were now set in motion which would end in Rev. Caldwell's historic utterance, "Give 'em Watts, boys."

The British used the port of Elizabethtown to bring in troops and supplies, and there was constant skirmishing throughout the area. On June 6, 1780, six thousand British and Hessian troops commanded by Generals Knyphausen and Stirling marched out of Elizabethtown Point to gain a foothold in the Watchung Mountains. After accomplishing this they planned to attack the main American Army, which had been keeping a wary eye on the British from the safety of the mountains. Any thought the British may have had of an easy march was soon dispelled. Almost immediately the British were fired upon by a small contingent of Americans. In this first exchange General Stirling, who was second in command of the Redcoats, was seriously wounded. The British, however, were not to be deterred that easily, and continued their march toward Springfield via Connecticut Farms.

In the meantime word had reached Washington of this British advance, and American forces were sent to intercept them. Fired upon from practically every tree and fence, the British troops nevertheless continued their line of march until they reached Connecticut Farms. Here, the American forces under General Maxwell had taken strategic positions, and it was obvious to General Knyphausen that any further advance would be disastrous. The British troops engaged the Americans in battle, attempting to dislodge them. This was not to be, however, and late in the afternoon the British and Hessians started their retreat to Elizabethtown.

Rev. Caldwell, his wife, and their nine children had moved into the Connecticut Farms parsonage when their parsonage in Elizabethtown had been burned down. With the impending arrival of the British, Rev. Caldwell attempted to send his wife and family to a place of greater safety. She refused to leave, thinking that her presence might save the parsonage. She took her children to the little bedroom on the first floor to wait out the fight. There are many versions concerning the actual events that took place that day. According to one, she saw a Hessian soldier coming into the backyard, and for safety's sake she gathered her family into a corner of the room. Her youngest son, 2-year-old Elias Boudinot, ran to the window to see what was going on. Mrs. Caldwell dashed to the window to pull her son back, but at that instant the Hessian soldier fired his musket, killing her instantly. Another version places Mrs. Caldwell in a rocking chair with her youngest son in her lap when the Redcoat put his musket through the window and shot her without any provocation. Still another explanation has its origin in an event that took place in the British camp the night before the battle. A quarrel developed between a lieutenant of the famed Coldstream Guards and two Hessian soldiers. The disputants were taken before General Stirling, who sided with the Hessian soldiers. Not only did he censure the lieutenant, but he praised the two Hessians as brave and valuable soldiers. General Stirling knew that he needed the loyalty of the Hessian troops in the upcoming battle the next day, and did not consider it wise to alienate them. Early the following day General Stirling was mortally wounded by a sniper's bullet. The Hessian soldiers, whom General Stirling had defended, shot the sniper, an 18-year-old boy named Moses Ogden. On his body they found a letter written by Mrs. Caldwell, the boy's aunt, which had on it the address of the parsonage at Connecticut Farms. In the letter Mrs. Caldwell mentioned that her husband was with General Washington at Morristown, and urged the young soldier to be courageous in fighting the British. When it became apparent that the British were losing the battle, these two Hessian soldiers sought other means to wreak their vengeance. What could be better than to kill the wife of the hated parson and the aunt of General Stirling's killer? If this could be accomplished, their revenge would be complete. With this thought in mind they went looking for the manse. It did not take them long to find it, and looking through the window, saw Mrs. Caldwell. They didn't hesitate a second, but fired, killing her instantly.

It was not at this battle that Rev. Caldwell was to be dubbed the "Fighting Parson." On June 23rd, the British again attempted to reach the Watchung Mountains in an effort to dislodge Washington from his hideout. The Tories called Rev. Caldwell the "High Priest of Rebellion." The Hessian commander, General Knyphausen, said, "This fighting parson with his tongue of fire can do more to harm England's cause than a dozen regiments."

Nothing could keep the Reverend from preaching on Sunday and fighting with Washington's troops during the rest of the week. When he was in the pulpit, armed sentries guarded the doors to the church, and he began his services by placing loaded pistols on each side of the Bible.

The British advance from Elizabethtown met fierce resistance at Connecticut Farms. The battle lasted three hours, but the Americans were forced to give way and to join the troops at Springfield. Here the

Rhode Island troops, under the command of Colonel Israel Angell, had made good use of their single cannon, but they began to run out of the paper wadding used to ram down the powder and shot. Rev. Caldwell, sensing the seriousness of the situation, raced to the nearby Springfield church and brought out arms full of Watts hymnals. He tossed them to the troops, shouting all the while, "Give 'em Watts, boys. Put Watts into them." Although the American troops prevented the British from reaching the Watchung Mountains, from where they could launch an attack on General Washington's main army, they could not prevent the pillaging of Connecticut Farms. It was after this battle that the church and most of the houses were burned down and the church records destroyed.

Connecticut Farms had the same problem experienced by most colonial churches—raising money to pay the minister's salary. Connecticut Farms, however, developed a very ingenious and successful resolution; bar days were inaugurated. These were gala days in the village, when it was customary for the minister to serve drinks, and in those days this was done without any twinge of conscience. The receipts for the day were then used to pay the minister's salary. The congregation would arrive at the designated inn, and the most faithful members were often the ones that drank the most, since otherwise it would look as though they were not supporting the minister. Rev. Caldwell refused to follow this custom, and, in fact, accused his congregation of drinking too much. He considered it a disgrace for them to boast of the number of barrels of rum they kept in their cellars. During the entire time that he was the minister at Connecticut Farms, he refused to attend bar.

Although their houses and church were destroyed during the holocaust of 1780, the villagers were not discouraged. They set to work immediately to rebuild the town. The rubble and charred timbers of the old church were removed, and plans were made for the construction of a new building. Materials were gathered, and the building was started in 1783. By 1788, the building was completed, but it was to be many years before it was completely furnished. On Sunday mornings the congregation would arrive, carrying their own benches, boxes, or chairs, since there were no pews in the church.

Difficult times were in store for the church. Membership was declining, and along with this decline came a reduction in the church's revenues. Shrinking church rolls were typical throughout the area at that time, as only eight percent of the American population belonged to a church in the year 1800. The Session minutes of 1807 refer to a meeting "being spent in prayer for revival." For many years these themes ran through the church records: "Neglect of the house of God," "Intemperate use of alcohol," "Neglect of public worship and baptism." In 1830, the church was behind in paying the salary of the minister. The church did own land, and repairs to the church and the parsonage were financed by selling wood from the church's property. It also owned an apple orchard, and every year two trustees were chosen to have the apples picked and sold. The grass in the orchard was cut every year, and half of it was sold while the other half was given to the minister for his horse and cow.

The earliest rules and duties for the church sexton were listed in 1834:

> The house be swept clean and brasses cleaned previous to each communion day, which shall be four times a year.
>
> The sexton ring and toll the bell fifteen minutes.
>
> All candles furnished for meeting in the church be lit and used for that purpose.
>
> The sexton to have the privilege of mowing the burying ground.
>
> The gates to be locked except on days when there is a meeting when the small gage shall be unlocked.
>
> To attend all calls for graves, as soon as called for, and the price to remain as formerly.

The stove in the church to be taken down in the spring of the year and put up in the fall and to make and keep good fires.

To keep the church glased and to be paid for the same separate and apart from his yearly salary.

To cut the wood for the stove and to be paid for the same.

To see that a pitcher of water is set under the pulpit on days of preparatory lectures previous to communion.

For all these duties the sexton was paid a yearly salary of $20 plus the hay from the burying ground.

Not only was the sexton expected to attend to his duties in a conscientious way, but the trustees were to take their responsibilities seriously also. In 1835 the Session book records the penalty for a trustee late to a business meeting—23 cents.

By the 1900s the spiritual and financial affairs of the church were improving. In 1923 a new parish house was built at a cost of $35,000. On one Sunday in 1927, sixty-eight people joined the church. The Rev. Fred Druckenmiller became pastor in 1928, and guided the church through the difficult days of the great depression. During his 34 years of service, church membership increased from about 300 to a peak of 2,169. The parish house was enlarged in 1950 at a cost of $150,000.

During the last decade the number of church members declined, and with it a reduction again in revenues. A changing population has been taking place in Union with many of the old members moving out and people from the cities moving in. A large percentage of the new people are not Presbyterians. As of December 1975, the congregation numbered 958. Most of the custodial and grounds work is now done by volunteers. But the heritage of the church lives on, and in 1970 Connecticut Farms Church was the first site in New Jersey to be listed on the National Register of Historic Places.

XXI

First Presbyterian Church

Newark, 1791

From its early Puritan beginnings to its present multiracial, multiethnic congregation, Old First Church, as it is commonly called, has ministered faithfully to the community surrounding it. Throughout its history the First Presbyterian Church of Newark has kept pace with the changing scene, having the courage, flexibility and resourcefulness to be a vibrant influence on the lives of the people in the area.

It was just forty-six years after the pilgrim fathers had set foot at Plymouth, Massachusetts when a small group of forty men, women, and children, led by Robert Treat, crossed the Passaic River to found a new colony. These pilgrims came from Milford, Connecticut, which they were forced to leave because of a Royal Charter that was fundamentally opposed to their concept of church and state. They believed that the church was the greater of the two and should govern the state. Their first act was to provide themselves with a constitution, a Magna Carta of religious and political liberty. This constitution consisted of four texts taken from the Hebrew Scriptures which expressed their ideas of self-government. The first was from Jeremiah (30: 21): "And their nobles shall be of themselves, and their governor shall proceed from the midst of them." The second and third were

The First Presbyterian Church in Newark, built in 1791.

from Deuteronomy (17: 15; 1: 13): "Thou shalt in any wise set him King over thee, whom the Lord thy God shall choose; one from among thy brethren shalt thou set King over thee; thou mayest not set a stranger over thee, which is not thy brother.

"Take your wise men, and understanding, and known among your tribes, and I will make them rulers over thee." The fourth was from Exodus (18: 21): Moreover thou shalt provide out of all the people able men, such as fear God, men of truth, hating covetousness; and place such over them, to be rulers of thousands, rulers of fifties, and rulers of tens."

Under this concept only church members could hold political office and transact civil affairs. The Royal Charter which united the two colonies of New Haven and Connecticut did not adhere to these principles and allowed men who had no connection with the church to hold public office.

New Jersey Governor Phillip Carteret was anxious to settle his colony, so he offered these pilgrims concessions and land together with liberty of worship and government as their conscience dictated. New Jersey was described to them as a place of pure, healthful air, wholesome springs, waters, and rivers along with a variety of flowers, trees, and forests. As New Jersey once was so it should be now, but man in his "wisdom" has polluted the waters and fouled the air to the extent that, if the same offer were made today, these pilgrims would never accept.

Their arrival almost met with disaster—not because the description given them of the land wasn't true, but because of the feelings of the earlier inhabitants. The Hackensack Indians claimed that the land was theirs, and for a time it looked as though the pilgrims would be forced to return to Connecticut. But negotiators met with an Indian by the name of Perro, the representative of Chief Oraton, and an agreement was reached. A fairer bargain was made with these Indians than had been made with the Indians in the purchase of

Manhattan Island. The pilgrims paid the Hackensack Indians in goods valued at about $750. The date of the agreement was July 11, 1667 and included the land to the top of the Watchung Mountains. The price paid included fifty double hands of powder, one hundred bars of lead, twenty axes, twenty coats, ten guns, twenty pistols, ten swords, ten kettles, four blankets, four barrels of beer, ten pairs of breeches, fifty knives, twenty hoes, eight hundred fifty fathoms of wampum, thirty-two gallons of liquor or something equivalent, and three troopers coats. These new settlers named the town "Milford" in memory of the place they had recently left. Within a year, June 1667, a second group arrived from Guilford and Branford, Connecticut. These newcomers had to be assimilated into the community. The first settlers had already grouped their houses together. Therefore the town was divided into quarters. Two broad avenues were laid out at right angles to each other, and each group was allowed to select the quadrant in which it would settle. Where these two broad avenues crossed was the center of town, and it is still known as "The Four Corners." The land set apart for the meeting house was diagonally across from where the church now stands, with ground staked out behind it for the first burying ground. Land for the parsonage was set aside opposite the meeting house. The minister was given 80 pounds to use in building the parsonage, along with the expenses of his transportation and the digging of his well. He was to receive 80 pounds annually for his salary, and various persons were designated each year to go into the forests to cut a sufficient amount of firewood for the pastor's use.

The Branford pilgrims had brought their minister with them. Abraham Pierson had been born in Newark-on-Trent and educated at Cambridge, England. He had ministered in the New World on the western shores of Long Island, and in 1644 had moved his congregation to Branford, Connecticut. This was the Branford pilgrims' third attempt to establish a "pure and Godly Government in the wilds of

America." This new community came under the congregational form of worship and government, and this continued until 1719. Under the congregational form of government the minister was the chief spiritual and temporal administrator, so for the next seventy years the town's records are indistinguishable from the church's records. The minister was elected by the inhabitants of the town, and his salary was voted upon by the town. Only church members could vote or hold public office.

The life of this little community was simple but not devoid of comfort or dignity. The people lived in log cabins, the logs for which were cut in surrounding forests. Large lots surrounded the log cabins, and the cabins themselves were often covered with roses. The spinning wheel was used in every cabin, and all the linen and woolen fabrics were homemade. To make a suit of clothes took about six months. A traveling shoemaker came once a year and stayed with each family until he had made a pair of shoes for each member. The beating of a drum took the place of an alarm clock, calling the people to work shortly after daybreak. This same drum called the people to church on the Sabbath and warned them when danger threatened.

The ministry of Abraham Pierson lasted eleven years, from 1667 to 1678. Under his leadership the first meeting house was built. On September 10, 1668, probably at a meeting in the parsonage, the decision was made to proceed with the erection of a meeting house. It was called a meeting house because all the town's business was conducted there, temporal as well as spiritual. A committee of five men was selected to oversee the construction. Every male member of the congregation was required to work two days in building the house when called upon. By March 12, 1669, the timber was cut and hewn and the frame ready to be raised.

It was a humble affair, thirty-six feet square, sixteen feet high in front under the eaves and somewhat less in the rear, without chimney or cupola. In 1675, at the time of Phillip's War in New England, structures were added at two corners called "flankers." These were built with palisades, or sharpened stakes, driven into the ground close together. These "flankers" housed sentries who would guard all sides of the house. The settlers were appalled at the stories of the Indian massacres taking place in New England. At all services sentries were posted, and one-fourth of the men were authorized to bear arms during Sunday worship services. Fortunately, for these residents, there are no records of any Indian uprisings, probably a result of the fine treatment accorded to them. Rev. Pierson had done missionary work among the Indians while in New England, and he continued to do so in his new location.

Inside the meeting house seats were arranged through the middle and along the sides, and every man, woman, and child took the seats assigned to them by the town's committee. The front seats were given to the men and women while the children sat in the back, with an elder appointed to see that they behaved.

Pierson was much beloved by his congregation, and on his death in 1678 they renamed the town "Newark," presumably in honor of his birthplace. But the congregational form of government which Abraham Pierson had striven for all his life had not long to last. In the very year of his death the town meetings were opened to others than those who were members of the church. Abraham Pierson, Jr., who succeeded his father as pastor of the church, was to continue this trend toward a more democratic form of government.

Although the early years of his ministry were harmonious and there was great affection between him and his congregation, his advocacy of a Presbyterian form of government for the church soon led to a serious rift. On January 2, 1687 the town meeting voted against a fixed salary for the pastor. His salary was to come from voluntary contributions, which unfortunately, did not equal his agreed-upon salary, and in 1692 he accepted a call from a church in Killingworth, Connecticut. This turned out to be a providential move, since he started a small school which became the nucleus for Yale College. Today there is a statue on the Yale University campus of Abraham Pierson, Jr., its first president.

With the removal of Rev. Pierson, Jr. the tension eased and the life of the community returned to its placid existence. In 1709, the Rev. Nathaniel Bowers took over the ministry, and during his pastorate the second meeting house was built. History does not record the exact date that it was constructed, but it was probably between the years 1714 and 1716. It was much larger than the first building, being forty feet square. In fact, its very size caused some consternation in the community as it was not thought possible that the inhabitants of the town would ever become numerous enough to fill it. It was built of stone with a steeple and a bell, and was considered the most elegant structure for public worship in the colony.

Times were changing. Many of the original pilgrims had died, and the feelings they had for the congregational form of government were not held as strongly by their offspring. Some of the new settlers did not adhere to the congregational doctrines, and, in fact, some remained outside the church. Thus, there was no wrenching of the spirit, no general upheaval when, after the death of Rev. Bowers, a new minister was installed by the Presbytery of Philadelphia in 1719. In fact, there is no record of a formal decision to break away from congregationalism and to embrace Presbyterianism.

The new minister was Rev. Joseph Webb, and during his tenure the final break came for civil authority over the ecclesiastical domination. This momentous event came about rather unsuspectingly. The controversy centered around Colonel Ogden, whose mother was Elizabeth Swaine, the first settler to touch ground at Newark. Colonel Ogden had a large wheat field which was being threatened by heavy rains. In order to save his crop he harvested his wheat on Sunday. This was against the rules of the church, and, despite the fact that he was a pillar of the church, he was censured by the congregation. The dispute was brought before the Presbytery, which ruled in Colonel Ogden's favor. But it was too late. Colonel Ogden, along with many of his followers, left First Church and started an Episcopal Church. This was the first independent, organized religious activity in Newark, and broke forever First Church's ability to rule in temporal affairs.

For reasons known only to Pastor Webb he took no sides in the dispute with Colonel Ogden. As a result he did not earn the respect of either group in the quarrel. The wounds were never healed, and upon application of a majority of the congregation, Pastor Webb was dismissed by the Presbytery in 1736.

There now came to Old First a minister who was to have a profound effect upon the congregation and community. Aaron Burr, Sr. was only twenty years old when he took over the pastorate, but he possessed such a sweetness and grace of character and mind that any animosities about his youth soon melted and a feeling of goodwill took their place. For a man of such tender years this was quite remarkable. Three very important events took place during his ministry. In May 1744, David Brainerd was ordained as "Missionary to the Aborigines." The ordination of this most famous of all missionaries to the American Indians was the first bit of direct missionary work undertaken by First Church, work which continues today, giving First Church an active interest in the affairs of the needy in its own community as well as in many parts of the world.

On June 7, 1753, the Church received its charter from King George II. This marked the final separation of church and state, as it restricted the Church's right to rule to the land and buildings which had been committed to its trust.

Undoubtedly, the most important achievement of Rev. Burr's life was the founding of a university. He had established a classical school in connection with his pastorate. In Elizabethtown, the College of New Jersey had been founded by Rev. Jonathan Dickinson, who died within the first year of its operation. The eight students were moved to Newark, and Rev. Burr assumed the presidency of the college. In 1756, the college moved to Princeton and eventually became Princeton University.

Rev. Alexander Macwhorter became the ninth pastor of Old First, and his ministry was to last 48 years, through the difficult years of the Revolution. He was a fiery preacher, and left an indelible mark on First Church as well as on the community of Newark. Much of his time was devoted to building a new church. The subject was discussed in town meetings from 1755 to 1774. Subscriptions were being taken, and by 1775 materials were being assembled and the trenches for the foundations dug. Then the war broke out, and the plans for the new church had to be shelved for a more propitious time.

Lord Cornwallis and the British army chased Washington and the Revolutionaries through Newark, looting the parsonage and stealing or destroying all of Dr. Macwhorter's books and papers. In recent years cannon balls have been dug from the cemetery grounds. Dr. Macwhorter had to flee for his life. He joined Washington's army as chaplain and participated in the discussions on the crossing of the Delaware and the attack upon the Hessians at Trenton.

Dr. Macwhorter returned to Newark at the close of the Revolution in 1783. He found a town devastated by the war, the church building old and badly in need of repair, and the religious spirit of the people at a low ebb. A leader was badly needed, and Dr. Macwhorter proved equal to the task. As a result of his indomitable spirit and fiery sermons, a new revolution—a spiritual revolution—spread through Newark. Over 100 converts were added to the church which was remarkable in a town with a population of only 1,200. The desire for a new church building was rekindled and ground was broken in September 1787. A building committee was chosen, consisting of Caleb Wheeler, Caleb Camp, Nathaniel Camp, Joseph Banks, Isaac Alling, William P. Smith, Samuel Hays, Benjamin Coe, Joseph

Davis, Daniel Johnson, Moses Farrand, Isaac Plum, Abiel Camfield, and Abraham Ward. The architect was Eleazar Ball.

The construction of the church was a community affair. To John Tichenor and Phineas Baldwin went the credit for hauling the first loads of stone. Others shoveled sand, cut timber, carted clay, donated teams of horses, and even supplied cider and rum. While the men did the construction work, the women cooked the meals and saw to it that the men were well fed. The general interest of the public was so great that all materials used in the construction of the building were exempted from tolls on the ferries and highways. By these combined efforts the total cost of the building was kept to 9,000 pounds, an immense sum for those days.

By January 1, 1791 the building was ready for use, although it was not fully completed until 1794. It was a magnificent structure, and to some critics known as "Macwhorter's Folly." It was 100 feet in length with a steeple 204 feet high. It contained 180 seats and twenty-four pews. In those days seats were what we now call pews, while the name pew was reserved for what we now call a box pew. One hundred twenty of the seats were on the ground floor, and sixty were in the galleries. True to the custom of those days, the church featured a high pulpit which the minister reached by climbing ten steps on the north side, walking along a platform in the rear of the pulpit, then ascending two or three steps on the south side where he found the door to the pulpit. Behind the pulpit was a large Venetian window. The illumination of the church was derived from tallow candles, and if evening services were held, the hour of assemblage was usually at "early candle light."

It was decided to sell seats and pews at public auction. They were all numbered, marked, and appraised at the supposed relative value, so that the total amounted to 7,000 pounds. Bidding had to start at the appraised value, and then the seat was sold to the highest bidder, who held title to it for his lifetime and that of his heirs. The public auction was held on Tuesday, February 1, 1791.

By 1801 Dr. Macwhorter's health was failing, and Dr. Edward D. Griffin became assistant minister. Upon Dr. Macwhorter's death in 1807, Rev. Griffin assumed full responsibility for the ministry of Old First Church. He continued the tradition of illustrious pastors for First Church, being a man of powerful intellect, enthusiastic temperament, and lively imagination. In 1809 he left Newark and eventually became president of Williams College in Williamstown, Massachusetts.

Dr. James Richards became pastor in 1809. During his ministry the first Sunday school in Newark was started. Miss Anna Richards, his daughter, gathered a group of children together in 1814 for religious instruction, and from this beginning the idea spread throughout Newark. Attendance increased rapidly, and the school met in the Church. Boys sat on one side of the gallery and the girls on the other. So fast was its growth that classes were soon held in the square pews and later in the vestibule. The Sunday school has continued uninterrupted to the present.

Dr. William T. Hamilton came to Old First in 1824, just one year after the Synod of New Jersey had separated from the Synod of New York. With Newark's fantastic growth Presbyterianism began to flourish. Fifty-six members left Old First to form the Third Presbyterian Church in 1824. This was due partly to the overcrowding of Old First and partly to the congregational split over the installation of Dr. Hamilton as pastor. Actually, it was necessary for the Presbytery to step in and force the formation of the new church. In the end the parting was amicable, and an additional 73 members joined the new Third Church. Old First, as the mother church, gave the Third Church two-sevenths of the land that it owned in 1809. In 1835, fifty-nine members were dismissed to form Park Presbyterian Church and in 1849 another group started the Sixth Presbyterian Church.

It was under the guidance of Dr. Jonathan F. Stearns, who took over the ministerial duties in 1835, that First Church started its backyard ministry. Bethany Chapel was begun as a Sunday school mission by one of the elders, and First Church assumed responsibility for it in 1864. It was maintained until 1916 when Old First turned it over to the Home Mission Board for use as a Jewish Mission. In 1872 the first Women's Foreign Missionary Society was formed.

Missionary work was continued under the guidance of Dr. David R. Frazier, pastor from 1883 to 1909. Some members of the First Church worked with the Newark Tract Society in starting a Sunday school in a frame building which cost $600 to build. Later the Tract Society felt unable to continue its responsibility and offered it to the Session of First Church. The Session turned it down, but the Sunday school of the Church enthusiastically accepted the responsibility. So successful was this project that the Session reconsidered and decided to sponsor it after all. They purchased property and erected a building on the northwest corner of Lafayette and Tyler Streets, costing $13,000. This work was carried on until 1931, when changes in population forced it to close its doors, and the members united with First Church.

During the time that Dr. Frazier was minister at Old First, there was a large Italian immigration to this country. Newark, being a large industrial city, received its share of these immigrants. Members of the First Italian Presbyterian Church established Olivet Chapel to minister to these newcomers. Unfortunately, they could not meet the expenses and offered the project to the Session of First Church. At first the work was conducted in a twenty by thirty-foot store front at 14th Avenue under the supervision of an Italian pastor. After an impassioned plea by Dr. Frazier, the congregation of Old First raised $4,500, and a new building was erected at a cost of $11,000. First Church ministered to the Italian population until 1951, when it was no longer necessary to hold services in the Italian tongue, and the congregation signified its desire to unite with First Church.

First Church responded to the need of the community and nation during the first World War. Collections of material, money, and old clothes became a way of life. The church was a central shipping point for the Belgian Relief Committee. Surgical dressings were made by the Women's Guild. Unfortunately, because of the severe fuel shortage, it was necessary to curtail all young people's activities. The South Canal Street Mission was founded to minister to poor Italians who lived in ramshackle houses along the old Morris Canal. An Italian minister was supported for Sunday services, and the young people of First Church ran a Sunday school several times a week. Various clubs for boys and girls were started, and a welfare clinic took care of the more material needs of these poor people. The South Canal Street Mission was run by Marie Schultze, one of the outstanding women of First Church. When the city tore down the mission and demolished the neighborhood to make way for a new market in 1920, she went into training at the Presbyterian Hospital in Newark, and later did missionary work in Santiago, Chile. There she directed a hospital and was decorated by the Chilean Government for her unselfish devotion to the needs of the people.

Down through the years, from its earliest beginnings in 1666 to the present day, Old First has faithfully looked after the need of its people whomever they were. It started as a dream of the pilgrims to found a "pure and godly government." Since then Old First has successfully met the challenges of a changing population. Starting with the Hackensack Indians, with whom they worked out a fair settlement for the lands which they occupied, Old First has ministered to and assimilated into its congregation the Italian immigrants, the Chinese, and the Blacks as each of these groups moved into its neighborhood. Truly a multiracial, multiethnic congregation, it has found its strength and vitality by pursuing its original purpose of attending to the spiritual and material needs of its neighbors.

XXII

First Reformed Church

Hackensack, 1791

The First Reformed Church of Hackensack, fondly known as "The Old Church on the Green," has a long and illustrious history. Rev. Peter Tesschenmaker, in the year 1686, is credited with organizing the Dutch Reformed Church in Hackensack, although he was never its ordained minister. He had been the dominie of a church in New Castle, Delaware, but due to financial reasons had been forced to leave. The records are not clear concerning his reason for being in Hackensack, but it is possible that he was considering a multiple pastorate, consisting of the churches at Bergen (Jersey City) and Staten Island. It was not unusual for a pastor in those days to have more than one church under his charge. Whatever the reason for being there, he found 33 people of the Dutch Reformed faith desirous of being organized into a church, so with his assistance they were formed into the Consistory of Ackensack, as it was known then.

The name Hackensack is apparently derived from the name of the Indian village of Achkinhesaky, which was located on the Overpeck Creek, probably in the present day location of Teaneck.[1] The church property is located in the Township of New Barbadoes, which was given its name by the first proprietors, Captains John Berry and

The First Reformed Church in Hackensack.

William Sanford. New Barbadoes was the name originally given to the entire peninsula formed by the converging Hackensack and Passaic Rivers. Both Berry and Sanford had lived and transacted business in the island of Barbados, it was logical for them to call the land they had acquired in the New World New Barbadoes. Captain Berry, upon learning of the desire of the Dutch settlers of Hackensack and Acquackanonk (Passaic) to build a church, gave them on April 20, 1696, 2.75 acres for this purpose. An old map identifies the location as "Berry's Grant, 1669."

At this time they had no regular minister, as Rev. Tesschenmaker had simply helped them in their organizational plans. It was customary in the Dutch Reformed Churches for a layman, or voorlesor, to conduct the services in the absence of a regular pastor. He led the congregation in singing, prayer, and in the reading of the scriptures. This same person was also the catechizer and schoolmaster. For all this he received a yearly salary of four pounds, four shillings, and sixpence.

The combined congregations of Hackensack and Passaic were unusually fortunate in having in their midst Guilliame Bertholf, who was to become the founder of the Dutch Reformed Church west of the Hudson River. Although he died over 250 years ago, it has only been during the last 75 years or so that his work has received the recognition that it deserved.

His work as voorlesor was performed so acceptably that the united congregations wanted him as their regular pastor. To accomplish this they sent him to Holland in 1693 at their expense to be examined by the Classis of Middleburgh. On September 16, 1693 he gave his discourse, which was so well received that he was admitted to the full examination by the Classis. In this examination he completely satisfied the Classis as to his qualification and was unanimously ordained and installed to the pastoral charge of the two congregations which had called him.

Five months later he arrived back in America and assumed his full ministerial duties. He thus became the first regularly installed pastor in a Reformed Dutch Church in New Jersey. On March 18, 1694, the combined congregations of Hackensack and Passaic were formally organized by the election of elders and deacons. The election was held at Acquackanonk (Passaic) and Hendrick Jorese was elected elder for Hackensack and Elyas Vrelandt for Acquackanonk. The deacons chosen were Hendrick Epke and Jurriaen Vestervelt for Hackensack and Bastiaen Van Gysse and Hess Pieterse for Acquackanonk.

Hackensack now lacked but one thing to make it one of the leading Dutch Reformed Churches in the New World—a church building. Where the congregations had been meeting is not definitely known, but according to legend they first met in a building belonging to Hendrick Jorese Brinkerhoss on the east side of the Hackensack River. Later they are supposed to have met in a building on the west side of the river, one or two miles south of the present building.[2] But beyond question, the united congregations must have been planning for a church building while their pastor-to-be was in Holland for his examination by the Classis.

Two and three-quarters acres were obtained from Captain John Berry for the building site, and William Day and John Stage (Stagg) were commissioned as the builders. The members supplied the stone and lumber, the stone being local sandstone. It was built in a style typical for those days, and was octagonal in shape, thirty to forty feet wide. Inside, wooden seats were built abound the walls while the center of the building was left completely empty. The men sat in the wooden seats while the women brought their own chairs and placed them in the open space in the center of the building. Opposite the door was a high, wine-glass shaped pulpit with a sounding board. The pulpit was reached by a curved staircase on one side. When finished, the church building cost about 2,600 guilders. This was all these early settlers could afford, so there was no steeple on the original building even though a steeple, topped by a weathercock, was the mark of a Dutch church. The steeple was finally built in 1708, making their little church complete.

On November 15, 1696, the united congregations gathered to hear their first pastor preach the first sermon in their new church. How satisfying it must have been, having paid the expenses of sending the man of their choice to Holland to be officially examined and recognized as their pastor, having built their own church, and then finally, gathering together to worship and praise God for their blessings. The service was in Dutch, and although there is no record of the service, it would have followed a typical Dutch church program. The voorlesor, from his seat below the pulpit, would read the scripture, and then lead the congregation in singing a psalm. Congregational singing in those days was quite different from what it is today. The voorlesor would read a line of the psalm, and then the congregation would sing it. After the singing the offering was taken. This was done with long poles, to which were attached black velvet bags. In the bottom of each bag was a bell which was to wake any worshipper who might be nodding. A sermon, no less than an hour in length, would follow, and then it was time for the midday break. The families were prepared with picnic lunches, which on mild, summer days would be enjoyed out of doors. After this respite another sermon would be given by the pastor, and then the families would climb into their wagons for the long journey home. Sunday was a day of worship for these early settlers, and that meant the *entire* day.

Dominie Bertholf's ministry lasted for just shy of thirty years. During that time he had a profound effect on the united congregations of Hackensack and Passaic, receiving into membership a total of 286 persons. During his active ministry, he became the founder of most of the early Dutch Reformed Churches in New Jersey. His final accomplishment, just before his death, was the establishment of the Schraalenburgh (Dumont) church as a separate congregation. The history of these two churches was to be intertwined over many tumultuous years. Dominie Bertholf died in 1724, much beloved and mourned by his faithful followers. With his death the connection between the congregations of Hackensack and Acquackanonk (Passaic) was ended.

The Schraalenburgh congregation was organized in 1724, and they built their first house of worship in 1725. It was located just east of the present South Presbyterian Church of Bergenfield. The two congregations, Schraalenburgh and Hackensack, sent a call to Holland for a young preacher, and Reinhard Erickzon accepted. However, his tenure was a short one, as he left the Hackensack Valley in 1728 to accept a call from the Schenectedy congregation, which, at that time, was considered the most prestigious Dutch Reformed Church in the colonies.

By now the original Hackensack church building had become too small for the fast growing congregation. Even though they were without a pastor, the members decided that a new building was necessary. In the same year that Rev. Erickzon left, the old building was completely torn down, and a new one erected on the same site. It followed the same design, octagonal in shape, with seats around the walls for the men and the center reserved for the women who brought their own chairs every Sunday morning. In keeping with the Dutch tradition a belfry was erected in the center of the roof.

With the pulpit vacant, the congregation sent a call to the Classis of Amsterdam for a new minister. In the meantime, Rev. Gualtherius Dubois, one of the most prominent Dutch preachers, supplied the pulpit on a part-time basis. At the time, the congregation had no way of knowing that this was a quiet prelude to the tumultuous years that were shortly to follow.

Rev. Dubois supplied the pulpit until 1730, when Antonius Curtenius became the regular pastor. He arrived in Hackensack on October 25, 1730, and it was expected that he would take full charge of the Hackensack and Schraalenburgh congregations, as his predecessor, Rev. Erickzon, had done. Rev. Curtenius soon let it be known, however, that he preferred to be pastor of the Hackensack church only. Fortunately for Schraalenburgh, Dominie Curtenius's decision did not deprive them of a preacher. An opportunity presented itself almost immediately for the churches of Schraalenburg and Paramus to call Rev. William Mancius. But this arrangement lasted only nine months, until Dominie Mancius left to accept the assistant pastorship at Kingston, New York. The Schraalenburgh church made several efforts to secure the services of another pastor, but to no avail. During this period, Rev. Curtenius had time to think over his previous decision to serve only the Hackensack church. Undoubtedly, influential members of both churches helped him come to a new decision, and by 1737, if not before, he agreed to minister to both congregations.

It is not hard to imagine that his relationship with the Schraalenburgh congregation was not the most cordial. Surely these people would not easily dismiss from their minds the fact that Curtenius had at first refused to be their pastor and, as a result, they had been without a pastor for several years. He remained the sole pastor of both churches until 1748, however, when Rev. John Henry Goetchius was engaged as co-pastor of both churches. Under this arrangement, the new minister was to spend one-third of his Sundays with the Hackensack church, and Hackensack would contribute one-third of his salary. On October 16, 1748, Rev. Goetchius was installed, and Rev. Curtenius preached the installation sermon.

This harmony was not to last very long. There were many factors at work which eventually were to cause great bitterness and to split the congregation irreconcilably. The perpetual conflict of youth vs. age may have been one factor, but certainly not the dominant one. Goetschius was 30 at the time of his installation while Curtenius was only 50. The personalities of the two men were certainly in conflict.

Goetschius was vigorous and active, traits which enhanced his popularity. Curtenius was quiet, reserved, and less partial to innovations. Before long, Curtenius was second to Goetschius in popularity, and the friends of Goetschius took control of both Consistories. The situation became so bad that Curtenius preached many a Sunday without a single elder or deacon in attendance. Goetschius and his friends did nothing to smooth over the situation. In fact, it must be said that Goetschius and his followers were not above tactics of a questionable nature. According to the records, Rev. Goetschius and his supporters traveled to Amboy and obtained from the Governor in an illegal manner a charter covering the church property. Rev. Curtenius had no knowledge of this act until after it was accomplished. He and his group thereupon made application to the Governor, and when the full facts were known, the charter was declared invalid.

All of these things were irritants which fed the flames of dissension. However, the main cause of the eventual split was an ecclesiastical one. Curtenius belonged to the Conferentie party, which believed in the formalism of the church, and that the authority of the church should remain in Holland. Goetschius belonged to the Coetus party, which wanted to rid the church of its formalism and to establish the authority of the church in America.

The bitterness became so great that it lasted for about 100 years, through the terms of eight pastors. This was no simple family quarrel, no mere internal strife. Its roots went deep to the very foundations of the church. Neither side exhibited that spirit of Christian love that might have solved the problem, or most certainly would have assuaged the bitterness. The results were that two separate congregations were formed at each church. Rev. Curteinus served a congregation at Hackensack and one at Schraalenburgh that followed the Conferentie line. Rev. Goetschius ministered to those at each location who followed the Coetus principles. The bitterness became so great that if the Conferentie followers, on their way to worship at the Schraalenburgh church, met the Coetus followers on their way to worship at the Hackensack church, neither side would give way so the other could pass. As a result, they sat there looking at each other, finally turning around and going back. At one time Rev. Goetschius, anticipating trouble in entering the Hackensack church, called for his sword, determined to take whatever action was necessary to protect his rights. Thus attired, he entered the pulpit, and was not disturbed.

In the midst of these problems, Dominie Curtenius resigned to accept a call from a church in Flatbush, Long Island in 1755. For the next year Rev. Goetschius was the sole pastor and tried to weld the congregation into one group under his leadership. But, the wounds were too great, and Curtenius's followers petitioned the Classis to permanently organize those belonging to the Conferentie into a separate body in each church. The Classis approved the petition over the strong objections of Dominie Goetschius. Rev. John Schuyler was called in 1756 to be the pastor for the Conferentie congregation.

Quite amazingly, the churches continued to function, and important events took place despite all the problems. Rev. Schuyler left in 1759, and in 1766, Rev. Goetschius became a trustee of Queens College (Rutgers University). Hackensack very nearly became the seat of Queens College, but after a long debate, lost out to New Brunswick by one vote. In 1772, a convention was held in New York City for the purpose of overcoming the differences between the Coetus and the Conferentie. The result was the formation of the Reformed Protestant Dutch Church in the United States of North America. At this convention Reverends Warmaldus Kuypers and Henry Goetschius represented the Hackensack and Schraalenburgh churches for the Conferentie and Coetus, respectively. Articles of Union were adopted, and an independent Classis and Synod were established on the order of the churches in Holland. This convention also met the longstanding demands of the Coetus group by agreeing that American ministers were to be educated at Queens College. The convention was a complete victory for the Coetus people.

More serious difficulties might have arisen between the Coetus and Conferentie groups as a result of this convention, had it not been for the fact that feelings were being inflamed by the conflict with England. Sides were being chosen according to this political struggle. The Conferentie leaned toward the Church of England and was Tory, while the Coetus group favored Presbyterianism and was revolutionary.

The factional strife continued throughout the entire war. Some of the members of the Hackensack and Schraalenburgh churches were intensely patriotic, others indifferent. Politics was often discussed from the pulpit, and the congregations were divided on political grounds. Rev. Dirk Romeyn was so ardently loyal to the cause of the colonies that the British called him the "Rebel Parson," and his life and freedom were often threatened. In March 1780, a detachment of British troops attacked Hackensack, took a number of people prisoner, burned the Court House, and carried off a large amount of booty. Dominie Romeyn escaped only by hiding in an attic. He and his family fled for safety to Marblehead, New York, but he continued to visit the congregation whenever he could.

With the cessation of hostilities on the national scene, the hostilities between the congregations at Hackensack and Schraalenburg did not diminish. In fact the dispute became so acute that it was finally placed before the Synod. After much discussion, Articles of Union were finally adopted on May 25, 1790. A new era had come. The energies of the congregation were now directed to a common cause. The old church at Hackensack, built in 1728, had to be either repaired or rebuilt. This was a cause in which they could all unite, but whether it would be rebuilt was a matter for some discussion. To resolve the arguments the congregations were to assemble on a given date to examine the building and come to a decision. The young people were anxious to have a new church building, and they took matters into their own hands. Hours before the time set for the members to meet, the young people had their own assembly. They tore down the pews around the walls, removed the chairs and benches from the center of the floor and took them out to the public square. When the older folks arrived and saw what had been done by the young people, there was only one decision they could come to—erect a new building.

The plan for the new building was agreed to in 1790. The old church was to be completely torn down, and a new one erected on the same site. The dimensions were to be forty-eight by sixty feet. It was to be built of stone, and inside there were to be two galleries. Pews were to replace the chairs, and there was to be no distinction in the seating arrangement between men and women. Special pews were to be assigned to the elders, deacons, and the families of the ministers. A magistrate's pew was to be constructed with a canopy. To help pay for the church, the pews were to be sold at public auction. Two subscription papers were circulated, one in Dutch and the other in English. A total of 132 signatures were obtained, with the subscriptions ranging from 4 shillings to 40 pounds. Altogether, 328 pounds and 9 shillings were pledged.

The building was colonial in design and true to Dutch tradition, with a weathercock on the steeple. Stones from the previous two buildings were worked into the new structure. Several members had their names engraved in stones for use in the new building. According to legend, the stone mason refused to set these special stones until the respective members paid a bonus for the privilege. Over the entrance was placed the red sandstone tablet bearing in Dutch the following motto: "Union Makes Strength." Below is a lion, which appears on the coat of arms of the Dutch King, William the Silent, containing the dates of the three church buildings. This coat of arms, with some variations, has been adopted by the entire Reformed Dutch Church as its own.

The use of the motto—Union Makes Strength—in the 1791 building seemed particularly appropriate in celebrating the union of the two congregations. As the worshippers gathered each Sunday, the stone was in plain view to help them consummate their shaky union. On Friday, July 19, 1795 a violent thunderstorm broke the tranquility of Hackensack. The steeple was struck and badly damaged by a bolt of lightning. The stone was also broken into three pieces, and many of the congregation regarded this as a symbol of Divine displeasure towards the bickering factions.

By 1792 the interior of the building had been completed. Two wood burning stoves on either side of the entrance provided the heat. Each stove had a pipe which extended along the full length of the building. In very cold weather women carried foot stoves to church. These stoves had small metal pans filled with live coals to provide additional warmth during the long services, which could last two or three hours.

The new building boasted a small, semi-circular pulpit, elevated about five or six feet above the floor and reached by a circular stairway on each side. Directly underneath was a desk and a chair occupied by the voorlesor. There was neither choir nor any musical accompaniment.

As the community continued to grow, so did the congregation. By 1847, the building had to be enlarged by adding ten feet on the rear, at a cost of $3,000. The broken inscription stone which had been damaged in the thunderstorm of 1795 was removed to the side wall and a new one put in its place over the entrance. In 1865, a bell was placed in the belfry, and two years later, the chapel was built at a cost of $8,500. The congregation continued to grow, and by 1869, the church was lengthened twenty feet to provide much needed additional space. The interior of the church was remodeled at the same time, and the result was basically the church building as it is today, with a seating capacity of 600. During these alterations the present stone was placed over the entrance.

After the end of the first World War there was considerable discussion concerning the desirability of leaving this old location. The neighborhood had changed from a residential area to a commercial environment. Most of the members had moved to the suburbs, and transportation to Sunday services presented a problem. Few people at that time could afford an automobile. But the congregation as a whole felt too attached to the historic site on the green and voted to keep the church where it was.

In 1937, at the height of the depression, shattering news was received by the congregation. Two of the trusses in the church roof needed to be replaced to prevent the west wall from buckling. The estimated expense was $10,000, which appeared overwhelming at the time. The congregation, however, with the help of some of the townspeople, met the crisis, as their predecessors had met theirs in the past, and oversubscribed the amount needed.

"The Old Church on the Green" has survived through many crises. It has seen internal conflicts that seriously divided the congregation, ministers who were openly in conflict with each other, and families that were divided against each other. It lived through the Revolutionary War, when some of its ministers were Tories and some were Patriots, some of the congregation loyal to the English Crown and others violently opposed to it. Despite all these harrowing experiences, one of which could have caused the church to dissolve, it has survived. "The Old Church on the Green" has been a vibrant force in the lives of its communicants, and spawned no less than 16 daughter churches between 1693 and 1855.

---

1. "The Old Church on the Green," published by the Congregation on the occasion of the NJ Tercentenary Celebration, 1964.

2. *The United Churches of Hackensack and Schraalenburgh*, by Adrian Leiby.

XXIII

Head of the River Methodist Episcopal Church

Estell Manor, 1792

No one could know that the loud, demanding knock on the crude front door of a house in Weymouth Township would result in the establishment of what is still the oldest church building in Atlantic County, least of all the principals of this little drama. It was the winter of 1780, and the fury of a blinding snowstorm made traveling impossible. A circuit rider, Reverend James, had lost his way, and when he spotted this house decided that it was time to ask for shelter.

David Sayrs had been a captain in the Continental Army and had settled in a small village, four miles from Tuckahoe, known as Head of the River. At this time it was a thriving, shipbuilding community at the head of the Tuckahoe River, which was the farthest point inland that the big, sea-going vessels could navigate. Reverend James was an Englishman sent over to this country as an itinerant preacher just at a time when the feelings of the colonists, especially Revolutionary soldiers, were not too cordial towards wandering strangers from across the seas.

Sayrs answered the knock at his door and, according to legend, berated the poor minister with his unflattering opinion of traveling parsons, especially those who had come from England. As is the

Head of the River Methodist Episcopal Church, built in 1792.

custom with old army men, his comments were sprinkled with a few oaths, just to be sure there was no misunderstanding as to the depth of his feelings. Undaunted, however, the visitor scolded the old army captain about his use of profanity and the reception given to a lost traveler looking for shelter in a raging blizzard. The courage and audacity of this man of the cloth in speaking sharply to the captain made Sayrs relent, and Rev. James was invited into the captain's home. The story goes that while nature's storm continued outside, the storm between the two men continued inside. All through the night and into the next day, until the snowstorm abated, the two men heatedly discussed their views on religion and the independence of the colonies. Rev. James must have been very persuasive, as he remained with Captain Sayrs for several days, and later returned to enlist his help in starting a mission at Smith's Hill. The mission was started in 1780, and from this mission the Head of the River congregation evolved.

By 1792, the congregation had grown to the point that a church building was necessary. Land was donated by Daniel Benezet, and the church was erected by Jeremiah and William Smith. The building resembles in many ways the early churches of New England as far as the outside appearance and construction are concerned. The design is similar to that of an old-fashioned farmhouse and just as severe in its austere simplicity. The clapboards were cut from local timber. The interior design consists of a large single room with a gallery around the back and two sides. The front of the church was dominated by a massive pulpit that was high enough for the minister to see those in the gallery as well as those on the main floor. Oil lamps were placed on either side of the pulpit. Plain pine board seats were provided for the worshippers, as comfort was not considered necessary for church-goers in those days. Box pews were later installed as a concession to the growing trend for more comfort. Unfortunately, records are not available as to the total cost of the building. Probably, in keeping with the custom of those days, most of the labor and material was donated by the members of the congregation. Dedication services were held the same year, and these were conducted by Benjamin Abbott, the famed Methodist Evangelist who traveled the Salem Circuit.

There was a definite need for a church in this area. At that time the Tuckahoe River was deeper and wider than it is today, and the big sailing ships could navigate the river as far inland as the village of Tuckahoe. The Revolution had created a huge demand for Jersey bog iron, and the iron furnaces of Etna and Ingersoll provided many jobs, so there were enough people to support a church. In fact, the Baptists had proceeded the Methodists in the vicinity and had tried to start a church across the road from the site of the Head of the River Church.

For whatever reasons the Baptists were unable to make a success of their venture, and the only memorials to their efforts are the grave stones which are still clearly visible. Among these stones are the ones for Reverend Peter Groom and his wife, Anne. Rev. Groom had been the preacher for the West Creek Baptist Church, but for unknown reasons left in 1807 and preached for many years at Head of the River Methodist Church. Despite the obvious approval with which the Methodists received the preaching of Baptist Groom, this was not sufficient reason to relent in their strongly held denominational beliefs. Since Peter Groom had been a Baptist, at his death he was refused burial in the cemetery that surrounds Head of the River Methodist Church where he had preached for many years. He was buried along with his wife Anne and their twins in the woods across the street from the Methodist cemetery. People took their religious beliefs very seriously in those days!

Head of the River prospered in those early years, and many well known evangelists preached there. Francis Asbury was one of these, preaching there on April 18, 1809, using as his text "Unto me, who am less than the least of all saints, is this grace given, that I should preach among the Gentiles the unsearchable riches of Christ." The pinnacle of the church's activities and influence was reached in 1842 with the ministry of Reverend William A. Brooks, when a great revival occurred. One hundred and fifty conversions were reported at this time.

A general decline in the prominence of Head of the River Church was precipitated by the building of a railroad through Tuckahoe. The demand for Jersey bog iron had practically ceased because of higher grade ore found elsewhere, and by 1863 this industry had practically died out. These two factors resulted in the abandonment of the Head of the River settlement, and other points in the Methodist charge were fast outgrowing Head of the River Church. However, through the efforts of many devoted parishioners, the church continued to hold weekly services until 1916. During this time many changes in its operation and organization took place, including an effort made by H. B. Beagle to have the church become an afternoon preaching station.

There was a split from the Atlantic Circuit when Jacob Price was hired as minister. His ministry lasted until 1866, when the church again returned to the Atlantic Circuit. In 1884, through the efforts of Captain Thomas Weeks, the plot of ground next to the church was purchased as additional space for the cemetery. Despite such personal efforts by these dedicated people, the general decline of the area was felt by the church as it saw its membership rolls decrease. By 1903, it was declared a mission of the growing Tuckahoe church. The remaining members of the congregation, however, were not easily discouraged. They came from tough, pioneering stock who had been influenced by such early giants as Francis and Benjamin Abbot, Daniel Ruff, and Dr. Thomas Coke. Despite their declining numbers, they continued weekly church services until 1916, and managed to keep the Sunday School going until 1935.

Now the church is open only once a year, on the second Sunday in October, for memorial services, attended mainly by the descendants of the early pioneers and history buffs interested in reliving for a moment, life as it was in the early colonial days of New Jersey. The church is maintained by a group of local citizens, from which a Board of Trustees is selected. The interior of the church has been kept very much as it was in those early days, with straight wood benches, oil lamps, and the ancient Bible. Missing from the scene is the iron fence that was taken down during World War II and used for scrap iron. The graveyard, which is the final resting place for soldiers of many wars, including the Revolution, the Civil War, the Spanish-American and World Wars, is immaculately kept. One can find here the grave of that vitriolic Revolutionary Army Captain, David Sayrs, who was converted by Rev. James and became the father of the church as well as the grave of one of the builders of the church, Jeremiah Smith.

Standing today as it did in 1792, the church is a quiet reminder to any modern day traveler who will pause long enough to be aware of its existence that the strength and character of our country was shaped by these early circuit riders who braved indescribable hardships. As a fitting climax to its historic origins, Head of the River Methodist Episcopal Church has been selected by the United States Department of Interior as a building to be included in the National Register of Historic Places because of its unusual historic and architectural importance.

XXIV

Old Stone Church

Swedesboro, 1793

n a tiny, neglected, country road that wanders between Bridgeport and Swedesboro is the oldest Methodist Episcopal Church building in South Jersey. Standing on a knoll in a grove of large white oak trees at the intersection of Oak Grove and Meeting House Roads, this old brown stone church has been known by many names: Adams Meeting House—Oak Grove Church—Old Stone Church. The early records have been lost, or possibly were never kept, so the name under which it was first organized is not known.

It was built in 1793 on a corner of the farm which belonged to Joseph and Elizabeth Adams. One acre of ground was deeded, on December 31, 1793, to Francis Asbury, John Earley, Daniel Bates, William Dilkes, Robert Newell, Michael Turner, and Samuel Adams, who, as trustees, were to pay the sum of five shillings for the use of the land. The deed was signed by the Adamses in the presence of William Adams and Joseph Blackwood. An interesting restriction to the deed was its exclusion from the pulpit any preacher who deviated from the doctrine contained in the form of Discipline revised and approved by the General Conference held in Baltimore in November

Old Stone Church, built in 1793.

1793. Later, the Adamses gave an acre of adjoining land for use as a burial ground.

The church, which was erected prior to the signing of the deed, was built of native dressed brown stone. With an artist's eye to the beauty of the structure, the builders used the best stones of uniform size on the front and side facing Oak Grove Road. The irregular stones were used for the walls on the side away from the road and in the back. The walls are more than a foot thick, and the stones were carted to the site by Robert Newell, one of the trustees. The roof was built of cedar shingles, which have since been replaced. The lumber was all hand-hewn and planed from oak, cedar, and heart pine. The few nails that were used were the crude, hand-forged type. A large center door leads into the auditorium with the high, old-fashioned pulpit directly in front. Although the present pulpit is not the original one, it is a reproduction of the type used at that time. On either side of the front door are stairs leading to the balcony, which runs around three sides of the auditorium. In the center of the room is a large chandelier holding four kerosene lamps. Although the kerosene lamps have had to be replaced, the chandelier is the original one. Two of the four posts supporting the balcony boast kerosene lamps, and these, along with the center chandelier, were the only lights available to the early worshippers. On the main floor are six long, narrow benches on either side of the aisle, and these are originals, which were made individually, as none of them are built exactly the same. The only back support is a single board about four inches wide and an inch thick, which adds nothing to the comfort of the bench, but instead guarantees that the worshippers will remain awake during the service. The floor is made of wide, oak planking, which was laid at the time the church was built.

When the church was erected it served a very large area, including communities which are now known as Clarksboro, Bridgeport, Center Square, Swedesboro, Pedricktown, Paulsboro, and other smaller villages. Members from the southwestern side of Raccoon Creek paddled small boats across the stream and walked from there to the church. Those from Center Square crossed in a barge, landing near the former Alexander Black's farm. The first members to worship in the meeting house were Joseph Adams, Benjamin Adams, Samuel Black, John Davis, George Horner, Malachi Horner, William Keyser, Isaac Shute, and David Shute. Several of these are buried in the churchyard, and descendants of many of these families still live in the area. In the burying ground are stones for Adams, Daniels, Fish, Horner, Shute, Dailey, Goff, and Davis. The oldest stone is for "Catherine wife of Meshack Fish died August 4, 1814 in her 39th year."

Like aging parents, the Old Stone Church is now cared for by one of her children: Bethesda United Methodist Church in Swedesboro. Called the "Mother of Methodism" in Gloucester County, Old Stone Church has an anniversary service once a year, when members of her children's churches throughout the area gather to worship as their ancestors once did. The center of activity in the late 18th and early 19th centuries, Old Stone Church may soon see a rebirth of religious activity around it. The Southern New Jersey Conference of the United Methodist Church has bought land adjoining the old property with plans to build a new church. The area is expected to be the center of a building boom in coming years, and if so, the new church will be built and Old Stone Church will be able to keep a watchful eye on another one of its children, just as a doting parent should.

XXV

Old Broad Street Church

Bridgeton, 1795

nlike the Quakers, who built a place of worship as soon as they settled in an area, the original inhabitants of Cohansey Bridge, as it was first known, did not get around to building a house of worship for approximately 107 years. Richard Hancock was the first known settler in the area, having migrated to this section about 1685, after leaving Fenwick's Colony, where he had been Surveyor General. The area was developed, however, by English settlers, who came from New England, and Scotch-Irish folk from Long Island. These people were not as insensitive to their religious faith as it might seem, since houses of worship were established in nearby towns to which the people of Cohansey Bridge traveled each Sabbath.

Their problem was not a lack of religious fervor, but rather one of affluence. Too many people were offering lots for the purpose of building a church. In addition to this, the town was growing on both sides of the Cohansey River, and agreement could not be reached as to which side of the river should be blessed with the church building. There were about 200 inhabitants and about 50 houses, equally divided on both banks of the river. In 1774, an unexecuted will of Alexander Moore, dated 1770, was discovered, which gave a lot of land on the east side of the Cohansey for a Presbyterian

The Old Broad Street Church in Bridgeton, erected in 1795.

Church and graveyard. The will also bequeathed $150 to be used toward the expenses of the church. The location of this lot was the northeast corner of what is now Commerce and Pearly Streets. A claim was filed for this bequest, and subscriptions were actually obtained sufficient to warrant the start of the project. Plans were made and stones were carted to the spot, but objections from those living on the west side of the Cohansey halted the project before construction actually started.

In support of those advocating the building of the church on the west side of the river, Dr. John Fithian offered a lot on the southeast corner of what is now Broad and Giles Streets. Several meetings were held, probably in Potter's Tavern, which was the common gathering place at the time, but with little result. An animated rivalry had developed between the east and west side inhabitants, and no compromise was possible. They all agreed that it was desirable to build a Presbyterian church in the community, but they could not agree as to its location. For years, the Presbyterians had been worshipping at the Presbyterian churches at New England Crossroads, just below Fairton, and farther along the river at Greenwich. Traveling preachers held services occasionally at the local courthouse, so the Cohansey Bridge Presbyterians felt no pressing necessity for a church building of their own, even though the town was now the county seat and was developing commercially and industrially.

In the spring of 1775, news of the Battle of Lexington reached Bridge Town, as it was called at this time, and with the start of the Revolutionary War, all talk of building a church ceased. The people of Bridge Town were ardent supporters of the Revolution. No Tories here! A company of soldiers was raised and many Presbyterians volunteered. Ebenezer Elmer, who later became a general and a member of the Senate and the U.S. House of Representatives, was a lieutenant in the company that was captained by Joseph Bloomfield, who was destined to become Governor of New Jersey. Dr. Jonathan Elmer was a member of the Revolutionary Congress and subsequently one of the first Senators of the United States. Approximately 300 Revolutionary soldiers are buried in the Old Broad Street Church cemetery. With the end of the war the question of a church building arose again. By now, however, the differences that had seemed so important a number of years ago had happily subsided, if not completely disappeared. In 1791, through the influence of Dr. Jonathan Elmer, Colonel David Potter, and General James Giles, Mark Miller gave two acres of ground "to be used, occupied and enjoyed by the inhabitants of Bridge Town forever, for the purposes of a burying ground for all said inhabitants generally, and for the erection thereon a house for the public worship of Almighty God."[1] Mark Miller was the son and heir of Ebenezer Miller, a member of the Quaker sect who had promised to donate these two acres to the Presbyterians. This lot consisted of the northeastern portion of the present cemetery, and included the ground on which the present building was erected.

A general meeting of the inhabitants of the village was held in May 1791, and agreement was reached to accept this lot and to proceed with the building of the church. Jonathan Elmer and Eli Elmer were unanimously chosen to take a deed in trust for the property. Later it was deemed advisable to add two additional members to the committee: namely, David Potter and James Giles. It is interesting to note that the members of this committee had outstanding records in the Revolutionary War. Giles had become a General, and Potter a colonel. Both Elmers were soldiers, with Jonathan later becoming a member of Congress.

With the decision finally made as to the location of the church, there was no problem in raising the necessary funds to start the building. Sixteen hundred dollars was immediately subscribed, and the work was begun in the spring of 1792. At the same time an additional half-acre of ground was purchased, making the total land available 2.5 acres. The cornerstone was laid July 26, 1792, with appropriate ceremonies and the participation of "the leading gentlemen of the town." On September 27th, the roof was raised, and in December the building was enclosed. By now, however, the initial funds had been completely exhausted, and the work which had started with such promise had to be stopped. Prior to this time, the enthusiasm generated by the actual construction of their own house of worship led the members, on October 14, 1792, to make application to the Presbytery of Philadelphia for the regular organization of a church. Jonathan Elmer was appointed to present the request, and, in amazingly fast action, on October 17, 1792 the Presbytery granted the petition. To encourage this new church, the Presbytery of Philadelphia met in Bridgeton on April 16, 1793, even though there was no church building to accommodate them.

Now that they were a formally organized Presbyterian church, they had to continue with the building of the church, even though their funds had been depleted. Casting about for ways to raise additional money, the trustees hit upon the idea of a lottery. In those days lotteries were often used to raise funds for charitable purposes, and the stigma that was later attached to such gambling efforts by a church was unknown. Possibly one factor that directed the attention of the trustees to a lottery was that General Ebenezer Elmer was a member of the Assembly. Authorization for a lottery had to be granted by a special act of the State Assembly, and with a member of the Assembly in their midst, what better means of raising money could be devised? General Elmer successfully prevailed upon his colleagues in the Assembly, and, in May 1793, a special Act was passed, authorizing the lottery.

The lottery was drawn in January 1793 and was successful in raising the authorized $2,000. What type of lottery was selected is not known, but tickets were sold over a wide area. In a letter to his brother-in-law James Ewing of Trenton, dated October 17, 1793, Colonel Potter writes; "I now take the liberty of enclosing fifty tickets which I hope you will be able to dispose of. General Elmer had fifty also, which I hope he can sell to the good men that passed the law for us."

In January 1794 work was resumed on the church building, and continued without interruption until May 1795, when the church, although not completely finished, was suitable for use. Altogether it took three years to build, but the time was well spent. It is one of the finest examples of colonial architecture found anywhere. It is described in the Library of Congress "as possessing exceptional historic and architectural interest, and as being worthy of most careful preservation for the benefit of future generations." It is of the meeting house design, two stories in height, and made of brick burned at the sight. The interior boasts a lofty, wine-glass shaped pulpit reached by a winding staircase, brick-paved aisles, and boxed-in-pews with high backs. Light was furnished by whale oil lamps, and heat by two Franklin stoves which were cast at Atison, New Jersey bearing the name "Jacob Downing," which is still visible. One of the outstanding features is the beautiful Palladian window directly above the pulpit. Only the finest buildings in early America exhibited this type of architectural refinement. It was a style of Renaissance architecture which derived its name from Andrea Palladie, the famous Italian architect of the 16th century. On the ceiling above the pulpit is the Seeing Eye of God, gazing critically at the minister as well as at the congregation. When the church was originally plastered, other quaint ornaments were molded into the plaster, such as wreaths and the heads of unknown dignitaries. Only the Seeing Eye of God now remains.

The back of the church faces Broad Street, and the front faces south and the cemetery. When the church was erected, the roads were not in their present locations. King's Highway ran through the present graveyard a little south of the church building, and as it was originally laid out, the church faced this road. The road to Roadstown also ran through the grounds of the present cemetery, but to the northwest. The church thus stood upon a plot of ground between these two roads. In later years the cemetery grounds were enlarged to approximately ten acres, and the roads were established as they are today. Total cost for the original construction was $4,200.

Dedicatory services for the new church were held on May 17, 1795, with the Rev. John Davenport, minister of the Deerfield Presbyterian Church, officiating. The text for his sermon was taken from the third chapter of Joel, verse 21:

> *For I will cleanse their blood that I have not cleansed;*
> *For the Lord dwelleth in Zion.*

Not waiting for the church building to be completed, the congregation unanimously agreed, in conjunction with the Greenwich Presbyterian Church, to call Dr. William Clarkson to be pastor of both churches. This action was taken on August 25, 1794, a full six months before the dedicatory services of the Bridge Town church. Dr. Clarkson accepted and was ordained in the Greenwich Church on November 14, 1794. The sermon for this auspicious occasion was given by Rev. Samuel Stanhope Smith, D.D., President of Princeton College. Dr. Clarkson preached in the Greenwich church on Sabbath mornings and in Bridge Town in the afternoon. Prior to the opening of the Bridge Town church, services were held in the courthouse.

Dr. Clarkson had received his education in medicine, and was a very skillful physician with a lucrative practice in New York City. Shortly after his marriage to Miss Floyd of Long Island, he and his wife became dedicated Christians, and he was licensed to preach the gospel. It was at this stage in his life that the call came from the Bridge Town and Greenwich churches. He first made his home on the parsonage farm near Bowentown, but after four years he moved to Bridgetown, where he resided until he resigned in 1801.

On May 19, 1795, two days after the dedicatory services, a committee was formed to number the pews and to establish a rental value for each. It was common practice in those days to charge a yearly rental for the pews as a means of raising money to support the church's activities. The committee's plan was unanimously accepted by the congregation and immediately put into effect. The pews were numbered, starting from the pulpit and progressing to the rear of the church, with the side pews being numbered first and then the ones in the center. The numbers ran from 1 to 38 and were rated as follows:

Numbers 2 and 11	$10 each
Numbers 4,5,8,9,10,12,13,14,18, & 20	8 "
Numbers 6,7,15,16,21,22,23,24,30,31,32, & 33	7 "
Numbers 1,3,17,25,26,27,28,34,35,36, & 37	6 "

Numbers 29 and 38 $5 each
Total $260

The parson's pew was number 19, and this, of course, was not included in the rentals. The money that was obtained from the pew rentals was designated to be used for church furnishings and was entrusted to Eli Elmer. The money obtained from renting the pews was only $77.25 in excess of Bridge Town's share of Dr. Clarkson's salary. When he accepted the call from the two churches, it was agreed that his combined salary would be $365.50 yearly, which would be supported equally by Greenwich and Bridge Town. Thus, Bridge Town's share was $182.75.

In the early days of the church, before trustees were elected, a standing committee performed those functions. The first committee consisted of David Potter, James Giles, Jonathan Elmer, and Eli Elmer. Ruling Elders were not elected until 1796. The first communicants numbered only 35, and the church was not incorporated until December 4, 1802. At this time Jeremiah Buck, John Moore White, David Bowen, Samuel Moor Shute, and Stephen Miller were the trustees, and they filed a Certificate of Incorporation in accordance with the laws of the state. The corporate name became "The Presbyterian Congregation of Bridge Town," which it still retains.

In 1797, a murder took place which greatly inflamed the populace. Feelings ran so high that it was impossible to hold the trial in the courthouse. It seemed as though all of the inhabitants wanted to be at the trial, and the courthouse was not large enough to handle the crowd. Since the Presbyterian Church had the largest seating capacity of any building in town, permission was granted for the trial to be held there. The trial started in September and the meeting house was literally packed to the rafters. According to the reports of the day, men and boys were sitting on the beams, so anxious were they to see and hear the drama first-hand. John Patterson, an Irishman, was the defendant, and the subject of all the animosity of the townspeople.

The charges were that Patterson murdered Captain Andrew Conrow and had attempted to kill two other crew members of the boat they were sailing on the Maurice River between Dorchester and Leesburg. The chief witness was the cabin boy who had escaped the same fate by climbing the rigging. During the course of the trial, as the cabin boy was giving testimony, Patterson, frenzied with anger, seized the boy by the throat and tried to choke him to death. This act so inflamed the spectators that they would have torn Patterson to pieces if they had not been forcibly restrained. Patterson was convicted and sentenced to be hanged for his crime, but the crowd was denied this final excitement as Patterson hanged himself, using his handkerchief attached to the upper hinge of his cell door.[2]

Dr. Clarkson submitted his resignation in 1801, after serving the congregations of Bridge Town and Greenwich faithfully for seven years. It seems that some conflicts had arisen among the parishioners over the fact that Dr. Clarkson had found it necessary to supplement his meager income by practicing medicine while he was their pastor.

From 1801 to 1805 the church was without a pastor. Two attempts were made in 1803 to call a minister, but in neither case could the Greenwich and Bridge Town congregations agree. Finally, on July 4, 1804, at a joint meeting of both congregations, agreement was reached, and a call was extended to the Rev. Jonathan Freeman of Newburg, New York. The call was accepted, and he was installed in the Bridge Town church October 16, 1805. His assigned duties were to preach in Bridge Town in the morning and evening and in Greenwich in the afternoon. Although this was a rather one-sided arrangement, Greenwich had reluctantly agreed to it. Rev. Freeman was able to maintain a harmonious relationship with both congregations, and he served the two churches for eighteen years, until his death on November 17, 1822. Dr. Enoch Fithian described him as follows: "His prayers were remarkable in language, matter, and manner, for their solemnity, impressiveness, and appropriateness; his sermons were prepared with care and read from manuscript. The same sermon, ordinarily that was preached to one congregation in the morning of the Sabbath, was preached to the other in the afternoon." No mention is made of the sermon for the evening service, so we might assume that a different subject was selected.

Rev. Freeman's salary was $666.66 yearly, the responsibility for which was shared by both churches. During his pastorate, he received 183 members by examination and 11 by certificate, solemnized 197 marriages, and baptized 234 children. It was during his ministry that the "Cent Society" was organized. This group of 80 women contributed one cent weekly to assist poor students who were training for the ministry.

From 1822 to 1824 the church was again without the services of a pastor. Although Bridge Town had been a regularly organized church since 1792, it had never felt strong enough to support a pastor by itself. With the growing importance of the town, the congregation now felt that it could maintain the full services of a pastor. In the spring of 1824, a call was extended to the Rev. Brogan Hoff, who was then pastor of a Dutch Reformed church in Philadelphia. The Bridgeton congregation (the town's name had been officially changed to its present form) took this action on its own, without consulting the Greenwich church. The protest filed by the Greenwich church shows their feelings about this action: "In justice to ourselves we declare that this separation has not been sort for on our part, if in the event, it should be attended with inconvenience or prejudice to either of the churches, we absolve ourselves of the consequences, and enter this our dissent to the manner in which the separation has been effected, for the satisfaction of those who may interest themselves in the subject, and for the information of our successors and posterity."[3]

Despite this protest from the Greenwich church, the Bridgeton congregation went ahead with its plans. Rev. Hoff was installed on June 10, 1824, and served the congregation for almost nine years, resigning because of poor health in April 1833. He had been born in Harlingen, New Jersey in 1794, graduated from Queens College (now Rutgers) in 1818, and licensed to preach that same year by the Classis of New Brunswick. He became pastor of a Dutch Reformed church in Philadelphia and was then called to Bridgeton.

During his ministry the church thrived, and the old church which had served its people so well no longer seemed adequate. On January 1, 1835, a congregational meeting was held to decide the question of building a new church home. This time the people were united, and a unanimous vote was recorded to build a new edifice immediately. Liberal subscriptions were made, and five months later, on May 31, 1836, the new church was dedicated, and after 41 years of being the spiritual home for the Presbyterians in the area, the doors of Old Broad Street Church were closed. Fortunately, the building was not demolished, and it is now maintained as a spiritual shrine for all the generations that have come and gone since then. Its influence is felt in even a wider area now, as annual Thanksgiving Day services are held, and are attended by hundreds of people from near and far. Occasionally, a picturesque wedding is held within its doors, and during the summer months the gospel is preached from its lofty pulpit as in the days of old.

---

1. From a sermon given in the Old Broad Street Church, July 1, 1962, by the Rev. John W. Hutchinson.

2. *History of Cumberland County*, by Evert and Peck.

3. *Outline History of the Presbyterian Church of West or South Jersey from 1700–1865*, by Rev. Allen H. Brown.

XXVI

Friends Meeting

Mickleton, 1798

riginally known as Lippincott's Meeting, the Mickleton Monthly Meeting was also called the Upper Greenwich Preparative Meeting before its present name was finalized. The Lippincott name came from the fact that Solomon Lippincott donated a portion of the 200 acres conveyed to him by the trustees of Edward Byllinge[1] to the Meeting for a graveyard and meeting house. The name Upper Greenwich was used to distinguish it from the Friends Meeting at Greenwich. On June 1, 1954 the Meeting separated from the Woodbury Monthly Meeting to become the Mickleton Monthly Meeting. The names of some of the early families which constituted this meeting were Lippincott, Fisher, Faucit, Hooten, Cozens, Zane, Mickle, Wood, Bickham, Bates, and Clayton. As early as 1736, Richard Bickham requested permission from the Haddonfield Monthly Meeting, to which these Friends belonged at that time, to hold meetings in the house of Grace Faucit, and the Haddonfield Meeting agreed.[2] This arrangement apparently continued until December 13, 1756, when permission was granted by the Haddonfield Monthly Meeting to "divers Friends who live near Raccoon Creek" to hold "indulged" meetings for worship at Solomon Lippincott's home.

Mickleton Friends Meeting House, built in 1798.

In 1759, a meeting house was built near Lippincott's house. The first reference to building a meeting house is found in the minutes of the Haddonfield Monthly Meeting, dated December 13, 1756: "David Cooper from ye Preparative Meeting at Woodbury Creek, reported that divers Friends who live near Raccoon Creek had requested to hold a meeting of worship in the neighborhood, on First days, which said meeting condescends to their having during ye Winter and part of ye Spring to be held at Solomon Lippincott's." Permission was granted by the Haddonfield Monthly Meeting, and Friends met in Lippincott's home until 1758. On September 11th, 1758, the following minute appears: "David Cooper from ye Preparative Meeting at Woodbury Creek requested leave for Friends to build a meeting house near Solomon Lippincott's." A committee was appointed to meet and to view the place proposed, and to consider the advisability of such a move. By January of 1759, the committee had met, viewed the location, and given their approval as recorded by this minute: "Ye Friends concerned are at liberty to build one, where ye committee of this meeting appointed, and to hold meeting at Solomon Lippincott's on trial as heretofore." This trial period was renewed and continued on a six month basis, until March 2, 1773, when approval was finally granted for an "established" Meeting—almost seventeen years after the first request! As was their custom, the Friends did not act with undue haste.

Upon receipt of the official approval in 1759, they immediately built their own meeting house. It was a one-story, frame building constructed of "good cedar material." Its location was about 1.5 miles from Mickleton near Walfreth's Station. This frame meeting house served the needs of the Friends in the area for almost forty years, until it was seriously damaged by fire. Solomon Lippincott had conveyed four acres, three roods, and twenty perches[3] to the Society, upon which they had built the meeting house. However, he did not relinquish title until February 5, 1795, when David Brown, Samuel Mickle, Samuel Tonkin, William Lippincott, and William White were appointed by the Preparative Meeting to receive the deed. The land was purchased for 16 pounds, 15 shillings in gold and silver money. The first trustee of which there is a record was Benjamin Hooten. An informal note dated 1788 mentions William White as clerk of the Meeting, and that he, Samuel Mickle, and Samuel Paul were the graveyard committee.

After the frame meeting house burned, consideration was given immediately to building a new one. By this time the population had considerably diminished along the river and to the west of the meeting house, but had increased on the eastern side. Lively discussions ensued as to the advisability of building on the same site or of selecting a new one more central to the homes of the majority of the members. The idea of a more central location prevailed, and two alternate sites were proposed—one on land owned by Samuel Tonkin and another on land owned by Samuel Mickle. These were adjoining properties on what is now known as King's Highway. One of the members of the committee reviewing the sites was William White, a deputy surveyor. When the committee was at the Samuel Mickle site, White emphatically stuck down his compass staff, and declared, "This is the spot."

Both Samuel Mickle and Samuel Tonkin deeded 1.5 acres to the Society for the new meeting house. The deed was made out to Samuel Paul, David Brown, George Brown, William Wood, Joshua Lippincott, and William White on August 15, 1799. Samuel Mickle's donation of land was part of 160 acres he had bought in 1796, from Samuel Phillip Paul. Samuel Tonkin's share was part of 100 acres he had purchased in the same year from Bodo Otto's heirs. Bodo Otto was the famous Revolutionary doctor who had befriended Rev. Nicholas Collin of the Swedish Lutheran Church at Raccoon.[4]

Although the title papers had not yet been conveyed to the Meeting, the Friends proceeded with the construction of the new meeting house. The bricks were burned on the farm of William Batten, near Clarksboro, with William White, master of the kilns. The building was two stories high, with a small, covered porch at each of the doors. In keeping with Quaker tradition, the meeting house was partitioned in the center, allowing separate meeting rooms for the men and women. These rooms were used for business purposes, as the men and women met together for worship services, although they sat on opposite sides of the room. What useable lumber could be salvaged from the old meeting house was used to build the horse sheds. The burial ground at the old site was maintained and became known as Solomon's Graveyard. It still exists, and is enclosed by a brick wall, which was erected in 1850.

The Quakers have always placed a high priority on the education of their children. On March 19, 1808, the same two men, Samuel Mickle and Samuel Tonkin, contributed one acre and five perches each to the Meeting for the purpose of building a school house. The Meeting accepted the responsibility of building the school house, and sufficient funds were pledged to pay for its erection. Those subscribing and the amounts pledged were as follows:

Samuel Paul	$60.00
Edward Gill	20.00
Samuel Tonkin	96.00
Issac Reeves	15.00
Samuel Mickle	100.00
William White	13.00
George Mickle	50.00
Thomas Clark	45.00
Issac Jones	20.00
William Beckett	20.00
Issac Cooper	50.00
William Haines	10.00
William Pine	66.00
Cooper Paul	20.00
William Lippincott	40.00
Jedidiah Allen	10.00
William Allen	20.00

The total amount subscribed was $655, which was considered adequate to meet the construction costs. On January 5, 1809, the meeting agreed to proceed with the building of the school. The plans specified a brick building with dimensions of twenty-five by thirty-three feet, one-story high. The building committee consisted of Samuel Tonkin, Samuel Mickle, William Allen, William Pine, and George Mickle. The bricks were burned on the farm of William Pine.

A large, ten-plate, wood stove heated the room. The smoke was carried to the roof by a long pipe connected to a chimney in the south end. This stove was used for about eighty years, keeping the children warm as they pursued their studies.

The school house was finished by January 16, 1810. The trustees were Samuel Paul, Thomas Clark, Joshua Stokes, William Beckett, and William Haines. George Mickle was hired as the first teacher, and the first class was held on the 8th of January. The Friends were among the first to recognize the responsibilities of society in educating all children, poor or otherwise, black or white. On the 13th of August, 1791 the Woodbury Monthly Meeting started a fund for this purpose. One of the by-laws was a requirement that the benefits from this fund should be extended to the black children. This fund exerted an extensive influence in Woodbury and Upper Greenwich on the poorer classes without distinction until the advent of the public schools in 1874. The building continued as a Friends school until 1908. The Greenwich Township Board of Education rented the building as a school for the lower grades from 1910 to 1928 for the sum of $15 per year. For a number of years after 1928 it was used as the local YMCA. In 1941, through the inspired leadership and generosity of Dorothy and Amos Peaslee, the "little red school house" was restored as a recreation center for the entire community. In 1957 the Peaslees donated over half an acre of land across the road from the school house to the Meeting. On this land tennis and basketball courts were built for the enjoyment of the people of the community. The building is still in use, and every year all the people from the neighborhood work together in preparing a strawberry festival and chicken salad supper to raise money for its maintenance.

The meeting house also continues to this day to serve the community in its spiritual needs. For over 100 years the meeting house remained as it was originally constructed, with only minor changes being made. A covered porch replaced the original stoops, the horse sheds were taken down, the partitions separating the men from the women were removed, the interior woodwork was painted, more comfortable benches were installed, and the gallery was converted to classrooms. In around 1918 a two-story annex containing an assembly room and kitchen was added to the back of the meeting house. This cement block building was later covered with red brick, and the asbestos shingle roof overlaid with wood shingles to harmonize with the architectural features of the meeting house itself. The wainscoting around the meeting room was replaced by knotty pine paneling. This paneling was made with old Jersey pine boards, which were taken from the loft of the meeting house where they had been laid to make a rough floor. Wall-to-wall carpeting has been installed, cushions adorn the hard benches, and central heating takes the chill out of the air on cold, wintry First days. A satisfactory compromise has been made in maintaining the beauty and quaintness of the original design with modern comforts.

Beautifully maintained, combining the old with the new, the meeting house reminds the casual visitor of the spiritual vigor of the early Friends, and at the same time provides the present day worshipper with a modern, comfortable means of seeking the "inner light." Possibly not as influential as it was in those early days when it was the only place of worship in the vicinity, the Meeting is, nevertheless, a vital force in the neighborhood with about 200 members, including "convinced" as well as "birthright" Quakers.

---

1. One of the purchasers, along with John Fenwick, of West New Jersey, from Lord Berkeley in 1673.
2. *Notes on Old Gloucester County, Volume 3*, page 282, by Frank H. Stewart.
3. A rood is a square measure equal to one-fourth of an acre. A perch is a measure of length equal to 5.5 yards.
4. See Chapter XVII on the Trinity Episcopal Church in Swedesboro.

XXVII

South Presbyterian Church

Bergenfield, 1799

ust when the first settlements were made in the Bergenfield area is unknown, but there is evidence that plantations had been established prior to 1640. The chances are that these were all abandoned during the Indian Wars of the 1640s, as the records indicate that the inhabitants of the outlying settlement fled to New Amsterdam for protection from the savagery of the marauding Indians.

Known as the Dutch Reformed Church of Schraalenburgh until 1913, when it joined the Presbyterian denomination, it received its name from the area which it served. Schraalenburgh was a farm community encompassing what is now Bergenfield, Dumont, and Haworth. An itinerant preacher, Petrus Taschemaker, with thirty-three people of Old Hackensack (Ridgefield Park), formed the Consistory of Ackensack. The year was 1686, and Taschemaker had come from New Castle, Delaware. Under his guidance, these people elected elders and deacons, who were formally installed on July 25th of the same year. Before coming to this area, Rev. Taschemaker had been involved in a controversy with both the church and government authorities that cost him his pulpit. Turning to the traveling ministry, he served a number of churches so that he was able to visit the Old

South Presbyterian Church in Bergenfield, erected in 1799.

Hackensack group only about four times a year. In 1690 he became the pastor of the Schenectady church where he and his wife, along with two black servants, were murdered during a raid by the French and the Indians.

There was no separate Schraalenburgh church until the year 1724. Previously, the people worshipped with the Old Hackensack congregation. In that year Rev. Guilliame Bertholf, the minister of the Old Hackensack church, died, and many changes took place. One of these changes was the formation of a sister church in Schraalenburgh. These two churches remained under the same pastoral care for the next 100 years, and their histories became intertwined.

The first records of the church are dated May 3, 1724, but the actual organization of the church must have taken place sometime earlier. In 1723 Rev. Bertholf announced to the congregation that he intended to retire, and that they should make plans for the future. A small piece of ground was obtained from Benjamin Demarest on the north side of the county road, which had been laid out in 1717, and just west of Long Swamp Brook. This was a convenient location for the people of Englewood, Tenafly, River Edge, and New Milford. Until a new building could be erected, however, they continued to worship at the Hackensack church. When it was decided to split the Hackensack congregation and to form the Schraalenburgh church, the congregation decided to build a new church located in present day Hackensack. To this new church the Schraalenburgh people journeyed every Sabbath until their own church could be completed.

Construction started in 1725 under the supervision of Ryer Ryerson, David and Daniel Demarset, Carrel DeBaun, Jan Durie, and Cornelius Leydecker. Although other early Dutch Reformed Churches were built in an octagonal shape, it appears that this building was square. Regardless of which shape it took, the interior followed the standard arrangement for churches of this denomination. The men sat on benches placed along the walls, while the women sat in chairs in the center of the building which they had brought with them from home. The building had no heat to comfort them on cold winter days. The children and slaves sat by themselves in the back. The pulpit was a high, wine-glass shaped affair which the dominie reached by a spiral staircase. The roof was two stories high, topped by a small steeple or cupola. Mounted at the very peak was a weather-cock, which was the mark of the Dutch Reformed Church. Originally, the church did not have a bell, but one was obtained around 1775 and mounted in the steeple. A rope from the bell hung straight down to the center of the building, where the sexton stationed himself at bell-ringing time. The services were far longer than they are today, continuing through the morning and afternoon. Each family would bring its own lunch and picnic on the lawn in good weather during the break between the morning and afternoon sermons. It was a pleasant location, with a nearby spring to satisfy the thirst of the worshippers. The availability of this spring water was one of the factors in the original selection of the site.

The new church was hardly built and in use before tensions began to develop, created, strangely enough, by one of the greatest revivals the world has ever seen. It was known in America as "The Great Awakening," and was brought about by a group of sincere, devout, articulate ministers who rebelled against the cold, ritualistic religion then being practiced. The teachings of Frelinghuysen, Edwards, and Tennent in the United States and Wesley and Whitefield in England had a profound effect on the people. They were fiery orators, and people by the thousands came to hear them preach. As a result, congregations became divided among themselves and were soon at odds with their ministers. Feelings were so intense that the controversies found their way into the very homes of the congregations with brother against brother and parents against children. Those who supported the established practices belonged to the conferentie group, and those who were in favor of the new teachings were members of the coetus group. In the approaching conflict with Great Britain, the conferentie supported the British and were Tories, while the coetus favored the Revolution.

The Schraalenburgh worshippers were not spared from this tremendous upheaval. The minister of the combined congregations of Hackensak and Schraalenburgh was Antonius Curtenius. He had been called from Holland in 1730, and shortly after his arrival had made it clear that he preferred to be the dominie for the Hackensack congregation only. For a short time Schraalenburgh united with Paramus, but, being unable to secure a minister of their own, returned to the Hackensack church after Rev. Curtenius agreed to serve both congregations. In 1748, the two congregations called Rev. Henry Goetschius to be co-pastor with Dominie Curtenius. The reasons behind this move may not have been so stated, but they were directly related to the conferentie-coetus conflict. Rev. Curtenius was a member of the conferentie while Goetschius was a well-known leader of the coetus.

The young, more aggressive Goetchius soon captured the hearts of many of the people, and Rev. Curtenius found himself preaching to smaller groups and, on some occasions, without even having one officer present. A definite split in the two congregations developed so that there was a conferentie faction and a coetus group in the Hackensack and Schraalenburgh congregations. By 1754, Dominie Curtenius decided that his work was finished in this area, and he accepted a call in 1755 from a church in Flatbush, New York.

This left the field entirely to Dominie Goetschius, who tried unsuccessfully to unite the warring parties. The followers of Curtenius were so incensed over his leaving that they decided to leave the united churches and to found churches of their own. The move was approved by the Classis of Amsterdam, resulting in two church groups meeting in both the Hackensack and Schraalenburgh church buildings. Rev.

John Schuyler was called as the minister for the conferentie group, and each faction met on alternate Sundays in each of the two churches.

Time did not heal the wounds. In fact, things became much worse with the advent of the Revolution. Instead of petty arguments among themselves, their differences now became much more serious. The conferentie were Tories and did all they could to help the cause of the British, while the coetus were patriots, devoted to helping the cause of the Revolution. It was impossible for them to live together in peace. Tory neighbors turned against patriot neighbors, and atrocities were committed by each group which inflamed the already hard feelings.

The Schraalenburg church was greatly damaged by the war and neglected by the people. It had seen the armies of both sides pass by its doors, fortifications were dug almost next to its walls, and cannons were fired but a few hundred yards away. On Tuesday, June 5, 1798, at a meeting of the joint consistories, a plan was approved to tear down the old building and to build a new church. It was hoped that this action would not only solve the problem of the inadequate building, but might also ease the tension that still existed between the two groups. Rev. Warmoldus Kuypers, the conferentie minister, had died on September 10, 1797, and the coetus group hoped that this would be the start of a new era, with only one minister for the church. This hope was soon to be shattered. On September 22, 1799, the conferentie congregation petitioned the consistory to call Rev. James V. C. Romeyn as the conferentie minister. The petition was rejected, and the conferentie congregation then appealed to the Dutch authorities, who granted their petition. This action resulted in the formal separation of the two congregations. The coetus congregation decided that if the conferentie faction wanted a separate minister they could also have a separate church building. A lot was purchased from Hendrick Zabriskie, and Captain James Christie, Simon Demarest, and Douwe and Jacobus Westervelt were appointed overseers. The conferentie congregation offered to share in the cost of the new building, but the coetus group would have none of it. They had decided that they would go their own way. Having been turned down in their offer, the conferentie congregation decided, on September 6, 1780, to build a new church of their own, about a mile to the north of the old building. This subsequently became know as the North Church.

Plans proceeded for the erection of the South Church. The dimensions were fifty by sixty feet, with a single door in front, two windows on either side of the door and three windows on each side of the building. The second floor consisted of a gallery on three sides, which was reached by a staircase on each side of the door. The traditional arrangement of benches around the walls for the men with the center open for the women to occupy with their own chairs gave way to the more modern idea of pews. There was no distinction as to pews for men and women, and these pews were sold at public auction to the highest bidders, except for those that were reserved for the minister's family, the officers, strangers, and black people. The cost of the pews ranged from a high of 70 pounds to a low of 15 pounds in the gallery. A high, hexagonal pulpit faced the door, reached by a flight of narrow stairs. A tower protruding out from the front of the building supported a steeple, on top of which was the traditional weathercock of the Dutch Reformed Church.

Unfortunately, the separation of the conferentie and coetus congregations, each with its own church building, did not abate the antagonism between them. Rev. Solomon Froeligh, dominie of the South Church, refused to recognize Rev. Romeyn's church, and received into the communion of his church members of Rev. Romeyn's church without proper letters of dismissal. In retaliation, the consistory of the North Church suspended all such members. Other similar events occurred, and, in 1822, Rev. Froeligh convinced the congregation of the South Church, along with the coetus group from the Hackensack church, to secede from the Dutch Reformed Church. For some time Rev. Froeligh had been at odds with the church authorities, and after his failure to be elected to a theological professorship at Queens (Rutgers) College, became openly critical of the orthodoxy of the Dutch Reformed Church. Rev. Froeligh's group then formed the True Reformed Church, which flourished in Bergen County and upstate New York for several years. By the end of the century, a number of the churches merged with the Christian Reformed Church and others joined the Presbyterian Church.

By 1866, the South Church was no longer adequate for the needs of the congregation. In the meeting of May 24th, the consistory decided to remodel and enlarge the building. It was agreed that at least 15 feet should be added to the north end of the building, and a committee was formed to carry out the work. This committee consisted of George Hayler, Henry H. Voorhis, Ralph S. Demarest, Cornelius R. Christie, and Andrew D. Westervelt. Since the church's records had become quite confused concerning the ownership of pews in the old church it was decided that no allowance would be granted for the purchase of pews in the remodeled building. Not quite a year later, the work was completed, and the rededication services were held on April 21, 1867. Despite its enlargement, the church was not big enough to hold all the people who attended. Over 1,000 people were present. The total cost of the reconstruction exceeded $19,000 and was paid by the sale of ninety-two pews for between $120 and $280 per pew.

The town was growing, new people were moving in, and it became evident that the church should supply a center for the young people where they could meet under the atmosphere of the church. At a meeting held by the consistory on February 22, 1909, it was agreed to tear down the old buildings on the parsonage property so that a parish hall could be erected. No formal plans were drawn, but the construction and design were left in the hands of Harry Bogert, who was an active member of the church and an excellent builder. The result was a building of no remarkable architectural design, but a solid, well-built structure that served the youth of the church for nearly forty years. By the end of World War II, it was in such dilapidated condition that it was beyond repair. The idea of building a new parish hall was broached, but many people were dubious about the church's ability to raise the funds, having recently gone through a severe depression and suffered through the sacrifices demanded by the war. It was estimated that $30,000 would be needed, and Mrs. Adrian C. Leiby headed the committee to raise the money. The drive was successful, but by the time the pledges were paid, which was over a three-year period, the cost of construction had risen so that the original estimate was no longer adequate. Enthusiasm had mounted over the successful drive, however, and it was now decided that the hall should be considerably larger than originally planned. Mr. George M. Cady of Teaneck was retained to design the building, in keeping with the architecture of the period. At a congregational meeting in April 1951, a building committee was named and authorized to proceed with the construction of a building costing not more than $100,000, an indication of the enthusiasm that the initial fund drive had created. Mrs. Leiby co-chaired the Finance Committee with Mr. Mark R. Lockwood. This fund drive was also successful, and construction of South Church House was begun. It was completed and formally dedicated on September 28, 1952, and six years later the mortgage was burned, leaving the building free and clear of any debt.

By 1900, the consistory of the Schraalenburgh church had unofficially sent representatives to the Classis of Hackensack of the Christian Reformed Church. By 1908, the churches within the jurisdiction of the Classis were directed to hold congregational meetings to vote upon an organic union with the Christian Reformed Church. Although the Schraalenburgh consistory did not consider itself bound by the directive from the Classis, it, nevertheless, held a congregational meeting on May 20, 1908. Instead of voting to unite with the Christian Reformed Church, the consistory was directed to cease all relations with the said church. In 1910, a delegation from the

Hackensack True Reformed Church met with the consistory of the Schraalenburgh church to discuss the desirability of uniting with some other church group. At a congregational meeting held on September 25, 1910, the Schraalenburgh congregation voted that it was desirable to unite with another denomination. When the question was raised as to which denomination to join, the Presbyterian Church received the highest number of votes. On May 5, 1913, the congregation voted formally to join the Presbyterian Church, of which it is a member to this day.

XXVIII

Bloomfield Presbyterian Church on the Green

Bloomfield, 1799

"**S**trangers once, we came to dwell together," was the dedication theme for the reunion in 1970 of four Presbyterian churches in Bloomfield. It was an historic reunion. The German Presbyterian Church, Westminster Presbyterian Church, and the Ampere Parkway Community Church had all been formed at different times from the congregation of Old First. As the changing conditions had necessitated the formation of these "daughter" churches in the 1800s and early 1900s, so the changing situation in the latter half of the 20th century brought them back together again.

The creation of Old First itself had been caused by the population movement from Newark to the suburbs. Newark had been the "mother" town, and as its inhabitants increased in number, many peopled moved out in search of more land. In 1794, ninety-eight families living in the area known as the Wardsessing section of Newark began meeting together for religious services. This section included the towns now known as Bloomfield, Glen Ridge, Montclair, Verona, and Caldwell—an area of scattered farmhouses and dirt roads. It had been necessary for these families to travel each Sunday all the way to the Presbyterian Church in Newark or to the one in Orange. It was a long and arduous journey, and despite their religious fervor, such

Bloomfield Presbyterian Church on the Green.

journeys were difficult, especially during the long, cold winters. No luxurious cars or smooth, concrete highways made their travel easier. Horse and buggy trips over almost impassable roads were their lot.

Deacon Joseph Davis offered the use of his stone house on Franklin Street as a meeting place for these families, and they gladly accepted. On May 7, 1794, a petition signed by these families was presented to the Presbytery of New York, requesting permission to establish their own church. The churches of Newark and Orange were members of this Presbytery. Since the churches of Newark and Orange were not aware of this petition, the Presbytery requested that committees from all of the interested groups meet with a committee from Presbytery to discuss the separation. The committee members were as follows: Ebenezer and Joseph Baldwin from the Newark church; John Peck, Joseph Baldwin, and Joseph Pierson from the Orange church; John Dodd, Ephraim Morris, Nathaniel Crane, Joseph Davis, and Issac Dodd from the Wardsessing Society. The meeting was held at the home of Joseph Davis on the 16th of June. The Wardsessing committee explained the reasons why a separate church was necessary, and the committees from Newark and Orange raised no objections. In fact these two committees encouraged the Wardsessing group in their efforts. In view of this favorable response, the Presbytery approved the petition. On July 23, 1794, the Wardsessing Society was organized as the Third Presbyterian Congregation of the Township of Newark.

In October 1976, the congregation incorporated under the laws of the State of New Jersey as the Presbyterian Society of Bloomfield. The name of Bloomfield was chosen in honor of Major General Joseph Bloomfield, a Revolutionary War hero who later became governor of New Jersey. Sixteen years later, the town of Bloomfield was established. Thus, the town was named for the church and not the church for the town, which is a rare distinction.

On October 27, 1796, a subscription list was started for the purpose of erecting a church building. On the same date, Joseph Davis and his wife conveyed to the trustees, for the sum of eight pounds, the beautiful plot of ground at the head of the green on which the church still stands. Plans for the new building were drawn by architect Samuel Ward, and the cornerstone was laid on May 8, 1797. Deacon Joseph Davis not only supplied the plot of ground for the church building, but also, unofficially, established the building's dimensions. Davis was convinced that the size of the building as laid out by the surveyors was too small. Therefore, in the middle of the night, he took a lantern, went to the site and moved the surveyor's stakes two feet outward in each direction. His little stratagem was not discovered immediately, and the foundations were laid according to the new location of the stakes. Most of the actual labor of building the church was provided by the men and boys of the congregation under the direction of Aury King. As a result, the cost was held to a modest $1,400.

On July 6, 1797, General Bloomfield and his wife visited the congregation. He contributed $140 to the building fund and Mrs. Bloomfield presented a Bible that is still one of the church's prized possessions. The Bible was printed in Trenton, New Jersey in 1791.

During the actual period of construction the congregation continued to meet at the home of Joseph Davis for worship services. By the summer of 1799, Sunday services were held in the new church even though the windows were not in and the floors were not laid. The exterior of the church was basically the same as it is today, but the interior was completely different. As was typical for that period, box pews with individual doors were provided for the worshippers. But this was the only "luxury." The building had no heat so that the doors on the pews were necessary to keep out the cold drafts. The women brought foot warmers, which were small, metal boxes in which hot coals were placed. The doors to the pews had the added purpose of keeping in whatever little heat was provided by these small stoves. The original windows were made of small panes of clear glass. The gallery was arranged to accommodate the organ, which was installed in 1800 over the front entrance. In 1819, the steeple was erected. It contained a clock, which was the gift of Major Nathaniel Crane. It was his family who gave its name to Cranetown, now known as Montclair. It wasn't until 1896 that the chimes were added, and these were replaced in 1940 by the electronic carillon.

The first minister was the Rev. Abel Jackson, who came to Bloomfield in December of 1799. He became very active in the Associate Presbytery of Morris, which was formed in Hanover, New Jersey on May 3, 1780. This group advocated the independence of the local church, rejecting all ecclesiastical authority of the Presbyteries and Synods except from an advisory capacity. They declared that each congregation was its own final authority in government and discipline, whose decisions were not appealable. During Rev. Jackson's entire pastorate the Bloomfield church conducted its affairs under the Congregational form of government rather than the Presbyterian. Other groups with a similar philosophy sprang up in other parts of the country, flourished for a period of time, but disappeared in the early years of the 19th century. Its adherents eventually joined either the established Congregational or Presbyterian churches.

Rev. Jackson's duties with the Bloomfield Society were terminated in 1810. On November 8th of that year, a committee was formed to approach the Presbytery of Jersey for the supply of substitute ministers while they were without a pastor. One man they approached was Rev. Cyrus Gildersleeve, who was called as the pastor on February 6, 1812, and installed on March 31st. In November of the same year, the church elected ruling elders. Those elected were Joseph Crane, Joseph Davis, Ichabod Baldwin, Israel Crane, David Taylor, Nathaniel Crane, Moses Dodd, John Dodd, Hiram Dodd, and Josiah Ward. These men were ordained on November 19th, and with their ordination the Bloomfield Society became a fully organized Presbyterian church.

Growth was inevitable. More people were moving to the area, and in 1840, the church found it necessary to build a parish house. This building was used by the town as well as by the church. Town council meetings were held in it for many years, and it was in this building that the First Baptist Church was organized in 1851. During these years a large number of immigrants came to the shores of this new country, and many of them settled in the Bloomfield area. By 1854, a number of German-speaking residents expressed the desire to have their own services. They began meeting in private homes and conducting their services in German. When their number became too great to comfortably meet in private homes, Old First offered them the use of its chapel. On January 1, 1855, thirty-seven men and women separated from the Presbyterian church and formed the German Presbyterian Church of Bloomfield.

Continued growth resulted in the formation of still another "daughter" church. The accommodations of Old First became inadequate to handle the crowds that sought to worship there each Sunday morning. Fifty-one members of the congregation started holding separate services. At first these were held in the Old Academy, which was the forerunner of Bloomfield College. Later services were conducted in Eucleian Hall, located over Horace Pierson's store at the corner of Glenwood Avenue and Washington Street. On December 31, 1869, this group became known as the Westminster Presbyterian Church of Bloomfield.

The town of Bloomfield continued to expand, and the membership of Old First continued to grow despite the formation of these two "daughter" churches. By 1924, there were enough members living in the eastern end of town to justify a church in that location. These people began meeting in private homes for worship services, and by 1926, they were able to build their own church under the name Ampere Parkway Community Church.

The influence of Old First was not limited to the three churches that it spawned. The old chapel, which had been the first home of the Westminster Presbyterian Church, was rebuilt and enlarged. By means of greased timbers and a horse-drawn winch, it was moved in 1901 to the corner of Liberty Street and Austin Place to be used by St. John's Lutheran Church. Some of St. John's founders were members of the German Presbyterian Church.

By 1965, there were seven Presbyterian churches in Bloomfield, and many people felt that the work of the churches could be better accomplished through a consolidation. Talks were conducted, and by 1966, a merger took place with Old First and Westminster. A few months later the Park Avenue and Ampere churches joined with Old First and Westminster. The Presbytery of Newark recognized the new, consolidated church by granting it the name of the Bloomfield Presbyterian Church on the Green.

"Strangers once, we came to dwell together." These words were spoken at the rededication service on April 26, 1970. In its early days as the Presbyterian Society of Bloomfield, the church had made welcome all those strangers that came from foreign soils and from other parts of the New World. Now, in keeping with the present needs of the town and its people, the church welcomed back into its fold all those from other churches, uniting with them in the common purpose of spreading the Gospel.

XXIX

Old Paramus
Reformed Church

Ridgewood, 1800

The Indians called it Peremessing because it abounded in wild turkeys. The white man first called it Peremesse, evolving into Peremes, Paremes, Parmes, and, finally, Paramus. The title to this land was obtained from the Indians by Albert Saboroweski, who had arrived in the New World from Poland in 1662. But it was not until about 1700 that settlers began to arrive, and it was another quarter of a century before there were enough inhabitants to consider forming a church. Dutch churches had sprung up in Hackensack, Tappan, Passaic, and Dumont before Paramus was ready.

The first record of a church at Paramus is found in a letter from Rev. Reinhart Erickzon to his brother-in-law, Henrious Coens, in 1725, in which he mentions that he is the minister for the people at Hackensack, Schraalenburgh, and Peremes. By the end of 1733, the people at Paramus felt strong enough to consider the possibility of erecting their own church structure. On January 15, 1734, the congregation assembled at the house of Johannes Wynkoop and authorized the building of a church. Chosen to oversee the work were Conradius Van Derbeck and Johannes Wynkoop. This action was taken even though they had no deed for the land on which they intended to build. They did, however, have a promise from Peter

Old Paramus Reformed Church, Ridgewood.

Faucounier that he would deed a parcel of land to them, provided they erected a church building and obtained a protestant minister to serve the people. Based upon this promise, they proceeded to build their first church.

Very little is known about this building except that the cornerstone was laid on April 21, 1735, and it was probably completed during the fall or winter of the same year. All indications are that it was built of native sandstone with an octagonal roof and a steeple in the center. Inside there were no pews, but the worshippers sat on ladder-back chairs, each chair identified with the owner's name on the back. There was no heating system, of course, and the only heat came from foot warmers which were brought to church each Sabbath filled with live coals. In consideration of Peter Faucounier's generosity, the Consistory agreed to reserve seats for him, his wife, and his heirs. These seats were to be exempt from all charges except the assessment for the minister's salary.

For the deed to the land to become valid the congregation had to build the church and secure a settled minister. Although they now had their church, it was thirteen years before they called a minister. In 1748, Rev. Benjamin Van Der Linde accepted the call to become the dominie for the churches at Paramus and Ponds (Oakland). The daughter of Peter Faucounier, Mrs. Magdelene Faucounier Valleau, then executed the deed, giving forty-five acres of land to the "Elders and Deacons" of the Paramus church. According to the call to Dominie Van Der Linde, the congregation agreed to pay him a yearly salary of sixty pounds, plus firewood, and to build a parsonage for him. He in turn agreed to preach four Sundays at Paramus and the fifth at Ponds. Rev. Van Der Linde served both churches for a period of forty-one years, guiding them through two wars and a division within the Dutch Reformed Church that very nearly ended its existence.

The question of becoming independent from the Dutch Church in Holland had begun to surface just prior to Van Der Linde's arrival in

Paramus. Nine Dutch Reformed ministers had met in New York in 1737 to discuss separation, and from this meeting had come the germ of an American ecclesiastical organization. This group called themselves "the coetus" and was composed of those ministers who had been born in America, but had to go to Holland for ordination. The older ministers, who had been educated in Holland, opposed the movement and called themselves "the conferentie." Feelings became so inflamed that, by 1771, the Consistory of the Collegiate Church in New York had issued a call to all Consistories to send a delegation to discuss ways of reconciling the differences. The first meeting was held in October 1771, and Rev. Van Der Linde and Stephen Zabriskie were the delegates from Paramus. A second meeting was held one year later, at which time Articles of Union were agreed to, granting the coetus group most of what they had demanded. An uneasy peace was maintained between the contending parties, mainly due to the preoccupation with the approaching war with England.

The Paramus church was greatly affected by the war. Geographically the church was located where key roads, north, south, and west converged, making it a strategic military location. Services were interrupted, and the church was used for various military purposes. In December 1776, a military outpost was placed at the church, which included a picket guard for the bridge over the Saddle River. Local legend claims that the church was used on occasion as a hospital and prison. During the course of the war, Washington spent 10 days at Paramus, as indicated by twenty-seven letters signed by Washington that have the heading "Paramus." Since the church was the only public building in the area suitable for housing a staff headquarters, it is believed that the church was used by him as a temporary headquarters. In 1778, the church was the scene of a portion of the court-martial trial of Major General Charles Lee, second-in-command of the American Army to General Washington. The trial, which had started four days before at New Brunswick, had moved to Morristown and then Paramus. Since many top-ranking army officers were required to attend the trial as witnesses, Washington had asked Lord Stirling, President of the Court-Martial Board, to hold the trial at different places, depending upon the location of the Army. Otherwise it would be injurious to the conduct of the war if key officers had to spend a considerable amount of their time away from their units. The trial brought to the church many high-ranking army officers, among them Lieutenant Colonel Alexander Hamilton.

In 1780, the army post at the church was attacked by two different British forces approaching from opposite directions. Early in the morning of March 22nd, the Pennsylvania Regiment, under the command of Major Christopher Stuart, was attacked first by British troops along the West Saddle River Road. A second British unit following Paramus Road attacked the post sometime later. They had just come from Hackensack, where they had burned the court house. The initial raid scattered the American forces, but when the combined British units withdrew along Paramus Road, they were pursued and harassed by the remnants of the American post as well as local militia. As a result of these raids, a plan was drawn up to fortify the church and the surrounding area. The plan was never carried out, however, since the British surrendered a year later at Yorktown.

In 1789, Dominie Van Der Linde passed away, worn out by the rigors of the war. He had managed to keep the Paramus church alive and functioning, and, in fact, personally attended every meeting of the Classis as well as the Synod, even though these meetings were held in remote places because of the dangers of the war. With his death, the connection between Paramus and Ponds was terminated. For the next ten years, Paramus was served by only two ministers. Rev. Isaac Blauvelt occupied the pulpit for only five months, and Rev. William P. Kuypers was suspended after completing barely three years. The congregation dwindled in number, and the church faced a critical period in which its very existence was at stake, but the elders and deacons, along with the faithful members of the congregation, managed to keep the church alive.

On May 7, 1799, a call was issued to Rev. Wilhelmus Eltinge, who was but twenty-one years of age and had just been licensed to preach the year before. When he arrived at Paramus, he found a disorganized congregation. The records of the church could not be found, and there was no list of the members. By actually canvassing the area he eventually located 171 members. The building was in a deplorable condition, having suffered from the ravages of war and the neglect of the people. At a meeting on August 12, 1799, the congregation decided to enlarge and repair the old building. Eight months later, however, a second congregational meeting decided to demolish the old building and to erect a completely new one. The dimensions were to be sixty-five feet long and fifty feet wide. John D. Berdan, Christian Zabriskie, and Casparus Bogert were selected as managers to oversee the construction.

The old church was demolished in April or May 1800, and worship services were held in a barn on the opposite side of Saddle River. The new building was completed on September 2, 1800. The total costs, including a new barn for the parsonage as well as repairs to the parsonage itself, were approximately $6,600. A new church bell was secured from Thomas Mears of London, which is the bell that still calls members to worship at the present time.

By 1805 Dominie Eltinge had added 314 members to his combined Paramus and Saddle River congregations. By this time he felt that more emphasis should be given to the English language in the services. This departure from the traditional caused considerable turmoil, particularly among the Saddle River members. The dissension did not diminish, and in 1811 Rev. Eltinge submitted his resignation. This was followed by the separation of the Saddle River members from the Paramus church in 1813. The Paramus congregation immediately recalled Rev. Eltinge to their pulpit, and in 1816 the Totowa Reformed Church allied with the Paramus church.

Following Rev. Eltinge's death, Dominie Aaron B. Winfield became the pastor. At the time he was only 36 years old, but in frail health. During his tenure, several improvements were made to the church building. Blinds were added to the windows, horse-sheds were built, and carpeting laid on the floor. He died in 1856.

Rev. Edward T. Corwin accepted the call in 1857, and turned the attention of the congregation toward the improvement of their house of worship. Two doorways were cut through the front wall, one on either side of the original entrance; new pews replaced the ones that had been in use since 1800; new flooring was laid; and the gallery, which had been sagging, was raised to its proper level.

The outbreak of the Civil War created discord within the church membership. Pro-slavery and anti-slavery forces clashed, causing serious friction despite Rev. Corwin's attempts to conciliate the disputants. By 1863, things were so bad Rev. Corwin felt that his efforts were to no avail, and he submitted his request to dissolve the pastoral relationship, effective December 1st. He was a gifted scholar, and in 1872 was granted the degree of Doctor of Divinity by Rutgers College. While at Paramus he had compiled and published the *Manual of the Reformed Protestant Dutch Church*, which, along with his other ecclesiastical works, established him as the most distinguished historian of the Reformed Church in America.

The next few years after Rev. Corwin left were ones of despair and apathy. In addition to the dispute over the slavery question, the congregation engaged in squabbles over pew ownership. With the building of the church in 1800, members bought pews, against which assessments were made to pay the minister's salaries and the upkeep of the property. Through the years the ownerships of the pews had changed, and some of the new owners had not taken the responsibility of pew ownership very seriously. As a result, the church treasury was badly depleted. The Consistory records of June 14, 1870, show what a sad state things were in by the following entry: "Cash received from treasurer $3.60 last year. Total amount of bills—$140." From early 1870 to late 1871, at least 30 Consistory meetings and 15 congregational meetings were held, trying to find the ways and means to keep the church in existence. When Rev. Goyn Talmage accepted the call in November 1871, the church had but 125 members on its rolls.

Never again was the church to fall to such a low ebb. Under the leadership of Dominie Talmage, the congregation experienced a rebirth of faith and enthusiasm. They set to work restoring the dilapidated sanctuary. The church was remodeled to its present Victorian style, new pews and windows were installed, the galleries were lowered, a recess was built for the pulpit, and the steeple was restored. Not satisfied with this major effort, a new parsonage was built and the other buildings repaired. The total cost for all of this amounted to $11,378. Not only was the renewed spirit of the congregation manifested in these material improvements, but it also reflected in the spirit of the people. The forerunner of the Women's Guild for Christian Service was started, pew ownership was replaced by a system of pew rental, for which bidding was so enthusiastic that the treasury was again in a sound condition. By 1880, the church was free of debt.

As the twentieth century approached, attention was focused on the music of the church. In 1892, a new pipe organ was presented to the church by Mrs. Elizabeth M. Blauvelt in memory of her parents, with the proviso that a suitable place be arranged to house the organ in the sanctuary. To comply with her request, a brick addition was built on the west end of the church for the organ and the choir. Other improvements were made as the years rolled by. In 1909, a full basement with a complete kitchen and a new heating system made the chapel more useful. A porch was also added to the front of the chapel, and a small steeple placed on the roof. In 1918, the East Paramus Religious Association was formed, to provide for those living in the East Ridgewood Avenue section known as "The

Point." A small chapel was built there to encourage attendance. The by-laws of the Valleau Cemetery, which was incorporated in 1802, were changed in 1920 to make it nonsectarian. Until this time, only Protestants were allowed to purchase plots in the cemetery. Dominie Henry Cook, who shepherded the congregation through both World Wars, was keenly interested in the church's historic background. In 1949, he organized the Paramus Historical & Preservation Society to encourage and sustain interest in the heritage of the church. At first, elected officers had to be members of the church, but the interest became so great that others were allowed to participate. In 1955, it opened the doors of the Schoolhouse Museum, a frame and clapboard building erected in 1871–73, to better house and display the articles of antiquity the Society had acquired.

In the early 1950s, the Paramus church found itself suffering from the problem facing most churches. It had a static membership with very few young people joining. Dominie William Babinsky launched a drive to increase church membership, with emphasis towards young parents newly settled in the area. Within five years the size of the congregation tripled. This growth emphasized the need for additional religious educational facilities, and in 1958 the present Religious Education Building was dedicated. The old chapel, which was a village landmark, was torn down. In 1969, the old brick addition to the church built in 1892 to house the organ, gave way to a new, architecturally compatible structure. The organ was completely rebuilt and rehoused in this new area, which provided additional space for the choir. Dominie Babinsky was responsible for another innovation in the life of the congregation; the old pew rental system, which had been in effect since the days of Dominie Talmege, was discarded for the more modern method of annual pledges to support the work of the church.

The Indians called it Peremessing because the area abounded in wild turkeys. The wild turkeys are gone, but the church, which was organized in 1725, is still there. Its future looks bright. If the past is any indication of the future, the faithfulness of its ministers and the devotion of the congregation will enable it to meet tomorrow's problems, which are certain to arise, successfully.

XXX

Cohansey Baptist Church

Roadstown, 1801

"The oldest church in South Jersey except for Friends Meeting," the historical marker in front of the church proclaims to all visitors, but it may be that some literary license had been taken by the author of this marker. Certainly the statement is not true if it refers to the church building itself. At least six church buildings in South Jersey still standing, not counting Friends meeting houses, predate the Cohansey Baptist Church. Obviously, the author referred to the organization of the church itself and not to the building, but then a further explanation is required, since early pioneers at New England Town Crossroads[1] had erected a church by 1680, ten years before the organization of the Cohansey Baptist Church. To build a church they must have been an organized congregation. But then let us not quibble, since it is true that the Old Stone Church in Fairton is no longer in regular use, and the descendants of those early pioneers no longer belong to the same denomination.

In 1683, Baptists from Tipperary County, Ireland, settled along the north side of the Cohansey River. About this time Rev. Thomas Killingsworth, fresh from his success in organizing Baptist churches in Middletown, near Red Bank, in 1688, and in Piscataway, near New Brunswick, in 1689, arrived in the Cohansey area. These Irish

Cohansey Baptist Church, built in 1801.

Baptists, who had been holding worship services in their homes, were anxious to form a regular church. There are supposed to have been only nine Baptists in the area at the time, including Rev. Killingsworth: Obadiah Holmes, Jr., John Cornelius, David Sheppard, Thomas Abbot, William Button, Reneer Van Hyst, John Child, and Thomas Lamstone. Researchers, however, have discovered that there were other Baptists in the surrounding countryside who were to become members: David Sheppard's brothers, John, Thomas, and James; John Gilman; John Lacrey; and Alexander Smyth. These people banded together in 1690 to form the Cohansey Baptist Church with Rev. Thomas Killingsworth as minister. Although they were scattered around Penn's Neck, Cohansey, and Salem, the distances involved in traveling to worship services did not prevent them from organizing the church.

In 1687, Welsh Baptists settled in the neighborhood of Bowentown, where they built a log meeting house and organized a church on the south side of the Cohansey River, with Rev. Timothy Brooks as their pastor. They had originally come from Swansea, Wales in 1663, and settled in Swansea, Massachusetts. It was from this area that they migrated to Bowentown. They differed in doctrine from their Baptist brethren in Cohansey over the questions of pre-destination, laying on of hands, and singing of psalms. For twenty-three years they maintained a separate church. The families who composed the church were the Bowens, Brookses, Barrets, and Swinneys.[2]

Rev. Killingsworth died in the spring of 1709, and, with the help of the Rev. Valentine Wightman, the two churches united, despite their philosophical differences, under the principle of "bearance and forebearance."[3] It is interesting to note that the Rev. Wightman was a descendant of Edward Wightman of Burton-upon-Trent, the last man in England to die at the stake for his religious faith. Accused by the Bishop of Lichfield of heresy because of his rejection of infant baptism, he was burned to death on April 11, 1612, one year after the publication of the King James version of the Bible.[4] Timothy Brooks became pastor of the united churches.

Prior to this union, in 1707, the Cohansey branch had joined with the Baptist churches in Middletown, Piscataway, Pennepeck (Pennsylvania), and Welsh Tract (Delaware) to form the Philadelphia Association, believed to be the oldest Baptist association in the colonies.

Since each group had its own meeting house which was inconvenient for the other to use, it was decided to obtain ground halfway between each meeting house and near the Cohansey River. By having the new meeting house near the river, those living on the south side could cross over in boats for worship services, while those at Bowentown could travel on horseback. It must be remembered that at this time all traveling was done by boat or on horseback. Wheeled vehicles for private use were unknown in the colonies prior to 1760. The site selected was in Lower Hopewell, known as Mount's Run and now known as Sheppard's Mill. Roger Maul gave them the land by a deed dated December 28, 1713, and additional land was given by Nathan Sheppard by a deed dated February 6, 1779. With this acquisition, the site consisted of about 1.25 acres of land. Here they erected a church, probably in the year 1714. The landing for those living on the south side of the river was about a mile south of the church. It became known as Baptist Landing, a name that it maintained until recent years. Rev. Brooks was the pastor for the united church until his death in 1716 at the age of fifty-five.

During Rev. Brooks' ministry, the membership was increased, due largely to the activities of the same Valentine Wightman. On one occasion in 1714, Mr. Wightman was invited to preach at the Presbyterian Church in Fairfield. As he spoke he became so involved in his sermon that he forgot where he was, and preached as though he were in the Baptist pulpit. So persuasive was he that eight Presbyterians sought him out afterwards and requested baptism by immersion. Only four of the eight, however, united with the Baptist church. Apparently the other four, concerned by Mr. Wightman's dire predictions, wanted to make sure that they were covered by the doctrines of both faiths!

After the death of Rev. Brooks, the church was without a pastor until 1721, when the Rev. William Butcher was ordained. He was a young man from Chester, Pennsylvania, who was attracted to Cohansey by a young lady whom he subsequently married. His career came to a sudden end, however, when he died December 12, 1724, at the early age of twenty-seven. A period of six years elapsed before the church had another minister. At the death of Rev. Brooks, Rev.

Nathaniel Jenkins, minister of the Cape May church, supplied Cohansey until Rev. Butcher was ordained. After Rev. Butcher's untimely death, Rev. Jenkins again supplied the church. Finally, by 1730, he accepted the pastorate of the Cohansey church. He was a man of many talents, and while at Cape May had been a member of the Assembly of that county for many years. While he was in the Assembly, a bill was introduced "to punish such as denied the doctrine of Trinity, the divinity of Christ, and the inspiration of the Scriptures." Rev. Jenkins opposed the passage of this bill with all his strength, declaring that he believed in these doctrines as firmly as the warmest advocate of the ill-conceived bill, but that he would never consent to oppose those who rejected them with law or with any other weapon except argument. Mainly due to his efforts, the bill was defeated, thus assuring that the Jerseys would enjoy religious freedom and not participate in the persecutions that prevailed in New England.

The church grew under his leadership, and mission outposts were established at Pittsgrove, Alloways Creek, Dividing Creek, and Great Egg Harbor. So inspirational was Rev. Jenkins that three young men of his congregation went into the ministry and were licensed to preach. One of these, Robert Kelsey, served as Cohansey's pastor for thirty-three years. Such inspired leadership resulted in the need for a new meeting house, which was built on the same site at Sheppard's Mill in 1741. It was their third meeting house, and this one was a frame building thirty-six feet long and thirty-two feet wide.

All was not harmonious, though, during Rev. Jenkins's tenure. The Welsh Baptists, who had united with the Irish Baptists in 1710, were never completely assimilated. Apparently they never felt quite at ease in the united church despite the accepted principle of "bearance and forebearance." A number of them became Sabbatarians, broke away from the Cohansey church and formed the Seventh-Day Baptist Church at Shiloh in 1737.

The frame meeting house erected in 1741 served the congregation until 1801. Talk of building a new church started in 1796. In the next year a subscription was started, and consideration was given to the most convenient site for the new building. In 1798, the three acres across the street from the Roadstown school were chosen. One of the considerations in favor of this location was the fact that the direct road from Roadstown to Bridgetown had been constructed a few years before, in 1792, and this meant easy access to the meeting house for most of the members. However, clear title could not be obtained until 1799 because of the death of Thomas Sheppard. In August 1799, David Gilman and Isaac Wheaton were appointed to purchase the land at a price of $120. The subscription list was again circulated, authorizing the pledged amounts to be paid in four installments. In March 1800, the subscription list had 108 subscribers, whose pledges totaled 1,131 pounds. Three months later seventy-eight pounds, ten shillings were added, and continued efforts were made to obtain additional subscriptions. Unfortunately, no information is available concerning the cost of the meeting house, but it was necessary to circulate the subscription list four times before the pledges were sufficient to allow construction. In May 1801, the committee was instructed to proceed with the raising of the walls, and by September the building had been enclosed. David Gilman, Isaac Wheaton, and Uriah Bacon had been appointed to superintend the making of the bricks and the purchasing of all other materials. The bricks were formed and fired in the field southeast of the meeting house.

The building was sixty-three feet wide and forty-five feet long with a high pulpit on the north side and an entrance door on each side of the pulpit. Opposite the pulpit, on the south side, was the main entrance. Galleries were on the south, east, and west sides, with stairs on each side of the main door. The ceiling was arched to the center from all four sides. The doors of the church were patterned after those of churches designed by Sir Christopher Wren, the famous English architect. In January 1802, a plan for improving the church lot and burying ground was presented. To the back and the east side of the church, a section was reserved for a stand for the horses and carriages. Burial lots were laid out and given to church families. Space on the south side was reserved for the internment of white "strangers"—nonmembers. Space below the west side was reserved for the internment of black people.

The new church was dedicated in 1802, during the ministry of the Rev. Henry Smalley. He was one of Cohansey's own licentiates who had been licensed to preach by them in 1786. He had taken charge of the church on July 3, 1790, and was ordained pastor on November 8, 1790. For almost forty-nine years he was their spiritual leader, baptizing over 500 people before his death on February 11, 1839.

The building of the new church was not to be accomplished without a tragedy. In December 1802, Isaac Wheaton was commissioned to select a stone for the church doorstep. Philadelphia was the only place that an item of this nature could be secured, and since his daughter was about to be married and had to purchase her trousseau, they decided to make an outing of the occasion by traveling to Philadelphia together. They went to nearby Greenwich, where they boarded a sailing vessel bound for Philadelphia. All went well. The trousseau was purchased, and an appropriate stone of which Wheaton was justifiably proud was loaded on board for the return voyage. As they were sailing down the Delaware River headed for Greenwich, a storm arose, causing heavy waves. The ship listed dangerously, and the stone slid to one side of the vessel, causing it to capsize. All the passengers were drowned. When the boat was finally righted, the stone was still there. It was brought to Roadstown where it is still in use at the south door.

In 1803, true to the custom of the times, the church pews were rented to the highest bidders. Quite probably the owner of each pew furnished it to his own satisfaction and convenience with bench cushion, floor covering, footstools, and foot stoves. Since some of the people of the surrounding neighborhood had neither contributed to the building fund nor rented pews to help with the work of the church, it was agreed that, if they should desire to bury their dead in the church cemetery, they should pay one dollar for each grave, provided that the sexton and two of the trustees thought that they were capable of doing so.

In 1806, as a concession to modern desires, a stove was ordered, a rare item for a church to have in those days. In 1811, the New Jersey Association of Baptist Churches was formed, with the Cohansey church being one of the guiding forces. One of the Association's recommendations to the individual churches was "to hold three-day meetings as an important means of advancing the interests of Christ's Kingdom." These were called "Protracted Meetings," and in 1833, Cohansey adopted protracted meetings as part of its program. A Sabbath School was organized in 1830, and the Watts & Rippen's *Selection of Hymns* was adopted as the hymn book in 1838. The Rev. Edward D. Fendall came as pastor in April 1843, and under his leadership the principle of total abstinence from intoxicating liquors was adopted for the first time. It was forty-three years later, however, on March 6, 1886, that unfermented wine was used for the first time in communion service!

The Roadstown meeting house was remodeled in 1851. The pulpit was moved to the west and lowered. The galleries and stairs were relocated to face the pulpit, the two doors in front were replaced by one in the center, a main entrance door was put in the east end, and more modern pews were installed. In 1864, the pulpit recess was built, and the baptistery added. Up to this time, baptisms had been conducted in the nearby ponds and streams. Musical instruments had never been allowed in the worship services, but in 1854, this rule was relaxed and an organ obtained. By 1862, the organist was voted a salary of fifty dollars per year, which was later reduced to forty-five dollars. On April 9, 1864, the corporate name of the church became "The First Cohansey Baptist Church of Roadstown."

Subscriptions were started for the chapel in 1875. The church's records state: "Resolved that a building be erected at the west end of the church after a sufficient amount has been subscribed." By 1876, $1,100 had been pledged, and since the church had received a low bid of $912.00, construction of the chapel was authorized.

Through the years, the Cohansey Baptist Church has continued to move ahead. Today it is particularly proud of its debt-free education building, costing over $75,000 when it was finished in 1964. One of its prized possessions, and a visible link to its past, is its communion table. This table was first used in the little frame meeting house built in 1741. The pioneer forefathers built the table similar in design to the one used for the Last Supper. When the frame meeting house was no longer in use, it was moved to Greenwich, where it was used as a barn. The communion table went along with the meeting house, and the farmer made use of it as a table for his milk cans. Many years later, it was found in a home in Lower Hopewell after an extensive search by T. B. Nixon, William Mackenzie, and Mrs. Bradway. Although the table is now used during the communion service of the church, it is practically the only similarity to the early communion services. After today's sacramental service the communicants rush home for Sunday dinner and to engage in whatever secular activities are planned for the day. In the little frame meeting house where the communion table was first used, the members did not rush home. They came prepared to stay all day, having brought their Sunday dinner with them.

Those of us today are apt to look upon the present generation as being the first to recognize the worth of all men whatever the color of their skin, and to accuse our forefathers of a serious failing in this respect. Therefore, an event in the history of the Cohansey Baptist Church is one that the present generation needs to reflect upon and to become a little more humble in its own evaluation. The September minutes of 1802 read: "This day divine service was performed to a numerous assembly of people to general satisfaction by a black man named Alexander Bishop." This event took place sixty years before the Civil War!

The old graveyard at Sheppard's Mill is still there, but it was turned over to the Cumberland County Historical Society. Still to be seen is the stone marking the grave of Deborah Swinney, daughter of one of the original Welsh families, "the first white female child to be born in Cohansey Precinct."

---

1. See Chapter XVI on Old Stone Church in Fairton.
2. *History of Salem County New Jersey*, by Joseph S. Sickler.
3. *History of Gloucester, Salem, and Cumberland Counties*, by Cushing & Sheppard.
4. *Glimpses of Old Cohansey*, by Alice Ayars Elwell.

XXXI

Friends Meeting

Moorestown, 1802

It was Sunday morning and Henry Warrington rode into the village of Chester, now Moorestown, on horseback to attend First day services as had been his custom for many years. He dismounted and threw the reins of his horse around a buttonwood sapling that stood just to the west of the old stone meeting house on Salem Road, now Main Street. In 1740, he had planted this sapling, to be used as a hitching post for his horse when he attended meetings. As he entered the old stone meeting house, little thought did he give to the likelihood that this sapling, in the full bloom of its years, would still be guarding the ground where these early Quakers met for worship more than 200 years later, even though its use as a hitching post would have long since disappeared.

The meeting house that Henry Warrington entered that Sunday morning was known as Adams Meeting. Dr. John Rodman of Rhode Island owned a considerable amount of land in this area, and on June 10, 1692, conveyed 500 acres to John Adams of Flushing, Long Island.[1] The next year, John Adams divided his holdings between his two sons, John and James, with James taking the western portion. On April 9, 1700, John and his wife, Hester, conveyed one acre of his estate to the Society of Friends for the consideration of seventy-one

Moorestown Friends Meeting, built in 1802.

pounds, fourteen shillings current money. This lot was located on the corner of Main Street and Great Road or Meeting House Lane, now Chester Avenue.

The desire for a meeting house must have been strongly felt, as the Friends apparently did not wait for the signing of the deed before starting construction of the building. The Articles of Agreement found in Chester Preparative Meeting folder in the Archives at 302 Arch Street, Philadelphia, Pennsylvania, state the purpose of the transaction: "...for the building of a Meeting House thereon for the Worshiping of God in Spirit & in Truth which said Acre of Land is already purchased and the sd house built accordingly." For the past fifteen years the Friends had been meeting on alternate Sundays at the homes of Timothy Hancock and John Kay. Hancock lived along the north branch of the Pennsauken Creek above Camden Avenue and Kay lived along the north branch of the Cooper River near Ellisburg. The first recorded meeting in the village of Chester was held by Thomas Story in the home of John Adams on March 19, 1700.[2] John Adams's home was on Salem Road. These meetings were sanctioned by the Burlington Monthly Meeting; but fifteen years is a long time to be meeting under such unfavorable conditions, so it is not surprising that they started construction as soon as preliminary arrangements for the lot had been made.

The meeting house that they built was made of logs, but there are no surviving records indicating its size or interior arrangement. It stood on the corner lot between Main Street and Chester Avenue and faced Main Street. It served their purpose until 1719, when it was completely destroyed by fire. Arrangements were immediately made to replace it with a larger stone building. This was erected in 1720 on the site of the old log building, facing Main Street with, in all probability, an entrance on Chester Avenue. The horse sheds were located back of the meeting house and extended as far as the present bank property. It must be remembered that prior to the Revolutionary War, both men and women traveled mainly by horseback. Since the entire family would attend First day services, it must have been a picturesque sight, with the Quaker ladies in their hoods and cloaks, and the men in their beaver hats, muslin cravats, and knee britches riding their horses to meeting. The Quakers believed in plainness of attire, and so that none would be tempted otherwise, the Philadelphia Yearly Meeting went on record with the following admonition: "Keep to Plainess in Apparel as becomes the Truth." None were supposed "to wear long lapped Sleeves or Coats gathered at the Sides or Superfluous Buttons or broad Ribbons about their hats or long curled periwigs. Women must be careful about making, buying or wearing strip'd or flower'd Stuffs or other useless and superfluous Things."

The old stone meeting house served the community for a period of eighty years, during which time it witnessed many historical events, and many famous and controversial figures spoke within its walls. Although there is no record that the most renowned American Quaker, John Woolman (whose *Journal* was one of the first books selected by Dr. Elliot for his famous "Five Foot Shelf of Books"), ever attended the Moorestown Meeting, it is logical to assume that he was here quite often. Although he is associated with the Mount Holly Meeting, his sister, Patience, who was married to Joseph Moore, lived in Moorestown. He had another sister, Elizabeth, who lived in Haddonfield, so it can be reasonably assumed that he visited his sisters from time to time and in doing so attended Adams Meeting. His appearance at meeting most certainly caused a stir. His clothes were out of the ordinary, even for the Quakers. He was clad in unbleached homespun and wore an undyed beaver hat. It was probably difficult for the parents to restrain the snickers of the young people as he strode into meeting. The parents themselves might have some qualms, since some of them were slave holders, and Woolman was one of the first to seek the freedom of the slaves.

In 1741, Thomas Chalkley attended the old stone church. He was a sea captain described by the Quaker poet Whittier as "Gentlest of Skippers rare sea saint." Since he had preached to negroes, a slave owner once peppered him with bird shot.

June 19, 20, and 21, 1778 were days that the local Quakers were not soon to forget. The British Army, under General Clinton, who had succeeded General Howe as Commander of the English troops in Philadelphia, crossed the Delaware River on the 18th and started its march across New Jersey. Part of the army went through Evesham and part through Moorestown. The brigades that marched through Moorestown left Haddonfield the morning of the 19th, taking the King's Highway route through Ellisburg, arriving in Moorestown that night. They camped in the vicinity of the meeting house, and some of the soldiers were quartered in the old stone house itself. The story is told, probably without foundation, of a greatly agitated person who rushed into the meeting house and shouted, "here you are all sittin with your hats on and the British just down at Neddy French's." As the story goes, the meeting adjourned and "the horses of the worshippers were driven out of the meeting house yard at a pace that astonished them and startled the neighbors." Whether there is any truth to the story doesn't really matter, because there was plenty of cause for alarm. The records show that the British troops, mainly Hessians, took the horses and plundered the houses of the Chester residents. A stout-hearted Quaker who had been victimized by the Hessian troops was not willing to let the theft of his horses go without a challenge. He presented himself to General Knyphausen, who was in charge of the Hessian troops, and demanded the return of his two horses. The General, impressed by the courage of this Quaker gentleman, gave him the following order, written in both German and English: "Moors Town June 20, 1778. The bearer, Joseph Roberts, has my permission to go through the camp and look for some horses he lost. Wherever he finds them it is ordered hereby to deliver them up immediately. Knyphausen."[3] Joseph Roberts apparently was highly incensed over his loss, as he followed the Hessian troops all the way to Mount Holly before he found his horses. Things quieted down after the foreign troops left, and life returned to a fairly normal routine.

As early as 1746, the Philadelphia Yearly Meeting had urged that schools be established, and that the Monthly Meeting assist each other in this endeavor. There is no recorded date indicating the start of a school by the Chester Meeting, but an Evesham Monthly Meeting minute of 1779 states that a school was opened at Chester, but that ground had not been secured on which to build the schoolhouse. At this time, the Chester Meeting was part of the Evesham Monthly Meeting. Arrangements were finally made in 1781 to purchase a lot from Ephraim Haines, which was across King's Highway, now Main

Street, from the stone meeting house. Classes were held in the stone meeting house until 1785, when a school building was erected.

By 1800, the Adams Meeting House had about fulfilled its purpose, and the members began considering the construction of a new place of worship. A committee was appointed, consisting of John Roberts, John Collins, Robert French, Abraham Rakestraw, Jacob Hollingshead, Samuel Roberts, Isaac Roberts, Abraham Warrington, William Evans, and Samuel Roberts, Jr.[4] After due consideration, the committee reported that they were united in proposing that a new meeting house be built on the south side of the road, across the street from the old stone meeting house. The committee further proposed that the building be sixty-six feet long and forty feet wide, with a partition across the center, that it be built of brick, and estimated its cost at not less than 1,000 pounds. In 1802, according to plan, the new meeting house was erected and is still in use today. The date 1802 can be plainly seen on the western gable.

For a quarter of a century the Moorestown Friends led a relatively placid existence. There were no major upheavals, and the War of 1812 barely affected them. But this peaceful life was not to last. A Long Island farmer was to cause a major split in their ranks and disrupt the entire Quaker sect. Elias Hicks had come into prominence as one of the three outstanding Quaker preachers of his time He opposed the "arbitrary authority" of the big city elders in imposing any type of doctrine, believing that the "Inner Light" was sufficient guidance for each individual. When it became apparent that his views would be sustained by the Philadelphia Yearly Meeting, his followers formed their own group, still maintaining the name "Society of Friends." This group became known as "Hicksites," and in 1827 they took over the Moorestown Meeting House. The remaining Friends, known as "Orthodox," retained possession of the schoolhouse built in 1785. Title to the old graveyard apparently was never surrendered by either side, and it was finally placed in the hands of joint trustees.

Moorestown Friends Meeting

In 1839, the Orthodox Friends, tired of meeting in the school-house, built a frame meeting house, which stood on the same site as the present brick building on Main Street, opposite the former location of Adams Meeting House. This frame building served the needs of the Orthodox Friends until 1896, when the question of erecting a larger meeting place was put before the Preparative Meeting. Agreement was reached, and on June 30, 1897, William Evans reported that the contract had been given to John L. Rogers. The new meeting house was completed one year later at a total cost, including the furnishings, of $15,708.47.

In 1883, the Hicksites built the first kindergarten school in Moorestown. The Friends Academy and the Friends High School on Chester Avenue were united, bringing the two groups of Friends into closer fellowship, and in 1929, the present Friends High School building was constructed. The old high school on Chester Avenue was abandoned, and the lot was sold to the federal government for the construction of the present post office.

Many interesting and accomplished people have been members of the Moorestown Friends, and their influence has been spread far beyond the borders of this Quaker community. Certainly all the boys and girls who have spent joyous winter days sledding down snow-covered hills have no idea that their fun was made possible by the inventive genius of a Moorestown Friend. The home gardener, as he toils in the hot, sultry weather of a Jersey summer, does not know that his task has been made lighter by this same Moorestown genius. What possible connection can there be between the young people's fun in the cold, exhilarating winter days and the joyous harvest anticipation of the home gardener as he tills the soil in the sweltering heat of the summer? The connection is Samuel L. Allen, who started as a farmer near Westfield, now Cinnaminson, but found inventing more to his liking. He invented a seed and fertilizer spreader, and later a hand cultivator under the name "Planet Jr." Another one of his

307

patented inventions was the Flexible Flyer sled, which has given uncounted hours of joy to thousands of young people.

George Abbott became the founder of Abbott's Alderney Dairies. He had the distinction of earning the incongruous titles of "minister" and "Quaker Fighter." He fought hard in the state capitals of Trenton and Harrisburg for good milk legislation. Thus the nickname "Quaker Fighter" was rather humorously bestowed upon this dynamic person by his Quaker friends as well as by his many friends in both the New Jersey and Pennsylvania state governments. As a recorded minister for the Friends, he was a member of the committees of Friends Academy and Westtown School, as well as serving as a member of the Meeting for Sufferings. He founded a Friends Meeting as far away as Orlando, Florida. Little do thousands of residents of Orlando realize that they owe a debt of gratitude for at least part of the beauty of this lovely city to a Moorestown Quaker. Not only did George Abbott found the Friends Meeting there, but he was responsible for obtaining the hardy palms that line the roads and beautify the landscaped grounds of the city buildings. Although his ambition of becoming a millionaire was never reached, he maintained a zest for business activities in becoming the first president of Pocono Manor Inn.

Dr. James Warrington was the originator of a lying-in charity. He was its sole director, and he had working for him a dozen nurses who visited indigent mothers in their homes. In 1832, a charter was granted, and in 1839 a Nurses Society was formed. He was an inspiring person, able to command the allegiance of those working for him, attested to by the fact that his 6 A.M. class for nurses was well attended.

John Hunt, a cousin of John Woolman, lived near Fellowship but attended Moorestown Meeting. In addition to being a farmer, he was a cabinet-maker, wheelwright, cooper, and shoe-maker. He was also a minister, actively engaged in preaching, visitations, and looking after the poor. He became much concerned over the "sins" of the world, which the Friends were adopting; the shiny new carriages, the broad-cloth suits, the excessive use of liquor, and the intermarriages with people of other beliefs. He did not spare his energy in preaching against these worldly traits and admonishing the Friends to forego such pleasures. In his well-known journal, which he kept religiously from 1770 to 1824, he sees God's just judgments upon man's sinfulness in the droughts, blights, epidemics, and, especially, in the ravages of the Revolutionary War.

Emmor Roberts, clerk of the Philadelphia Yearly Meeting for fifteen years and a member of the Board of Swarthmore College for thirty years, had a sense of humor as well as an understanding of young people. The story is told of an escapade on Halloween. A young boy had placed a ladder against a maple tree and was putting Emmor's front gate high up in the tree. Emmor watched the boy's efforts for awhile, and then said, "Harry, I think thee has done a remarkable piece of work to put the gate up there. How would it be now to bring it down?"

The old buttonwood tree, planted as a sapling by Henry Warrington in 1740 as a hitching post for his horse, has seen many changes. No longer do Friends ride to meeting on horses or in the shiny new carriages so feared by John Hunt. But these are superficial changes. The old buttonwood tree is a witness to the faith and devotion of the Friends of the present day, which have not changed from the time when the buttonwood was a sapling.

1. *Moorestown and Her Neighbors*, by George DeCou.
2. 250th Anniversary Publication.
3. *The Historic Rancocas*, by George DeCou.
4. 250th Anniversary Publication.

XXXII

Weymouth United Methodist Church

Weymouth, 1807

eymouth was a thriving industrial city in the early 19th century, famous for its iron works and paper mills. Its iron products were shipped to many parts of the young nation, and there is a story that the first iron water pipes in Philadelphia came from Weymouth. Its paper mills made manila paper, from old ropes and abandoned riggings of ships, as well as waterproof building paper.

The first meeting house was built here long before the famous Weymouth Iron Works or its paper mills existed—while the area still belonged to the West Jersey Society. It was a log building erected in 1754, and stood in what was known as "The Grove." It was built about seventy-five feet west of the present church in a stately grove of oak trees close to the bank of the Great Egg Harbor River. The building was large for the time, being fifty-five feet in length, forty feet in width, and thirty feet in height. The logs were "clayed," not plastered, as native material was used entirely. There were three windows and a door at each end. The pulpit was reached by a winding stairway on either side. In back of the pulpit were two small window sashes, eighteen inches square, and over the pulpit was a high sounding-board. The pews were made of cedar, high, straight-backed, uncushioned, and uncomfortable. In those days it was not considered proper

The Weymouth United Methodist Church.

to be comfortable during worship services, as comfort was thought to be the handiwork of the devil. The pews were arranged in a center block, with two side aisles and a square pew in the front on each side. A large, tin plate, cast-iron stove stood at the window near the entrance. Lard lamps were used on the pulpit, and sconces on the walls held candles. The services were nonsectarian, with traveling ministers of various denominations presiding when they were in the area. During the week the meeting house was used as a school, and children walked great distances to attend.

This place of worship served the community until 1807, when the "New Meeting House," which was started in 1806, was completed at a cost of over $3,000. This cost was borne by the proprietor of the

Weymouth Iron Works, and in most historical accounts of the meeting house the proprietor is identified as Samuel Richards, son of William Richards, of Batsto fame. But the records do not substantiate this claim, and, in fact, cast doubts upon it. The Weymouth Iron Works was built in 1801 and 1802 by five partners, none of whom were Samuel Richards. In 1806, the Weymouth Iron Works was put up for sale, since the manager, George Ashbridge, had died. Samuel Richards and his cousin, Joseph Ball, were interested. Richards had been trained in iron making at Batsto and knew the iron market thoroughly. Ball had managed Batsto during the Revolution, and since then had amassed quite a fortune. Between the two of them they had the money and the know-how to run the iron works. In April 1808, three-fourths interest in the Weymouth Iron Works was deeded to Richards and Ball. Since construction of the "New Meeting House" started in 1806 and Samuel Richards did not appear on the scene until late 1807 and early 1808, it is highly unlikely that he was in any position to commit any funds from the Weymouth Iron Works to the construction of a church for the iron workers.

The time books of the Weymouth Iron Works show the carpentry to have been done by Eziel Prickett and his son. The father received $1.25 per day and worked three hundred and sixty-five days. The son, apparently less skilled, received only $1.00 per day, but worked one day more than his father. The plastering and mason work was done by C. McCormick. Altogether the material and labor for the construction of the meeting house came to $3,690.

All of the work was done by hand. The weather-boards were of hand-grooved cedar. The cedar joists were held in place by wooden pegs, turned from the hard wood of locust trees. Originally, the pulpit and pews were the same ones used in the log meeting house. A stove, cast at the Weymouth foundry, took the chill out of the air for Sunday services.

In the cemetery, which was laid out in 1754, the grave markers cast of Jersey bog iron can still be seen, as well as wooden markers more than a century old and stones of a more recent vintage. Perplexing to the champion of modern-day technology is the fact that the grave markers made from Jersey bog iron have not rusted, despite being exposed to the elements for almost two hundred years!

The Weymouth meeting house was originally established as a non-sectarian place to hold religious services for the benefit of the Weymouth iron workers. The records show that it was used chiefly by the Presbyterians and Methodists, although services were conducted by Episcopalians, Baptists, Dutch Reformed, and, in February 1825, a Miss Miller, probably of the Quaker faith, preached a sermon there. The incorporation of the Board of Trustees of the Weymouth Methodist Episcopal Church in 1810 was recorded on May 25, 1811, at the Court House in Woodbury, but there is no evidence that they ever owned the meeting house. In 1853, Weymouth was listed as a class meeting on the Mays Landing circuit.

The fortunes of the Weymouth meeting house were directly connected with the fortunes of the Weymouth iron and paper industries. By 1862, the Weymouth Iron Works had closed, and, although the paper mills survived for a few more years, they succumbed by the turn of the century. With its industry gone, Weymouth became a ghost town, and regular services at the meeting house ceased. Except for an annual anniversary service and an occasional church school, Weymouth slept until 1959. The decay of the iron and paper industries became its death-knell in the later 1800s. The decay of the big cities was to be its resurrection in the middle 1900s. A great exodus from the cities began in the 1950s, and homes were reestablished in this forgotten area. In April 1959, services in a church school were again organized under the Mays Landing Church. In October of the same year, the congregation was constituted a Methodist Society. Dr. John Henry Trescher of Baltimore, who had become the owner of the old Weymouth plantation, donated the meeting house and four acres of land to the new Methodist congregation.

The pendulum has swung, and once again regular services are held every Sunday in this historic old meeting house, which served the spiritual needs of the iron and paper workers so many years ago. Repairs to the building have been made and automatic heating added to comply with the necessities of modern-day living, but the old meeting house remains basically as it was when the sounds of the iron works and paper mills could be heard throughout the area.

XXXIII

Batsto-Pleasant Mills United Methodist Church

Batsto, 1808

cottish exiles were the first white settlers in the Batsto-Pleasant Mills area, refugees from the brutal war waged by Charles II against the Church of Scotland. Having fled to this land, they found sanctuary at first with the Quakers who had settled in southern New Jersey. Desiring a place of their own in this virgin wilderness, they followed in the footsteps of one of the earliest explorers, for whom the Mullica River is named. A Swede, Eric Mullica, sailed up the river which now bears his name in 1645 and established the first white settlement around Lower Bank. Friendly Indians, the Lenni Lenape, traveled throughout this region, and, according to tradition, spent the summer at a place about eight miles northwest at the forks of the Mullica and Batsto Rivers. The Indians called it "Nescochaque," and a lake and stream still bear this name.

To the early settlers it was known as "The Forks"; it was referred to by this name until 1821, when William Lippincott built a cotton mill there. The plant was called "The Pleasant Mills of Sweetwater," and from that time on the town was called "Pleasant Mills."

It was in 1707 that the Scottish exiles settled at The Forks. They were deeply religious people, and, according to legend, immediately erected a meeting house for worship services. In fact, this was the first

317

Batsto-Pleasant Mills United Methodist Church, erected in 1808.

building they constructed. As can be imagined, it was not very elaborate. The twenty-five by thirty foot building was erected in one day between sunrise and sunset. The walls were simple, unhewn logs, and the floor was just the native clay. To complete the construction by sunset, they thatched the roof with dried, matted grass. Later, a more permanent roof of cedar boards covered with cedar shingles was constructed.

This meeting house was in use for over fifty years, serving an everexpanding community. The Forks, located at the confluence of two navigable rivers, attracted settlers, smugglers, and entrepreneurs of various types. Because of the abundance of Jersey pine and cedar, and the ease of transportation down the Mullica River, sawmills became a flourishing industry. Jersey cedar was used for paneling in houses as far away as New York. Piracy and smuggling were not uncommon occupations at the time, and The Forks provided an ideal haven, located a considerable distance inland for protection, and yet on a navigable river with plenty of inlets and wooded areas for hiding places. For the settlers, although the "livin" was not easy, there were large, pleasant meadows in which to build their log cabins and to grow food. The woods nearby provided game aplenty for their table, and the many streams, unpolluted in those primeval days, abounded in fish of all kinds. It was an attractive, picturesque area, with pleasant surroundings and the opportunity of making a livelihood in whatever direction a man's inclination turned.

But progress brings change, and the little log meeting house was no longer able to serve the needs of the growing community. Although the actual dimensions have been lost to history, a larger structure was built in 1762. This became known as "Clark's Little Log Meeting House," named for the man who built and donated it to the people of The Forks. Elijah Clark was the youngest of four sons of Thomas and Hannah Clark, who had established a home as well as a town seven miles below The Forks known as "Clark's Landing." Just before reaching his thirtieth birthday, young Elijah decided to make The Forks his home. He acquired a total of seventy acres, fifty of which were on Lake Nescochaque, and it was here in 1762 that he build his homestead. Clark was a deeply religious Presbyterian, as were the majority of the people in the area at that time, being descendants of the original Scottish exiles. As a result, it was the Presbyterian itinerant preachers who visited the new meeting house. The Reverend John Brainerd records in his journal of April 26, 1762 that he "preached for the first time in the new meeting house." This would indicate that the meeting house was erected in the early part of 1762. Rev. Brainerd was so impressed by the new structure that he leaves a picture of it for posterity, describing it as small in size, built of hand-hewn logs with great red cedar beams, a clapboard floor, and hand-hewn shingles for the roof.

Unfortunately, very few records of its early activities exist. Apparently the meetings were conducted by traveling preachers when they reached the area. When such professional help was not available, Elijah Clark would conduct the services. In those days, the itinerant preacher was the backbone of the small wilderness churches. They were very devoted and devout men who covered an immense wilderness on horseback, undergoing extreme hardships to follow their calling.

Besides John Brainerd, another well-known itinerant preacher who conducted services in Clark's Little Log Meeting House was the Reverend Phillip Vickers Fithian. He was a frequent visitor to the area, and described Elijah Clark as a man "of integrity and piety," and had high praise, also, for the "good and useful Mrs. Clark." The members of the meeting must have been very astute and critical subjects, not given to blind acceptance of whatever sermons the traveling men had to offer. Rev. Fithian sounds a little plaintive in discussing the reaction of the audience on the occasion of one of his preaching missions there. He states that it would be a natural assumption for the natives of such a wilderness area to admire anyone who had enough assurance to stand up and be heard. Instead, the audience was not very receptive unless there was "good speaking, good sense, sound divinity, and neatness and cleanliness in the person and dress of the preacher." This does not sound like a "backwoods" congregation.

It was understandable that the congregation wanted good preaching, as a certain amount of courage was required to travel about in those days and to attend services. The Forks was not only a haven for smugglers, but was a stamping grounds for a notorious gang of more than one hundred ruffians who burned and plundered wherever they saw fit and whatever would benefit them. This was Joe Mulliner's gang, feared throughout The Forks area. A story is told that a widow,

Mrs. Bates, whose four sons were serving in the Continental Army, was returning from a meeting at Clark's Little Log House, and found Mulliner's gang ransacking her house. Mrs. Bates, a courageous woman, did not flee the scene, but instead told the gang in no uncertain terms her opinion of them. Whereupon they set fire to the house and tied the widow to a nearby tree, as she helplessly watched her home burn to the ground. Mulliner was not with them at that particular time, and, according to the story, a few weeks later the widow received an anonymous gift of three hundred dollars. Supposedly, this was sent by Mulliner to make amends for the heinous crime committed by his gang. Few people believed, however, that Joe Mulliner was graced with such a repentant nature. He finally paid for all his crimes by being tried, convicted, and hanged in Burlington. His body was returned to his wife, who buried him alongside the Weekstown-Pleasant Mills Road.

Clark's Little Log Meeting House faithfully served the community for almost forty years, but, like the little meeting house before it, the time of its usefulness was quickly drawing to a close. Charles Read had started his Batsto Furnace in 1766, and the Revolutionary War had helped this enterprise grow into a large industrial complex. By now the descendants of the Scottish exiles were the minority, and Methodism was on the rise. The first Methodist Bishop in America, Francis Asbury, had been active all through this region, and the fruits of his inspirational organizational ability were evident in the number of his converts.

By this time, Elijah Clark's property had changed hands a number of times, and was now owned by Joseph Ball. He in turn sold it to Samuel Richards and Clayton Earl on August 24, 1796. One important aspect of this sale was the fact that Joseph Ball excluded from the sale the two acres occupied by the meeting house and cemetery. Title for these two acres remained with Joseph Ball and his wife, Sarah. Measured by the standards of his day, Ball was a wealthy man.

Besides owning vast tracts of land in New Jersey and surrounding states, he was involved in the founding of Weymouth Iron Works and was an original director of the Insurance Company of North America.

By the turn of the century, it was apparent that Clark's Little Log Meeting House would have to be replaced with a larger structure. Simon Lucas was pastor at the time, and he was indeed a colorful character. At various times he was a farmer, philosopher, Captain of the Gloucester Militia, and lay preacher. According to the folklore of the area, he "got religion" from the itinerant preacher, John Brainerd, and was very definite in his opinions and vocal in their dissemination. He diligently watched and jealously guarded the morals of his flock in the entire Forks area. Who is to argue whether the growth of the congregation was the result of Simon Lucas's flaming oratory or the natural growth caused by the expanding Batsto Iron Works? Suffice it to say that a board of trustees was formed to consider the construction of a larger place of worship. The members of this board were Simon Lucas, William and Jesse Richards, George Peterson, G. Gibson Ashcroft, John Morgan, and Laurence Peterson. Romantic legend would have us believe that Jesse Richards, the Baron of Batsto, donated the land for the new church. Actually, the two acres on which the present church stands were deeded by Joseph Ball to the trustees on October 10, 1808. The romantic notion that Jesse Richards donated the land is easily understood since Jesse, an Episcopalian, was a very religious man who offered his home to the traveling preachers of all denominations, and who loved to argue with the Quakers and Presbyterians. He believed completely in religious freedom, employing for his ironworks those of different persuasions so that many sects were represented. Since there was no Catholic church in the area, he built St. Mary's of the Assumption for his Catholic workers.

Batsto-Pleasant Mills United Methodist Church

The new church was built in a pleasant grove of Jersey cedars, pines, and oaks, practically on the foundations of Clark's Little Log Meeting House. It took three months to build, and was dedicated by the first Methodist Bishop of the United States, Francis Asbury. But Jesse Richards's influence was still strongly felt, as the church was made nondenominational and was to be used for public worship by the ministers of any Christian denomination.

Simon Lucas, minister of Clark's Little Log Meeting House, continued his ministry in the new church, much loved by his parishioners despite his austere manner and forthright condemnation of the pleasures of the world. Apparently, he ruled his flock with an iron hand, and was not bashful in publicly denouncing any breach in strict Christian deportment as judged by him. Flashy clothes might be alright at certain times, but certainly not in church on a Sunday morning, where such attire could distract the minds of the congregation from the sermons being preached. One Sunday morning a young woman, not known to the congregation, entered the church very scintillatingly dressed and sat in the front pew. As Simon arose to announce the hymn, the reflection from a large brooch she was wearing flashed in his eyes. Distracted himself, Simon roared, "Young woman, do you know that shiny thing on you dress reminds me of the devil's eye?" Flustered and embarrassed, the young lady left the church. Simon Lucas had saved his congregation from the "handiwork of the devil," and went on to preach a powerful sermon.

Another story is told which reflects his understanding, rather than his austerity. One Sunday morning a large run of herring appeared in Atison Creek. The stream was so full that both sides of the bank were covered with flopping fish. People in the area depended a great deal on fish for food, so the temptation to fill their larders, Sunday or not, was too great to resist. Therefore, when a man came into church during services and announced "herrings up," the male members quickly fled the church to take advantage of a God-given opportunity.

Greatly shocked at their irreverent action, Jesse Richards's daughter asked her father why he didn't stop the men from fishing on Sunday. Replying that he didn't think he had the right, he volunteered to ask Rev. Lucas. Later in the day, when his daughter asked him what Rev. Lucas had said about such misconduct, Jesse Richards replied that the Reverend had advised: "The time to catch herring is when the herring are here to catch." Remembering the lady with the brooch, Jesse Richards's daughter might have thought that Simon Lucas, being a man, did not condone the favorite pastime of women, but condoned the favorite pastime of men.

Simon Lucas lived to be 87 years old, dying on August 10, 1838. Hannah, his wife, died February 5, 1836, at the age of 83. Both of them had been members of the church for more than sixty years, and, as the epitaph on their stone reads, "during that time were distinguished as most exemplary and zealous followers of Christ."

Mrs. Elizabeth Mick, a present member and life-long resident of the area and who has many ancestors buried in the cemetery alongside the church, gave us the following account of earlier services:

> We used to have very severe winters, and we didn't have anything but the old pot-bellied stove. We'd go out and get twigs, or maybe send the children out to get twigs to burn in the stove. The minister used to come down and stand around the stove and gather his congregation and preach from there, instead of from the pulpit. The pot-bellied stove is the original stove that was in the church from the beginning. We used to have quite a time. We would polish the stove, which was a very mean and nasty job, with the black stove polish. We would sort of take turns with the polishing.
>
> The doors of the church have never been closed. They have had services ever since the church opened. But the

doors would have been closed if it hadn't been for Rev. Charles Evell. He used to come and preach and the people would give whatever change they had. In the olden days we didn't give like we give now. Of course, they didn't have it. His salary was whatever the collection brought. I remember one Sunday when there was only thirty cents in the collection plate. He wore glasses and quite often would forget them. I would say, "Reverend, use mine!" Many times he preached the sermon using my glasses.

One of the ways we had of raising money for the minister was to sell honey. There are a lot of bees around here, and we would gather the honeycombs and sell the honey.

An exciting evangelist who would preach occasionally was Finney Mahan. He had been a jockey, but had been sent to prison for crowding another jockey off the course. While in prison, he studied to become an evangelist, and was ordained a minister in the Methodist church. When he preached, he would get so excited he would jump over the altar rail and show us how he used to ride the horses.

In recent years the development of the historic Batsto area by the state of New Jersey has created many problems for the church. Because of the many visitors to the Batsto historic site, the church is no longer able to post signs directing people to the church, as the signs are taken as souvenirs. Many things have been taken from the cemetery, and the stones broken or desecrated. This has placed an added burden on the church, since it is supported only by private contributions and the weekly offering. No special funds are received from any other source, despite the historical importance of the church and cemetery, not from the Methodists, not from the state, nor from any historical society.

The church has been proud of its heritage, and had preserved many of its important possessions in a trophy case in the back of the church so that members and visitors alike could enjoy them. As if to emphasize the problem the church has experienced in recent years, this trophy case was broken into in August, 1975, and all of these irreplaceable articles stolen. Among the stolen items was the first Bible used by Bishop Francis Asbury. The pages were turning yellow and the cover was worn smooth. It was presented to the church on November 4, 1810, by Mrs. Elizabeth Richards Haskins, sister of Jesse Richards. There were two other Bibles in the trophy case, one published in 1858 and the other in 1861. These were taken along with two hymnals for Sunday school, one published in 1856 and the other in 1869.

As tragic as this loss is to the church and to the community at large, the Batsto-Pleasant Mills United Methodist Church is looking to the future. The doors of the church have never been closed, and it is the intention of the present members that they never will be. Although the hey-dey of the church has passed, a small, loyal group, consisting to a great extent of the descendants of the early members, keeps the church alive and active. Even though the number of worshippers cannot compare to the crowds of the early 1800s, when as many as 3,000 would come to hear the Rev. Charles Pitman preach, the church provides an active ministry for those in the area and to any of the visitors who might be interested in attending one of the oldest churches in South Jersey.

XXXIV

Friends Meeting

Medford, 1814

ioneer Robert Braddock arrived from England in 1702 and in 1709 married Elizabeth Hancock, daughter of Timothy Hancock, who had settled on Pennsauken Creek near Moorestown. He departed this life a short five years later in 1714. It was his son, Robert, who conveyed one acre of ground to Hugh Sharp and others for the use of Friends on December 11, 1759. On this acre the first schoolhouse was erected, and it was in this schoolhouse that the Friends held their meetings for worship as early as 1761. Approval was given by the Evesham Monthly Meeting according to the minute of December 12, 1760: "Friends from ye preparative meetings at Evesham request that a meeting for worship might be held at ye Schoolhouse near Robert Braddocks, on ye first first Day and on ye Second Sixth Day in each month: which was granted until our general Spring meeting next." Medford Friends had been attending worship services prior to this time at Evesham, now know as Mount Laurel.

It was obviously their intention to build a meeting house of their own since a subscription list was started in 1760. In 1762, a frame meeting house was built about fifty yards southwest of the present structure as an L-shaped addition to the schoolhouse. This was the

Medford Friends Meeting, built in 1814.

only house of worship in the entire area until 1805, when the Baptists erected a church at Eves Causeway east of Marlton. The meeting house was built facing south, which was a common practice in those days, since this gave the greatest protection to the worshippers from the cold north winds. It faced the road or lane leading down to Landing Bridge. At that time Union Street, on which the present meeting house stands, was not yet surveyed.

Upper Evesham was considered an "Indulged Meeting" until 1782, when the Preparative Meeting of Upper Evesham was established, according to the December 1782 minute of the Evesham Monthly Meeting: "Most of the committee appointed in consequence of a request made by this Meeting respecting the establishment of a

Meeting for worship at upper Evesham now attended; and informed that they had a solid opportunity with Friends of that Meeting & are united in Judgment that may be for the benefit of Society that not only a Meeting for Worship but also a preparative meeting be established there; which after mature deliberation, this Meeting unites with the Judgment of the said Committee therein."

In 1782 Hugh Sharp, the only surviving trustee of the acre of land given by Robert Braddock, conveyed the same acre to John Haines, Jr., Daniel Braddock, Job Collins, Joseph Sharp, Josiah Stratton, and Joshua Owen. These men had been named by the Meeting to take title to the land. Upper Evesham Monthly Meeting was established December 1793, and the first session held on January 11, 1794. The Monthly Meeting was composed of Cropwell, New Hopewell, and Upper Evesham Preparative Meetings.[1]

Medford Friends met in the old frame meeting house for over fifty years, after which it was no longer considered adequate. At a Preparative Meeting held July 30, 1812, a committee was chosen to consider the feasibility of enlarging the existing frame building or of constructing a new one. Members of the committee were John Haines, Job Haines, Benjamin Davis, Josiah Reeve, Joshua Stokes, Joseph Haines, William Page, William Stockton, and Japhet Garwood. At the Preparative Meeting held on September 3, 1812, the committee reported that it was their considered opinion that a new meeting house should be built rather than the old one repaired. They estimated that a meeting house seventy-six by thirty-eight feet in overall dimensions would be necessary to accommodate the members, and that the cost would be about $3,600. The Meeting lost no time in accepting the committee's report and in authorizing Job Collins, Josiah Reeve, Brazilla Braddock, Core Haines, and William Reeve to take subscriptions to cover the cost of the building.

In the meantime the building committee was busy laying out plans for the new Meeting house, and the dimensions were fixed at seventy-four feet long and forty-two feet wide. At the Upper Evesham Preparative Meeting held on September 30, 1813, the building committee recommended that the Meeting accept the plans and that construction should start the following summer. Managers were appointed to employ workers and to oversee the actual construction. These men were William Reeve, Joseph Haines, Robert Braddock, Joshua Stokes, Josiah Reeve, Benjamin Davis, and Isaac Wilson. Apparently no major problems developed, and the managers were able to report to the Preparative Meeting on August 4, 1815, that the job was completed. They submitted the following report:

On the first subscription paper	*$3,229.56-1/2*
On the second subscription paper	*710.00*
From non-subscribers	*223.40*
Private sale materials	*56.55*
Interest on vendue book	*1.08-1/2*
Last public sale of remnants	*33.52*
Sale of old meeting house, etc.	*326.32-1/2*
	$4,580.44-1/2

Accounted for as follows:	
To offset with various subscribers for	
Material and labor furnished	*$1,521.44*
Cash paid for white pine logs	*254.00*
Cash paid for making bricks	*380.00*
Cash paid for bricks bought	*70.50*
Cash paid for lime	*192.00*
Cash paid for stone	*60.00*
Cash paid for shingles	*240.00*
Cash paid for carpenter work	*990.00*
Cash paid for mason work	*378.25*

Cash paid for stoves and pipes	*125.00*
Cash paid for nails, spikes, hinges, paint, etc.	*339.42*
	$4,550.61
Leaving in the hands of the treasurer	*29.83-1/2*

Although the building was not quite finished, the first Meeting, a Monthly Meeting, was held in it on February 15, 1815. As soon as the meeting house was completed, the trustees took the unusual step of contributing $10.00 towards the purchase of a fire engine. Leather buckets costing $8.00 were also purchased, to be used for carrying water from an old well on the meeting house grounds. The firehouse stood on the northeast corner of the meeting house yard, and on the right was the old well. At that time the horse sheds came up to the firehouse, and the property was enclosed by a wooden fence.

Of prime concern to the Friends was the education of their youth. Despite the heavy expenses of building a new meeting house, the members of this Meeting built school houses at Medford, Fostertown, Southampton, and Hartford, now known as Shamong. The Hartford school was on the Reservation at Indian Mills. None of these schools is now under the care of the Friends. The one in Medford was closed in 1898 because of small enrollment. In 1905, it was remodeled as a lunchroom and used especially by the Quarterly Meeting. Through the years, as a result of the generous donations of time and money, the school house has been made more serviceable by the addition of electricity and an oil burner. It is now used for many purposes including First-day school.

The Separation of the Society of Friends in 1827–28 affected the Upper Evesham Meeting as it did so many others.[2] The majority of the members were Orthodox, and they maintained control of the meeting house. However, there were some who had been influenced by the theology of Elias Hicks, the Long Island farmer, and they withdrew from the Meeting. In 1842–43, the Hicksites built their own meeting house on Main Street, just around the corner from the Orthodox meeting house. The ground and a large part of the funds used to build the meeting house were donated by Benjamin Davis, but he died in the meeting house before it was finished. He was on his way to Philadelphia to buy some hardware needed for the building, and had stopped at the meeting house to look around to see what else was required, when he had an apparent heart attack and dropped dead on the floor.

The Separation caused many problems, not the least of which was the control of the property and the division of funds. The plight that the Hicksite Friends found themselves in is graphically portrayed by this excerpt from one of their minutes: "The treasurer of the school funds and the settlement of his accounts is wholly confined within the power at this time of our opposing Friends, the treasurer being one of their number."

For the next one hundred years these two groups went their separate ways. On November 29, 1928, a concern was expressed by Emily Forsythe in the Upper Evesham Preparative Meeting that the principles of peace should be extended to the Main Street Friends. However, the bitterness generated by one hundred years of separation could not be easily overcome, and it was not until 1941 that committees were appointed by the two groups to confer on First-day school and on Meeting matters as they came up. This was the start of cooperation between the two opposing groups. In 1945, a joint First-day school was started, and the two Meetings worshiped together once a month. Finally, in June 1955, the two Monthly Meetings appointed a joint committee to explore the possibilities of uniting Upper Evesham and Medford Monthly Meetings. Edward T. Pennock and Justus C. Brick were clerks of their respective Monthly Meetings at this time. The Quarterly Meeting held in Moorestown in December 1955 granted permission for these two Meetings to form one

Monthly Meeting under the name Medford United Monthly Meeting. The properties are still held separately, however. The Union Street meeting house and grounds are under the care of Upper Evesham Preparative Meeting, and the Main Street property is cared for by the Medford Preparative Meeting.

Extensive repairing and remodeling was done to the Orthodox meeting house during the years 1845 through 1847. At that time the lobbies were added, new porches built and the horse sheds enlarged to accommodate thirty-four carriages. Such a program costs money, and each of the members was assessed a fair share of the expenses. Apparently all assessments were met, as there are no records of delinquent accounts. In keeping with their beliefs, the Friends were sympathetic to anyone in distress. One member fell and broke his leg just at this time and was unable to work. Rather than letting his assessment fall into arrears, it was assumed by other members, and he was completely released from his obligation.

A campaign was started in 1911 to improve and beautify the graveyard. Considerable effort was made to locate old stones, some of which were nearly a foot underground. An iron probe was used to find their location. Some of the stones were in perfect condition and bore dates from the middle 1700s. The oldest stone is dated 1759 and marked M.S. This is considered to be the stone that marks the grave of Mark Stratton, who died on April 3, 1759, at the age of sixty-nine. It is believed that he came from England in 1702 with Robert Braddock. Elizabeth Collins is also buried in this old graveyard. She was the first recorded minister of the Evesham Meeting. She became a minister in 1779 and died on February 1, 1831 in her seventy-seventh year, having been a minister for over fifty years. The stone marking the grave of Isaac Walton can also be found. He was a soldier in the Civil War and was buried by the government in the Friends graveyard.

Over the years, additional land had been obtained by the Meeting. The following is an account of the deeds by which the property is held:

Robert Braddock	December 22, 1759	one acre
John Braddock	November 20, 1784	one-quarter acre
Cornelius Brannin	August 20, 1786	four acres
Daniel Braddock	August 28, 1790	small strip
Nicholas Hoile	May 3, 1810	16 square perches
Jane Sleeper	May 3, 1810	6 square perches
Mark Reeve	June 5, 1811	6-4/10 perches
John Taylor	November 23, 1814	5-9/10 perches
Lawrence Webster	April 29, 1812	5 rods
Daniel Braddock	July 1802	1 acre, 4 perches
Job Lippincott	March 25, 1830	27 perches
Robert B. Stokes	October 27, 1847	12 perches
Barclay E. Haines	December 30, 1852	8/100 acres

First day services are still held in these two beautifully maintained red brick meeting houses. Worship services from June through September are held in the Main Street meeting house, and during the rest of the year in the Union Street meeting house. Although the congregation of the Meeting is not as large as it once was, there are still about 135 adults, with twenty to thirty members in attendance at the First day services.

---

1. *The Historic Rancocas*, by George DeCou.

2. See Chapter II on Friends Meeting, Woodbury.

XXXV

Cold Spring Presbyterian Church

Cold Spring, 1823

ounded by whalers in 1714, Cold Spring Presbyterian Church has seen the area change from a wild, forbidding peninsula of marsh lands three miles inland from the ocean with thick cedar forests to the north, to a fashionable resort area famous for its beaches and beautiful climate. Whaling was the first occupation for the Dutch settlers in the Cape May area, which had been discovered by Captain Cornelius Jacobsen Mey in 1620. It was the British, however, who made whaling a successful commercial venture. It was they, rather than the Dutch, who left a lasting impression on the area by Anglicizing the name to May. These hardy pioneers ventured out in the waters of the Delaware Bay in small boats to battle huge mammals weighing as much as 250 tons. Strange as it may seem to us today, whales were very numerous then, and the British made large quantities of "oyle and whalebone" from their catches. William Penn took notice of this lucrative enterprise when he wrote that one whale could bring as much as $4,000.

It was in September 1714 that a petition was presented to the Philadelphia Presbytery for the ministry of John Bradner. The petition was presented by David Wells in the name of the people of Cape May. Families of Presbyterian persuasion had been meeting for some

Cold Spring Presbyterian Church, built in 1823.

time at Coxe Hall, the home of Dr. Daniel Coxe. Mr. Bradner was a Scotchman, educated at Edinburgh University, who had been preaching to these people for some time without official authority. According to Presbytery's records, he was licensed to preach in March 1714. After preaching a trial sermon on Philippians 2: 12, 13 he received a call from the congregation and became the first settled minister. His ordination took place on May 6, 1715.

A log meeting house was built in the year 1718. It was erected in the center of a compact, almost solid Presbyterian constituency of sixty families in an area seven miles long and from one to seven miles wide. Those within hearing distance were summoned to worship services by the bellowing of a conch shell, or by the beat of a drum, or by the town crier. The meeting houses were plain in those days, in keeping with their hard lives and their strict Calvinistic principles. The morning service started at nine o'clock and lasted for several hours. In front of the pulpit on a low platform sat the deacons facing the congregation. On a platform a little higher than the deacons sat the ruling elders. Above them was the pulpit. The minister started the service with a solemn prayer lasting about fifteen minutes. After the prayer the minister read and discussed a chapter from the Bible. Then a psalm was sung by the congregation, but no musical instruments were allowed. The precentor stood in front of the pulpit, and he would read two lines of the psalm and then lead the congregation in singing it. This would be repeated for the entire psalm. Finally came the sermon, which could last well over an hour, timed by an hourglass resting on the pulpit. The congregation was dismissed after a short prayer, the singing of another psalm, and the benediction.

This log structure stood near the road and to the right of the present building. The road was then just a sand trail made by the Indians. Nearby are the shell mounds where the Indians made wampum. The building was called simply "The Meeting House." Rev. Bradner remained as minister until 1721, when he left to become pastor of the church in Goshen, New York. Before leaving, he deeded to the Board of Trustees his estate of about 200 acres in perpetuity for the use of the pastors of the Cold Spring Presbyterian Church. The Board of Trustees was composed of the following thiry-two men:

Humphrey Hughes	Nathaniel Hand
Yelverson Crowell	George Hand
Barnabas Crowell	Josiah Crowell
John Parsons	Jehu Richardson
William Mulford	Joseph Whildin
George Crawford	William Matthews

James Spicer	Benjamin Stites
Samuel Bancroft	Shamgar Hand
Jeremiah Hand	Eleazer Nocault
Joshua Gulickson	Samuel Eldredge
Joshua Crawford	Samuel Johnston
Ezekiel Eldredge	Samuel Foster
Constant Hughes	Eleazer Newton
John Matthews	Cornelius Schellenger
Nathaniel Norton	Nathaniel Rex
John Hand	Recompense Furman

These thirty-two men and their descendants have been the principal supporters of the church ever since.

After Rev. Bradner left there wasn't a settled minister until 1752, except in the year 1726, when Hughston Hughes was pastor. His ministry was terminated quickly when it was discovered that he had a great fondness for intoxicating liquor. Traveling ministers supplied the pulpit with marked ability. One of these, Rev. Samuel Finley, became the fifth President of Princeton College. In the winter of 1745, Rev. Daniel Hunter, pastor of the Greenwich Presbyterian Church, preached there and appointed the first elders. Unfortunately, their names have been lost, since the earliest available records start from 1754. The names of the ruling elders in that year were James Whildon, Richard Stillwell, and Samuel Bancroft.

In 1761, a frame meeting house was built to replace the log structure. This, too, was called simply "The Meeting House." It was built during the pastorate of the Rev. Daniel Lawrence, was larger than the log meeting house, and was built close to the road near the old cemetery gate. Rev. Daniel Lawrence has an interesting background, as he was first a blacksmith and then had worked with the renowned Indian missionary, Rev. John Brainerd. After Lawrence's death in 1766, Rev. Brainerd supplied the pulpit during the winter of 1769–70.

The next settled minister was the Rev. James Watt, who took charge on May 12, 1770, and served for over 18 years until his death in 1789. Rev. Watt was a sincere and dedicated pastor, with a sense of humor and a forceful personality. One Sunday Rev. Watt preached a sermon on the evils of strong drink. A drunkard in the neighborhood was offended, thinking that the minister was pointing a finger at him. On a subsequent Sunday he accosted Rev. Watt and demanded an apology. The minister denied any personal application of the sermon to the offended man and refused to apologize, whereupon the man slapped him. Following the biblical injunction Rev. Watt turned the other cheek, and the drunkard immediately slapped him again. According to the story, Reverend Watt addressed the man as follows: "The Bible tells me if a person slaps me on one cheek to turn the other cheek. I have done all the Bible instructs me to. Now I am going to give you a thrashing." This he proceeded to do until the man cried "enough." The minister then helped to bathe the man's wounds and took him home in his own carriage. On the way he stopped the carriage, got out with the drunkard, knelt down on the ground with him and prayed that the drunkard might be given strength to overcome his weakness. Much to the amazement of the congregation, the drunkard, his wife, and children came to church the following Sunday. The story ends there, but we might assume that he became a member of the church and found the strength to resist his fondness for strong drink.

One of Rev. Watt's favorite pastimes was fishing, and this hobby can either demonstrate a man's ill-temper or his good humor. On one occasion, when he was fishing in the Delaware Bay with two other clergymen, Rev. Watt caught a large devil fish. The fish was so powerful that it began to pull the boat toward the open sea. While the others became alarmed, Watt saw the humor of the situation and broke forth with peals of laughter. Indignantly the other two clergymen asked him what was so hilarious. Rev. Watt replied that he couldn't conceal his mirth at the thought of three ministers being abducted by the devil.

One of the elders of the church was Isaac Smith, who was an undertaker, coffin maker, and justice of the peace. Between 1793 and 1821, he made 327 coffins. It is interesting to note the charges that applied in those days:

Opening grave	*$1.00*
Shroud	*2.00*
Cap and handkerchief	*1.00*
Walnut coffin	*12.50*

It had been apparent for some time that the old frame meeting house was no longer adequate for the needs of the congregation. The present beautiful brick church was erected in 1823, after considerable discussion as to its size and structure. One of the strongest proponents for a large, spacious, brick building was the energetic Thomas H. Hughes. Mr. Hughes refused to accept any arguments for a smaller church saying, "My head will not be laid in the grave before this church is full." He lived to see his hopes and prophecy fulfilled.

The bricks were brought from Philadelphia by boat to Town Bank, and then hauled by wagon teams to the building site. Two stoves were provided in the church, one near the pulpit and one near the center of the sanctuary. Candles were used for lighting, later replaced by kerosene lamps. It was not unusual for landowners in New Jersey to own slaves in the early days of the church, and stalls were provided in the east end of the gallery for them so that they, too, could worship in the church. However, there was a considerable difference in the accommodations provided the slaves and those provided the plantation owners. The slave stalls did not have pews, and the slaves had to stand throughout the lengthy service.

As was the custom then, the pews were auctioned off to the highest bidders, the pews on the main floor going for a higher price than those in the gallery. The original pulpit stood high above the main floor and was reached by a winding staircase. The church was affectionately known as "Old Brick," and was the first brick church in the county.

One of the most prominent clergymen of the 19th century in this section of the country was the Rev. Moses Williamson. He was pastor of the Cold Spring Presbyterian Church from 1831 to 1873. Born May 7, 1802, in Newville, Pennsylvania, he graduated from Princeton Theological Seminary in 1828 and came to Cape May for his health in 1829. On August 16th of that year, he was asked to supply the pulpit and remained as supply until 1831, when he received a call from the congregation to become their settled pastor. He served the church for 44 years until April 18, 1873, when he asked to be relieved of the charge. He died at Cape Island October 30, 1880, at the age of 78, and is buried near the front entrance of the church where a beautiful marble monument was erected in his memory.

Rev. Williamson was an effective and hard-working minister. He preached every Sunday morning and Thursday evening at Cold Spring. At stated periods, he preached at Fishing Creek and Green Creek, and occasionally at Cape Island, formerly the name of Cape May City. Sensing the urgent need for a church for summer visitors, he set about with characteristic energy and perseverance to collect the necessary funds, largely from the summer visitors themselves.

In 1848, the "Visitor's Church" was dedicated, and Rev. Williamson conducted regular services on Sunday afternoons and Tuesday evenings. With the help of others, these services were continued until members of Cold Spring Church residing on Cape Island decided that they would like to organize their own congregation. A petition for such action was forwarded to Presbytery in 1850 and finally approved in 1851. This congregation used the Visitors' Church until 1853, when they decided to build a new sanctuary on Lafayette Street. The Visitors' Church was sold to the Methodists in 1854.

Important to seafaring men is the availability of fresh water. It is no wonder, then, that the original whalers who founded this church settled in this area. There was a cold spring of pure, fresh water constantly bubbling up in the midst of a salt marsh about 140 yards south of the church. It was from this spring that the church derived its name. Serving men of the sea in its early years, the church soon found itself serving the spiritual needs of nationally famous personages. Cape Island became the earliest bathing resort along the Atlantic Coast, and the fashionable resort visited by the early Presidents and members of congress. On August 24, 1890, Benjamin and Mrs. Harrison attended Sunday services. Henry Clay and Rev. Williamson became close friends as a result of Henry Clay's visit to Cape Island on August 16, 1847. John Wanamaker and Russell Conwell are other noted figures of their day who attended Cold Spring Presbyterian Church.

Another person who is not as well known but who has a vast following all over the Christian world was E. P. Stites. It was he who penned the famous hymns "Beulah Land" and "Simply Trusting, Every Day." The son of a Delaware River pilot by the name of Page Stites, he signed many of his hymns, including "Beaulah Land," under the pen name of "Edgar Page." When Uncle Joe Cannon, famous speaker of the House of Representatives, visited Cape Island, Stites wrote a poem in his honor. Cannon thanked Stites for the poem saying, "I would rather have written 'Beulah Land' than to have been President of the United States." This famous hymnologist died at the age of eighty-four and was buried in the "Old Brick" cemetery. He was a direct descendant of the first whalers who had come to Cape May in search of these huge mammals and in the process founded this venerable old church.

XXXVI

The Presbyterian Church at Woodbury

Woodbury, 1833

host stories have been told throughout the ages, but rarely have there been such ghosts as those that "haunted" the old log meeting house in Woodbury. These ghosts must have been very active and energetic, because their presence was so strongly felt that the brave patriots who had so valiantly fought in the Revolutionary War refused to enter their meeting house once it had been occupied by the British. History does not record the nature of these ghosts nor their appearance and particular activities, but some historians tell us that the British used the building as a commissary depot and others that it was used as a hospital. The weight of logic comes down heavily on the side of the hospital legend, however, since surely the ghosts of a commissary depot would not be as foreboding as the ghosts created by its use as a hospital.

Be that as it may, the fear engendered by the supposed presence of the ghosts was so overpowering that the log meeting house remained unused from the close of the Revolutionary War until 1803, when it had become so dilapidated that it was necessary to tear it down. The meeting house was built on one acre of land deeded by John Tatem, August 10, 1721 to William Allen, Joseph Redman, Joseph Shippen, Humphrey Morrey, and John Snowden, all from Philadelphia; Peter

The Presbyterian Church at Woodbury, built in 1833.

Long, John and Richard Crew, John Browne, and Alexander Randall, all from Gloucester County, for the sum of five pounds. This land was located at the north end of Woodbury, and one of the conditions under which the land was deeded was that it was to be held in trust for the purpose of a meeting house and burial ground for the Presbyterians. It is interesting to note that in those days the Presbyterians referred to their house of worship as a "meeting house," as did the Quakers.

Although their numbers were small, they immediately built their log meeting house. No records exist concerning the size of this building, nor the interior design, but it is known that it was located in the front center of the lot and partially across the present North Broad Street. In keeping with other log structures of the same type, it probably had wooden benches with straight backs for the "comfort" of the worshippers. The only heat would have been that created by the fervor of the worshippers. Outside, along the south side of the grounds, a row of carriage sheds was built. In 1731, the group was organized into a congregation consisting of ten families, who were ministered to by itinerant preachers. It was not until 1751 that the congregation enjoyed the services of their own minister. At that time a call was issued to the Rev. Benjamin Chestnut, who was installed and ordained in 1752. The call was issued jointly by the congregations of Woodbury and Timber Creek, now Blackwood, and was the beginning of the union of the two congregations that was to last until 1843, when the church at Blackwood felt strong enough to support its own minister. There was but one church until 1770, after which the two churches divided, although they had the same Session until 1828 and the same minister until 1843. The first Elders were Elijah Clark, John Sparks, and Charles Ogden.

For over fifty years the log meeting house served the people well. But then the shadow of the Revolutionary War fell over this small congregation, and many of its members volunteered their services.

Over two score of these early patriots are buried in the cemetery, including Elijah Clark and John Sparks, two of the three original Elders, both of who were prominent members of the Provincial Congress in 1776. The church was used by both the British and Continental Armies, and troops were bivouacked in the burying ground. As a result, the "ghosts" of the British occupation of the building prevented its further use, and it was allowed to deteriorate to the point that it was beyond repair and was finally sold for the value of the lumber.

These were hard times for the congregation. Rev. Andrew Hunter, nephew of the Rev. Andrew Hunter who had been pastor of the Greenwich and Deerfield Presbyterian Churches, reluctantly accepted the pastorate in 1787. He had an extensive army record as a chaplain with the Continental Troops. At the close of the war he was publicly thanked by General Washington for his valuable service at the Battle of Monmouth. In 1787, he served as a member of the Convention that met in Trenton to ratify the Constitution of the United States. His first wife, Nancy Riddle Hunter, is buried in the cemetery.

Rev. Hunter left Woodbury in 1797 and was followed by a number of supply ministers, none of whom stayed very long, as the congregation found it very difficult to pay their salaries. Despite these problems the people were not lacking in religious ardor. Maria Ogden, daughter of Charles Ogden, one of the original Elders, became one of the first missionaries to the Sandwich Islands in 1821. Serious thought, however, was given in 1824 to the idea of disbanding and uniting with the Episcopal Church at Clarksboro, even though they had the use of the Woodbury Academy building, which had been erected in 1791. The history of the Academy is interestingly intertwined with that of the Presbyterian Church. The land upon which the Academy was built was deeded by Joseph Bloomfield,[1] later Governor of New Jersey, to, among others, Rev. Andrew Hunter, who was the second stated minister of the Woodbury Church. The Academy was erected opposite the present church building, and permission was granted for church services to be held there. At first a portion of the school room was curtained off for this use, but in 1821, a second story was added to the building. The trustees of the Academy deeded the entire first floor to the church for the "free use and enjoyment of the celebration of divine worship as long as the present building shall stand." Two years earlier, the first trustees of the church had been elected, legally incorporated, and qualified before James Matlack, Justice of the Peace. They were Charles Ogden, Thomas Hendry, James Jaggard, Ephraim Miller, Amos Campbell, William A. Tatem, and James Dorman.[2] Twenty-six pews were installed and auctioned off, raising $460. Benjamin Smallwood was engaged as sexton at a salary of $18 per year. He was to sweep the floor as often as he found necessary, and to scrub the floor at least twice a year. Later the ringing of the bell was added to his duties with no increase in pay.

Slowly the congregation grew in numbers and spirit, and gradually the desire to erect a new church building began to surface. Mentioned at first by only a few, the idea took hold and the congregation began to give it serious thought. Finally, in 1833, under the leadership of Pastor Charles Williamson, construction was started on a two-story colonial style building with red brick and white trim. The following year the building was completed, and dedication ceremonies were held September 16, 1834. The trustees were Robert L. Armstrong, John Cade, William Scott, Ephraim Miller, William Roe, Dr. Joseph Fithian, and Richard Wells. Rev. Williamson personally took the job of collecting the pledges and negotiating a mortgage. Two years after the dedication, although his salary was only $300 per year, the congregation owed him $150 with no funds in sight. When the committee called upon him to discuss the situation, he resigned immediately, saying "they should not expect me to appear among them anymore in the future." The only income the church had came from the pew rentals. Rents were charged as follows: pews opening into the center aisle, $10; those opening into the wide aisles, $6; and those on each side of the pulpit, $4. The full amount was to be paid when they had the services of a regular minister and half the amount when the pulpit was empty. Whenever the church was behind in paying the minister's salary, the pew rents were raised. Since the congregation was almost always in debt to the minister, the rents were constantly being raised. Pew rents became so high that many families could not afford them. Some families found it necessary to rent only half a pew, and finally, for only one or two sittings. It soon became necessary to have special collections at some of the services, and eventually the special collection became part of each service. The system of pew rents was finally discontinued in 1921, when Rev. Herbert Ure was pastor.

By 1847, it was decided that definite regulations were necessary to govern the operation of the cemetery. The following rules were established: persons not belonging to the congregation at the time of a burial shall be required to pay the sum of $3 for each grave. Anyone having bought a grave could then buy a lot eight by fifteen feet at the time of the burial or within one year thereafter. The cost for this lot was $3 for every two-and-a-half feet, payable within one year of the time of purchase. Members of the congregation could select a lot not larger than eight by fifteen feet, free of charge.

Despite the attraction of the beautiful new building, the growth of the congregation was slow, as was the growth of the community. By 1862, there were only 58 members, with 70 enrolled in the Sunday School. Fifteen years later the membership was only 71, a net gain of only 13, but despite the slow growth, continued progress was made. For the first time, a parsonage was provided for the ministers. In July 1868, a lot was purchased on Euclid Street, and a few months later the manse was built. This served the various ministers until 1946, when it was sold and a new house purchased at 323 Delaware

Avenue. In 1878, a wooden chapel was built, about sixteen feet behind the church, which was used for a Sunday School until 1895, when it was replaced by a larger stone building. By 1906, the trustees became convinced that additional pew space was necessary to accommodate the increased membership. At this time a major renovation took place. The church building and chapel were connected, and the walls of the church were faced with the same type of stone used for the chapel; in fact, the stone was obtained from the same quarry. A pipe organ was installed, as were stained glass windows.[3] Finally, a tower for a church bell was added to the chapel, and therein lies an interesting story.

In 1789, there was an insurrection in Santo Domingo, and objects of great value were shipped out of the city to prevent their destruction. In one of the missions there was a bell that had been cast in Bordeaux, France, probably in the 12th century, the date of which can be determined by the relationship of its height to its width. Exactly how this bell reached Woodbury is another of those mysteries of early church history, but according to legend, General Franklin Davenport, nephew of Benjamin Franklin and one of the founders of the Woodbury Academy, is credited with the feat. Davenport and Stephen Girard, Philadelphia's business tycoon, were contemporaries. Girard had a fleet of boats that plied the seas from America to the West Indies. It may well be that one of Girard's boats brought the bell to Philadelphia, from where it was transported to the Woodbury Academy in around 1791. It was placed in the belfry of the Academy, where it was used to call the children to school and the congregation to church until the new Presbyterian Church was built in 1834.

By 1844, the Academy could no longer meet its financial obligations, and was sold by Mark Ware, the Sheriff, on June 23rd. The sale was held in the house of Richard Humphreys, who was an innkeeper in Woodbury. The entire property, including the bell, was purchased by John Harrison, who sold the bell on December 26, 1844, to the

Trustees of the Presbyterian Church for $100. Since the church building had no belfry, it remained in the belfry of the Academy, which was purchased by the Woodbury Free School in 1851. This brings us to 1906, when the renovation of the church took place, and a belfry was added to the chapel to accommodate the bell. The church could not use the bell, however, since the belfry, along with the rest of the building, was enclosed in stone. Apparently the esthetic beauty of the church property was considered more important than the beautiful tones of the tolling bell.

This situation was appropriately corrected in 1965, when the church undertook another major remodeling job, this time to restore the building to its original colonial appearance. The stone exterior was removed, along with the arched stained glass windows. A new red brick exterior, covering the old scarred bricks of 1834, and tall, graceful colonial-style windows of softly tinted glass restored the church's original look. At this time, the front of the church was extended to include a narthex, cloak-room, board room, and pastor's study. A cupola was added, which houses the convent bell brought from Santo Domingo in 1791. Now the beautiful sound of the bell, which was so unfortunately silenced for so many years, can be heard around the community, calling the people to worship.

---

1. See Chapters XXV and I, respectively, on Old Broad Street Church in Bridgeton and St. Mary's Protestant Episcopal Church in Burlington.

2. *History of the Counties of Gloucester, Salem and Cumberland,* by Thomas Cushing and Charles Sheppard.

3. The organ was built by Estey Organ Co. of Brattleboro, Vermont, at a cost of $3,000.

XXXVII

First Presbyterian Church

Greenwich, 1835

The night was cold and dark, as mysterious, shadowy figures moved in and out of a house just a few hundred yards from the river. As one's eyes became adjusted to the darkness, it could be seen that they were carrying large chests on their backs. It wasn't long before the darkness was dispelled by the light of a huge bonfire. Soon, the whole village was bathed in the glow of the crackling fire, and the figures of a score or more painted, feathered, Indians could be seen dancing around the bonfire.

For the past ten days the town had been buzzing about the arrival of the brig *Greyhound* with its consignment of tea from the East India Company in London. For several years now, the colonists had been infuriated with the various taxes placed upon them by the English government. There was a tax on almost everything, even the number of window panes in a house. Finally, a tax was placed on tea, which was one luxury the colonists could afford, and which they loved. On December 16, 1773, the Boston Tea Party had taken place, and on December 18, 1774, the people of Annapolis, Maryland forced a ship owner to burn his own vessel, the *Peggy Stewart*, which carried several chests of tea. The citizens of Philadelphia had turned back the

First Presbyterian Church of Greenwich, erected in 1835.

ship, *Polly*, which had a load of tea, refusing to allow it to dock in Philadelphia.

So it is no wonder that J. Allen, the Captain of the brig *Greyhound*, fearing the wrath of the colonists, put in at Greenwich on the night of December 12, 1774. He knew the name of a local loyalist, Daniel Bowen, who was considered "a safe man." In the darkness of the night, Captain Allen unloaded his cargo of tea and hid it in the basement of Daniel Bowen's house. Such an act could hardly be kept secret, however, and by noon of the next day word had spread all over town that English tea had been stored in Daniel Bowen's house. An indignation meeting was scheduled for Friday, December 23rd in Bridgeton, the County seat. There were others, however, who felt that direct action would accomplish more than any indignation meeting. On the night of the 22nd, these men gathered at the home of Richard Howell, near Shiloh, about four miles from Greenwich. It was from there that they rode down the Greenwich Road to the home of Phillip Vickers Fithian. They painted their faces and dressed like Indians so that they would not be recognized. Protected by the darkness of the night, they stole down to Daniel Bowen's house, carried the chests of tea outside, and set them on fire. The residents of Greenwich had declared their independence from the hated tea tax!

Practically all the "Indians" who participated in this raid were members of the First Presbyterian Church of Greenwich, including the nephew of the minister, Andrew Hunter, and the famed Phillip Vickers Fithian. Such a spirit of independence came naturally, as these men were descendants of the original Presbyterian settlers who had come from Scotland and Ireland to escape the tyranny of the Old World. They were joined by a large number of Congregationalists from Long Island and New England. They had never formed themselves into a religious society, but had worshipped as often as possible at Fairfield, on the south side of the Cohansey River, where a society of Congregationalists had been established with a settled minister. As their numbers increased, this practice became less desirable, and, in 1707, they formed a religious society for the purpose of securing ground on which to build a house of worship and for use as a burial ground.

As the original church records were destroyed in a fire that consumed the parsonage in 1739, their early activities are not precisely known. A Reverend Samuel Black apparently supplied the church for about three years, leaving in 1706 for Lewes, Delaware. The first meeting house was built of logs, across the street from the present church building in the area know as Head of Greenwich. A deed for one acre of land was given by Jeremiah Bacon to Henry Joyce and Thomas Maskell, trustees for the Society, on April 24, 1717. This acre of ground was given as a gift "for the love, affection, and good will which I bear to the people of the north side of the Cohansey, commonly called Presbyterians."

After Rev. Black left, the pulpit remained vacant until 1728. During those years, they invited supplies as often as they had the opportunity, either Presbyterian or Congregational, without any denominational distinctions. In 1721, an arrangement was made with the Fairfield congregation to share the services of their minister, an Irishman by the name of Henry Hook.[1] He agreed to devote one-third of his time to the Greenwich church, an arrangement which remained in effect until Hook was suspended by the Presbytery in 1722. Another effort by the congregation to secure a settled minister was made in 1724, when they called a young man from New England named Paris, but before he was ordained or installed, he became mentally deranged and was forced to leave the ministry.

A successful call was finally made to Rev. Ebenezer Goold (also spelled Gould), who was installed as pastor in 1728. He was born in Guilford, Connecticut, and had graduated from Yale College in 1723. Upon his installation the congregation appointed two deacons, and the church assumed the Congregational form of church authority, in accordance with the philosophy of the new minister. A year later, a piece of ground consisting of six acres was secured for five shillings, on which a parsonage was built. A deed, dated January 13, 1730 was given by Nicholas and Leonard Gibbon to "Josiah Fithian, Thomas Maskell and Noah Miller, in behalf of the Presbyterian or Descenting Presbyterian inhabitants of the north side of the Cohansey." The Gibbons were wealthy Episcopal landowners. While pastor, Rev. Goold married Amie Brewster, a sister of Francis Brewster, one of the elders of the church and a descendant of Elder Brewster, who landed with the *Mayflower* at Plymouth in 1620. The pastor and his wife lived in the newly erected parsonage until July 16, 1739, when Amie died at the age of 36.

During Rev. Goold's ministry, the congregation increased to the point where the old building was no longer adequate. It was decided to erect a new building, and in the spring of 1735, subscriptions were taken to defray the cost of construction. Sixty-six subscribers pledged a total of 234 pounds, 10 shillings. Although the building was not completed until 1751, it was in use for services several years before it was finally completed. It was built of brick, forty-four feet in length, thirty-four feet wide, and two stories high. The pews, which were built at pew holders' expense, were placed on raised platforms around the walls. In the center of the auditorium benches were placed on the brick floor for those of the congregation who could not afford the pews. A broad aisle extended from the entrance on the east to the pulpit at the west. There were deep galleries in the front and on the sides, and the stairs to the gallery were at first constructed on the outside of the building and later changed to the interior. The pulpit was a magnificent piece of woodwork, supposedly made in Boston. It was a high pulpit, hexagonal in shape with a sounding board of the same design. Adding special beauty were the inlaid woods of different colors. When the church was completed, it was the largest and most imposing structure in this part of West Jersey.

Rev. Goold did not stay for the completion of the new church. Shortly after his wife's death the parsonage burned, destroying all the furniture and the church records. Although the church expanded rapidly under his leadership, he became dissatisfied, and difficulties arose between him and the congregation. The problem may have been caused by his preference for the Congregational form of government opposed to the Presbyterian. Whatever the cause, Rev. Goold left the congregation without notifying the Presbytery or being dismissed by it.

After Rev. Goold's exodus the church remained pastorless until 1746. During this time the people were fortunate that some of the most eminent preachers of the day supplied the church. In the fall of

1740, Rev. Gilbert Tennent stopped at Greenwich on his tour through the Jerseys. He remained about one week, preaching once or twice each day. His visit had a tremendous effect upon the people, and the church was filled each Sabbath, a situation that lasted well into the fall of the year. At that time the celebrated Whitefield arrived, preaching with his usual eloquence. On one occasion 3,000 people came to hear him, and the meeting had to be held in the nearby woods, since the church could not accommodate such a large crowd. In 1744, the congregation applied to the Presbytery of Philadelphia to be organized as a regular Presbyterian church. In the fall of that year a Mr. Campbell was sent by the Presbytery to formally organize the Greenwich church as a Presbyterian church. At this time the former two deacons were ordained, and six elders were chosen and ordained, in compliance with the Presbyterian form of government.

In 1746, Mr. Andrew Hunter supplied the Greenwich church. The congregation approved of him, and a call was issued in conjunction with the Deerfield Presbyterian Church, which was having difficulty in securing a settled pastor. On September 4, 1746, Rev. Hunter was ordained and installed as pastor of the Greenwich and Deerfield churches. According to the arrangement agreed to, Rev. Hunter was to spend two-thirds of his time in Greenwich and one-third in Deerfield. This arrangement lasted until 1760, when dissension between the two congregations made it impossible for the arrangement to be continued.[2] On May 3, 1754, a farm was purchased from Joseph James for 250 pounds, to be used as a parsonage. It originally consisted of 105 acres which, on April 23, 1784, was increased by an additional 28.5 acres of woodland, purchased from John Reeves for three pounds per acre. The land was conveyed to Joel Fithian and Thomas Brown in trust for the congregation. The total amount subscribed was 213 pounds, 10 shillings, but there had to be other donations, since a statement in the original records mentions that the subscriptions were sufficient to pay for the glebe. This farm became one of the best in the area, with the most modern farm buildings of any farm in the congregation. It was finally sold in 1811 to Abijah Harris for $2,400.

Rev. Hunter was an able scholar and pastor, and his influence on the congregation was great. From the very beginning he was an ardent patriot and was undoubtedly partially responsible for the flame of patriotism that burned so strongly in the citizens of Greenwich. No wonder, then, that most of the tea burners were members of his church, including his own nephew. A considerable number of them are buried in the old burying ground of the church. Rev. Hunter's influence can be judged by the prominence later obtained by some of these men: Richard Howell, Governor of New Jersey; Elias Boudinot, President of the Continental Congress; Johnathan Dickinson, principal founder of the College of New Jersey; Joseph Bloomfield, member of the Provincial Congress and Governor of New Jersey; and Phillip Vickers Fithian, the outstanding preacher whose journal was largely responsible for the authentic restoration of Williamsburg, Virginia. Rev. Hunter died of dysentery on July 28, 1775, after almost thirty years of devoted ministry to the Greenwich church. His remains were interred under the middle aisle of the church, near the pulpit. During his pastorate the Greenwich church reached the height of its prosperity and influence, and was one of the largest and most influential in West Jersey.

After the death of Rev. Hunter the pulpit remained vacant for six years. On August 18, 1781, Rev. George Faitoute was called to take pastoral charge of the church, and was installed as its minister on April 8, 1782. He received a salary of 75 pounds per year or the equivalent in provisions. Since produce was more available than money, most of his salary was provided in the form of farm products. He became dissatisfied with this arrangement, so the congregation increased his salary and gave him some land to farm. As he was unaccustomed to farming, he did not manage the land very well, and in 1789 asked to be dismissed as pastor.

Around this time a Presbyterian congregation was formed at Bridgeton, which drew largely for its congregation on the members of the Greenwich church. Since both congregations were in need of a pastor, they unanimously agreed to call Rev. William Clarkson as minister for both churches. Rev. Clarkson accepted and was ordained and installed in the Greenwich church November 14, 1794. It became his practice to preach at Greenwich in the morning and in the afternoon at Bridgeton. Rev. Clarkson took up residence on the parsonage farm, but he too was not a farmer, and became dissatisfied with the arrangement. In the spring of 1798 he moved to Bridgeton. Finding it impossible to support his family on the yearly salary of $365.50 paid him in total by both churches, he resumed the practice of medicine, in addition to continuing his pastoral duties. Rev. Clarkson had been an eminent physician in New York City before studying theology. This action, however, caused dissension among his parishioners, and he applied for dismissal from the Presbytery in 1801.[3]

It was not until 1805 that the congregations of both churches agreed on another pastor. At that time a call was extended to the Rev. Jonathan Freeman of Newburg, New York. The call was accepted, and Rev. Freeman was ordained and installed in the Bridgeton church on October 16, 1805, as pastor of both churches. After living a few years at the parsonage farm he and his family became dissatisfied with their isolated situation and the arduous labors connected with running the glebe. In 1811, they too moved to Bridgeton, where they lived in the home of his mother-in-law, Mrs. Ker. This move made it mandatory that he change the preaching arrangements so that his sermon was now given in the morning in the Bridgeton church and in the afternoon in the Greenwich church. Although this new schedule was not popular with the Greenwich congregation, they acquiesced to it. During his tenure as pastor of both churches from 1805 to 1822, Mr. Freeman was the most prominent minister of any denomination in South Jersey. He was an old-fashioned Calvinist, and had little toleration for those who differed with these beliefs. On November 17, 1822, he died of a fever at the age of 57.

Rev. Samuel Lawrence was called as stated supply for both the Greenwich and Bridgeton churches, and preached his first sermon in the Bridgeton church on November 23, 1823. With the growing importance of the Bridgeton area, the Bridgeton church felt that it was now strong enough to support its own minister, and in the spring of 1824, without consulting the Greenwich church, issued a call to Rev. Brogan Hoff to be its full-time pastor. The Greenwich congregation was stunned by this unilateral action, and the cooperative arrangement between the two churches, which had been maintained since 1794, was severed.[4]

The Greenwich church issued a call to Rev. Lawrence, and on November 10, 1824 he was ordained and installed as pastor. During his ministry the church building became so dilapidated that a congregational meeting was held on February 14, 1835, at which time it was decided to build a new sanctuary. Thomas E. Hunt, Phillip Fithian, and Enoch Fithian were selected as the building committee. A lot was purchased across the street from the old church, and the cornerstone of the new church was laid May 7, 1835. The church was built of brick at a cost of $4,475. The last service in the old building was held Sunday morning, April 12, 1835, and dedicatory services in the new church were held May 5, 1836. A near catastrophe occurred Tuesday morning, December 23, 1845, when the church was damaged by fire. The sexton had placed a box of ashes containing live coals in one of the closets under the stairs. The coals burned through the box, and a current of air fanned the ashes into flames, causing considerable damage.

The old elm trees that line the street and add beauty to the church grounds were planted by Dr. Enoch Fithian, a member of the building committee and a trustee for many years. As a young man he had gone to Boston, where he gathered the seeds from the elm trees in Boston Common and planted them on the church grounds.

By 1860, the congregation had outgrown the building, and during the ministry of the Rev. Shepherd Koscinske Kollock an addition to the east end was built. In 1894, the church was modernized; the organ was taken from the gallery and placed in the recess in back of the pulpit, the pew doors were removed, and, as a concession to the comfort required by the worshippers of that day, cushions were placed in the pews and the aisles carpeted. In 1934, acknowledging the changing lifestyles of the members, the horse sheds were removed. Under the leadership of the Rev. John E. Slater, Jr., a new chapel and Sunday school rooms were added in 1949, at a cost of $10,642.

Quaker Fenwick designed the town and named it Cohansey. But the Presbyterian and Congregational influence of the early settlers prevailed. Many of these people had come from Connecticut, and they referred to it as Greenwich, after the town of the same name. This explains the statement made by a lifelong resident and a descendant of one of the original settlers, that those who have "lived" in the area for only a short time, such as a hundred years, pronounce the name "Green Wich," while those who have lived there from the beginning pronounced it "Gren-ich," as it is pronounced in England.

The Presbyterian Church was once the most prosperous and influential church in the area. The most eminent of ministers have preached to its congregations and the people of the area. Now it maintains a quiet dignity at the end of Ye Greate Street at Head of Greenwich, nestled among the tall trees overlooking the final resting place of many noted figures who helped gain this country's independence and prevent the tyranny of the Old World from gaining a foothold in the New.

1. For further information on Henry Hook see Chapter XVI on Old Stone Church in Fairton.

2. For further details see Chapter X on the Deerfield Presbyterian Church.

3. For more information on Rev. Clarkson see Chapter XXV on Old Broad Street Church, Bridgeton.

4. Ibid.

XXXVIII

Saint John's Church

Salem, 1838

Despite the fact that people had fled the Old World for the New to escape the tyranny of a state religion, supporters of the Church of England were living in Salem as early as 1691. This is confirmed by the fact that a marriage performed according to the rituals of that Church took place that year. Joseph Burgin and Jane Silver were married "after the manner of the Church of England" on March 23, 1691.[1] Nelson Burr, author of *The Anglican Church in New Jersey*, believes that members of the Anglican Church actually arrived with John Fenwick and his band of Quakers when the first colony was established in Salem in 1675. These early Anglicans had no church in which to worship, but met in private homes. The rector of Immanuel Church in Newcastle, Delaware held occasional services for them in the Salem Court House. After St. Mary's in Burlington was established in 1702,[2] Rev. John Talbot visited Salem at irregular intervals.

A building, probably made of logs, was started as early as 1708. John Talbot mentions an unfinished church that had been generously aided by Colonel Francis Nicholson. In 1708, Queen Anne of England sent the church Glass Pulpit Cloths and Altar Cloths. Why it was never finished is not answered by any of the records. It is

Saint John's Church in Salem.

known that Benjamin Vining, Joseph Coleman, George Trenchard, John Rolfe, Alexander Grant, James Sherron, and the Dunlap family were among the first Episcopalians. The Reverends Hesselius and Lidenius, Swedish Luther ministers, read prayers and preached at Salem. The Society for the Propagation of the Gospel paid each of them ten pounds for their efforts and gave Rev. Hesselius an additional thirty pounds to help him return with his family to Sweden.

By 1722, this group of adherents to the Church of England desired their own missionary, rather than having to rely on the occasional services of traveling ministers. They wrote to the Society pleading for a missionary, stating that they had "never been so blessed as to have a person settled amongst us to dispense the august ordinances of religion; in as much that even the name of it is almost lost among us..."[3] Such a pathetic appeal could hardly be overlooked by the Society, and in 1722 Salem was constituted a mission under the care of Rev. John Holbrooke.

It was two years before Holbrooke arrived in 1724, and he didn't like what he saw. Shortly after his arrival he wrote to the Society: "The place lies between two branches of a large creek that falls into the lower part of ye River Delaware. The shores of this creek are prodigiously rotten, marshy and fenny for several miles, and are as bad as any of the hundreds. My constitution being but weak, I am persuaded I shall never be able to outweather ye unwholesomeness of this place."[4]

Not only were the geography and climate disappointing to him, but also the religious attitude of the inhabitants. Again he wrote to the Society, this time with an assessment of the possibilities for the Church of England: "This part of ye country being first settled by Quakers, Quakerism has taken such root here that of all ye weeds of Heresies and Schism, this is by far ye most flourishing. The Quakers are about five time ye number of those of ye Church of England who are about seventy adult persons. Besides Quakers there are no other sort of Dissenters near Salem Town except three families of Anabaptists, and as many of Independents. I do not know if there is one Papist in ye whole country."[5]

Despite Holbrooke's misgivings, he set to work to build a suitable place of worship for the seventy people who espoused the Anglican faith. One acre of land on the south side of Bridge Street (now Market) was deeded by Samuel Fenwick Hedge, grandson of John Fenwick, to Benjamin Vining and Joseph Coleman, wardens "for the sole use and behoof of the members of the Church of England, of the Church of Salem." The land fronted 165 feet on Bridge Street, and was 254 feet in length. The deed was dated February 5, 1727. Although the people were generally poor, they contributed generously toward the building of the church, which was started May 7, 1725, only one year after Holbrook's arrival and two years before the land was actually deeded. Contributions were received from places as far distant as Philadelphia, and the Governor of the Colony, William Burnett, donated ten pounds. The church was formally opened for services on June 24, 1728, and accordingly named Saint John. About seventy people attended the opening, although Holbrooke reported that there were only fourteen communicants from February 1726 to February 1727. The building was chapellike in appearance, forty feet long, twenty-eight feet wide, and made of brick. It had a high peaked roof and a small, square belfry, topped by a short spire with a weather vane. The double leaf front door had a narrow window on each side, and a large fanlight several feet above it. There were side porches opening into the cemetery. The church and cemetery were separated from the street by a wall with a double gate in front.[6]

The erection of the new church attracted a large congregation. It would be expected that such a major accomplishment so soon after his arrival would have overjoyed Holbrooke, but he was not happy. He was concerned over the fact that the church owned no rectory or glebe, so he had to pay fifteen pounds yearly for the rent of a house in which to live. He received twenty pounds yearly from the congregation and another sixty pounds from the Society, but he complained about his financial straits. Besides these frustrations, he had a congregation at Cohansey and another at Maurice River, forcing him to travel considerable distances in order to minister to these people. Finally, in 1732, he resigned his post.

Since this was the only mission between Burlington and Cape May, the Society in London could not let it fail. They, therefore, appointed the Rev. John Pierson, who arrived on January 30, 1734. In the interim, the congregation had been held together by the Swedish Lutheran pastor at Penn's Neck, Rev. Peter Tranberg. Rev. Pierson was a New Englander, a graduate of Yale College, and a convert from dissent. In a joint letter which he and six others presented to the trustees of Yale College on the day after commencement in 1722, Pierson states: "Some of us doubt the validity of the Presbyterian ordinance in opposition to Episcopal."[7] A little over six months after his arrival, he was able to notify the Society that upwards of 100 people attended services on Sunday mornings, and that on some Sundays the congregation was close to 200. Even though he reported that his congregation was flourishing in 1735, by 1737 he sounded a little discouraged when he wrote: "The Generality of the people of Salem are very ignorant, more especially in regard to the Sacraments, and not only neglect, but have them in great contempt, through a deep tincture of Quakerism."[8] Apparently he had not been as successful as he had originally hoped in convincing the people of the importance of the rituals of the Anglican Church. Pierson conducted one of the first census-takings in the colony, listing the number of inhabitants as 2,700; the number of baptized inhabitants 1,400; the number of actual communicants, 23; those who professed allegiance to the Church of England, 207; dissenters of all sorts, 2,430; Catholics, 60; number of heathen and infidels, uncertain.[9] Pierson died in 1745 and is buried in Saint John's cemetery.

The area was without a missionary until 1747, when the Rev. Thomas Thompson arrived. Since he was expecting his wife to arrive shortly, he was horrified to find that the parish had no rectory for him. Disgusted, he resigned the post and went to Chester, Pennsylvania. Feeling that he might have acted impulsively, he returned to Salem and rented a house for his wife. The Society tried to help him by ordering the Vestry to give him a rectory and a glebe and to add twenty pounds to his salary. This dictatorial action by the Society so infuriated the congregation that they flatly refused, and told the Society that no minister was necessary nor wanted. This was enough for Mr. Thompson, who left Salem for good in 1749.

From then until 1792, the parish had no settled Anglican priest. The action by the Vestry in 1749 was undoubtedly instrumental in causing the Society to formally abandon the mission in 1751. The church was kept alive, however, through the ministrations of Rev. Eric Unander of the Swedish Lutheran Church in Penn's Neck.

The parish reached its lowest ebb during the Revolutionary War. Without a regular pastor interest waned. During the war the British soldiers used the building for a barracks, and in their raid on Salem in March 1778, Colonel Charles Mawhood's troops completely wrecked it. The troops vented their spite on the church, since so many members of the congregation were patriots. When Colonel Mawhood posted as list of Salem "rebels," three-quarters of them were Episcopalians.

Until 1807, there were no regular ministers, and the building as well as the congregation suffered through neglect. The church had fallen into ruins and become a "burrow for rabbits and a resting place for swallows."[10] By 1812, with the help of Presbyterians, it was repaired, and from then until 1820 Presbyterians and Episcopalians worshipped together, with Presbyterian ministers occasionally preaching from the pulpit. In 1820, the Rev. Richard F. Cadle became rector and was aghast to learn that others than those ordained by the Episcopalian Church were allowed to preach within its walls. The controversy he aroused threatened the peace of the parish, but was finally solved when the Presbyterians withdrew. With this problem out of the way, the parish began to grow, and it was necessary to erect a gallery in 1825 to accommodate the increased congregation.

Talk of building a new church began as the old one was over a hundred years old, had been wrecked by the British troops, and was no longer suitable for the needs of the congregation. In 1836, during the rectorship of the Rev. Henry M. Mason, final plans were made to build the new church. William Strickland of Philadelphia was hired as the architect, and a new structure was erected on the site of the old one. It was dedicated on February 8, 1838, by Bishop G. W. Doane. The hard times the parish had experienced from its beginnings were now over. From this time forward, the history of Saint John's was to be one of growth and improvement. In 1840, the membership had increased to the extent that there were sixty pews on the lower floor, all occupied. From 1842 or '43 to 1845, a new Sunday school building was erected, a Vestry room constructed, and the chancel enlarged. A gift from Colonel Robert G. Johnson and his wife in 1847 enabled the cemetery to be enlarged. The church edifice was improved in 1880 by the addition of a recess chancel, an organ chamber and robing room, and a beautiful memorial chancel window, at a cost of $8,131.83. In 1884, the old brick church was torn down and a chapel erected on the site, connected to the church by a cloister in 1911. In 1914, a memorial brass pulpit was installed, the funds for which were given by the joint will of Mrs. Mary Sinnickson and her sister, Miss Margaret Prescott Stoughton. A new parish house was built on a side street at the rear of the rectory.

The present pastor, Rev. F. B. Schultz, conducted his first service on November 23, 1952. He soon learned that the church was so badly divided that it was impossible to get the wholehearted support of all the members and organizations. He invited the congregation to a special service on Palm Sunday, at which time he announced that "the honeymoon was over," and it was time for all members to work for the good of Saint John's. A program of renovating and restoring the interior of the church was completed in 1956 at a cost of almost $100,000. It was then decided to dismantle the 127-year-old "temporary steeple." A Norman tower, in keeping with the architecture of the church, was completed in 1962. The property on Grant and Market Streets was purchased, and a new parish house completed the same year.

Saint John's has had many outstanding citizens as members of its congregation. Father Schultz and Senior Warden Howard B. Keasbey received the Bishop's Medal of Honor in 1962. The church also has the distinction of having more congressmen elected from its rolls than any other church in South Jersey. To help celebrate its 250th anniversary in 1972, the church brought to this country the Right Reverend Robert W. Stopford, Lord Bishop of London.

1. *Minute Book #2*, Court of Salem, New Jersey.

2. *History of the Church in Burlington*, by Jeremiah Bass.

3. *The Anglican Church in New Jersey*, by Nelson R. Burr.

4. *History of Salem County New Jersey*, by Joseph S. Sickler.

5. Ibid.

6. *The Anglican Church in New Jersey*, by Nelson R. Burr.

7. *Historic Episcopal Churches of New Jersey*, by William W. Klenke.

8. Ibid.

9. *The History of Salem County New Jersey*, by Joseph S. Sickler.

10. *History of Gloucester, Salem and Cumberland Counties*, by Cushing & Sheppard.

XXXIX

Winslow Methodist Church

Winslow, 1840

"They owned the factory, they owned the store, they owned the homes, they owned you!" Mr. Lamond Smith, trustee of the Winslow Methodist Church, was describing the conditions that existed in Winslow Village during the early days of the church. He didn't mention ownership of the church, but well he might have, since the entire village and hundreds of acres surrounding it were owned by the Winslow Glass Works. This was typical of the factory-owned towns of the early 19th century. The only industry was the factory, and the factory was the only employer. In fact, the workers were not paid in money but rather in script, which was redeemable only at the factory-owned store.

William Coffin, Sr. was the founder of the enterprise that eventually included two large window-glass factories, a large steam grist mill, a hollow-ware factory, a large store, and about 100 tenements. He formed a company with his eldest son, William, who felled the first tree to start clearing for their endeavors, since the area was nothing but a dense forest. But the place needed a name, so the father called it "Winslow" after his youngest son, Edward Winslow Coffin. When the township was formed, the name "Winslow" was officially adopted.

Winslow Methodist Church.

The elder Coffin retired in 1833, and William Jr. and a brother-in-law, Thomas J. Perce, joined forces until the latter's death in 1835. William Coffin, Jr. was then sole owner of the Winslow Glass Works until 1838, when he sold a half-interest to another brother-in-law, Andrew K. Hay.

In the meantime, a young church was struggling valiantly to get started and to minister to the spiritual needs of the people of this community, which at that time consisted of about 300 people. As early as 1833, Winslow Methodist Church is recorded as being part of the Gloucester Circuit of the West Jersey District under the Philadelphia Conference. Rev. Edward Stout was the circuit rider, and the credit must go to him for the founding of the Winslow church. He established group meetings that, for the lack of more suitable quarters, assembled in the members' homes. Use was also made of the local schoolhouse, which was available on Sundays for services. Richard Watcoat Petherbridge was the presiding elder at the time. Rev. Stout was indefatigable in his labors, traveling the circuit alone and enduring many privations. In no year did he receive more than $400 for his efforts, and in many years it was less.

In 1840, William Coffin, Jr. and Andrew K. Hay donated one acre of ground to the church on which to erect a church building. The church was built that same year, with Hay furnishing the materials as well as the carpenters needed. It was a small, frame, story-and-a-half construction, built along the lines of a country farm house. Although the church was not owned by the Glass Works, it certainly owed a great deal to it.

Rev. William Lummis was the Gloucester Circuit rider at the time the church was built. He had it dedicated by Thomas Neal, presiding elder of the Gloucester Circuit, and preached the first sermon there. If he had not been disabled by severe attacks of rheumatism, Rev. Lummis might have been the first stationed pastor. But since he could not physically handle the task, Rev. G. A. Raybold became the first stationed pastor. The trustees at this time were Reuben Westcoat, E. Wolf, I. Cline, J. Murphy, and C. L. Stanger.

In 1842, Winslow church became a station in the Burlington District, New Jersey Conference. The minister's salary was fixed at $600 yearly, and he was supplied without cost all his meats, vegetables, and groceries by members of the congregation. The money to cover his salary was raised by a door-to-door canvass. Men in an official capacity would go from house to house and inquire as to the amount each person desired to give for the support of the ministry. The pledges were recorded by the payroll department of the Glass Works, and deducted from the wages of the workers each week. The total amount deducted from the wages of all the employees was then placed in a special envelope marked "The Preacher's Salary." Each week the minister would appear at the payroll window along with the company's employees and collect his salary. This was an unfailing way of making sure that the pledges were kept! In addition to collecting the pastor's salary the company also paid for all his clothing and took care of all repairs to the church building. As a result, the minister's salary of $600 was practically clear.

In the early years the church enjoyed considerable success, since it was the only church in the area, and it had the backing of the Glass Works and its executives. At various times it was on the same circuit as the Pleasant Mills, Waterford, and Hammonton churches. Missionary work was one of its main endeavors, and it was responsible for the establishment of churches in Berlin, Blue Anchor, and Hammonton. In 1860, the Hammonton classes were under the leadership of J. Trafford and H. Feris, and they called upon the Rev. S. H. Johnston to receive them into the full membership of the Methodist church. Conklin Mayhew was the Sunday School superintendent for the Winslow church in 1853, when he was responsible for starting a Sunday School at Berlin. Mayhew was an inspirational leader; by 1868, as a result of his magnetism, it was necessary for the Winslow Sunday School to meet in the Lodge Hall to accommodate the large attendance. The average attendance under his administration was 90. This was in addition to the infant class, which met in the church and had an average participation of 60.

Unfortunately, at the same time, the attendance at the prayer and class meetings declined, and it was necessary for the pastor, Dickerson Moore, to report that these were poorly supported. Rev. L. O. Manchester became the minister in 1870, and interest in these meetings again flourished. Some of the credit for the increased participation and enthusiasm must go to the evangelist, Rev. Thomas Cole, who conducted revival meetings in the church in 1871.

The influence of the Glass Works was still an important factor in the financial success of the church. In 1875, the hall, known at one time as the "Big School," was deeded to the church, along with a half acre of land by A. K. Hay, John B. Hay, and his wife, Louisa Hay. By 1885, the prospects of future support by the Glass Works looked dim as the company was leased to Tillyer Brothers, and there were rumors that the works would be closed and moved to Vineland. These fears were confirmed in the fall of 1888 and the spring of 1889, when the Tillyer Brothers moved their interest in the Glass Works to Vineland. The membership of the church was affected, as some of the members found it necessary to move with the jobs. There was a short respite for the church as a new proprietor took over the Winslow Glass Works until they burned down in 1892. Before their demise, however, the works deeded one acre of ground to the church for the sum of $1, to be used for a cemetery.

During these uncertain times and the insecure future of the church, it never lost interest in its missionary work. In 1879, the Sunday School was organized into a Missionary Society. The trustees of the church were Conklin Mayhew, Reuben Boulton, William Brayman, L. D. Richman, and Charles Wescott. Although no longer superintendent of the Sunday School, Mayhew's influence in his capacity as a trustee must have been strongly felt in the activities of the Sunday School. In 1887, Emma and Nettie Wood started a Sunday School at Blue Anchor, which resulted in a church being built there ten years later.

During the ensuing years, the fortunes of the church rose and fell, depending upon the leadership of the laity as much as on the leadership of the ministers. During the pastorate of Richard Smith in 1898, camp meetings were held in the pleasant church grove. Such activities brought out large gatherings. The building was kept in good repair, and additions and improvements were made at different times. In 1904, Isaiah Morgan was appointed to put a front entrance on the church and to erect a place for a church bell. The parsonage was deeded to the church in 1914 by the Robert's estate for $750. Then came World War I, and with most of the men away in military service or wartime industries, it was necessary to close the church.

The church reopened in 1919, and has continued holding services and conducting its usual activities to the present day. The Winslow Society was formed in 1931, on the occasion of the church's 98th anniversary. This Society took upon itself responsibility for the repair and improvement of church property. One of the first things it did was to install electricity in the parsonage in 1932. A new driveway was put in at the church and cemetery. This was accomplished at a total cost of $69.53, with the labor being supplied by the men of the church and some of the equipment by the town. Lamond Smith, church trustee, remembers the operation. "They used mules and they had two mules from the brick yard. Aaron Chew furnished the mules and the rooter. The gravel was given to us by the township. We had two trucks. There was an awful lot of work. Each man got paid 25 cents an hour, and there was about 230 hours of labor. Surveying was done by Mr. Baker and this cost $12.50."

A new heating system became necessary, and to make room for the boiler the cellar had to be dug. It seems as though one of the trustees was doing most of the digging without getting much help from the rest of the men. After this had been going on for some days without any appreciable change for the better, the trustee threw down his shovel and went home. It wasn't too long after this when another member went by and asked him to come over to the church and help dig the cellar. At first the trustee refused, but upon being reassured that he would have some help, he agreed to go. The trustee had no sooner reappeared at the church when the helper showed up, armed with a bottle of rock and rye. In no time at all, the cellar was dug. When the minister realized that the job was done, he congratulated them upon the speed with which it was accomplished. According to the trustee, the minister never did discover the real reason why the job was finished so quickly, and the congregation, enjoying the warmth of the new heating system, attributed the speedy accomplishment of the job to the devotion of the workers.

Indebted to the Winslow Glass Works for the help needed in its early history, Winslow Methodist Church is now indebted only to the devotion of its faithful members. Through the years, these people have kept the church alive, despite misfortunes of local industry. Now the area is once again experiencing a rebirth of activity, with new housing developments bringing many residents. Winslow Methodist Church will continue ministering to the need of these new arrivals, just as it had served the needs of the people in the days when the Winslow Glass Works owned the town.

XL

Old Bergen Church

Jersey City, 1841

This Reformed Dutch Church was affectionately known as "Old Bergen Church" long before its name was officially changed in the 1970s to reflect the popular usage. It is the oldest organized church congregation west of the Hudson River. In the cornerstone of the present building is a charter certificate, dated November 27, 1660, which notes that Gerit Gerritse and his wife were considered "Orderly, honest, and pious people" by the Mayor of Wagening, The Netherlands. Gerritse's descendants became known as Van Wagening, "van" meaning "from" in Dutch.

Unlike the Puritans, Presbyterians, and Quakers, the Dutch did not flee the Old World because of religious persecution. In 1629, the West India Company agreed to consider anyone who established a community of 50 people or more outside Manhattan a patroon. Even with this encouragement it was not until 1660 that there were enough people on the west bank of the Hudson River to establish a town. In the fall of that year a site was chosen, streets laid out, and the name "Bergen" selected. It is possible that the town was named for Bergen-op-Zoom in The Netherlands, but more likely the name was chosen as a description of the area, which in Dutch, simply means "hills." Because of serious troubles with the Indians, particularly in 1655,

379

The Old Bergen Church in Jersey City.

when the Indians had driven the settlers back to the protective arms of New Amsterdam, Governor Stuyvesant had forbidden any settlements on the west bank of the river, unless the population was concentrated in villages which could be defended. That was the reason these pioneers had selected this high ground about two miles from the river. Besides its geographical advantages, the town was protected by a rectangular palisade with a gate at the center of each side.

In those days, the Dutch Church was the official church of the Dutch people. Just as Gerit Gerritse carried a document signed by the Mayor of Wagening attesting to his piety, so it was that the civil authorities of Bergen petitioned the governor and his council in 1662 to send a minister. One of the conditions agreed to by each settler in accepting a village lot was his obligation to contribute to the support of a minister and schoolmaster. The civil authorities included with their petition a list of 25 people who had agreed to pay 417 guilders yearly for the support of a minister, but it was to be almost a full century before the people of Bergen were to enjoy the services of their own minister.

Church membership in the Dutch Reformed Church was not automatically bestowed in those early days. Before being accepted, one had to pass a rigid examination given by the minister and the consistory. This examination covered Bible history and the evidence of the truths of Christianity as well as the doctrines of the Dutch Reformed Church. If the applicant passed this examination, he was then accepted into church membership provided no complaint had been made against his moral character. It took several years of study before young people were able to pass such an examination.

The first schoolmaster, Englebert Steenhuysen, arrived in 1662. He was also the voorleser, and in this capacity conducted religious services for the townspeople. According to his contract, he was to teach the children in his own home, and to conduct church services each Lord's Day. For these services he read from a printed sermon, supplied by the Classis of Amsterdam. These early church services were probably held in private homes also. The records do not disclose the date that the first schoolhouse was built, but it was probably erected soon after the town received its charter. The schoolhouse served the double purpose of a school during the day and a church on Sundays.

The first church was built in 1680. It was located near what is now the corner of Bergen Avenue and Vroom Street, but at that time was south of the village and actually outside the palisade. It was octagonal in shape, built of stone, and about 20 feet in diameter. Plain wooden seats lined the walls, except for the one opposite the door, where the high pulpit was located. The men occupied these wooden seats while the women sat in straight-backed chairs in the center. The voorleser sat at the foot of the pulpit, where he was able to hand up announcements to the minister on a forked stick. Over the front door was a stone, on which was inscribed "W. Day, 1680." W. Day was the builder. At the peak of the roof was a cupola, which housed the bell. The bell rope dangled down to the center of the building, where the sexton stood. Deacons collected the offering in small, black velvet bags attached to long poles. At the bottom of these collection bags was a bell, used to awaken any drowsy worshipper. The offering was made in Indian money known as wampum, which was made of conch shells. The shells could either be black or white, the black shells being worth twice as much as the white ones. Three black or six white shells were equal to a stiver, with 20 stivers to a guilder. The wampum was owned by the deacons, and they sold it to the head of each family, who deposited the wampum in the collection bags on Sundays.

The services were conducted by the voorleser until arrangements were made with Rev. Henry Seluns, the minister of the New Amsterdam church, to conduct the sacramental services three times a year. Since Rev. Selyns had no one to take his place in New Amsterdam, the services were held on Mondays for the people of Bergen, both in the morning and the afternoon. The first service under this arrangement was on October 2, 1682, to a congregation of 134 people. This arrangement continued until 1699, when the responsibility for the Bergen congregation was turned over to Rev. Selyn's colleague, Rev. Gualtherus Dubois. Rev. Dubois continued the practice for over half a century, until 1751.

On April 1, 1750, a call was made to Petrus DeWindt by the churches of Bergen and Staten Island. Bergen was to furnish him with a parsonage and firewood, Staten Island was to give him a riding horse. DeWindt was a native of St. Thomas, Virgin Islands. In 1749 he had presented to the New York Coetus (an assembly of Dutch Reformed Churches in America) a certificate of church membership and a license issued by the Classis of Harderwyk in The Netherlands. Based upon these credentials, he was recommended to the Classis of Amsterdam for ordination. After examination by the Classis of Amsterdam he was ordained in 1751, even though the Classis was not completely satisfied with his knowledge of doctrine. In May of that same year the Classis received word that the documents presented by DeWindt were forged. The Coetus in New York was immediately notified, but not in time to prevent his installation at the church in Bergen. Pending a further investigation, DeWindt was suspended. By 1752, sufficient evidence was on hand confirming the forgeries, and DeWindt fled to St. Thomas.

This was a bitter blow to the people of Bergen, who had been seeking their own minister since 1662, and had to resume their search. At that time William Jackson was studying privately under the renowned Rev. John Frelinghuysen at Raritan (now Somerville). The Staten Island and Bergen churches again united and issued a call to him on June 22, 1753. One of the requirements of the call was that Jackson was to go to Holland to finish his studies and be ordained by the Classis of Amsterdam. While he was studying in Holland, the two churches were to pay him 100 pounds for his support. In September 1753, Jackson formally accepted the call, and spent the next four years in Holland completing his studies. He returned in 1757 and was installed in the church at Bergen on September 10, 1757. For the first time since its founding in 1660 the church had a legitimate pastor. Jackson was its dominie for over 30 years, earning the devotion of his congregation and the respect of the entire Christian community.

During his years of service, the separation of the Dutch Reformed Churches in America from the authority of the church in Holland took place. The separation battle had been raging for many years and had created many hard feelings. Congregations were split over the issue, and the Bergen church was no exception. Rev. Jackson was on the side of those who wanted the church in America to be independent of the church in Holland. This group saw no reason why the ministers should not be educated and ordained in America. They also promoted the idea of services in English, rather than in the Dutch language. Both groups met in 1771 and signed the Articles of Union. This was a victory for the separatists, and in 1772, the Reformed Protestant Dutch Church in America was established.

During Jackson's ministry, the old octagonal church became much too small to handle all those who came to hear him preach. He was a fiery orator, with a reputation second only to Whitefield in the power of his sermons. A new sanctuary was erected in 1773. It was built of stone, with dimensions of forty-five by sixty feet. Projecting somewhat from the front wall was a tower, on top of which was a steeple. At first, the only entrance to the sanctuary was through the tower. The archways over the doors and windows were covered with decorative brick, imported from Holland. Stones from the old church were used, along with others taken from the fields. Inside was a high pulpit, large enough for only one person, with a large sounding board overhead.

After serving the Bergen church for over a quarter of a century, Rev. Jackson began suffering from mental illness. He occasionally would make remarks from the pulpit that were very disturbing to the devout feelings of the congregation. While preaching to a large group in New Brunswick, he lost all track of time. A friend in the audience finally held up his watch, hoping that this would make Jackson realize how long he had been talking. Undaunted, Jackson simply reminded his audience that Saint Paul preached for long periods of time, and continued on with his sermon. Finally, his behavior reached the point that the consistories of Bergen and Staten Island presented the Classis of Hackensack with a united petition to conduct a hearing into the situation. Starting on December 8, 1789, the commission met for several days and finally came to the conclusion that Rev.

Jackson's condition was such that he should relinquish his charge. The dominie complied with the commission's request, and the consistory of the Bergen church granted him the use of the parsonage and about four acres of ground for the rest of his life. Rev. Jackson died on July 25, 1813, nearly twenty-four years after being removed as minister. At the time of his death he was 81 years old.

Upon the termination of Rev. Jackson's ministry, the connection between the Bergen and Staten Island churches came to an end. On November 28, 1792, the churches of Bergen and English Neighborhood united in calling Mr. John Cornelison, at that time a candidate for ordination. On May 26, 1793, Mr. Cornelison was ordained and installed as the pastor of the two congregations. The arrangement was that he was to preach in Bergen two-thirds of his time and one-third in English Neighborhood. By 1806, the church at Bergen felt that it could support a minister full time, and on December 1, a call to this effect was submitted to Rev. Cornelison. The call was accepted, and the connection between the Bergen and English Neighborhood churches was dissolved.

During Cornelison's ministry, the church was thoroughly repaired and the interior more comfortably arranged. A new, more modern pulpit was installed, and family pews replaced the "sittings." The total cost was about $2,000, but this was amply covered by the sale of the pews, which brought in nearly $4,000. Rev. Cornelison's health began to decline in 1827, and on March 20, 1828, he died at the age of 58.

Rev. Benjamin C. Taylor, pastor of the Dutch Reformed Church at Acquackanonck, was called, and he was installed on July 24, 1828.

By 1841, the church was once again too small to accommodate all those who wished to worship. Three petitions were presented to the consistory, signed by heads of families, stating that they had no seats for their families. After due consideration, the consistory agreed that a new, larger church was necessary. On July 22, 1841, contracts were signed with M. H. Kirk & Co. and Clark & VanNewt of Newark for the construction of the building. As a matter of prudence, before signing the contract, the consistory had insisted that the seats for the new church be offered for sale to the highest bidders. This was done, and the amount received was $9,905.

The last services were held in the old church on July 25, 1841, and the work of demolishing was started the next day. The old church had been in use for sixty-eight years. As before, the stones from the old church were used for the new one, the cornerstone being laid on August 26th. The dimensions of the new church were sixty-eight by eighty-four feet, with a ten-foot portico in front. The building was of stone, except for the front and portico columns, which were stucco-coated brick. On the main floor were 144 pews, with seventy-eight in the galleries and a seating capacity of 1,200 people. The dedication service was held July 14, 1842. The entire cost of the building and its fixtures, excluding the furniture, was $15,477.04.

In the years since the church was built, many repairs, alterations, and improvements have been made. The church has ministered to the needs of its community since its organization in 1660—more than 319 years. Twelve pastors have served the congregation and the sur-rounding community. Among its prized possessions are two silver communion cups, which replaced pewter cups on January 26, 1731. These were made in 1730 by Hendrikus Boele from silver coins con-tributed by the congregation. These cups have been exhibited twice at the Metropolitan Museum of Art. The cups are so highly valued that they are kept in a bank vault between communion services, when they are used for decorative purposes only, since the church uses a set of silver trays and individual cups for regular communion services. It also has the original baptismal bowl made of coin silver. It is not used today, however, as the church has a baptismal font which came equipped with its own baptismal bowl.

XLI

St. Peter's Church, Berkeley at Clarksboro

Clarksboro, 1845

lthough this area was mainly settled by the Quakers, there were some followers of the Church of England who, as early as 1765, had been meeting in private homes, but were desirous of having a church of their own faith in which to worship. Nathaniel Evans, who had been sent to Gloucester as a missionary by the Society for the Propagation of the Faith, wrote in December 1766, that he had preached on week days in several parts of the county where church families had settled. Among the places he mentioned was Mantua Creek, which was the name given to this area by the early settlers. It was later to become known as Sandtown, Berkeley, and Mount Royal. When Nathaniel Evans died on October 19, 1767, there was no missionary from the Society to take his place. His father, Edward, who was a Methodist preacher, took over his son's congregations, particularly the one at Mantua Creek.

On November 29, 1770, the people of Mantua Creek bought from Uriah Paul half an acre of land for a church and cemetery. The purchasers, who were called managers and trustees, were Robert Friend Price, Esq., and Isaac Inskeep of Deptford Township; Thomas and Timothy Clark, Jonathan and Jesse Chew, Joshua Paul, and Thomas Thompson of Greenwich Township; George VanLeer, Esq., Jacob

St. Peter's Church, Berkeley at Clarksboro, built in 1845.

Jones, and Samuel Tonkin of Woolwich Township; and Edward Evans of Philadelphia.[1] The land was located at Mantua Creek on the Salem-Gloucester Road in Greenwich Township, and because of this location the church was often called "Greenwich."

Immediately after the acquisition of this half-acre of ground, a substantial frame structure was built, about forty-five feet square with a hipped roof. Inside there was a gallery, with stairs both left and right leading to it. A broad middle aisle ran from the door to the Chancel. The pulpit was the old-fashioned kind, called the three-decker, consisting of one piece of furniture divided into three parts, a communion table at the bottom, above that a reading desk, and above that the pulpit. The reading desk and the pulpit were reached by winding stairs. The interior was not plastered, but the interior wall and ceiling were formed of neatly-fitted white boards. Heat was supplied by a ten-plate stove.[2]

One of the prime motivating forces in the organization of St. Peter's was Thomas Clark. He was one of the most outstanding residents of the county at that time, serving as a State Assemblyman for many years. In recognition of his services to the parish, a movement was started to name the newly built church after him. He refused the honor, and reported in his journal: "I built a House of Worship in Greenwich Township which was then wanted to be called Saint Thomas and which name I refused to be called in the year 1770 but now called Berkeley, a Church in Memory of John Lord Berkeley the Proprietor of West New Jersey."[3]

It was difficult to secure ministers, especially those affiliated with the Church of England, so in the beginning the church building was used by any denomination. Edward Evans preached there until his death in October 1771, and was so successful that he was called the father of Methodism in Gloucester County. There is a record that Francis Asbury preached there in June 1772. In fact, the activity of the Methodists was so strong that Nicholas Collin, minister of the

Trinity Church in Swedesboro, wrote in his journal in 1773: "The Methodists have recently nestled themselves in, and roamed around especially in the woods east of Raccoon among the wild people, who had for the most part not confessed any particular religion before." This experiment in a community church was bound to cause problems, since by far the greatest number of contributors were followers of the Church of England.

The arrival of Rev. Blackwell in April, 1773 as Rector solidified the feelings of the Anglicans in the congregation that St. Peter's should be an "established church" in the fold of the Church of England, and this view was encouraged by Rev. Blackwell. At a congregational meeting held on June 30, 1774, it was decided that since the greatest number of subscribers were persons who professed themselves to be members of the Church of England, the church building should henceforth be used only by the clergy ordained by that Church. In a spirit of conciliation it was agreed, however, that other ministers could use the church if permission first had been obtained from Dr. Bodo Otto, Jr., who was charged with the responsibility of investigating the abilities and morals of each applicant. It was also agreed that any subscribers who were displeased with this arrangement could have their money returned to them upon proper application to Thomas Clark, Esq. The church was to be included in the charter with Saint Mary's, Waterford (Colestown). This resolution was signed by Timothy Clark, Isaac Inskeep, Thomas Thompson, Samuel Tonkin, Jonathan Chew, Gabriel D. Viber, and Bodo Otto, Jr. To make sure that this resolution was kept, the door of the church could not be opened without getting a key from the sexton, Gabriel D. Viber.[4]

This restrictive action was justified on the basis that the original deed given by Uriah Paul stated that the land was "for the use of an English Church to be built and a Burying Ground."[5] The Methodists were not disturbed over this turn of events, since they were planning the construction of their own church and agreed to abide by the resolution. Other groups, however, did not take kindly to this restriction, as is evident from the action the managers took on March 9, 1775, forbidding the use of the church to any but ordained priests of the Church of England, and reserving the cemetery for the exclusive use of subscribers.

Far more serious trouble, however, was in store for this little parish. The Revolutionary War divided the congregation. Jonathan Chew and Gabriel D. Viber were loyalists, while Dr. Bodo Otto, Jr. became Colonel of the Gloucester County Militia and a surgeon with the Continental Troops. He suffered the privations experienced by Washington's Army at Valley Forge, and his health was seriously impaired. Rev. Blackwell tried to remain neutral, while staying at his post as Rector of St. Peter's. Being an Anglican priest, he was suspected of Tory sympathies and was subjected to many indignities. He finally left in March 1779. The forlorn little church was closed, and the managers held no meetings for a period of about fifteen years. The church continued in existence, however, as shown by the records of the Conventions. At the Convention of 1792, St. Peter's was represented by Jeffrey Clark. According to "The Greenwich Church Book," which was the first book of records, the parish was known as Sand-town through the Conventions of 1808, 1809, and 1810. At the Convention of 1811, it appeared as Berkeley for the first time. In 1813, the Vestry reported that there were thirty-seven families, fifty-two communicants, and that Divine services were held every Sunday. A remarkable record for a church that still had no regular minister. By 1820, thought was given to uniting with some other vacant church to call a minister. The Rev. Jacob M. Douglas, Rector of Trinity Church in Swedesboro, officiated at St. Peter's in the afternoon of every second Sunday.

By 1824, the loyalty and devotion of its members was rewarded by the appointment of Rev. Richard D. Hall, who became the parish's first regular priest. He was an indefatigable worker, serving St. Mary's in Colestown as well as St. Peter's, adding St. John's of Chews Landing to his charge, and starting a mission at Mullica Hill. The records fail to give the year and reasons that he left St. Peter's, but it was prior to 1827, when the Rev. William Bryant served for one year. The church was vacant for the next six years, and then had the services of two ministers for short periods.

In 1836, the fortunes of the parish were again to change, this time for the better, as the Rev. Hiram Harrold arrived on the scene, staying for nearly fourteen years. Rev. Harrold had been a Methodist minister stationed in the vicinity, but became an Episcopalian and was ordained in that denomination. Not only did the parish gain the service of a dedicated rector, but benefited also from the energy and devotion of his wife. It was through her efforts that the parsonage in Clarksboro was obtained in 1838, at a cost of $900 plus an additional $600 for repairs. The acquisition of this property was to lead to the eventual erection of the present church building in Clarksboro, so that her influence is still enjoyed by the members today.

By 1845, the old church was badly in need of repair, so a special meeting of the congregation was called on November 18, 1845. At this meeting a discussion was held as to the advisability of repairing the old church or building a new one. If it was decided to build a new church, then it was necessary to determine if it should be built at the present site, or on land made available in Clarksboro, opposite the parsonage, by one of the members. The congregation voted unanimously to raise funds to build a new church, and that it be located in Clarksboro, the location that was most convenient for the members. At the same meeting, Dr. J. C. Weatherby, James M. Wolf, Esq., William Rambo, and Mrs. Hiram Harrold were appointed a committee to solicit and collect funds for the purpose of building the new church.[6] The Vestry met immediately after the congregational meeting and appointed the following persons to carry into effect the resolutions agreed to by the congregation: Dr. J. C. Weatherby, David B. Gill, Jas. M. Wolf, Esq., Chas. Wolf, and Hanson Cade. It also directed this committee to commence building when $1,200 was subscribed.[7]

The necessary funds were pledged in short order, the lot purchased from Dr. J. C. Weatherby for $100, and the new church erected across the street from the parsonage. Dedication ceremonies were conducted on December 17, 1846, by Bishop G. W. Doane.

On April 24, 1848 the building committee filed their report with the Vestry:

The whole amount of monies collected	$1837.59-1/2
The whole amount of monies paid out	1831.65-1/2
Balance on Hand	5.94
From which deduct a counterfeit note	5.00
And there remains	.94

Which was paid over to the vestry.[8]

If it was known, the records make no mention of the person who, knowingly or unknowingly, contributed the counterfeit note!

To the great regret of his congregation, Rev. Hiram Harrold resigned in December, 1849, after a rectorship of nearly fourteen years which witnessed many major accomplishments, not the least of which was the erection of the church which still stands today.

The church was to be fortunate again, when the Rev. Samuel C. Stratton became rector in 1850 and stayed for six years. Besides the major problems that confront a church, many unheralded ones crop up and must be resolved. On April 11, 1850, Jonathan Egee was appointed to remove the privy in the corner of the parsonage garden, as "Mr. Zebulon Locke designs to run his fence where it now stands."[9] Apparently Mr. Locke had a right to run his fence through the garden, which would indicate that the garden was not part of church property.

Over the ensuing years, the parish has been fortunate in the caliber of the rectors who have served the church. Many advances were made both in spiritual and temporal affairs. In 1872, the Rev. James Hart Lamb became rector and immediately reawakened interest among the parishioners in church work. He started a mission in Paulsboro and built St. James Church. Major improvements were made to the church building in 1911. New pews were installed, the church was piped for gas, and everything was completely repainted and redecorated. The total cost was $1,083.33. In 1919, the church was incorporated for the second time. The first time was on April 23, 1835, when the corporate name was designated as "The Rectors, Wardens, and Vestrymen of Saint Peter's Church in Berkeley." The incorporation of 1919 changed the name to "St. Peter's Church, Berkeley at Clarksboro, NJ."

Under the dynamic leadership of the present rector, St. Peter's continues to move forward. In 1964, a new vicarage was procured on the south side of the church. In 1967, a new parish house was built, with a capacity for nine church school class areas, a worship center and a large kitchen. The building was dedicated by the Rt. Rev. Albert W. VanDuzer, Suffragan Bishop of the Diocese of New Jersey. In the same year, additional ground was purchased from Gilbert Justice in the rear of the parish house to be used for a parking facility.

---

1.   *The Anglican Church in New Jersey*, by Nelson R. Burr.

2.   *Historic Episcopal Churches of New Jersey*, by William W. Klenke.

3.   A pamphlet entitled "St. Peter's Episcopal Church 1770–1970."

4.   *Saint Peter's Episcopal Church at Berkeley and Clarksboro,* by Paul Minotty.

5.   Ibid.

6.   Ibid.

7.   Ibid.

8.   Ibid.

9.   Ibid.

XLII

Friends Meeting

Haddonfield, 1851

No church has had a more romantic love story told of its beginnings than the Haddonfield Friends Meeting. To delve into the history of this old Quaker meeting house is to discover the love of a woman for a man profoundly shaping the events that transpired during its early years. Elizabeth Haddon and John Estaugh were the parties involved, and so warm hearted was the tale that Henry Wadsworth Longfellow immortalized it in his *Tales of a Wayside Inn.*

The story begins in the Quaker home of John Haddon in London, England in 1694. John Haddon was a devout Quaker who had already suffered at the hands of the authorities for his determination to follow his religious beliefs. As early as 1670, in Yorkshire, he was fined the equivalent of eleven dollars for attending a Quaker meeting at the home of Anne Blackburn.[1] This was his first offense, but not his last, as in 1687 he again ran afoul of the law, this time forfeiting over one hundred dollars. However, the Haddon's were made of stern fiber, and these episodes did not deter John Haddon from practicing his faith and from trying to influence others. And influence he had, as he was a prosperous blacksmith with a shop located between

Friends Meeting, Haddonfield.

Ratherhithe Street and the Thames, where he specialized in making anchors for a seafaring nation.[2]

The London Yearly Meeting was in session, and John Haddon was impressed by an earnest young man, just barely twenty years old, who had preached that day at the Yearly Meeting. John Estaugh was invited to the Haddon homestead for dinner that evening, and for a discussion of Quaker concerns. Although we have no record to prove it, very likely William Penn was also one of the guests, since Haddon and Penn were friends of long acquaintance, and Penn certainly would have been in London for the Yearly Meeting. It was during this evening that John Haddon's daughter, Elizabeth, first met John Estaugh. Although she was only fourteen years old, Elizabeth

Haddon was deeply impressed by this fervent young man, who had expressed a strong desire to go to the New World and become a missionary to the Indians and colonists. This is the only recorded meeting between Elizabeth Haddon and John Estaugh, but it is not hard to believe that they met many times in the six years that were to elapse before John Estaugh received the necessary authority and backing to sail for the colonies. In fact, in 1698, four years after this particular meeting, John Haddon purchased 500 acres of land in West Jersey from Thomas Willis, who had purchased it from William Penn. Since John Estaugh was determined to go to the New World, he was probably a constant visitor at the homes of all the influential Quakers, particularly those holding land in the colonies, to press his cause and to obtain the needed backing for his missionary ventures.

Finally, in 1700, John Estaugh received permission to visit the colonies on a preaching tour. Sailing from England late in the year, he arrived at Patuxent, Maryland, in January 1701.[3] By this time, Elizabeth Haddon had made up her mind that her life revolved around John Estaugh. Having inherited her father's determination and pluckiness, she soon obtained her parent's permission to leave her comfortable home in London for the uncertainties, hardships, and inconveniences of colonial America. Being impatient, she didn't wait for good sailing weather but left England early in the spring of 1701 and arrived in Philadelphia before summer.

What a courageous young lady! Barely twenty years old, yet willing to leave behind the security, comforts, and social life found in a fashionable capital. History tells us of only one occasion when she met John Estaugh, and that at the tender age of fourteen. Could it have been love that made her leave her homeland for the wilderness life of the New World? She was well aware of the persecutions suffered by those of her faith, and the difficulties they experienced in worshipping God as they wished. Was it her religious faith that made her leave her parents and married sister in London and follow other

Quakers to the New World, where she knew religious liberty existed? Her father had five hundred acres in West Jersey that needed managing and developing. Was it the spirit of adventure that lured this young woman to the excitement of life in a new environment? Nowhere does history tell us her reasons or motives, but they must have been compelling. It was not the usual custom in the 1700s for a young lady to travel alone upon such an adventure. Sixty-two years later, her epitaph was to describe her as "Remarkable for Resolution," and she was already demonstrating this trait by securing the blessings of her parents for her perilous journey. Armed with her father's power of attorney and the necessary funds, she set sail for the fields of Haddon with the avowed purpose of managing her father's estate, and joining other Quakers in religious freedom. Her love for John Estaugh was kept close to her heart.

The Quakers had already been established in the area for nineteen years, and were a growing organization. A small group of Irish Friends had arrived in West Jersey in the spring of 1682, establishing a colony along the middle branch of Newton Creek, which they fittingly called Newton.[4] A meeting was established that same year, and, until a meeting house was built, the members met in Mark Newby's log cabin. In 1694, the same year that John Estaugh was invited to John Haddon's home in London, the Newton Friends built their first meeting house. Although very small and lacking any but the most primitive comforts, it served their purposes until 1720. This was the meeting house that Elizabeth Haddon and John Estaugh were to call their first religious home.

Upon her arrival in 1701, Elizabeth Haddon remained for a time with friends in Philadelphia. Anxious to be about her father's business and to have things ready for John Estaugh when he came north from his preaching tour, she soon left her friends for her new home. Taking Daniel Cooper's Ferry, she crossed the Delaware River and landed in Camden at the foot of what is now Cooper Street.[5] Traveling by horseback ten miles up the Cooper River through a forest of Jersey pines and oaks, she arrived at Mountwell, the plantation estate of Francis Collins, a friend of her father's. She remained here for a short visit before continuing on to her own home, probably a log cabin, on the crest of a hill at a place afterwards known as Coles Landing, about two miles from the present borough of Haddonfield.[6]

Eventually John Estaugh found his way back from Maryland to Philadelphia. Historians disagree as to whether Elizabeth and John first met in Philadelphia or in Elizabeth's wilderness house. The actual location of the meeting is important only to the strict historian, while the fact that they met at all is important to this story.

Apparently John had no idea of Elizabeth's intentions toward him, or he was an extremely bashful lover. Having met several times, with no words coming from John as to any plans for the two of them, Elizabeth found it necessary to set aside her Quaker modesty and do the speaking. The opportunity came on a beautiful spring day, when she joined John with a group of Quakers on their way to Quarterly Meeting in Salem. As the group started off, Elizabeth leaned over to John and whispered, according to Longfellow, "Tarry awhile for I have something to tell thee, not to be spoken lightly, nor in the presence of others." John was puzzled and curious as to what Elizabeth had to say that required such secrecy. So they rode slowly through the woods, letting the others get ahead of them, while Elizabeth selected in her mind the right words to use. Finally she turned to John and said, "I will no longer conceal what is laid upon me to tell thee; I have received from the Lord a charge to love thee, John Estaugh." John, surprised by these forthright words and needing time to compose his thoughts, replied that he enjoyed her conversation, her ways, the meekness of her spirit, and the frankness of her speech. Not to be rushed, he spoke gently to her, saying, "I have yet no light to lead me, no voice to direct me ... I will gather into the stillness of my own heart awhile, and listen and wit for His guidance."[7] So it was left, the seed having been sown, time was now needed for it to germinate.

John left on another missionary trip to the south, and for the next six months or so listened to the stillness of his heart, and came slowly to the conviction that he must return to the fields of Haddon and take Elizabeth as his wife. They were married December 1, 1702, at the Coles Landing home that they lived in until 1713. In that year, they moved into a red brick, two-story home, much more commodious, comfortable, and nearer the present Borough of Haddonfield.

During this time John Estaugh continued his missionary journeys, and Elizabeth busied herself in the affairs of the Newton Meeting, having been selected clerk of the Women's Meeting in 1705. By 1720, a more central site for the meeting house was desired. A log meeting house, covered with shingles, was built that year on Haddon Avenue near King's Highway, on the site of the present firehouse. This church was larger and more comfortable than the one in Newton, built in 1684. Its cost was approximately $560. John and Elizabeth Haddon Estaugh returned to England and secured a deed from John Haddon for one acre of land, on which the log meeting house was built. The deed was dated July 1, 1721, and given in trust to William F. Evans, Joseph Cooper, Jr., and John Cooper, trustees of the Newton Meeting. The meeting house was opened for worship on December 22, 1721, and was the only place of worship in Haddonfield for the next ninety-seven years.[8]

By 1732, the ownership of the Haddon property had been transferred to John and Elizabeth Estaugh. Since the Meeting was in need of additional ground for burial space, John and Elizabeth conveyed an addtional 1.25 acres adjoining the meeting house lot to the Society of Friends. The trustees were John Mickle, Thomas Stokes, Timothy Matlack, Constantine Wood, Joshua Lord, Joseph Tomlinson, Ephraim Tomlinson, Joseph Kaighn, John Hollingshead, Josiah Foster, and William Foster.[9] In March, 1754, the Township of

Newton bought from the Estaughs a half-acre plot for a burial place for the poor. The location was inconvenient, and in 1755 it was exchanged for one-quarter acre of land adjoining the Friends Meeting House. It had been called "Poors Burying-Ground." But the stigma became objectionable, and by a vote of the township government on March 8, 1808, the name was changed to "Strangers Burying-Ground." The plot is in the northwest corner of the cemetery in an area called "The Glen" and is under the care of the Friends.

By 1760, the congregation had outgrown the facilities of the old log meeting house. It was moved to the opposite side of Ferry Road (Haddon Avenue), and a larger brick house was erected on the site. The old log house served as a horse shed for the First day worshippers in the new brick meeting house. Since the borough government had no place to meet, both meeting houses were used for this purpose until 1786, when the Friends school was built and put to this use.

Although the Friends built their meeting houses for the peaceful worship of God, the advent of the Revolutionary War saw these houses being put to other than peaceful purposes. The Haddonfield Meeting House was no exception, being used as a hospital and as quarters for both the British and American troops. On the morning of June 18, 1778, the British forces, under General Clinton's command, evacuated Philadelphia, crossed the Delaware River, and started their march across New Jersey. They reached Haddonfield that night, and used whatever facilities they could find for shelter, including the Quaker Meeting House. As no engagement took place, the meeting house was not damaged, and the troops pushed on toward Moorestown and Mount Holly in the morning.

With peace came a period of quiet industry, when the Quakers were able to pursue their normal occupations, and to meet for First day services in the quiet manner they loved so much. They still traveled by horse, or horse and buggy, and each First day would find them going to Meeting at a respectful "Quaker-trot." However, the peaceful scene was soon to erupt into a grievous internal fight. Elias Hicks, a farmer from Long Island and one of the most prominent Quaker preachers of the early 19th century, precipitated a split in the Quaker fold that none would have thought possible a few years earlier. The Separation, as the division became known, occurred in the early years of 1827–28, when the Friends split into two groups, Orthodox and Hicksite. Elias Hicks traveled through Haddonfield and visited the Friends Meeting House, where he won many converts. Opposing feelings became so intense that it was impossible for the two groups to meet together. But Haddonfield was more fortunate than some other Meetings, in that they continued to use the same meeting house until 1851, worshipping in opposite sides of the building.

In 1851, they separated physically as well as spiritually. The Orthodox Friends bought land behind the burial grounds, and built what is now the present meeting house on Friends Avenue. The bricks from the old meeting house were used in the wall surrounding the cemetery. The Hicksite Friends bought property at Ellis and Walnut Streets, and built their meeting house at that location. This meeting house is no longer in use, having been sold to the American Stores Company with the stipulation that the meeting house be incorporated in the building of the Acme Super Market.[10]

There is a story told among the local residents that the idea to build separate meeting houses in 1851 may not have arisen naturally. The story, which is not substantiated by historical records, credits a group of about thirty Orthodox Friends, versed in the building trades, with secretly entering the meeting house grounds one night and demolishing the building. Naturally, with no meeting house standing, it was necessary to build a new one, and since they would not meet together, two separate meeting houses were built.

For over one hundred years the two groups worshipped in their own meeting houses, but were finally reunited in 1952. The United Meeting decided to use the Orthodox meeting house as its place of worship, and the Hicksite property was sold. A Day School and a First Day School were housed in a new facility, built in 1956, adjacent to the meeting house. Services are still held in this historic old building each First day, although the membership has dwindled to about 180.

Although the story of Elizabeth Haddon has been justifiably recorded in history and recounted in prose and poetry, the story of another famous Quaker lady is not as well known. Living in Philadelphia at the time, Miss Dorothea (Dolly) Payne frequently visited her uncle in Haddonfield, who was proprietor of the Indian King Tavern. In 1790, she married John Todd, and in 1798 she became a 23-year-old widow, as her husband was one of the many victims of Philadelphia's yellow fever epidemic. The following year she met and married James Madison, and went on to fame as Dolly Madison, the First Lady of the country. Since she was a Quaker who spent considerable time in Haddonfield, it is not too remote an assumption to believe that she worshipped many times in the red brick meeting house on Haddon Avenue.

---

1. *Jersey Wagon Jaunts*, by Alfred M. Heston.

2. Ibid.

3. Ibid.

4. *History of Camden County, New Jersey*, by Geo. R. Prowell.

5. Ibid.

6. *The New Jersey Sampler*, by John T. Cunningham.

7. *Tales of a Wayside Inn*, by Henry Wadsworth Longfellow.

8. *This is Haddonfield*, Haddonfield Historical Society.

9. *History of Camden County, New Jersey*, by Geo. R. Prowell.

10. *This is Haddonfield*, Haddonfield Historical Society.

XLIII

First Presbyterian Church

Salem, 1856

I t was Sunday morning, December 3, 1820, and a large crowd had gathered outside Saint John's Episcopal Church in Salem, anticipating the arrival of the Rev. Ashbel Green, a Presbyterian minister and President of Princeton College. He was scheduled to preach that morning in the little Episcopal Church where Presbyterians as well as Episcopalians had been holding services. The church had been wrecked by the British troops in the Revolutionary War, and in 1812, Presbyterians along with Episcopalians had contributed to its restoration. Part of the arrangement was that Presbyterians would be allowed to conduct services when the church was not occupied by an Episcopalian minister.

This Sunday morning, though, when Rev. Green arrived with his friend and former classmate, Colonel Robert G. Johnson, the church doors were barred and locked. After appropriate apologies were made to the assembled members, Colonel Johnson went to the home of Dr. Robert Hunter Van Meter to discuss the unfortunate occurrence. Both were aware of the increasingly strained relations that now existed between the two groups since the arrival of the new rector for St. John's. As it was against the Canons of the Episcopal Church for the pulpit to be used by anyone not ordained in that Church, Rev.

The First Presbyterian Church of Salem.

Richard Cadle, who had just arrived that year, was dismayed to find that such arrangements existed, and intended to enforce the Church laws. As Johnson and Van Meter discussed the bleak outlook, Colonel Johnson suddenly said, "Dr., if you will help me, I will build a Presbyterian Church in Salem."[1]

Out of this incident the First Presbyterian Church in Salem was born. Plans were quickly made. Dr. Johnson had a notice printed and distributed all over town stating that Rev. Ashbel Green would preach that evening in the court house. Dr. James Van Meter, brother of Robert, was told of Colonel Johnson's plans to build a new church and quickly approved. These three men became the leaders of the new movement. Since Dr. Robert Hunter Van Meter was the only church member of the three, the responsibility for organizing the Presbyterian Society and arranging for services to be held in the academy and the court house until a church could be built fell upon his shoulders. Johnson came from an Episcopalian family, and the Van Meter brothers were the sons of Benjamin Van Meter, a Ruling Elder in the Pittsgrove Presbyterian Church. All three had received their early education at the Pittsgrove Log College, under the tutelage of the Presbyterian minister there. Johnson had come under further Presbyterian influence when he studied at Princeton College.

The enthusiasm of the Van Meter brothers was contagious, and they raised $400 in one day toward the expenses of building the new church. Colonel Johnson gave $1,200 and half an acre of ground on East Griffith Street (now Grant). The balance was donated by various citizens of Salem, Cape May County, Elizabethtown, Kingston, Princeton, and Philadelphia.[2]

No time was lost. On March 6, 1821, the cornerstone of the new church was laid, just three months after the withdrawal from the Episcopal Church. The ceremonies were conducted by the Reverends Freeman, Janvier, and Ballantine. Rev. Janvier preached the sermon, using his text Second Chronicles, Chapter 12, verses 13 and 14. The building was completed and opened for services on July 14, 1821, just seven months after the Episcopalians had locked their doors.

The First Presbyterian Church of Salem was organized by a committee of the Presbytery of Philadelphia on November 13, 1821, four months after the dedication of the building. The committee consisted of the Reverends Freeman, Janvier, Biggs, and Ballantine. It was organized with six members from other churches in Salem County, three men and three women. The three men were immediately elected as Elders. They were Samuel Burden, Esq., a former Elder of the Penn's Neck Presbyterian Church; Dr. Robert Hunter Van Meter and Robert McMillan, both from the Pittsgrove Presbyterian Church. The three women were all from the Pittsgrove Presbyterian Church: Mrs. Robert (Lydia) McMillan, Miss Sarah McMillan, and Mrs. Lois Powell. Six others were transferred from the Penn's Neck Church: Mrs. Samuel (Martha) Burden, John Congleton, Mrs. John (Sarah) Congleton, Sarah Kean, Mrs. Lambson, and Mrs. Sarah Lumley.[3]

This first church was built of brick, with a gallery across the northern end and lighted by long windows. The pews were plain wooden benches with straight backs. The men and women sat separately on opposite sides of the aisle. Besides his other gifts, Colonel Johnson donated a mahogany pulpit, and Mrs. Ruth Van Meter gave the velvet pulpit hangings. The pulpit Bible was a gift from a bookseller in Philadelphia. Small, globe-shaped whale oil lamps lighted the pulpit, one on each side. Stairs on one side led to the high pulpit. The precentor used the desk below the pulpit, which was nearly level with the floor. Tin reflectors, each holding a tallow candle, were placed around the walls of the building. The offerings were collected by means of long black poles with black velvet bags suspended at the ends. The entire cost of the new church was $2,443.[4]

When the building was erected, East Griffith Street had not been laid out. The church was reached by a private road, and the front of the church and the steeple faced north. When East Griffith Street was put in, it ran within a few yards of the rear of the church so that it became more convenient to enter the church from the rear.

On January 24, 1822, the following were elected as trustees: James Bartram, Dr. James Van Meter, Dr. Edward J. Keasbey, Joel Fithian, Samuel Copner, and Samuel Dunn. Supplies were furnished by the Presbytery until the fall of 1822, when the trustees hired Rev. Moses T. Harris of Philadelphia to perform pastoral duties. Rev. Harris acted in this capacity until October 1823. In November of that year, Rev. John Burtt was invited to preach as stated supply for the next six months. At the end of his trial period he received the unanimous call of the congregation to become their first pastor. He was accepted, and was ordained and installed on June 8, 1824. The trustees agreed to pay him $300 yearly and to supply his house and firewood. Rev. Burtt began his pastorate with thirty members and ended in 1830 with fifty-two.

In 1831, during the term of Rev. Alvin H. Parker, who was a supply minister, a wealthy mahogany merchant donated enough mahogany to make the benches into pews. Until this time the benches had been rent-free, but now income was provided the church by pew rental. In 1835, under the leadership of Rev. Alexander Heberton, the church building was enlarged by lengthening the south end and making room for an additional twenty pews. A wing was added on each side of the new addition, the floor was raised three feet, and the ground under the front end was dug out four feet, providing a basement lecture room that was used for Sunday school and weekly meetings. The building now resembled a T, with a door on each side of the pulpit. The pews faced the doors so that upon entering the church, a visitor faced the congregation. With the added pews the church now seated 300. The total cost for these improvements was $3,000.

Rev. James I. Helm was called as stated supply on June 25, 1840, and continued as supply until October 1, 1842, at which time he received a call from the church to become the regular pastor at a salary of $500 yearly. During his pastorship of nearly 12 years, including his supply time, a farm in Pittsgrove Township was bequeathed to the church by Dr. James Van Meter. Since his will was not signed, the church could not legally claim the bequest, but Dr. Van Meter's son, Dr. Thomas J. Van Meter, deeded the property to the church in accordance with his father's wishes. In 1849, a parsonage was purchased and furnished at a cost of $2,800. Rev. Helm was dismissed at his own request on April 20, 1852 to enter the ministry of the Episcopal Church.

The present building was erected during the ministry of Rev. Daniel Stratton, who was ordained and installed on October 14, 1852. At a congregational meeting held July 5, 1853, it was unanimously resolved "that in view of the inadequate provision now offered by the building in which we statedly worship and in view of the increase of population in this town we believe it to be expedient, in dependence upon God, to erect a more commodious house of worship for the church and congregation."[5] A lot was purchased from Calvin Belden on the east side of Market Street. The cornerstone was laid July 17, 1854, and the building was completed in two-and-a-half years. The architect was John McArthur of Philadelphia; the mason, Richard C. Hallinger of Salem; the builder, A. Van Kirk of Trenton. The dimensions were forty-eight by eighty-six feet, and the steeple, an outstanding architectural feature of the church, rose 184 feet from the ground. The total cost, including the lot, sheds, and furniture was $27,047.50, while total contributions were $13,723.50.[6]

Rev. Robert Burtt, son of the first installed pastor, filled the pulpit as supply after Rev. Stratton's death and aspired to be his successor. The Elders did not think this wise, however, and called Rev. Frederick W. Brauns, who was installed April 25, 1867. He received

$1,500 annually, along with the free use of the parsonage. He remained only 18 months and left to accept a call from a church in Cincinnati.

On January 25, 1869, the congregation called the Rev. William Bannard, D.D. from the Presbytery of Albany, New York. He was installed April 27, 1869, remaining as pastor for nearly fourteen years. Early on the morning of October 23, 1878, winds of nearly hurricane force roared through Salem. The slate roof of the church was ripped off and fell into adjoining yards with a great crash. Bricks and timber from the eastern gable crashed through the building to the lecture room in the basement, wrecking everything in the way. The tall steeple swayed but was not damaged. Total repairs amounted to $6,590. Dr. Bannard paraphrased Isaiah 64, verse 11 for his text the first Sunday after the disaster:

Our holy and beautiful house,
Where our fathers praised thee,
Is destroyed by wind;
And all our pleasant things are laid to waste.

Rev. William V. Louderbough was installed on November 11, 1883. His long pastorate of nearly thirty-six years ended with his untimely death in the vestibule of the church on a Sunday morning, May 18, 1919. Rev. Louderbough was loved and respected not only by his congregation, but by all the citizens of the area. On the day of his funeral, places of business throughout the city closed as an expression of respect.

Although Rev. Louderbough's pastorate was the longest in the history of the church, many excellent men have faithfully served the church through the succeeding years, leaving their own indelible impressions and accomplishments. Today the church is a vibrant part of the community with 354 members.

---

1. *First Presbyterian Church, Salem, NJ. 1821–1921*, by Anna Hunter Van Meter.

2. Ibid.

3. *History of Gloucester, Salem and Cumberland Counties*, by Cushing & Sheppard.

4. *Sketch of the First Presbyterian Church of Salem, NJ*, by Quinton Gibbon.

5. Ibid.

6. Ibid.

XLIV

United Methodist Church of Absecon

Absecon, 1856

"We the people of Absecon and its vicinity at a public meeting held in the Meeting House in Absecon on the 3rd day of March A.D. 1823 pursuant to the Act of Assembly of the State of New Jersey for incorporating Religious Societies in order the more effectually to accommodate ourselves and our posterity with a House in which we many more comfortably and quietly assemble to worship Almighty God have agreed to build a house for that purpose and likewise to procure a suitable Burying ground for the dead."*

With these words the local Methodists incorporated an official church body known as the Methodist Episcopal Church at Absecon. Their purpose at this time was to build a meeting place where they could "more comfortably" worship, and yet the house that they built would be anything but comfortable by modern standards. There were no pews, just benches with one board across the back for a backrest! One cannot help but wonder how full our churches would be today if such "comfortable" benches were provided instead of the pew cushions and air-conditioning that is considered so essential now.

Actually, the Methodist Society had been in existence almost thirty years before this meeting was called. There had been a Methodist revival in this area in 1796–97, organized and led by that

The United Methodist Church of Absecon.

most dynamic of all itinerant preachers, Francis Asbury. He was sent to America from England by John Wesley in 1771. Asbury traveled the length and breadth of New Jersey, inspiring the local inhabitants and organizing them into classes. The determination of this outstanding preacher can be understood better, perhaps, if we note the difficulties under which he traveled. The following quotation from his writings is interesting: "We have ridden about one hundred and fifty miles over dead sands and among a dead people and a long space between meals ... preached in a close hot place and administered the sacrament. I was almost ready to faint."

By 1796, the Salem Circuit was already in existence, and its preachers were Anthony Turk and Richard Sneath. Under their guidance classes were formed in Absecon, with Rev. John McCloskey as preaching elder. There is very little information concerning the activities of these early Methodists, but we do know that they built a frame meeting house. In fact, it was in this house that approximately twenty-six men and women met to incorporate on March 3, 1823. It can logically be assumed from comments in Francis Asbury's journal of 1809 that he preached in this same frame meeting house on April 18th of that year. This meeting house was located on Kings Highway, a short distance to the north of the present church building. The chief builder was Robert Doughty, a ruling elder of the Clark's Mill Presbyterian Church. The ceiling was wood rather than plaster, and it had a gallery along two sides and the back. According to the present minister, Rev. James McGowan, the original frame meeting house was moved in 1829 to Pitney Road, where it became a general store.

"We the people of Absecon ... have agreed to build a house ... " and with the determination so expressed by those words, the people of Absecon did build a more commodious house in which to "assemble to worship Almighty God." Built of brick, it was completed in 1829, with dimensions of forty by thirty-six feet. Unfortunately, there appears to be no recorded information concerning the cost of this new building. Since it took six years from its conception to the completion of the building, we can assume at least part of the delay was caused by the problem of raising sufficient capital. Sarah Ewing and Robert McMullin list the original subscribers in their interesting book, *Along Absecon Trail*:

Absalom Doughty	$100.00
Daniel Adams	25.00
Parker Cordery	100.00
Joel Adams	5.00
Enock Doughty	100.00
Bice Adams	5.00
Daniel Doughty	100.00
Uriah Adams	5.00
Absalom Cordery	50.00
Thomas Chamberlain	25.00
Jn. Pitney	100.00
James Covenover	15.00
James Smith	50.00
Israel Shillingsworth	25.00
Ezra B. Risley	25.00
Daniel Reed	15.00
Enoch Risley	50.00
Harbour Hughes	5.00
Joab Chamberlain	10.00
Daniel Steelman	10.00
Alexander G. B.	20.00
Daniel S. Risley	10.00
Michael Frambes	10.00
Thomas C. Marshall	25.00
Capt. John M.	10.00

But this comes to less than $1,000, and unquestionably much more was needed, so the assumption that part of the six-year delay was caused by the necessity of raising additional funds seems to be a safe theory. When completed, the building was of plain brick with no porch, narthex, or steeple. Inside, there were simple benches with one board for a backrest for the worshippers, and an old-fashioned high pulpit with a winding staircase. The altar was arranged in the center, and the high pulpit was to the left. According to Rev. McGowan, the pulpit was placed to the left because the "scriptures teach that Christ sits on the right hand side of God, and, in the tradition of the church, the clergy never felt that it was worthy enough nor had the right to sit on the same side."

On a recent visit to the church we were invited by Mr. Francis Jones to climb to the top of the steeple to view the bell. Since this seemed to be essential to our research, my wife and I happily agreed. It proved to be quite an adventure, and well worth the arduous climb. Mr. Jones took us to the back of the gallery, where he opened a very narrow door. In fact I didn't think I could fit through but somehow managed. This door simply opened into the superstructure of the steeple, which boasted nothing but a very primitive, narrow ladder going straight up. Half way up, this ladder abruptly ended, and it was necessary to navigate a few beams of the superstructure to reach another ladder of the same type that led to the top of the belfry. At the end of this ladder was a slab, which Mr. Jones pushed aside, and we were inside the peak of the bell tower. The bell was supported by wooden framework, and the top of the steeple had nothing but wooden supports and framework all in excellent condition. On the bell itself is the following inscription:

Cast by Jos. Bernhard & Co.

No. 120 Nth 6 St.

Phila.

1858

Rev. Z. T. Dugan was pastor from 1896 to 1899, and during his ministry the church celebrated its 100th anniversary. Considerable interior redecorating was done at this time, and the beautiful stained-glass memorial windows were installed in 1898. Electricity displaced the old oil lamps in 1902, and Reuben Babcock presented the church with a chapel. The Babcock family have been members of the congregation for many years, and a descendant of this family is still a member and active in church affairs. The chapel, fittingly enough, carries the Babcock name, as do two of the memorial windows.

It was rather daring and very modernistic of the church in 1864 to use a melodeon in the service. By 1916, however, the use of a musical instrument was so commonplace that a pipe organ was installed, a project sponsored by the young people of the church. The organ was built by A. B. Felgemaker Organ Company of Erie, Pennsylvania. By 1968, it needed major overhauling, requiring replacement of over 900 leathers and rebuilt foot pedals. According to Francis Jones, the cost was over $18,000.

Over the years, many improvements have been made, reflecting the interest and devotion of the congregation. The Christian Center was built in 1937 and added-to in 1957. The Children's Building was erected in 1964, adding six classrooms to the Sunday School. The congregation has a fondness for naming its buildings from Biblical passages. The Children's Building gets its name from the 19th chapter of Matthew, verse 14: "Let the little children come unto me and forbid them not, for of such is the kingdom of heaven." The Lamp Light Library was completed in 1970, and its name also comes from the Scriptures; in Psalm 119, verse 105 we read, "Thy word is a lamp unto my feet and a light unto my path." The entrance to the library boasts the oil painting "Lamp Light," which was given by the artist, Mae Townsend.

True to the words written by the Absecon pioneers of the Methodist faith in 1823, generations of dedicated Christian men and women have been just as strong in purpose and faith as those early pioneers. Perhaps the best way to express the devotion of this congregation is to quote from the Church's 1973 directory: "Our heritage comes from the devotion of many in the past. Our service is offered to those of the present. Prayerfully we try to anticipate the future and be ready for it in advance. Thus do we best serve God."

XLV

First Presbyterian Church

Mendham, 1860

ome of them had come from Southold, Long Island as early as 1713 or 1714, and settled on a tract of land in a place called Rocksitious. It was located on Indian Brook, a small stream that flows into the north branch of the Raritan River. Others were farmers who had worked their way from Perth Amboy along the Raritan River through Hanover, Basking Ridge, and finally to Rocksitious. Here they found the rich soil and the winding stream running through a wooded valley very much to their liking. Following a path westward across the stream and up the next steep hill could be found the neighboring settlement of Black River, now known as Chester. Rocksitious, also spelled Roxiticus, is now the town of Ralston.

At the top of the hill on the east bank of Indian Brook, these settlers built their first house of worship. Their need to build a church was twofold. The first reason was their love of God, and their desire to hear His word preached. Their second reason was found in the well-known English statute that defined a town as follows: "It cannot be a town in law, unless it hath, or in past time hath had, a church and celebration of divine services, sacraments and burials."

The First Presbyterian Church in Mendham.

Mendham First Presbyterian Church

Just when their church was completed is uncertain, but there was a small log meeting house in existence as early as 1738. In fact, their records show that they had a minister by 1734, Eliab Byram. What this building looked like has intrigued the fancies of many residents of Mendham. According to the stories passed on from one generation to another, it was a simple log house with two windows on the side. These were without glass but did have shutters. In keeping with the meeting house design there was no steeple, no belfry, and, of course, no heat. It was on the hill just east of Indian Brook and on the north side of the trail to Morristown and Whippany. Heating the meeting house in those rugged days was unheard of. The heat of the sermon, plus some heated bricks to keep the feet warm were considered sufficient. The meeting house accommodated fifty worshippers, and people came from as far as Chester.

The religious views of the congregation were undoubtedly influenced by events taking place around them. William Tennent had established his famous Log College in Neshaminy, Pennsylvania in 1726. Rev. Theodorus Frelinghuysen's revivals among the Dutch were being held at this time. Those who had come from Long Island were from a Congregational background. So the Dutch, the Presbyterians, and the Congregationalists certainly had an influence on the thinking of these early settlers. On May 24, 1738, however, Rocksitious became part of the Presbytery of New York, so the congregation was officially affiliated with the Presbyterian Church.

Over the next few years the area developed inland on both sides of the stream, and there was talk of building a new house of worship in a more accessible location. In November, 1745, a deed was given for the ground on which the church now stands. An elder, Ebenezer Byram, was instrumental in securing the services of John Cary from Bridgewater, Massachusetts, and it was he who built the church at Mendham in Rocksitious, as it was called in deeds through 1751.

In the spring of 1745, the new building was started and, no doubt, completed by the fall. It was a wooden structure with cedar shingles on the sides. There was no steeple or cupola, as bells were a rare luxury in those days. The main entrance was on the south side by way of double batten folding doors, with additional doors on the east and west sides. A broad aisle extended from the south doors to the pulpit, which was a box-like affair, raised high on a single pillar. Above the pulpit was an octagonal sounding board. Underneath the pulpit was a large square pew, in which the officers sat, facing the congregation. A gallery extended around three sides of the building, with the stairs inside the auditorium. The pews on the main floor were unusually elaborate for those days. They had very high backs, perpendicular to the seats, and the upper part was finished with upright spindles.

By 1791, the congregation was ready for a bell, and John Cary was hired to construct a belfry. The belfry was built in the center of the meeting house, with the bell rope hanging down in the middle of the main aisle. Elisha Beach, Jr. became the first bell ringer, and he performed admirably for the benefit of the entire congregation. He stood in the center of the meeting house with his hand on the bell rope until the entire congregation was assembled. At the proper moment he would leap high in the air, raise his hands high over his head and grasp the bell rope. As he descended, the bell would ring out victoriously. This act was repeated until there could be no doubt throughout the community that it was time for Sunday services.

During the winter of 1777–78, Washington's Army was encamped in and around Morristown. Some of the soldiers were housed in rude log cabins in Mendham. That winter, a smallpox epidemic broke out, and the church was used as a hospital for the victims. In order to provide sufficient space, the pews were removed from the assembly room, and the victims brought there for whatever aid and comfort could be given them. Twenty-seven soldiers succumbed to the smallpox scourge and were buried in the churchyard. A stone marking their graves can be found there today.

In 1763 Francis Peppard, a licentiate of the Presbytery of New York, came to preach. He received the call to be their minister, and was installed and ordained in 1764. Rev. Peppard has gone down in folklore as the one responsible for the town's name. He was an Irishman and a lover of music. He was also an admirer of George Whitefield, and a follower of the "New Side" of religious thinking. It is obvious that he was a free thinker. Ever since 1741, all the churches had been in turmoil over the use of Watt's psalms and hymns. Music or congregational singing had not been in common usage since the days of the Reformation, when no music was allowed in church services. Rev. Peppard, with his love of music, introduced the Watt's Hymnal to the Mendham church, thus causing a most unmusical uproar. Many of the older worshippers were offended at such liberal actions, and would leave the meeting house during the singing. He had considerable difficulty in teaching the congregation to sing, and legend had it that he often used an old Irish expression, "Never ye mind, I'll mend 'em." This was not a slang expression, but was his way of saying, "I'll reform them."

A conflicting tale credits the saying, "I'll mend 'em" to Ebenezer Byram, the same elder who secured the services of John Cary in building the church. When he arrived in town he established the Black Horse Tavern. Since he was new to the vicinity, he was not aware of the reputation for rowdiness that the area had because of a few unruly young men. Being advised of the situation, he is quoted as saying, "I'll mend 'em." He immediately took steps to make his boast come true, by giving generously of money and time in building the new house of worship.

Pursuing the riddle of the town's name a little further, it must be remembered that a number of the original settlers had come from England and Scotland. These folks loved to name their new homes after the ones they had left. There is no proof that this was the case in Mendham, New Jersey, but the name is known in England, "ham" being a good Anglo-Saxon suffix meaning home.

To further compound the riddle, it should be remembered that there is an Indian word "mendom," meaning huckleberry or raspberry. It is interesting to note that the oldest records of the church are contained in a book entitled "Mendom Congregation Book."

Whether Francis Peppard was responsible for naming the town is of little consequence, since he had a profound effect on the town as the third minister of Hilltop Church. He was born in Dublin in 1752. He had been educated for the priesthood and was soon to be ordained when he decided to sail for America. His parents objected so strongly that he sailed without their permission or knowledge, and landed penniless in Perth Amboy. His decision to come to America was not taken lightly, as he forsook a large fortune which would have been his had he remained in Ireland. Upon landing in Perth Amboy, he met Ebenezer Byram, who paid for his passage and hired him as a schoolteacher. He soon became friendly with Rev. Samuel Kennedy of Basking Ridge, a friendship that was to affect the entire course of his life. It was from Rev. Kennedy that he received his basic training for the Protestant ministry, and in 1762, he was graduated from Princeton University, and ordained in 1764.

Rev. Peppard became the third pastor of Hilltop Church, and, although he only served for a short three years, he had a profound effect upon the life of the church. Besides his obvious musical ability, he was a good organizer, a successful evangelist, and a dispenser of cures for the ailing body. During his pastorate, there was a widespread revival, and large numbers were added to the rolls of the church. Rev. Thaddeus Dod was converted at this time, the first of more than twenty-seven clergymen this church has given to the world. His notebook contained forty-eight prescriptions, covering cures for most of the common ailments.

During Rev. Peppard's tenure, the Session decided to raise the money for the minister's salary by renting pews. In their Session meeting of August 21, 1766, they voted to make it "a standing rule and abide in that Method in the Congregation to Support a Minister in paying ye Salary & all other Charges and arrears by Laying it on the Seats and pews in the Meeting house & that we will pay our proportion of all Such Charges According to the Seats or pews we improve." At the same meeting they voted to create a committee of eleven men to be "Managers of the Seats & pews." It was their job to seat every member to the best of their ability, assuring the harmonious working of this new plan. Certainly the men selected had to be endowed with attributes of firmness and diplomacy. These men were:

Jacob Wolf

Nathaniel Burt

Ezra Cary

Samuel McIlrath

Benjamin Pitney

John Cary

Samuel Day

James Jonston

Nathaniel Dotey, Jr.

Asa Cooke

John Carns

By 1791, the seating arrangement had become a serious problem, faced by the Session in a special meeting held in the spring. The plan of selling pews was discarded in favor of the modern method of subscription. The seating arrangements established by selling the pews had been causing problems over the years, and the crisis was met by the Session at their special meeting. Along with the change in the method of allocating the pews, the Session decided that the women should sit on one side of the church and the men on the other. What grave problems had arisen to cause the separation of the sexes is not known, but they must have been severe indeed.

The matter of the seats was not to rest easy for any length of time. On August 27, 1796, just five years later, Rev. Armstrong called a special meeting to once again consider the renting of the pews.

Apparently the subscription plan had not worked very well, and the congregation decided to revert to the rental plan. The seats were rented to the highest bidders, with the following conditions governing the arrangement:

"Any person that buyeth a Seat or pew to pay for the Same until given up to the Committee, and that not less than one year.

"And every person to have a right to hold their seats and pews until given up, and any person have a right to give up at the end of any year."

Lightning, of the man-made variety as well as nature's, became a problem for Hilltop Church. The church records show that drunkenness among the members was a serious threat to the tranquil life of the congregation. It is reported that twenty-seven members owned distilleries, and that Jersey Lightning was a favorite drink at many of the local inns. According to one report, most of the money that came into Mendham resulted from the sale of intoxicating liquor. William Phoenix owned one of the inns that maintained a bar. When he applied for a burial plot within the church's graveyard his application was refused. Not to be denied, he bought a large plot of ground adjoining the church cemetery and built a stone fence around it.

Nature's lightning had a much more devastating effect. On Sunday morning, May 16, 1813, a storm arose during the worship service, and a bolt of lightning killed one of the parishioners without damaging the church. A local newspaper, *The Palladium of Liberty*, reported the event:

> A most distressing event occurred here yesterday. At the close of the morning service, there appeared a shower to be rising from the west, which prevented most of the congregation from leaving the church during the interval of public worship. About half past twelve o'clock the shower began with hail and rain; and a bout a quarter before one

a stream of lightning was seen to descend from the cloud to the lightning rod on the church, and by the lightning rod down to within about eight feet of the ground (the lower part of the rod having been broken off and lost) the lightning there burst, and one part of it entered a window into a pew where several people were sitting, and struck the wife of Mr. John Drake, who expired instantly! Eight or ten others were injured, some of them very much ...

In the same year, other events resulted in the formation of the church's first Sunday School. A man of many years, Japhet Byram, lived about one mile from the Black Horse Tavern. He was an elder in the Hilltop Church and a very devout Christian. At the same time the Barnet family lived just a short distance away. They were Scotch people who had just recently arrived. Mrs. Barnet was a good, old-fashioned Presbyterian, and had been received as a member of the Hilltop Church. Elder Byram and Mrs. Barnet became very warm friends. One day Mrs. Barnet called on Elder Byram, but he had left the house to look at his farm. When he returned, he told Mrs. Barnet that he had to constantly check his farm, since there were some boys in the neighborhood who seemed to take delight in damaging his property. Mrs. Barnet described the Sabbath Schools they had in Scotland and suggested that he should start one here and get the boys in to it. Elder Byram had his doubts about the wisdom of such a move, but Mrs. Barnet was a persuasive lady, and by the spring of 1814, the first Sunday School was started.

In 1816, the church was no longer large enough to handle the congregation. In Rev. Armstrong's twenty-one years with the church, 260 members were admitted to church membership. Discussions had been carried on for several years as to the advisability of adding to the present building or of erecting a new church. Finally, in 1816, the old church was torn down and a new one constructed on the same site.

This building was forty-five by sixty feet, with a steeple at one end. The idea of a steeple at one end of the building was made popular by Sir Christopher Wren, the famous English architect. It was a feature of distinction, and was adopted quite often in the colonial period, when congregations could afford it. The building was completed in the fall of 1817 and dedicated on January 1, 1818. Apparently, there was only one gallery, with the seats reserved for the singers. Considerable progress had been made by now concerning the use of music in the Sunday services. Permission was granted to those leading the singing to use the bass viol when they considered it necessary.

Rev. Amzi Armstrong's pastoral relationship was dissolved by the Presbytery on October 2, 1816 because of his health. He had always been interested in education, especially the training of young men for the ministry. Upon his retirement from the active ministry, he took charge of Bloomfield Academy, which was the forerunner of Bloomfield College.

The church building erected in 1817 was consumed by fire on February 17, 1835. A new building was immediately erected on the same site, completed by November 24th of the same year. By 1848, an enlargement was necessary, and in 1849, a new Session House was built. The Session House was later called the Lecture Room, and still later the Chapel.

On April 7, 1852, Rev. Thomas S. Hastings came as supply minister and was installed as pastor on October 27, 1852. He was a graduate of Hamilton College and of Union Theological Seminary. He was the son of a famous hymn writer, Thomas Hastings of Utica, New York. Together they compiled the hymnal, *Church Melodies*, published in 1858. Rev. Hastings' son became a well-known architect. Some of the works for which his architectural firm is famous are the Memorial Amphitheatre in the National Cemetery in Arlington, Virginia, the Princeton Battle Monument, and reconstruction of the

Senate Chambers in Washington, DC. In 1888, Rev. Hastings became President of Union Theological Seminary.

This church building was to suffer the same fate as its predecessor. It was consumed by fire on Sunday morning, February 26, 1859. At about seven-thirty in the morning, the sexton had started a fire to warm the sanctuary for the morning services. There was a defect in the chimney, and by ten o'clock the flames burst through the roof. By eleven o'clock the building had been completely destroyed, although the members had been able to rescue some of the furniture and books.

The burning of the church was not the only problem that faced the congregation at this time. On August 18, 1856, the Rev. Theodore F. White had been called to succeed Rev. Hastings. He was a strong abolitionist, as was Dr. Hastings, but he was unable to handle this explosive question harmoniously within his own congregation. Difficulties arose which were severe enough to cause the formation of the Second Presbyterian Church. Rev. White's pastoral relationship with Hilltop Church was dissolved, and he organized and supplied the pulpit of the Second Presbyterian Church, but declined to be ordained and installed as its regular minister.

By the close of the Civil War, the necessity for a second Presbyterian church was less pronounced. At a Session meeting held on September 20, 1894, it was voted to disband the Second Presbyterian Church and to dispose of its property.

The fourth house of worship on the same site was completed in April 1860. The simple style of the colonial church was again chosen. The Steeple was on the west end over the entrance. There was a bowed gallery at the rear of the main room, which was considered especially beautiful. The building was heated by four large stoves, one in each corner of the auditorium, and each stove had its own chimney. The ceiling was spanned with wooden arches and girders, one upon the other in such a way as to form a network of open rafters, creating a beautiful effect.

The total cost of the new building was $9,588, including the furniture and a new 1,500 pound bell for the belfry. Even though there had been considerable opposition to building a new church, the congregation met the challenge by having the building paid for by its completion date, with the exception of a $50 debt.

The new bell was the cause of a near catastrophe. Shortly after its erection, the clapper, weighing about 70 pounds, broke loose and fell a distance of about 80 feet, crashing through two floors and landing near the ground. Fortunately, no one was in the way.

The Rev. James Carter was installed September 30, 1886. It was through his efforts that the Mendham church celebrated its 50th anniversary in 1888. In preparing for the event, Rev. Carter wrote the first historical account of the church, which he delivered at the anniversary services. To abbreviate the title for his address he made use of the Latin word "sesqui," in connection with the word "centennial." This was the first time the compound word "sesqui-centennial" was used, meaning 150 years. It was later used by Princeton University on the occasion of its 150th anniversary, which led to its common usage today.

The years that followed presented the normal problems confronting any congregation. In 1913, the church was remodeled, modern heating and lighting systems were installed, the ceiling was changed, and the gallery was enclosed. In 1917, and again in 1941, came the call to arms, and its young men responded to these national emergencies as their forefathers had during the Revolutionary War.

This church has inspired artists and writers; from it have gone missionaries, preachers, college professors, and university presidents as well as other men of distinction.

XLVI

St. Andrew's
Episcopal Church

Bridgeton, 1864

The first known adherent to the Episcopalian faith to live in Bridgeton is believed to have been James Giles, who resided there from 1789 until he died in 1824. To attend services, it was necessary for him to travel all the way to Salem or Swedesboro, since there was no Episcopal church in his home town, although the beginnings of the Episcopal faith in this area go all the way back to a group of Anglicans, who settled around Greenwich in the late 1600s.

John Fenwick, a Quaker who had purchased a large part of South Jersey from Lord Berkeley, donated an acre of ground at Greenwich for "the uses and profits of the Church commonly called the Church of England."[1]

That land was acquired by Nicolas and Leonard Gibbon, who owned a large portion of Greenwich Township. They were enterprising gentlemen who had migrated to West Jersey, erected one of the first grist mills near Cohansey, and had become influential and wealthy landowners. On the acre donated by Fenwick and used partly as a cemetery, they erected a neat and comfortable brick church for their families and relatives. It was built in "Old Cohansey," not far from Greenwich landing and on the main street of the settlement. It was completed in 1729; it was dedicated by the Rev. Phineas Bond of

St. Andrew's Episcopal Church in Bridgeton.

Newcastle, Delaware, and the Rev. John Pierson, missionary at Salem for the Society for Propagating the Gospel in Foreign Parts.

During the lives of the Gibbon brothers, the parish flourished, but after their deaths it slowly dwindled. Leonard Gibbon and his wife were buried in the chancel, and with their death went the spirit that had kept the parish alive. Settlers continued to arrive in Cohansey, but these were Quakers, Baptists, and Presbyterians who were not interested in the preservation of the Anglican church. Indeed, a number of them had fled England to escape the tyranny of a state church. For some years the building was used as a stable; later it was damaged by fire and finally demolished in the 1830s. Descendants of the Gibbons had their ancestors' remains removed and reinterred in the Presbyterian cemetery. This act marked the complete collapse of the Episcopal church in the area.

It was 1851 before regular Episcopal church services were held in Bridgeton. These were conducted at various times in the Baptist Session House, the Court House, Grosscups Hall, and Temperance Hall, with priests from Salem officiating. Dr. John S. Kedney conducted those held in the Baptist Session House in 1851. From 1852 until March of 1857, monthly services were held in the Court House by Dr. A. B. Patterson. Enthusiasm waned a bit from 1857 to 1860, and services were not held on a regular monthly basis. The Rev. M. Bradin officiated occasionally during this time and kept the spirit alive.

In 1860, the Rev. Dr. Franklin L. Knight arrived on the scene, and his dynamic personality was to have a profound effect on the history of the Episcopal faith in the area. That was the year in which he became the resident missionary for the Diocese of New Jersey in Cape May and Cumberland Counties. He wasted no time in gathering together the Bridgeton Episcopalians. They met at the home of Robert Nichols on the evening of December 21, 1860, "for the purpose of organizing an Episcopal Church in the town of Bridgeton."[2] At this meeting Robert Nichols and Stephen Cox were nominated as

Wardens; Percival Nichols, Jonathan Davis, John Salkeld, Charles Davis, and Charles B. Fithian were nominated as Vestrymen. Sunday, December 23, following Divine services at Grosscups Hall, a congregational meeting was held with Dr. Knight presiding. At this meeting these men were elected to hold office until Easter Monday, April 1, 1861. Despite the enthusiasm originally generated by Dr. Knight, they did not hold their first meeting until March 2nd, less than a month before their terms of office expired. Apparently they had been working independently, as they immediately authorized the Wardens to take the necessary steps to have the church incorporated. Dr. Knight appointed Robert Nichols and Stephen Cox, along with John Salkeld, to purchase a suitable lot of ground on which to erect the church building. The actions of the Wardens and Vestrymen proving satisfactory to the congregation of twenty-three people, they were re-elected to continue their efforts in establishing a church home.

A Certificate of Corporation was deposited on April 2, 1861, with Providence Ludlam, Esq., clerk of the Court of Common Pleas of Cumberland County.[3] In the meantime, Robert Nichols reported that he had purchased the home and grounds of Mrs. Emily Buck at the northeast corner of Pearl and Washington Streets for the sum of two thousand dollars. Since, at the time of the purchase, the church was not incorporated, the purchase was made in the name of Robert Nichols. At the annual convention of the Diocese of New Jersey, held in Trenton in the spring of 1861, St. Andrew's Episcopal Church at Bridgeton was admitted into union with the Diocese.

After this flurry of activity the Vestry and the congregation experienced a period of indecision, probably brought about by their worsening financial plight. Dr. Knight reported to the Vestry on July 2, 1861 that the Diocese had reduced his stipend to fifty dollars per year. In an effort to assist Dr. Knight, the Vestry authorized that the entire Sunday offering be given to him. Since the church had been using this money to pay their rent and other expenses, it was decided to assess each adult fifty cents per quarter year to cover these outlays. As the Vestry had previously accepted an offer to lease the Baptist Meeting House on Pearl Street, it now found it necessary to terminate this arrangement and to accept an offer from the Sons of Temperance to rent their hall for the small sum of fifty cents for each day the hall was used. These problems were apparently causing internal strife among the members of the Vestry, and at a special meeting held in the summer of 1862, Robert Nichols resigned as Senior Warden. Although the church was now incorporated and could purchase and own property, it had never purchased the house on Pearl and Washington Streets from Mr. Nichols, which he was holding for it. On September 18, 1862, the Vestry informed Mr. Nichols that the church had no legal nor moral obligation to him for this house and lot. He had paid two thousand dollars for the property, and had offered to assume half of this expense when the church bought the property. The Vestry released him from his $1,000 pledge at the same time that it informed him that it was no longer interested in the property.

In the meantime, Mr. Truman Chapman donated to the church a lot on the corner of Cohansey and Lamning Streets, provided the church would build on it within a year. For whatever reason, the church didn't find this property any more attractive than that originally secured by Mr. Nichols. Finally at a meeting held on April 26, 1863, a committee was appointed to consider an offer of a piece of ground from Mr. S. Emlen. This lot met the requirements of the Vestry and was purchased on May 12, 1863, for the sum of $400. Although the reasons for selecting this lot are not stated, they must have been compelling, because the church forfeited all claim to the free ground offered by Mr. Chapman. Within four months, on September 16, 1863, the Right Reverend William H. Odenheimer laid the cornerstone of St. Andrew's Church.

With the laying of the cornerstone for a permanent church building, the Rev. Dr. Franklin Knight considered his mission in Bridgeton accomplished. He severed his connections with St. Andrew's so that he might continue his missionary work in other parts of Cumberland and Cape May Counties.

With three well-attended services on July 31, 1864, St. Andrew's congregation celebrated the completion of their new church building. The Vestry reported that the total cost of the church, including Sunday School room and carriage shed, was $9,021.88. Subscriptions and donations received amounted to $6,061.22, leaving a balance of $2,960.66. By November 30, 1865, the balance was paid, and the church was free of all indebtedness. It was on this date that the church was consecrated by the Bishop of the Diocese. Robert Nichols, who had resigned in the summer of 1862 as the Senior Warden, still maintained his love for the church, as it was he who had made the early consecration possible. When the building committee announced the amount still needed to pay off the costs of construction, Nichols volunteered to pay this amount if the church would pay the balance he felt they owed on the lot. The offer was accepted, and the church was debt-free, due largely to the generosity of Mr. Nichols, who had earlier been rebuffed by the Vestry.

By 1867, the Vestry was considering the feasibility of purchasing a bell for the tower. A committee was appointed to collect funds for this purpose, and in the amazingly short span of four weeks, $956.80 had been collected. A bell weighing 1,095 pounds was purchased from E. R. Mencely Works in Troy, New York for $597.50, leaving a sizable balance to be used for other purposes. The bell was joyously rung for the first time at Easter Services in 1867.

On April 8, 1869, at a special Vestry meeting, Rev. Henry M. Stuart resigned as Rector of St. Andrew's. He had served the parish for five hectic years when it was first organizing, and through the strength of his personality had held it together. Now that the church was well established in its beautiful new building, he felt that his services were needed elsewhere.

Unfortunately, the next twenty-five to thirty years were unhappy ones for St. Andrew's. Plagued by financial difficulties, the church was unable to meet its expenses, and the Vestry found itself in the position of having to make up the differences on quite a few occasions. A large part of every Vestry meeting was devoted to the problem of augmenting the slim income of the parish. At practically every congregational meeting a deficit was reported. It was finally decided to rent or sell the pews to members of the parish, but even this measure failed to provide sufficient funds to cover expenses. As a result, there was a steady flow of priests in and out of the rectorship of St. Andrew's, with few remaining more than two or three years. Often they left with their salaries hundreds of dollars in arrears, even though they only received $700 to $1,000 per year, and had to provide their own rectory.

The situation in the parish reached its lowest ebb in October 1896. It was decided by the Vestry and the Bishop, the Right Reverend John Scarborough, that St. Andrew's could not support a rector. The solution agreed upon was to combine the rectorships of St. Andrew's in Bridgeton and Saint John's in Salem. The Rev. C. M. Perkins, who was Rector of Saint John's, would assume the Rectorship of St. Andrew's while still maintaining the Rectorship of Saint John's. He would continue to reside in Salem, but his curate, the Rev. C. G. Hannah, would live in Bridgeton. This arrangement worked so well that, by May 1897, just seven months later, the Vestry was able to call Rev. Hannah to be Rector of St. Andrew's and disassociate the church with Saint John's. He was hired at a yearly salary of $700.

Financial difficulties usually lead to other problems; this was true with St. Andrew's. Some members of the parish, along with three Vestrymen, had become dissatisfied with the way things were handled, and they began worshipping separately in a building on Elmer Street. The leader of this group was Mr. J. Dennington. A special meeting of the Vestry was called on September 19, 1896, and a letter was sent to Mr. Dennington reminding him that this action was contrary to the Canons of the Episcopal Church. The letter did not produce any results, so on September 23rd, another letter was sent and the Bishop was notified. At the regular meeting of the Vestry on October 8th, the three errant members of the Vestry resigned, and the schism was crushed by the Bishop. Time heals all wounds, even those of the church. The Vestry was unable to secure supply priests after Rev. Hannah resigned in 1899, and Mr. Dennington was asked to read Morning Prayer, which confirms that a Christian solution was found to their previous differences.

After the Rev. Hannah resigned, the Vestry found itself in the same untenable position of having to find a rector while at the same time the financial situation was such that it was difficult for them to pay the agreed salary. A special congregational meeting was called August 27, 1899, to discuss the advisability of St. Andrew's becoming a mission. It was finally decided to leave the decision to the Vestry. Several more attempts were made by the Vestry to obtain a priest, and, finally, Rev. F. Heisley accepted. During his two years as Rector, the pledge-and-envelope system was instituted as another attempt to solve their financial problems. Rev. Heisley resigned in 1901, and the Rev. Albert Monk became Rector the same year, but resigned October 4, 1903. After Mr. Monk's resignation the Vestry decided that the only solution was to make an arrangement with another church to share the rector. Such an arrangement, upon the approval of the Bishop, was made with Christ Church in Millville.

This solution turned out to be a happy one for St. Andrew's. The Rev. J. Clarke Robbins, who was officiating at Christ Church in Millville, became Priest-In-Charge of St. Andrew's. Dr. Robbins and the St. Andrew's Parish got along so well together that, in 1914, Dr. Robbins became Rector of St. Andrew's. He had served the parish as Priest-In-Charge for ten years and would be their Rector for an additional eight years. With such a long period of stability in their leadership, St. Andrew's made great progress. The first rectory was purchased, which was located at the corner of Walnut and Cedar Streets. The present parish house was built, and the altar was given to the church by the Altar Guild. After serving the church for eighteen years, Dr. Robbins announced his resignation to a stunned congregation on April 19, 1922. He had been greatly loved, and had brought a period of stability and harmony to the church that it had not known since its inception.

Rev. Ross Flanagan followed Dr. Robbins as Rector, but only remained for two short years. He in turn was succeeded by Rev. James S. Holland, D. D., who became Rector in August 1925. Rev. Holland was Rector for eighteen years, steering the parish through the turbulent times of the Great Depression and the beginning of World War II. In 1926, the Vestry purchased the present rectory on East Avenue for $7,385.30, and sold the old rectory for $3,881. With the deteriorating economic conditions in the country, the parish once again felt the bite of financial woes. Beginning in 1930, every Vestry meeting was occupied with efforts to find solutions to monetary problems. Many times the Rector, Wardens, and Vestrymen had to borrow money just to meet the operating expenses. Even as late as 1939, despite gallant efforts by the Vestry and the Women's Auxiliary, the Rector's salary was $220 short, the organist was owed money, and there was no sexton.

Dr. Holland resigned as Rector on December 27, 1943, and the Rev. W. Gordon Craig was Priest-In-Charge until he was killed in an accident in 1945. The Rev. Leon A. Shearer served as Rector until January 1959. Upon his resignation, the Vestry called the present Rector, Rev. E. Thomas Higgons, who was formally instituted by the Right Reverend Alfred L. Banyard on April 29, 1959. The work of rebuilding the church spiritually and financially started by Rev. Craig in the war years has been vigorously carried on by Rev. Higgons. On October 16, 1960, ground was broken for a new church school building. Taking part in the ceremonies were Rev. Higgons, John Toothaker, Jr., Donald Burton, Charles Craddock, and Howard Hensel. On Whitsunday, May 21, 1961, Rev. Higgons laid the cornerstone, and on the eve of St. Andrew's Day, 1961, the building was blessed by Bishop Banyard. The entire parish entered whole-heartedly into this project, assuring its success. When completed, the cost of the new building, without furniture and appurtenances, was $34,632.

St. Andrew's Episcopal Church has weathered many a storm, spiritual and financial, throughout its long history. Through the hard work, unflagging faith, and financial sacrifices of many of its Wardens and Vestrymen, as well as the Rectors, the church has continued to serve the needs of its community since 1851, when it had no place except rented quarters in which to hold worship services.

---

1.   *The Anglican Church in New Jersey*, by Nelson R. Burr.

2.   *History of St. Andrew's*, by Rev. Canon E. Thomas Higgons.

3.   Ibid.

XLVII

The Presbyterian Church at Absecon

Absecon, 1867

I t was election night in the small, shore community of Absecon. One would think that nothing of great significance could happen there, a town of only 7,000 people. Yet the election results in that seashore community, through which millions of shore travelers have sped but never seen, were to be reported in the large metropolitan newspapers of Philadelphia and as far away as Jacksonville, Florida. The new Mayor of Absecon was the minister of the Presbyterian Church.

The Reverend David Hodgson passionately believes that the sacred and the profane, the ministry and the market place, the religious and the political cannot be separated and placed in different worlds. To him the wisdom of the Old Testament is immaculate in its simplicity, and its truth is self-evident. As he informed his congregation in his sermon before announcing his candidacy, "Where there is ignorance of God, the people run wild; and every history book, if it is honest, will reveal a direct correlation between a society's ignorance of God and its level of social immorality and political corruption. And let's face it; our world is terribly ignorant of God." He goes on to tell his congregation that there has been a rule of thumb that ministers shouldn't get into politics. But, "… Moses never heard it! The disciples never heard it

The Presbyterian Church at Absecon.

from the lips of Jesus! The Reformers in the 15th century didn't believe it! The founding fathers of our country didn't bring it with them from England. It is of recent origin, a product of a dying church in a deteriorating country."

So after much soul searching and prayerful consideration, Dave Hodgson, minister of The Presbyterian Church at Absecon, announced his decision to run for the office of mayor of Absecon. Whether it was Divine Providence or not, he won over two other candidates by a plurality of 200 votes.

By such independent thinking, Dave Hodgson has taken his place among the other courageous ministers this historic congregation has encouraged over the years. Such men as Dr. Samuel Zwemer, pioneer missionary to the Arab world; Dr. Edward Roberts, beloved dean and professor of Princeton Theological Seminary; Harold Voelked, missionary to Korea—all were ministers or student preachers to this shore congregation.

The strong religious work in this area was begun by the dauntless and indefatigable John Brainerd. He was appointed missionary to the Indians in 1759, but he ministered to Indian and colonist alike. He was the only resident preacher between Mount Holly and the shore area. Another famous pioneer preacher of that era, Rev. Philip Vickers Fithian, preached at Absecon on February 26, 1775. At that time there was no church building, and the itinerant preachers were dependent upon sympathetic individuals offering a meeting place. In the Rev. Fithian's case the sympathetic individual was John Steelman, who provided the use of his home, which had a large single room on the second floor that made an ideal meeting place for public worship. Rev. Fithian records the occasion in his journal, "Sunday 26th. I preached to a thin assembly at Cedar Bridge meeting house. At 2 P.M. I preached at Absecon, at one Mr. Steelman's; a full house." From this brief, terse note we learn that even the early settlers of Absecon supported and encouraged the traveling preachers. It wasn't until 1841 that there was a permanent Presbyterian church in Atlantic County, and that was built at Mays Landing.

There can be no doubt that divine guidance directed Allen H. Brown to the ministry and the South Jersey area. He was graduated from Princeton Theological Seminary in 1843, and after a year of advanced study, followed a call to Mays Landing, where he became the second Synodical Missionary in New Jersey, following John Brainerd of ninety years before. The Rev. Brown devoted his life to organizing congregations and encouraging them to build churches. He was directly responsible for the organization of seven churches in Atlantic County alone, one of these being The Presbyterian Church at Absecon.

One of Rev. Brown's friends and strongest supporters was Dr. Jonathan Pitney. Dr. Pitney was an influential resident of Absecon, and still considered himself a Presbyterian, even though he had helped organize Absecon's Methodist Church more than thirty years before. The Pitney family apparently was deeply religious and committed to the furtherance of the Christian faith in this area, since we read in Mr. Brown's journal that he visited and dined at Dr. Pitney's frequently. The doctor's wife was also very much involved, since we learn that she presented Mr. Brown with a pulpit Bible, and made other contributions to encourage him in his work.

The actual beginning of the Presbyterian church took place on Saturday, June 29, 1850, when Rev. Brown and Dr. Pitney went to the new Odd Fellows Hall on Church Street to make arrangements for a Presbyterian service to be held there the next day. In keeping with his intense interest, Dr. Pitney donated the rental fee for the hall. Services continued there, and in 1851, the Presbytery sent the Rev. Edward Eells to assist Mr. Brown. Eells was the first of several ministers sent by the Presbytery who apparently found greener pastures elsewhere, as he did not linger long in this virgin territory. One who found the challenge to his liking, however, was James M. Edmonds, who was sent by the Presbytery in the summer of 1855.

Messrs. Edmonds, Brown, and Dr. Pitney met on June 17, 1856 to consider the purchase of ground for a church building and cemetery. Such a building seemed remote at the time, but the Camden and Atlantic Railroad had been in operation for two years and real estate values were rising rapidly. A committee to choose the site was formed, consisting of Enoch Doughty, James Edmonds, and Allen Brown. This committee selected four acres owned by Frederich Chamberlain, and this is the ground on which the church and cemetery are now located. It was necessary that a Board of Trustees be elected to purchase the land for church purposes, and on August 25, 1856, the Board was elected, with Edmonds as president. The deed from Chamberlain to the trustees of The Presbyterian Church at Absecon was dated October 16, 1856, and recorded at Mays Landing. The cost was $1,400.

Three years later, at seven o'clock on a Friday evening, February 11th, the Rev. Mr. Brown preached to sixteen persons in Odd Fellows Hall. The next afternoon the session of the First Presbyterian Church of Leeds Point met in the same hall, with Mr. Brown as moderator. In the evening a prayer meeting was held with Mr. Brown preaching. At this time the members of the session constituted themselves a committee of Presbytery and invited the Rev. Miles J. Merwin to sit as corresponding member.

The following Sunday, February 13, 1859, with Rev. Brown preaching, The Presbyterian Church at Absecon was formally organized. The text for Rev. Brown's sermon was, "We thank God for what we have seen and take courage." George W. Scott was ordained and installed as Ruling Elder. Felix Leeds, who recently moved from Leeds Point, was installed as Deacon. The new church was born with only eight members: George W. Scott and his wife Frances, Felix

Leeds and his wife Eunice, Rebecca W. Doughty, Mrs. Janet Fariah, John Weber, and Rev. Miles J. Merwin.

Church services were still held in Odd Fellows Hall. With their minister serving the congregation of Absecon and Leeds Point, the worship services at Absecon were held in the afternoon so that the morning and evening services at Leeds Point would not be interrupted. Although the congregation owned four acres of land, they were not yet strong enough to launch their own building program. In fact, a lot of work had to be done to clear the land for building. In 1861, on Washington's birthday, the gigantic task of clearing the lot for the cemetery was completed in just one day. This difficult task was achieved by good organization, hard work, and pleasant fellowship. Twenty teenaged boys had a good time keeping the huge bonfires going, and the loan of Luca Lake's stump machine probably carried the day. During the following fall, Eustice Johnson plowed the property, and D. E. Snow and Allen Brown laid out and surveyed the cemetery.

Atlantic Democrat and Cape May County Register, a weekly newspaper published in Egg Harbor City, printed a notice in the April 5, 1862 issue offering burial lots for sale at prices ranging from five to seven cents per square foot. The editor of the newspaper apparently read his own advertisements, since the earliest cemetery deed was executed between the trustees of the church and O. A. Douglas, the paper's editor. He purchased Lot No. 144, with a deed dated September 13, 1862. The first internment was that of the Rev. James S. Mayne, who died at Absecon on August 30, 1860, before the cemetery ground was cleared; but the grave was close to New Jersey Avenue, south of the main entrance, in an area probably not affected by the dense undergrowth.

Five years had gone by since the organization of the church, yet no regular minister had been ordained or installed, and the congregation continued to hold its services in rented halls. As mentioned earlier, the first services were held in Odd Fellows Hall on Church Street, and later they were held at Fithian's Hall of the store located at the corner of New Jersey and Station Avenues. On July 3, 1864, the Rev. Charles T. McMullin was invited to supply the pulpit until October 1st. He had preached at Leeds Point and at Absecon on May 29th. Mr. McMullin gladly accepted the opportunity to spend the summer at the shore. Not only did he enjoy the shore, but the congregation was so appreciative of his efforts in their behalf that they forgot about the October 1st deadline and made him their first installed minister.

The Absecon Academy had been built by the Presbyterians in 1856, and Mr. McMullin's first act as pastor was to change the place of worship from Fithian's Hall to the Academy. The first service was held there on August 14, 1864. It had been the custom for the morning services to be held at Leeds Point and afternoon services at Absecon. Rev. McMullin changed all this, and Absecon was no longer treated as the mission congregation. At this time a Sunday School was organized, and Rev. McMullin was invited in September 1864 to continue as stated supply for both Absecon and Leeds Point, and to teach at the Absecon Academy. He received an annual salary of $300. On November 1, 1864, he was ordained as evangelist by the Presbytery of West Jersey.

The enthusiasm generated by Charles McMullin resulted in efforts being made by the congregation to erect its own church building. The cornerstone was laid November 16, 1865. The congregation insisted on a traditional church building with a spire high enough to be visible by the entire community. This created an engineering problem, but was solved by assembling the framework in the vestibule and erecting it from there. One hundred and five feet tall, the steeple was raised August 2, 1886, and from that day has stood through the years, viewed by millions of shore travelers as a witness to the Christian faith of the early settlers. On June 20, 1867, the church was dedicated. The dimensions of the building were fifty by thirty-two feet, with fifty-six pews seating 250 people. The cost was officially given as $4,400. Furniture and fixtures cost $700, the four acres of land, $1,000, so that the total cost for the church was $6,100. At the time of the dedication all debts were paid, except a mortgage of $500 on the property and $300 still due on the bell and organ.

The present congregation is justifiably proud of the Schulmerich Carillon, which has replaced the original tower bell. In keeping with the congregation's involvement with the community, the carillon plays two concerts daily, one at noon and one at 6 P.M., to enrich the daily lives of the Absecon residents as well as shore travelers speeding along Route 30 who might have their windows open and their ears attuned to the joyous pealing of the bells. The carillon was a gift to the church in 1969, and consists of two sets of English bells.

Serious throat trouble ended Rev. McMullin's career as a preacher in January 1871. Lean years for the church followed. Supply ministers and students came to the pulpit, but the church was able to hold services only every two weeks. During the winter of 1881 there was no preaching at all, but members of the congregation made sure the Sunday school was continued. Hard times lasted until 1886, when a call was extended to E. Morris Ferguson, who accepted and became the second regular pastor of the church.

The first society of the church was organized at the home of John H. Doughty in May 1887. This was known as the Mite Society, and this group provided needed funds for the church's work. When one realizes that the dues for the devoted members of this Society were only ten cents, it becomes apparent that they worked hard on fund raising activities.

A church pamphlet says, "In 1866 the present spire was raised in the center of town, proclaiming then as it does to this day, that the church's place is in the midst of community life." The present pastor believes this statement and believes in putting it to work. That is why he ran for mayor. In fact he believes that such action by church people is essential if America is to reverse the history of the demise of the big civilizations. According to Rev. Hodgson, "There has always been a strong faith that the American dream had something to do with divine providence." He believes that Absecon can be an example for other cities and for the nation, that politics and religion are not only compatible but necessary to improve the quality of American democracy. His congregation agrees—not a single member left the church when he announced his candidacy for mayor.

XLVIII

Cathedral of St. John the Baptist

Paterson, 1870

atholicism was late in arriving in northern New Jersey. As early as 1678 Dutch settlers had traveled up the Passaic River as far as Acquackanonk Landing (Passaic), buying land from the Lenni Lenape Indians. Discovery of iron ore in the Ramapo Mountains by the industrious Dutch brought a wave of immigrants to the area to work in the mines. Among these imigrants were three families from the Black Forest of Baden—the Merrions, the Strubes, and the Schulsters—who are considered the founding families of Catholicism in the area. Feeling the need for religious exercises, these families requested the services of a Catholic priest. Responding to their call, Rev. Ferdinand Farmer, who was an itinerant missionary stationed in Philadelphia, arrived in Macopin (Echo Lake) and performed the first Catholic baptism in 1768. Thus Macopin became the birthplace of Catholicism in northern New Jersey.

Other Catholic families of Irish and German origins were soon settled in the area. To provide them with religious services, Father Farmer changed his itinerary to include this section. Each spring and fall he started from Philadelphia, traveling north along the Delaware Valley to the northern part of New Jersey into New York, then south

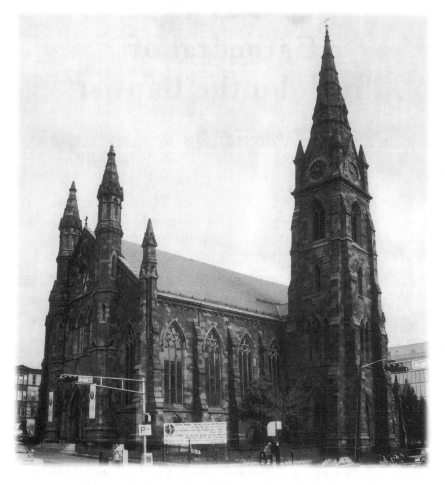

The Cathedral of St. John the Baptist in Paterson.

through Elizabethtown and Trenton, completing his journey in Philadelphia.

A number of trails and primitive roads soon connected the settlements of Long Pond (Ringwood), Mount Hope, Macopin, Bottle Hill (Madison), Pompton, Hackensack, and the little village at the Great Falls which was to become known as Paterson. These trails converged in the vicinity of the Great Falls at an area known as "Goffle," which in Dutch means "Fork in trails." Missionary Farmer tended to the needs of the Catholics in this area for many years, including the trying times of the Revolutionary War. He died in 1786, but many other missionaries followed him and kept the spark of Catholicism alive.

By 1791, there were only ten houses and a small Dutch Reformed Church clustered on the banks of the Passaic River just below the Great Falls. In that year, Alexander Hamilton, President Washington's Secretary of the Treasury, obtained a charter from the New Jersey State Legislature for "The Society for Establishing Useful Manufactures," known as S.U.M. William Paterson was Governor of the state at the time, and in recognition for the help he had given in obtaining the charter, Hamilton named the town Paterson. The S.U.M. was to figure prominently in the development of the Cathedral of St. John the Baptist.

The first Mass was celebrated in Paterson in 1817 by Father Lariscy at the home of Michael Gillespie. Some years later, when the Gillespies moved to Belleville, Mass was celebrated in the home of Robert McNamee at Broadway and Mulberry Streets. At that time there were only thirteen families comprising about fifty people who participated in these devotions. A room was set aside as a small chapel which Father Lariscy, and later Father Langdill, used to minister to the Catholics of Paterson.

The promise of work in what was now becoming an industrial town prompted a large number of people from Ireland to settle in Paterson. Since most of these people were Catholics, the need for a church was very apparent. Roswell Colt, a son of the first superintendent of S.U.M., was now president of the Society. He gave a small plot of ground at Mill and Market Streets to the Catholics on which to build a church. A small, frame building was erected the same year. It was a simple affair, containing only a table altar and rough, wooden benches without backs, and was named for St. John. One hundred people attended the first Mass, celebrated by the pastor, Rev. Richard Bulger. The parish consisted of the three counties of Passaic, Morris, and Sussex.

Not only were the industries of Paterson thriving, but work was started on the Morris and Essex Canal. All of this activity created many jobs, and soon additional immigrants were arriving from Ireland and Germany. The little Paterson church became too small to accommodate all these new arrivals. At first it was thought to build a new gallery around three sides of the old church to provide additional seating capacity. This proved to be impractical, however; a new, larger building was needed.

The arrangement with S.U.M. for the land on which the church was built provided that the land would revert to the Society if it was not used for religious purposes. Since a larger church could not be built on the original plot of ground, Roswell Colt came to the rescue. In 1828, he authorized the parish to sell the old church building, and then gave the parish a plot of land on Oliver Street. The sale of the old building realized about $1,600 for the parish. The value of the land on Oliver Street was about $2,000, which Roswell Colt paid to the Society out of his own pocket.

A large stone church was decided upon. The foundation was laid of stone hauled by boat from Little Falls, and the cornerstone was blessed in 1828 by Bishop DuBois of New York. Unfortunately, the War of 1812 had created a depression, and its effects, which were still being felt, caused a temporary delay in the construction of the new church. It was not until 1836 that the building was completed. It had a large, well-lighted basement, which was used for years by the German-speaking Catholics for their own religious services. Eventually they built their own church, St. Boniface, and the curate of St. John, Father John J. Schandel, became their resident pastor. In spite of the panic of 1837, the debt incurred in building this new church was paid in record time. By 1846, the church again needed to be enlarged. This was done by adding galleries to increase the seating capacity.

Paterson was growing rapidly. A thriving brewery, rolling mills, and the famous Rogers and American Locomotive Works supplied jobs for an expanding population. In 1853, the famous Colt revolver (first used in the Seminole War) was invented. But the greatest industry of all was the spinning and weaving of silk. Silk was to remain the largest, single industry in Paterson for nearly a hundred years. People flocked to Paterson seeking work.

The seating capacity of St. John the Baptist was inadequate to handle the additional worshippers brought to the area by this industrial activity. There was no way the Oliver Street church could be enlarged again. A new location was necessary. A large piece of ground on Main and Grand Streets was selected, even though the price was a forbidding $10,000. Despite the hardships imposed by the Civil War, which was in progress at the time, the entire purchase price was contributed in two months. During the lifespan of the Oliver Street church, the parishioners had been served by many zealous priests.

The scene was now set for one of the most inspiring periods in the history of the church. Paterson had grown from a village of ten houses in 1791 to a population of 10,000 in 1851, and to nearly 20,000 in 1861. By now the discriminating laws excluding Catholics from holding public office had been repealed, and the climate was right for the rapid growth of St. John.

Plans for the new church were prepared by the eminent American architect, P. C. Kieley. The land at Main and Grand Streets was cleared, and construction was started. Native brownstone from Little Falls was again the material used, which was hauled this time down the Morris and Essex Canal. On September 10, 1865, the cornerstone was laid by the Most Reverend James Roosevelt Bayley, Bishop of Newark. In 1853, New Jersey had become a diocese. Work was to move slowly, however, and the actual construction of the church took five years and cost $200,000. On July 31, 1870, the building was dedicated by the Most Reverend Bishop Wood of Philadelphia, acting for Bishop Bayley, who was in Europe at the time.

All of this was accomplished under the inspiring leadership of the Very Reverend William McNulty, who had arrived at St. John's in 1863 and was to remain for fifty-nine eventful years. During these years great things were done in the fields of education, orphaned children, and the sick and poor. Dean McNulty busied himself in these charitable endeavors, as the welfare of those in need was closest to his heart.

According to legend, the first Catholic school was started by Hugh Dougherty, an Irish schoolmaster, in 1826. There is no doubt, however, that the first Catholic school in New Jersey was opened by Father Richard Duffy in 1835. Classes were conducted in the basement of the Oliver Street church, which had just been completed. For a number of years, dedicated laymen taught the boys and girls. One of the most illustrious of these laymen was John Philip Holland. While living in Paterson he invented the first submarine, the *Fenian Ram*, which was successfully launched in the Hudson River in 1881. Eventually, Christian Brothers came to staff the boys school, and at the urgent request of Dean McNulty, sisters from Convent Station agreed to teach the girls.

At first the nuns were housed in the St. Agnes Academy on Church Street, but this meant a long walk for the sisters, which was particularly unpleasant on cold, winter days. Finally, the Dean was able to build a lovely convent on DeGrasse Street for them. School enrollment grew rapidly, and in the 1880s the Dean bought additional property on Oliver Street and built a three-story brick building. In 1895, Sister Regina Nevin, with the backing of Dean McNulty, opened St. John's High School for Girls. It was situated in a building on Church Street, but in 1923 most of the classes were moved to the Oliver Street school. Many changes and improvements were made over the years, including the admission of boys to the high school. Dean McNulty would have approved the attention given the young people by both the grammar and high school; unfortunately, because of economic reasons, it was necessary to close the high school in 1972.

Even closer to the Dean's heart than education was the care of orphaned children. Father Senez had opened a small orphanage in the 1850s on Church Street, but the carnage of the Civil War created more orphans than this small building could accommodate. When Dean McNulty bought the Sheppard farm, consisting of seventy-three acres in Totowa, for a new cemetery, the purchase included a large farmhouse. This he immediately equipped in 1867 to the use of the orphans.

When the orphanage was moved to Totowa, the building on Church Street was turned into a hospital, the first St. Joseph's, and placed in the care of the Sisters of Charity of Convent Station. In 1868, the hospital was moved to Main Street. At first this hospital had only twelve beds, but has since grown into one of the largest private hospitals in the state.

Besides the care of the poor, the sick, and the orphaned, Dean McNulty had another great passion—his fight against the abuse of alcohol. Many are the fond stories that are told about the Dean and his crusade against the use of liquor. He made a habit of visiting the saloons, a custom which was well known by all those living in the area. In fact, these visits were so frequent and so well known that a system was devised to warn the imbibers that the Dean was on his way. One man was posted near the door. When he saw the Dean coming, he would throw a stone into the saloon alerting those inside to the danger. They would disappear as fast as they could so that the saloon was empty when the Dean entered. The Dean would then use his cane to sweep all the beer glasses on the tables to the floor.

He did not limit his crusade to the saloons. Whenever he was out for a walk and saw women wearing shawls over their shoulders, he would stop them and inspect their shawls for hidden pails of beer. If he found any, he would immediately dump the beer into the street and send the women on their way, empty-handed.

Dean William McNulty served St. John into the third decade of the 20th century, and the city of Paterson reached its zenith during his lifetime. Many parishes and schools were opened, numerous institutions and societies were started, all of which he had a hand in. On the 18th of June, 1922, he was called from his earthly labors. He had lived ninety-four years, had been a priest for sixty-five, and had served St. John's Church for fifty-nine years. Not only was he mourned by his parishioners, but by all of the people of the city of Paterson. On the day of his funeral, all places of business were closed. It is reported that the funeral procession was still leaving St. John's Church when the casket arrived at Holy Sepulchre Cemetery for temporary interment.

A fitting memorial was deemed necessary for such a great man, and the task of creating such a monument was given to Paterson's gifted sculptor, Gaetano Frederici. A bronze statue representing the Dean listening to a small boy was finally finished. The Dean's remains were reinterred beneath this statue, on the ground of the church he loved so much. Father John O'Rourke, S. J., who preached the eulogy, called him, "The last of the pioneer priests of North America." Truly he was Paterson's "Grand Old Man."

Despite the passing of the great, life goes on. The Rt. Rev. James T. Delehanty led the church through the aftermath of World War I and the Great Depression. Even in these troublesome times the church was completely renovated and redecorated. New flooring, roofing, and lighting were installed. The sanctuary was enlarged, and a beautiful new marble pulpit and altar rail were added.

Paterson Cathedral of St. John the Baptist

With the tremendous increase in the population, the Holy See, in December 1937, divided the state into four Dioceses, with Paterson as one. Old timers claimed that this action fulfilled one of Dean McNulty's prophecies—that St. John's Church would one day become a cathedral. The territory of the diocese is the same as Father Bulger's original parish, the counties of Passaic, Morris, and Sussex. A three-story wing was added to the parish hall to house the chancery offices. New vestments and all other accessories needed for pontifical services in a cathedral were procured. Monsignor Delehanty was made Vicar-General, and Father Hill, Superintendent of Schools. In the spring of 1938, the installation of the first Bishop, Most Reverend Thomas H. McLaughlin, took place.

The Cathedral of St. John the Baptist continues to serve well the needs of its community. With the increase of Spanish-speaking people in the city of Paterson, services in the Spanish language have been included. As proof of its historic importance and its value to the surrounding area from its beginning in the 1700s, the Cathedral of St. John the Baptist has been named a national historic monument by the U.S. Department of the Interior.

Suggestions for Further Reading

Acrelius, Israel, *A History of New Sweden.*

Allison, Clyde M., *Deerfield Presbyterian Church 1737–1847.*

Anderson, Rev. Samuel R., *History of the Old Stone Church.*

Armitage, Thomas, D.D., LL.D., *History of the Baptists.*

Bass, Jeremiah, *History of the Church in Burlington.*

Beck, Henry Charlton, *Forgotten Towns of Southern New Jersey.*

Beck, Henry Charlton, *Jersey Genesis.*

Beck, Henry Charlton, *More Forgotten Towns of Southern New Jersey.*

Beck, Henry Charlton, *The Roads of Home.*

Boucher, Jack E., *Absegami Yesterday.*

Brown, Rev. Allen H., *History of Pittsgrove Church.*

Brown, Rev. Allen H., *Outline History of the Presbyterian Church of West or South Jersey from 1700–1865.*

Burr, Nelson R., *The Anglican Church in New Jersey.*

Cawley, James and Margaret, *Exploring the Little Rivers of New Jersey.*

Chalmers, Kathryn H., *Down the Long-A-Coming*.

Child, Lydia Maria, *Youthful Emigrant*.

Cochran, Jean Carter, *Church Street Stories of American Village Life*.

Cunningham, John T., *Colonial New Jersey*.

Cunningham, John T., *New Jersey—America's Main Road*.

DeCou, George, *Burlington: A Provincial Capital*.

DeCou, George, *Historical Sketches of Crosswicks and Neighbors*.

DeCou, George, *Moorestown and Her Neighbors*.

DeCou, George, *The Historic Rancocas*.

Elmer, Lucius Q. C., *History of the Early Settlement and Progress of Cumberland County, New Jersey*.

Elwell, Alice Ayars, *Glimpses of Old Cohansey*.

Ewing, Rev. John, *History of the Pittsgrove Presbyterian Church, Presbytery of West Jersey from 1812 to 1889*.

Ewing, Sarah W. and Robert McMullin, *Along Absecon Trail*.

Gibbon, Quinton, *Sketch of the First Presbyterian Church of Salem, New Jersey*.

Green, Charles F., *A Place of Olden Days*.

Hall, John, *History of the Presbyterian Church in Trenton, New Jersey*.

Hall, John F., *History of Atlantic City and County, New Jersey*.

Herner, Maurice W., *A History of Evesham Township*.

Heston, Alfred M., *Bicentennial Celebration of the Old Stone Church*.

Heston, Alfred M., *Jersey Wagon Jaunts, Vols. 1 & 11*.

Heston, Alfred M., *South Jersey—A History, Vol. 11*.

Suggestions for Further Reading

Higgons, Rev. E. Thomas, *History of St. Andrew's.*

Hills, Rev. George Morgan, *History of the Church in Burlington, New Jersey.*

Jacquett, Josephine, *The Churches of Salem County, New Jersey.*

Jamison, Wallace N., *Religion in New Jersey: A Brief History.*

Johnson, Amandus W., *The Journal and Biography of Nicholas Collin.*

Klenke, William W., *Historic Episcopal Churches of New Jersey.*

Leiby, Adrian C., *The Buildings of The South Church, Bergenfield, New Jersey.*

Leiby, Adrian C., *The Revolutionary War in the Hackensack Valley.*

Leiby, Adrian C., *The United Churches of Hackensack and Schraalenburgh, New Jersey, 1686–1822.*

Lippincott, Paul S., Jr., *Answered Prayers.*

Lippincott, Wm. R., *Traditions of Old Evesham Township.*

Macaltioner, George B., *Moravian Church at Oldman's Creek.*

Magee, James D., *Bordentown, 1682–1932.*

McGeorge, Isabella C., *Ann Whitall—Heroine of Red Banks.*

McMahon, William, *Historic South Jersey Towns.*

Mellick, Andrew D., Jr., *The Old Farm.*

Miers, Earl Schenck, *Crossroads of Freedom.*

Minotty, Paul, *Saint Peter's Episcopal Church at Berkeley and Clarksboro.*

Minotty, Paul, *The Moravian Church at Oldman's Creek.*

Mints, Margaret Louise, *The Great Wilderness.*

Oerter, M. F., *Moravian Church at Oldman's Creek.*

Palmer, F. Alan, *The Presbyterian Parish of Deerfield Street, 1737–1971.*

Pepper, Adeline, *The Glass Gafers of New Jersey.*

Pierce, Arthur D., *Family Empire in Jersey Iron.*

Pierce, Arthur D., *Iron in the Pines.*

Pierce, Arthur D., *Smugglers' Woods.*

Prowell, George R., *History of Camden County, New Jersey.*

Romeyn, Rev. Theodore B., *Historical Discourse on the First Reformed (Dutch) Church of Hackensack, NJ.*

Russell, Elbert, *The History of Quakerism.*

Schermerhorn, William E., *History of Burlington, New Jersey.*

Sickler, Joseph S., *History of Salem County, New Jersey.*

Sickler, Joseph S., *Tea Burning Town.*

Society of Colonial Wars in the State of New Jersey, *Historic Roadsides in New Jersey.*

Stewart, Frank H., *Notes of Old Gloucester County, Vols. 1 & 3.*

Stockton, Frank R., *Stories of New Jersey.*

Tayler, Rebecca Nicholson, *Small Adventures of a Little Quaker Girl.*

Taylor, Benjamin C., *Annals of Classis and Township of Bergen of the Reformed Dutch Church.*

Van Meter, Anna Hunter, *First Presbyterian Church, Salem, New Jersey.*

Versteeg, D., *Sketch of the Early History of the Reformed Dutch Church of Bergen, NJ.*

Suggestions for Further Reading

Wallace, Philip B., *Colonial Churches and Meeting Houses, Pennsylvania, New Jersey, and Delaware.*

Wallington, Nellie Urner, *Historic Churches of America.*

Weiss, Harry B. and Grace M., *Early Bricklaying in New Jersey.*

Weygandt, Cornelius, *Down Jersey.*

Wright, Helen Marth, *The First Presbyterian Congregation, Mendham, Morris County, New Jersey—History and Records, 1738–1938.*

Zimmerman, J. A. Ernest and Mabel C., *The Silent Bell.*

Index

B

Index

D

E

F

G

H

I

J

K

L

M

O

P

Index

Q

R

Index

Index

T

U

V

W

Index

Y

Z

More Great New Jersey Books from Plexus Publishing

...LD AND HISTORIC CHURCHES OF NEW JERSEY, VOLUMES 1 & 2

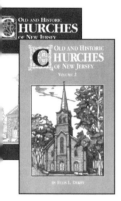

By Ellis L. Derry

These inspirational books allow us to travel back in time to the days when this country was new—a vast and dangerous wilderness with few roads or bridges, schools or churches. It tells the stories of how our forefathers established their religious communities and houses of worship, often through great hardship and sacrifice. To be included in this two-volume history, a church had to be built by the time of the Civil War. A history of each church is given, alongside a photograph or illustration.

Vol. 1/498 pp/hardbound/ISBN 0-937548-50-2/$29.95
Vol. 1/498 pp/softbound/ISBN 0-937548-52-9/$19.95

Vol. 2/372 pp/hardbound/ISBN 0-937548-25-1/$29.95
Vol. 2/372 pp/softbound/ISBN 0-937548-26-X/$19.95

...TRIOTS, PIRATES, AND PINEYS: SIXTY WHO SHAPED NEW JERSEY

By Robert A. Peterson

"*Patriots, Pirates, and Pineys* is excellent ... the type of book that is hard to put down once you open it." —*Daybreak Newsletter*

Southern New Jersey is a region full of rich heritage, and yet it is one of the best kept historical secrets of our nation. Many famous people have lived in southern New Jersey, and numerous world-renowned businesses were started in this area as well.

This collection of biographies provides a history of the area through the stories of such famous figures as John Wanamaker, Henry Rowan, Sara Spenser Washington, Elizabeth Haddon, Dr. James Still, and Joseph Campbell. Some were patriots, some pirates, and some Pineys, but all helped make America what it is today.

1998/155 pp/hardbound/ISBN 0-937548-37-5/$29.95
1998/155 pp/softbound/ISBN 0-937548-39-1/$19.95

...ATURAL PATHWAYS OF NEW JERSEY

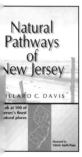

By Millard C. Davis

"Laden with keen observations of the unspoiled world, and the feelings these evoke in Davis, *Natural Pathways of New Jersey* represents a rare and genial wedding of science and heart." —*The Central Record*

Natural Pathways of New Jersey describes in eloquent detail over 100 natural places in New Jersey. Davis's descriptions of beaches, forests, and fields include not only the essence of the landscapes, but also portray the animals and vegetation native to the area.

Natural Pathways of New Jersey is divided into sections by county, making it very readable and easy for anyone to find the cited areas. The book includes over 100 original watercolor illustrations by artist Valerie Smith-Pope and two simple trips that anyone can take, showcasing the best that New Jersey has to offer.

1997/271 pp/softbound/ISBN 0-937548-35-9/$19.95

KATE AYLESFORD, OR, THE HEIRESS OF SWEETWATER

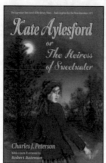

By Charles J. Peterson
With a new Foreword by Robert Bateman

"Plot twists, colorful characters, timely observations, lyrical descriptions of the Pine Barre
and ... an unusually strong and well-educated female protagonist." —*Robert Bateman, fr*
the Foreword to the new edition

The legendary historical romance, *Kate Aylesford: A Story of Refugees*, by Charles
Peterson, first appeared in 1855, was reissued in 1873 as *The Heiress of Sweetwater*, a
spent the entire 20th century out of print. As readable today as when Peterson fi
penned it, *Kate Aylesford* features a memorable cast of characters, an imaginative pl
and a compelling mix of romance, adventure, and history. Plexus Publishing is pleased
return this remarkable novel to print.

2001/276 pp/Hardbound/ISBN: 0-937548-46-4/$22.95

THE FORKS: A BRIEF HISTORY OF THE AREA

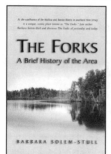

By Barbara Solem-Stull

Located on a navigable waterway, yet inland and remote, "The Forks" in South Jers
was a haven for smugglers at the dawn of the Revolutionary War. This short histe
describes the contribution of The Forks and its inhabitants to America's fight
independence and introduces a variety of colorful characters: early settler E
Mullica, the treacherous Benedict Arnold, visionary citizens Elijah Clark and Richa
Wescoat, ship builder Captain John Van Sant, highwayman Joe Mulliner, and
fictional Kate Aylesford—immortalized as "The Heiress of Sweetwater" in a popu
novel first published in 1855.

2002/48 pp/softbound/ISBN 0-937548-51-0/$9.95

OVER THE GARDEN STATE & OTHER STORIES

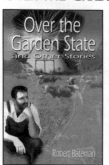

By Robert Bateman

Novelist Bateman (*Pinelands, Whitman's Tomb*) offers six new stories set in his na
southern New Jersey. While providing plenty of authentic local color in his portraya
small-town and farm life, the bustle of the Jersey shore with its boardwalks, and the s
tude and otherworldliness of the famous Pine Barrens, Bateman's sensitively portra
protagonists are the stars here. The title story tells of an Italian prisoner of war labo
on a South Jersey farm circa 1944. There, he finds danger and dreams, friendship
romance—and, ultimately, more fireworks than he could have wished for.

2000/296 pp/Hardbound/ISBN: 0-937548-40-5/$22.95

FIELD GUIDE TO THE PINE BARRENS OF NEW JERSEY

By Howard P. Boyd

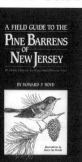

"...Howard Boyd has succeeded in the formidable task of bringing together definitive and detailed answers to questions about the Pine Barrens.... a must for anyone who is casually or seriously interested in the New Jersey Pine Barrens." —V. Eugene Vivian, Emeritus Professor of Environmental Studies, Rowan State College

With his 420-page volume, author Howard P. Boyd presents readers with the ultimate handbook to the New Jersey Pine Barrens. Boyd begins his book by explaining and defining what makes this sandy-soiled, wooded habitat so diverse and unusual.

Each entry gives a detailed, nontechnical description of a Pine Barrens plant or animal (for over 700 species), indicating when and where it is most likely to appear. Complementing most listings is an original ink drawing that will greatly aid the reader in the field as they search for and try to identify specific flora and fauna.

91/423 pp/hardbound/ISBN 0-937548-18-9/$32.95
91/423 pp/softbound/ISBN 0-937548-19-7/$22.95

PINE BARRENS ODYSSEY: NATURALIST'S YEAR IN THE PINE BARRENS OF NEW JERSEY

By Howard P. Boyd

A Pine Barrens Odyssey is a detailed perspective of the seasons in the Pine Barrens of New Jersey. Primarily focused on the chronology of the natural features of the Pine Barrens, this book is meant as a companion to Howard P. Boyd's *A Field Guide to the Pine Barrens of New Jersey*.

The two books form an appealing collection for anyone interested in the Pine Barrens of New Jersey. The *Field Guide* can be used as a reference tool for the types of flora and fauna and the *Odyssey* as a calendar of what to expect and look for season by season in this beautiful natural area of New Jersey.

1997/275 pp/softbound/ISBN 0-937548-34-0/$19.95

WILDFLOWERS OF THE PINE BARRENS OF NEW JERSEY

By Howard P. Boyd

Howard P. Boyd offers readers 150 detailed descriptions and 130 color photographs of the most commonly seen Pine Barrens wildflower species. Other useful features include a chapter on the flora of New Jersey, notes on threatened and endangered species, a primer on flower anatomy, a glossary of terms, references to literature cited and recommended reading, and indexes to both the common and scientific names of wildflower species. The author has avoided highly technical language, and employed a useful chronological organization (by blossoming times).

2001/176 pp/softbound/ISBN 0-937548-45-6/$19.95

Down Barnegat Bay: A Nor'easter Midnight Reader

By Robert Jahn

"*Down Barnegat Bay* evokes the area's romance and mystery."
—*The New York Times*

Down Barnegat Bay is an illustrated maritime history of the Jersey shore's A[ge] of Sail. Originally published in 1980, this fully revised Ocean Coun[ty] Sesquicentennial Edition features more than 177 sepia illustrations, includ[ing] 75 new images and nine maps. Jahn's engaging tribute to the region bri[ms] with first-person accounts of the people, events, and places that have cor[ne] together to shape Barnegat Bay's unique place in American history.

2000/248 pp/hardbound/ISBN 0-937548-42-1/$39.95

Boardwalk Empire
The Birth, High Times, and Corruption of Atlantic City

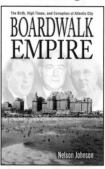

By Nelson Johnson

Atlantic City's popularity rose in the early 20th century and peaked dur[ing] Prohibition. For 70 years, it was controlled by a partnership comprised of local pol[iti] cians and racketeers, including Enoch "Nucky" Johnson—the second of three boss[es] to head the political machine that dominated city politics and society. In *Boardw[alk]* *Empire*, Atlantic City springs to life in all its garish splendor. Author Nelson Johns[on] traces "AC" from its birth as a quiet seaside health resort, through the notoric[us] backroom politics and power struggles, to the city's rebirth as an entertainment a[nd] gambling mecca where anything goes.

2002/300 pp/softbound/ISBN 0-937548-49-9/$18.95

Gateway to America
World Trade Center Memorial Edition

By Gordon Bishop
Photographs by Jerzy Koss

Based on the acclaimed PBS documentary, *Gateway to America* is both a comprehens[ive] guidebook and history. It covers the historic New York/New Jersey triangle that was [the] window for America's immigration wave in the 19th and 20th centuries. In addition [to] commemorating the World Trade Center, the book explores Ellis Island, The Statue [of] Liberty, and six other Gateway landmarks including Liberty State Park, Govern[ors] Island, Battery City Park, South Street Seaport, Newport, and the Gateway Natio[nal] Recreational Area. A must for history buffs and visitors to the area alike.

2003/188 pp/softbound/ISBN 0-937548-44-8/$19.95

To order or for a catalog: 609-654-6500, Fax Order Service: 609-654-4309

Plexus Publishing, Inc.

143 Old Marlton Pike • Medford • NJ 08055
E-mail: info@plexuspublishing.com
www.plexuspublishing.com